KIERKEGAARD, LANGUAGE AND THE REALITY OF GOD

Debate about the reality of God risks becoming an arid stalemate. An unbridgeable gulf seems to be fixed between realists, arguing that God exists independently of our language and beliefs, and anti-realists for whom God-language functions to express human spiritual ideals, with no reference to a reality external to the faith of the believer. Søren Kierkegaard has been enlisted as an ally by both sides of this debate.

Kierkegaard, Language and the Reality of God presents a new approach, exploring the dynamic nature of Kierkegaard's texts and the way they undermine neat divisions between realism and anti-realism, objectivity and subjectivity. Showing that Kierkegaard's understanding of language is crucial to his practice of communication, and his account of the paradoxes inherent in religious discourse, Shakespeare argues that Kierkegaard advances a form of 'ethical realism' in which the otherness of God is met in the making of liberating signs. Not only are new perspectives opened on Kierkegaard's texts, but his own contribution to ongoing debates is affirmed in its vital, creative and challenging significance.

Kierkegaard, Language and the Reality of God

STEVEN SHAKESPEARE

LONDON AND NEW YORK

First published 2001 by The Educational Publisher Inc.

Reissued 2018 by Routledge
2 Park Square, Milton Park, Abingdon, Oxon OX14 4RN
711 Third Avenue, New York, NY 10017, USA

Routledge is an imprint of the Taylor & Francis Group, an informa business

Copyright © Steven Shakespeare 2001, 2013

Steven Shakespeare has asserted his moral right under the Copyright, Designs and Patents Act, 1988, to be identified as the author of this work.

All rights reserved. No part of this book may be reprinted or reproduced or utilised in any form or by any electronic, mechanical, or other means, now known or hereafter invented, including photocopying and recording, or in any information storage or retrieval system, without permission in writing from the publishers.

Notice:
Product or corporate names may be trademarks or registered trademarks, and are used only for identification and explanation without intent to infringe.

Publisher's Note
The publisher has gone to great lengths to ensure the quality of this reprint but points out that some imperfections in the original copies may be apparent.

Disclaimer
The publisher has made every effort to trace copyright holders and welcomes correspondence from those they have been unable to contact.

A Library of Congress record exists under LC control number: 2001022837

ISBN 13: 978-1-138-63433-6 (hbk)
ISBN 13: 978-0-415-79287-5 (pbk)
ISBN 13: 978-1-315-21015-5 (ebk)

Contents

	Preface	vi
	List of abbreviations	vii
1	Kierkegaard and the question of language	1
2	In search of the perfect language	28
3	A Kierkegaardian theory of language?	56
4	The seduction of language	86
5	Significant silences	110
6	Kierkegaard's ethical realism	139
7	The analogy of communication	180
8	The passion of language	221
	Bibliography	240
	Index	249

Preface

I owe a number of people a large debt for ensuring that this book has seen the light of day. The staff of Ashgate and Martin Warner, the series editor, have been very helpful with comments and in putting the final text together. George Pattison has been a constant and generous source of insight and encouragement. Without him, I might have given up some time ago. Sally Bower has supported me throughout, and helped with the indexing (which has to go beyond the call of duty!). Many others have given me the opportunity to test my thinking and arguments, not least in the Cambridge Kierkegaard reading group and the Søren Kierkegaard Society of the UK.

Finally, I wish to acknowledge my debt to Don Cupitt, who instilled a love for philosophy of religion into me and taught me something about the courage of witnessing. It is to him that this book is dedicated.

Acknowledgements

The author and publishers are grateful to the following for permission to quote copyright material: Princeton University Press; Indiana University Press; Cambridge University Press; Blackwell Publishers; Harper Collins; Routledge; University of Chicago Press; Duquesne University Press; Florida University Press; Stanford University Press.

List of abbreviations

The following texts were used (passages marked with an asterisk [*] are my translation); they are cited with their standard abbreviation, which is used where appropriate in this book.

AN   *Armed Neutrality* and *An Open Letter*, trans. Hong and Hong, Indiana University Press, Bloomington, 1968 (*Den bevæbnede Neutralitet*, written 1848–9, post. published 1965; 'Foranledigt ved en Yttring af Dr. Rudelbach mig betræffende'. *Fædrelandet*, 31 Jan., 1851, SV 18).

C   *The Crisis [and a Crisis] in the life of an Actress*, trans. Crites, Harper, New York, 1967 (*Krisen og en Krise i en Skuespillerindes Liv*, 1848, SV 14).

CA   *The Concept of Anxiety*, trans. Thomte, in collaboration with Anderson, Princeton University Press, Princeton, NJ, 1980 (*Begrebet Angst*, 1844, SV 6).

CD   *Christian Discourses*, including *The Lilies of the Field and the Birds of the Air* and *Three Discourses at the Communion on Fridays*, trans. Lowrie, Oxford University Press, London and New York, 1940 (*Christelige Taler*, 1848, SV 13; *Lilien paa Marken og Fuglen under Himlen*, 1849, SV 14; *Tre Taler ved Altergangen om Fredagen*, 1849, SV 14).

CI   *The Concept of Irony* together with 'Notes on Schelling's Berlin Lectures', trans. Hong and Hong, Princeton University Press, Princeton, NJ, 1989 (*Om Begrebet Ironi*, 1841, SV 1).

COR   *The Corsair Affair*, trans. Hong and Hong, Princeton University Press, Princeton, NJ, 1982 (writings of Kierkegaard and others mainly from 1846; see SV18)

CUP   *Concluding Unscientific Postscript to Philiosophical Fragments*, trans. Hong and Hong, Princeton University Press, Princeton, NJ, 1992 (*Afsluttende uvidenskabelig Efterskrift*, 1846, SV 9–10).

ED   *Eighteen Edifying Discourses*, trans. Hong and Hong, Princeton University Press, Princeton, NJ, 1990 (*Opbyggelige Taler*, 1843–4, SV 4).

EO   *Either/Or*, trans. Hong and Hong, Princeton University Press, Princeton, NJ, 1987 (*Enten/Eller I–II*, 1843, SV 2–3).

EPW   *Early Polemical Writings*, trans. Watkin, Princeton University Press, Princeton, NJ, 1990 (*Af en endnu Levendes Papirer*, 1838, SV 1, plus early articles).

FSE *For Self-Examination* and *Judge for Yourself!*, trans. Hong and Hong, Princeton University Press, Princeton, NJ, 1990 (*Til Selvprøvelse*, 1851 and *Dømmer Selv!*, post. published 1876, both SV 17).

FT *Fear and Trembling* (with *Repetition*), trans. Hong and Hong, Princeton University Press, Princeton, NJ, 1983 (*Frygt og Bæven*, 1843, SV 5).

GS *Edifying Discourses in Various Spirits* (*Opbyggelige Taler i forskjellig Aand*, 1847, SV 11). Parts Three and Two, *The Gospel of Suffering* ('Lidelsernes Evangelium') and *The Lilies of the Field* ('Lilierne paa Marken og Himlens Fugle), trans. Swenson and Swenson, Augsburg, Minneapolis, 1948.

JC *Johannes Climacus* (with *Philosophical Fragments*), trans. Hong and Hong, Princeton University Press, Princeton, NJ, 1985 ('Johannes Climacus eller *de omnibus dubitandum est*', written 1842-3, unpublished, Pap. IV C 1)

JP *Søren Kierkegaard's Journals and Papers* (see 'Primary sources: English translations' in Bibliography).

KAUC *Kierkegaard's Attack upon 'Christendom'*, trans. Lowrie, Princeton University Press, Princeton, NJ, 1944 (*Bladartikler* I–XXI, *Fædrelandet*, 1854–5; *Dette skal siges; saa være det da sagt*, 1855; *Øieblikket* 1–10, 1855; *Hvad Christus dømmer om officiel Christendom*, 1855; all SV 19).

LD *Letters and Documents*, trans. Rosenmeier, Princeton University Press, Princeton, NJ, 1978.

OAR *On Authority and Revelation. The Book on Adler*, trans. Lowrie, Princeton University Press, Princeton, NJ, 1955 (*Bogen om Adler*, written 1845-6, unpublished, Pap. VII(2) B 235; VIII(2) B 1–27).

Pap. *Papirer* (see 'Primary sources: Danish' in Bibliography).

PC *Practice in Christianity*, trans. Hong and Hong, Princeton University Press, Princeton, NJ, 1991 (*Indøvelse i Christendom*, 1850, SV 16).

PF *Philosophical Fragments* (with *Johannes Climacus*), trans. Hong and Hong, Princeton University Press, Princeton, NJ, 1985 (*Philosophiske Smuler*, 1844, SV 6) .

PH *Edifying Discourses in Various Spirits* (*Opbyggelige Taler i forskjellig Aand*, 1847, SV 11). Part One, *Purity of Heart*, trans. Steere, Harper, New York, 1948 ('En Leiligheds-Tale').

PV *The Point of View for My Work as an Author* and *On My Work as an Author*, trans. Lowrie, Oxford University Press, London and New York, 1939 (*Synspunktet for min Forfatter-Virksomhed*, post. published 1859 and *Om min Forfatter-Virksomhed*, 1851, both SV 18).

R *Repetition* (with *Fear and Trembling*), trans. Hong and Hong, Princeton University Press, Princeton, NJ, 1983 (*Gjentagelsen*, 1843, SV 5).

SLW   *Stages on Life's Way*, trans. Hong and Hong, Princeton University Press, Princeton, NJ, 1988 (*Stadier paa Livets Vej*, 1845, SV 7–8).
SV   *Samlede Værker* (see 'Primary sources: Danish' in Bibliography).
TA   *Two Ages: The Age of Revolution and the Present Age. A Literary Review*, trans. Hong and Hong, Princeton University Press, Princeton, NJ, 1978 (*En literair Anmeldelse*, 1846, SV 14).
SUD   *The Sickness Unto Death*, trans. Hong and Hong, Princeton University Press, Princeton, NJ, 1980 (*Sygdommen til Døden*, 1849, SV 15).
TCS   *Three Discourses on Imagined Occasions (Thoughts on Crucial Situations in Human Life)*, trans. Swenson, Augsburg, Minneapolis, 1941 (*Tre Taler ved tænkte Leiligheder*, 1845, SV 6).
UG   *The Unchangeableness of God* in *For Self-Examination, etc.*, trans. Lowrie and Swenson, Princeton University Press, Princeton, NJ, 1941 (Guds Uforanderlighed, 1855, SV 19).
WL   *Works of Love*, trans. Hong and Hong, Harper, New York, 1967 (*Kjerlighedens Gjerninger*, 1847, SV 12).

For Don Cupitt

If anyone says that this is only an exercise in elocution, that I have only a bit of irony, a bit of pathos, a bit of dialectic with which to work, I shall answer: What else should the person have who wants to present the ethical?
Johannes Climacus

Our faith is not assured
Jacques Derrida

CHAPTER ONE

Kierkegaard and the question of language

The bankruptcy of language

In an early journal entry, Kierkegaard writes of a

> bankruptcy in an intellectual-spiritual sense ... that is, a confusion in the languages themselves, a mutiny, the most dangerous of all, of the words themselves, which wrenched out of man's control, would despair, as it were, and crash in upon one another. (JP 5: 5181; Pap. I A 328)

He goes on to complain:

> every Christian concept has become so volitilized, so completely dissolved in a mass of fog, that it is beyond all recognition. To the concepts of faith, incarnation, tradition, inspiration, which in the Christian sphere are to refer to a particular historical fact, the philosophers have chosen to give an entirely different, ordinary meaning ... We would also wish that powerfully equipped men might emerge who would restore the lost power and meaning of words. (ibid.)

What is at stake in this 'bankruptcy' of language? How does such a devaluation of concepts come about? How are concepts 'restored' to their lost and proper meaning?

Kierkegaard's remarks, written before his authorial career had begun, pose questions which open up new perspectives on his authorship. He is not well known for his views on language, but I will justify a reading of his work which makes his commitment to writing inextricable from the account of language implicit within it.

This book aims to explore Kierkegaard's theological language throughout his authorship, published and unpublished, in the light of his more general views on the nature and function of language. The investigation will be guided by the terms of a current debate within the philosophy of religion which has had a significant impact on Kierkegaard studies.

The debate concerns the proper way to interpret religious language.[1] It focuses on notions of reality, truth, objectivity and subjectivity. It is an argument that is often staged between 'realists' and 'anti-realists'.

---

[1] For recent evidence of this debate see the collection of essays *God and Reality. Essays on Christian Non-Realism*, ed. Colin Crowder (London: Mowbray, 1997).

More will be said about these categories in the theological context later. As an opening gambit, however, we might characterize the opposing sides along the following lines. If you interpret language about God in a realist way, it means that you believe that the reality of God is independent of that language. In other words, God's reality is 'objective'. It does not depend upon human experience or concepts. However metaphorical or analogical it may be, language about God refers to and is constrained by the objective truth of God. It does not create or project that truth out of 'subjective' human ideals, values or feelings.

Conversely, an anti-realist sees language about God as an expression of human ideals and needs. We do not know or need to know if that language has any objective referent. This is not necessarily intended to be a devaluation of language about God. A religious anti-realist claims that religion does not provide us with information about realities that exist prior to us. The function of religion is expressive. It is a means of articulating a way of life and a set of values. Within this picture, language about God provides a focus for our notions of the ultimate good in human life. As the sum or pinnacle of human aspiration, 'God' may not be entirely known to us, but this does not imply that 'God' exists in any objective, independent sense. Rather, 'God' is a projection, but one which is of profound spiritual worth.

Summarizing the debate in this way is inevitably unsatisfactory, as both positions need to be set in context before we rush to analyse and judge them. The theological aspect of this dispute is part of a wider controversy, one which not only affects specific areas of human discourse, but involves fundamental notions of truth and reality. For the past century – and arguably further back as we shall see – argument has centred on notions of meaning, reference and representation. In short, language itself has become the battleground.

Why is this? And what does the history and shape of this debate teach us when we approach the specific area of language about God? We can only begin to broach these questions, but doing so can orient us for the specific lines of enquiry that lie ahead.

Realism and anti-realism

The terminology of realism has a varied history in philosophical usage. Two significant moments can be distilled out of that development. In each case, realism is defined in opposition to something else, and so the nature of realism shifts in response.

Firstly, realism is contrasted with nominalism in medieval debates about the nature of universals. The nominalists – foremost among whom was William of Ockham – were taking up earlier investigations into the nature of signs (especially linguistic signs) and their relationship to reality. Platonic metaphysics, still profoundly influential upon Augustine, held that universal, eternal ideas or forms were the ultimate constituents and generators of reality. It was through participation in these ideas that particular things were what they were. In a sense, all particular things were signs, pointers to a more fundamental reality. Linguistic signs echoed this structure at a further remove. Attached to sensory impressions, they were able to bring ideas to mind. However, they were not productive in any fundamental sense – they did not create new ideas. The ideas themselves, for Augustine at least, were put into the mind and illuminated by God.

However, this priority of universal forms was questioned partly under the influence of the work of grammarians, for whom it was the naming of particular things that was primary. Following Boethius and Abelard, nominalists like Ockham denied that universal terms had any objective reality beyond their functional role in human thinking. Ockham claimed that everything that exists is particular. Universal terms are devices of convenience for relating particulars together, but they have no existence outside the process of thought.

Realism in this context meant asserting the independent and objective reality of universals (though this could be dealt with in more or less subtle ways). But it is associated with a whole metaphysics of how signs work, and how they can be the occasion for the human ascent to truth. Via particular things and signs, the mind is led to universal forms and thence to the illuminating presence of God. Nominalism threatened to interrupt this analogical ascent. It recast the relationship of God to the world in terms of arbitrary divine will, rather than the indwelling or participatory vision of Platonic Christian thought. We can begin to see how the evolving dispute about realism brings into play significant questions of the order of truth and the nature of divine reality.

The second major phase in the history of realism comes in the eighteenth and nineteenth centuries, when it is contrasted with idealism. Idealism is a term applied to a huge range of philosophical enterprises, which could have their roots in empiricism, rationalism or mysticism. Berkeley, Fichte, Schelling and Hegel were all idealists, yet all significantly different in their approach and conclusions. What brings them together is a shared concern to invert the empiricist claim that thought was dependent upon sense impressions which themselves were anchored in a reality which pre-existed thought. Berkeley, in particular, delighted in pushing the empiricist world view to its limit and seeing it flip over into something utterly different. The German idealists were more immediately motivated by a desire to overcome the dualism – the split between the human subject of knowing and the objective world that was known – which they believed to be the legacy of Kant's attempts to reconcile rational thought with empiricism. In each case, the antinomies of philosophy were overcome by asserting the priority of consciousness over 'objective' reality.

What this meant was that consciousness was seen not as a passive receptor of impressions, but as a creative and productive force, which generated the complexity of the world out of its own resources. Reality was thus not separate to or independent of consciousness save in appearance. Fundamentally, reality was rational, even spiritual through and through. There was a deep religious motivation behind the idealist move. In Berkeley's case, this took the form of a kind of revival of Augustine: giving honour to the God who put the ideas of things in our minds. For the German idealists, there was a more mystical sense of our participation in the unfolding of the divine Spirit in its journey through alienation to the eventual reconciliation of all things.

In this context, realism means a denial of the priority of consciousness in the construction of the real. The external world encountered in the senses has an independent existence which is not a projection of the mind, be it human or divine. A priori reasoning about the world has to give way to empirical observation and experiment, based on the assumption of the objective reality of the world and the natural laws which govern it.

A certain irony may be noticed in all of this. The realism that opposed idealism, and which was rooted in a 'common-sense' empiricism, could reasonably look back to the nominalism of the Middle Ages as its intellectual inheritance. Idealism seems to have more in common with the 'realism' of Augustinian theology, with its concern for the priority of 'ideas' and their capacity to lead us to participation in the divine.

Realism is thus a moving target, and one whose definition depends on what it is being opposed to. In each case we have looked at, realism is concerned to assert, in some sense, the objectivity of a class of entities: universals (the 'ideas' which through divine guidance give rise to universal terms in language) or empirically discovered physical objects (which give rise to the sense-impressions from which ideas are generated). Arguably, each version of realism tries to resist a conclusion that would make human beings the primary creators of the real. The difference lies in how the nature of that reality is defined.

In the last century, the issue of realism has been a particular concern of analytic philosophy, which takes its cue from the work on logic and meaning pursued by Frege, Russell and others. Drawing on the empiricism of the eighteenth century, analytic philosophy classically works by breaking down the components of the inputs and outputs of knowledge into their constituent parts. In other words, both the sensory impressions that give rise to knowledge and the sentences in which that knowledge is articulated are analysed into their irreducible parts and related according to logical principles. Questions about the objectivity of knowledge and the meaning, reference and truth conditions of our sentences take centre stage.

In this setting, it may be helpful to distinguish three aspects of the realism issue which have been important in analytic philosophy. First is the question we have identified in previous phases of the history of realism: does a certain class of entities possess an objective, independent reality or existence (the terminology may shift depending on what is being talked about)? For instance, Michael Devitt's defence of realism is specifically focused on arguing for the independent existence of physical objects as a necessary condition for the validity of scientific discovery.[2] He claims that this question is separate to the one about how we justify our claims to knowledge about such objects.

Related to this is a second question. Michael Dummett refers to this when he writes that 'A dispute over realism may be expressed by asking whether or not there really exist entities of a particular type – universal or material objects; or, again, it may be asked, not whether they exist, but whether they are among the ultimate constituents of reality.'[3] The latter part of this quotation raises the issue of reductionism: explaining the reality of an entity as an epiphenomenon of a more fundamental reality. An anti-realist about a certain entity may be concerned to deny its existence, but this is not the only option. She may also claim that it has only a partial or dependent existence, one which can be resolved into a more basic reality. For example, one may not want to deny that secondary qualities like colour are 'real', but that reality is dependent on our perspective. From an ideal, perspectiveless point of view, the world is not coloured. It has to be analysed into more basic constituents.

The third aspect of the realism issue is distinctively modern in its present form. It concerns verification. Logical positivism, deriving from the Vienna School of Carnap and others, and including the work of Ayer, claimed that utterances were only meaningful if they had some kind of determinate empirical verification. Michael Dummett develops this line in his own critique of realism. He argues that realists differ from anti-realists in whether they demand that a statement should be open to decisive verification before it can have a truth value:

> The realist holds that we give sense to those sentences of our language which are not effectively decidable by appealing tacitly to means of determining their truth-values which we do not ourselves possess, but which we can conceive of by analogy with those which we do. The anti-realist holds that such a conception is quite spurious, an illusion of meaning, and that the only meaning we can confer on our sentences must relate to the means of determining their truth-values which we actually possess. Hence, unless we have a means which would in principle decide the truth-value of a given statement, we do not have a notion of truth or falsity which would entitle us to say that it must either be true or false.[4]

---

[2] Michael Devitt, *Realism and Truth* (2nd edn, Oxford: Blackwell, 1986).
[3] Michael Dummett, *Truth and other Enigmas* (London: Duckworth 1978), p. 145.
[4] Ibid. p. 24

Dummett denies that what he calls undecidable statements, such as 'Jones was brave' or 'A city will never be built here', are either true or false, since there is, in principle, no way for us to verify their truth-value.

Anti-realism appears differently according to the aspect of realism one is focusing on. Anti-realism could be the denial that a certain kind of entity exists. It could be the denial that a certain kind of entity is ultimately real, and the assertion that it can be reduced down to, or explained in terms of a more fundamental reality. Or it may be the denial that truth can float free of verification, and that undecidable statements have any independent, objective truth or falsity.

It is important to point out that anti-realism can be quite selective. In other words, one can be anti-realist about certain kinds of entity. A logical positivist might be a realist about physical objects, but not about ethical values or the referents of religious language. The issue of realism is thus contextual. Ironically, it could be said that nominalism is realist about particular objects, or that idealism is realist about universals. It all depends on the ordering of reality in a particular philosophical account.

A further point needs to be noted. In its recent history, debate about realism has been intimately connected with the analysis of language, and with questions of truth, meaning and reference. Those who like Devitt try to isolate the question of realism from that of truth or meaning may have a certain logic on their side; but in practice, since any formulation of realism is inevitably mediated linguistically, no sharp division can be sustained. Attempts to devise a logical meta-language which would be entirely adequate to reality and thus render language invisible depend upon a number of questionable presuppositions, as we shall see in the next chapter. Modern analytic philosophy's attempts to work towards such a language, following Frege and Russell, have not been conspicuous in achieving successful consensus.

One reason for this is the shortcomings of the account of reference underlying such a project. It was claimed that reference – using language to pick out an object – works only if we have 'grasped the *sense* of the referring expression, that is, the various descriptions, criteria, or identifying attributes standardly imputed to the referent in question'.[5] The problem arises when descriptions accompanying words are found to be false or inadequate in some important respect. For example, if our historical knowledge of the person and career of Julius Caesar or our scientific knowledge of the chemical nature and behaviour of gold is significantly revised, it seems highly counter-intuitive to say that our previous uses of Julius Caesar and gold either failed to refer or referred to a different (non-existent) entity.

The descriptivist account of reference was an attempt to assure us that we

---

[5] Christopher Norris, *New Idols of the Cave: On the Limits of Anti-realism* (Manchester and New York: Manchester University Press, 1997), p. 166.

could successfully make contact between our words and the world out there. It was, in this sense, designed to support a kind of realism about the world. Unfortunately, its shortcomings meant it played into the hands of anti-realism, because it began to appear that our definition and redefinition of our words and ideas actually changed the nature of 'reality'. In other words, our language, and the conceptual schemes into which it was organized, was the primary factor in shaping the world we experienced. Through language, we were defining the world according to our arbitrary conventions.

To avoid such an anti-realist drift, a number of writers, notably Kripke and Putnam, developed causal theories of reference. According to these, words acquired a referent in an initial act of naming, which picked out an entity or substance. The attributes of that referent may then undergo further exploration, and more adequate descriptions of the referent may be devised. But the reference remains stable even through changing definitions.[6]

This account depends upon the idea that words are able to pick out 'natural kinds' – substances which have a certain essential nature, which may not yet be fully known by us. Successful reference depends not upon having exhaustive and absolute knowledge of the essential nature of a thing, but on being part of a linguistic community, in which there is a chain of usage linking our words to something whose true nature we are still discovering.

These debates may seem obscure, but they have consequences as wide as those entailed by earlier historical clashes over realism. For anti-realism has played its part in much more 'global' philosophies concerning the status of human knowledge. In particular it has been associated with the spectre of relativism. If our language and our knowledge do not give us access to some objective, independent source of truth, then factual and ethical critique and consensus seem to be under threat.

With this in mind, some have advocated a more overarching case for realism. One such is the critical realist account of science (which has been extended to fields such as social science, and to theology itself). Roy Bhaskar, one of the leading thinkers behind this project, argues that one can only account for scientific discovery and for progress in understanding on a realist interpretation of the objects of scientific research.[7] The descriptivist or anti-realist account leaves us with an entirely instrumental view of science. In other words, scientific theories cannot be judged true or adequate with reference to an independent, objective realm of entities and laws. Rather they are human ways of organizing our experience, projections on to the world rather than discoveries of objective features of that world. Such anti-realist

---

[6] See Saul Kripke, *Naming and Necessity* (Oxford: Blackwell, 1980); Norris, *New Idols*, pp. 164–73.
[7] See Roy Bhaskar, *Reclaiming Reality* (London: Verso, 1989) and the essays collected in Margaret Archer *et al.* (eds) *Critical Realism: Essential Readings* (London: Routledge, 1998).

relativism is able to appeal to a reading of cultural and historical difference that denies any universal criteria of truth. Meaning, reference and truth are determined by different criteria in different conceptual schemes, and there may be no valid way of linking them.

Bhaskar counters that this leads to the absolutization of our present state of knowledge and culture. It fails to provide any account of the progress of scientific knowledge or for our ability to have a critical relationship to current theories and practices: 'To be a fallibilist about knowledge it is necessary to be a realist about things. Conversely, to be a sceptic about things is to be a dogmatist about knowledge.'[8]

However, Bhaskar is aware that realism needs a degree of sophistication if we are not to assume that we can simply lift ourselves out of our existing knowledge and conceptual schemes through assuming a pre-ordained 'fit' between our words and things in the world. Critical realism argues that science searches for deeper generative mechanisms behind surface phenomena. Its working assumption is that reality is not shaped without exception by our mode of knowing, but that new discovery is possible because reality is stratified. It is not simply a collection of objects available to the senses, but is built up of layers of successive levels of natural necessity. Bhaskar hopes to resist the narrow verficationism and reductionism he ᴄ ·es in anti-realism.

Modern realism has thus taken on board some of the positions used by anti-realists. Causal theories of reference and critical realism acknowledge the historically evolving state of our knowledge, the multidimensional nature of the real and the rootedness of language in particular communities and their traditions. However, it rejects the anti-realist conclusion that any of this denies us access to independent and objective reality, for such anti-realism and global relativism are themselves partial accounts of how language works and how knowledge is discovered. Ultimately, thoroughgoing relativism is self-defeating, since one cannot assert relativism to be true without contradicting oneself ('it is a universal truth that there are no universal truths').

Such sophisticated realism has not, however, gone unchallenged. The most significant criticism has come from Hilary Putnam himself, who was at one stage a leading advocate of a causal account of reference. It is worth briefly examining Putnam's reasons for his change of mind, as it links with issues central to our concern in this book.

In *Reason Truth And History*, Putnam declares his aim to break the grip of dichotomies which are influential within philosophical and lay discourse: 'Chief among these is the dichotomy between objective and subjective views of truth and reason.'[9] Objective views in philosophy centre around a

---

[8] Roy Bhaskar in Archer *et al.*, *Critical Realism*, p. 32.
[9] Hilary Putnam, *Reason, Truth and History* (Cambridge: Cambridge University Press, 1981), p. ix. See also *The Many Faces of Realism* (La Salle, Ill.: Open Court, 1987), pp. 23–40.

correspondence theory of truth, the idea that statements are true if they correspond to states of affairs which are independent of the mind. Such is the strength of this view that both its supporters and opponents claim that if it is wrong, we are left with a merely subjectivist, relativistic view of truth, in which there can be no objective constraint upon the patterns we impose upon the world.

For Putnam, part of the problem with this dichotomy is that it relates to what he calls metaphysical realism. This is the belief that 'the world consists of some fixed totality of mind-independent objects'[10] and that there is one true and complete description of that world. Words or mental ideas are true insofar as they correspond to this reality. Putnam points out that the issue of realism, when set up in this way, sidesteps the issue of reductionism which we noted earlier. In other words, a reductionist who takes one limited set of realities to be fundamental is as much a metaphysical realist as someone with a more cluttered ontology.

Putnam agrees with the anti-realist that no exhaustive account can be given of how our statements hook up with or copy the world outside our language and theories. There is no way of climbing outside our language and conceptual schemes to judge how successfully what we say mirrors reality. Putnam argues at length that is is quite possible for the same truth conditions to apply to the same sentences in different possible worlds, and yet for those sentences to refer to different things. Following Quine, he points out that we can conceptually divide the world up in a multitude of different ways, all of which would fit our experiences and all of which would be true. The reason is that there is no one way of dividing up the world which forces itself upon us, no one way for signs to 'refer'. Reference is always indeterminate to some extent. Causal theories of reference will not solve the problem, since there is no way of specifying what 'appropriate type' of causal chain gives rise to certain signs without already having assumed that we can successfully refer. We cannot step outside language to say how it matches up with reality, since in the process we will use the very concepts of reference and truth that we are trying to explain.[11]

Putnam's own 'internal realism' denies that there is any God's eye view, or any one-to-one match between words and things. Crucially, he shows that 'signs do not interpret themselves'[12] apart from practices – there is no intrinsic connection between a sign and any part of the world before that sign is embedded in use and context. Putnam clearly builds upon Wittgenstein's

---

[10] Putnam, *Reason*, p. 49.
[11] Ibid., Chapter 2, 'A problem about reference', pp. 22–48; cf. pp. 65–6 and also *Renewing Philosophy* (Cambridge, Mass.: Harvard University Press, 1992), Chapter 3, 'A Theory of Reference', pp. 35–59.
[12] Putnam, *Reason*, p. 67.

arguments in *Philosophical Investigations,* which criticize the idea that our mental pictures have any a priori link to reality, or that a private language could be constructed *ex nihilo,* apart from all assumed standards of truth and reference.[13] To use an un-Wittgensteinian phrase, language has always already begun.

Wittgenstein's notion of language games attempts to elucidate this facet of language – that it is not simply a collection of signs which stand in one-to-one correspondence with things, but an activity, bound by rules which cannot be straightforwardly read out of the world by way of logical necessity. Thus, ostensive definition (saying 'apple' while pointing to an apple) is not the foundational act of reference it may appear to be. It presupposes what the whole activity of referring, pointing and signifying is about, and it always takes place within a context whose borders may not be determined with absolute assurance ('ostensive definition can be variously interpreted in *every* case'[14]). Wittgenstein reacts against his own former view that the world can be analysed down into simple constituents and then a language constructed which corresponds to those constituents point for point.

This is interestingly related to what philosophers of a different tradition – notably Derrida – have been saying about the problems language causes for a totalizing philosophical project.[15] And it is especially important to us in that it resists the pretensions of both metaphysical realism in Putnam's sense *and* subjective idealism and relativism. Remember that Putnam advocates *internal realism* – we cannot just say anything, there are constraints on our language – it is just that we have no access to the world in itself apart from its linguistic mediation. If objects 'are as much made as discovered'[16] it remains the case that they are not simply 'made'. It makes no more sense to say that we create the world from nothing than it does to say that truth and reference are forced upon us by certain irreducible physical causes. Language does not work like this, and any sensible idea of truth and reality cannot do without language.

Putnam's critics, however, worry that the divide between his internal realism and relativism is paper thin.[17] There seems little to separate it from the more cheerfully pragmatic projects of philosophers such as Goodman and Rorty. It is unclear just how much these thinkers draw back from a

---

[13] Wittgenstein, *Philosophical Investigations* (Oxford: Blackwell, 1958) §243ff.
[14] Ibid., §28.
[15] See for example, Jacques Derrida, *Dissemination* (London: Athlone, 1981), p. 340: 'My own presence to myself has always been preceded by a language' and *On the Name* (Stanford, Calif.: Stanford University Press, 1995), p. 30: 'As soon as there are words ... direct intuition no longer has any chance'.
[16] Putnam, *Reason,* p. 54.
[17] See Norris, *New Idols,* pp. 203–4; Curtis Brown, 'Internal Realism: Transcendental Idealism?' in Peter A. French, Theodore E. Uehling Jr. and Howard K. Wettstein (eds) *Realism and Antirealism* (Minneapolis: University of Minnesota Press, 1988), pp. 145–56.

thoroughgoing cultural relativism, which, as Bhaskar and others fear, leaves no room for rational and ethical critique.[18]

There is no disguising the fact that Putnam has no fully worked out theory of reality and truth. But this is because, on his view, there is no such all-encompassing theory that can stand on some extra-theoretical foundation. The point is that our ordinary notions of truth and reality, in the different contexts in which these terms are used, do not depend on such mythical foundations. Relativism is only a problem if metaphysical realism is accepted as the only acceptable account of reality.

Putnam's questioning of the dichotomy between objective and subjective views opens new perspectives on ethical and religious language. As Wittgenstein suggests, once we see how such language works, we may no longer be in thrall to a set of reductionist empiricist or idealist dogmas about how truth must be in all circumstances.

We can begin to see how this relates to our concern with realism in theology and in the works of Kierkegaard in particular. Expanding our initial definition to take into account the history of the general debate, we could say that realism about God is the claim that God's existence is objective and independent (of human words, ideas and experiences); that God's existence is an ultimate reality and that language about God cannot be reduced or translated without remainder into language about what is not God (assuming God's existence to be objective etc.); that language about God can be verified in some way.

Anti-realism could then be seen as the mirror image of this position, depending on precisely how it is expressed: that God does not exist as an objective, independent, ultimate reality apart from human words, ideas and experiences, that language about God can be translated into language about what is not objective and independent. For example, it can, according to logical positivists, be translated wholly into emotive expressions of human dispositions.[19] This is further associated with the verificationist view that the truth and indeed meaningfulness of statements depends on our possessing some decisive means for verifying them.

The problem here is that the debate seems to centre on ideas of existence, objectivity and independence which are themselves questionable. For instance, we have to recognize that the referent of language about God is not like other referents. God is not 'a' being or 'an' object or 'an' entity, since this

---

[18] See Richard Rorty, *Philosophy and the Mirror of Nature* (Oxford: Blackwell, 1980); Nelson Goodman, *Ways of Worldmaking* (Indianapolis: Hackett, 1979).

[19] For the classic interpretation of religious language as an emotive expression of ethical values, see R. B. Braithwaite, *An Empiricist's View of the Nature of Religious Belief* (Cambridge: Cambridge University Press, 1955). Note, however, that Braithwaite is intending to say something positive about religious language. For a logical positivist like Ayer, religious language was simply meaningless, because unverifiable.

would entail that God is one of a class of things, a finite part of the world – and therefore not God. The problem with the way we have set up the contrast between realism and anti-realism is that it seems to distort the very nature of what is being debated.

There are two further difficulties with this scenario. Firstly, it is hard to see what distinguishes anti-realism from straightforward atheism. Why say '*N* is an anti-realist about God' when we might just as well say that '*N* thinks that language about God is a lot of emotive nonsense'? And this is connected with the second point. As Putnam argues, an anti-realist about a certain area of discourse can still be a metaphysical realist – and logical positivists are a case in point. They are realists about what they take to be the ultimate constituents of the world. An atheist may share a surprisingly similar ontology to a theist – they just happen to disagree about the existence of an additional being in the universe.

If that is putting it too strongly, the point stands that if the debate about anti-realism is not to remain superficial, it has to lead us on to more 'global' issues, in which the status of ideas of reality, truth, objectivity and subjectivity is brought into focus. In targeting metaphysical realism, Putnam asks us to think through the potentially dangerous, reductionist implications of our philosophical pictures. From the other direction, Bhaskar and others are motivated by a political and ethical resistance to what they see as the alternately dogmatic and relativistic overtones of the view that our language is unconstrained by a complex, objective reality.[20]

The two perspectives converge on a concern to take seriously the ethical dimension of human life – and for Putnam at least, the religious dimension also. Indeed, it may be that interpretations of religious language become especially important, since the very nature of talk about what transcends all finite entities tests the limits of realist and anti-realist notions of reference and truth. It will be a hypothesis of this study that language about God, rather than being positioned and confined as an additional and optional part of discourse, may hold important lessons for understanding how language as a whole works. But this only happens if we do not define God in advance according to the standard we apply to other 'entities'.

As we shall see, Kierkegaard's searching, teasing authorship offers one of the most fertile grounds for such a raising of the stakes. It has already become a source of inspiration for philosophers of religion who question a metaphysically realist understanding of truth and how language – particularly language about God – works.

---

[20] See also Christopher Norris' attack on the political implications of relativistic thinking in *Uncritical Theory: Postmodernism, Intellectuals and the Gulf War* (London: Lawrence and Wishart, 1992).

An anti-realist Kierkegaard?

Kierkegaard's works have always been the subject of much fierce interpretative debate, not least between those who accuse him of 'subjectivism' in its pejorative sense (as a kind of irrationalism) and those who would maintain that Kierkegaard stresses the transcendence of God and the objective (in the sense of extra-human) truth of his revelation of himself, especially in the incarnation.[21] The very existence of such radical disagreement suggests that ambiguity must be a major characteristic of Kierkegaardian texts, and one which can be exploited to serve various ends. Kierkegaard's name can become a talisman for justifying the most diverse interpretations of Christian truth, and we will ultimately suggest reasons why that is so.

For now, however, it is important to see how Kierkegaard has entered into this particular controversy. Don Cupitt, one of the best known advocates of an anti-realist approach, suggests that, for Kierkegaard:

> everything is decided within the sphere of human subjectivity. All the different ways of life that he discusses ... appear simply as various possible forms of consciousness, shapes that the human spiritual life may assume and worlds that it may construct around itself. None was assessed in terms of its correspondence with objective facts and structures out there; all were assessed from within, and in terms of their inner logic and movement.[22]

He can thus claim Kierkegaard's support for the notion that 'For us, God is the various roles God plays in the formation of a Christian, and no more can be said.'[23]

Brian Hebblethwaite, in his reply to Cupitt defending objective theism,

---

[21] For a survey of the literature, see David Law, *Kierkegaard As Negative Theologian* (Oxford: Clarendon, 1993), pp. 90ff.

[22] Don Cupitt, *The Sea of Faith* (London: BBC, 1984), p. 153.

[23] Ibid., p. 154. See references to Kierkegaard in David Hart, *Faith in Doubt* (London: Mowbray, 1993), pp. 10–14, 121–2. The tension between Kierkegaard and Hegel is also clearly influential on the thinking of Mark C. Taylor, whose own postmodernist anti-realist theology is outlined in *Erring: A Postmodern A/theology* (Chicago: University of Chicago Press, 1984). Taylor stands in some continuity with the 'death of God' theology which was prominent in the 1960s. One of the leading exponents of that thinking, Thomas Altizer, describes Kierkegaard as 'the real creator of modern theology' (Thomas Altizer and William Hamilton, *Radical Theology and the Death of God* (Harmondsworth: Penguin, 1968), p. 28). Altizer sees the Kierkegaardian dialectic of faith in the absurd as requiring a negation of Christendom as a supernatural faith, and a following of Christ in the profane world: 'As Kierkegaard saw so deeply, faith in the Incarnation is faith in the truly absurd. Therefore the only language for the Incarnation is the language of paradox, of the deepest paradox, which may well mean that it is only the language of the radical profane that can give witness to the fullest advent of the Incarnation' (Ibid., p. 35).

rejects this reading, quoting Sutherland to the effect that 'Kierkegaard's thought and writing is dominated, one might even say "domineered", throughout by the conception of a transcendent and sovereign God.'[24] However, Cupitt has anticipated this. He argues that Kierkegaard's notion of transcendence does not signify the objectivity of God, but is a way of refusing any assimilation of the idea of God by speculative philosophy.[25] 'God' is an ideal which transcends any partial fulfilment or systematic comprehension, but it does not follow that the word 'God' corresponds to any objectively existing being. Cupitt claims that Kierkegaard's language about God implies that 'the reality of God *is identical with* the awesome challenge and promise of becoming an individual'.[26]

It is important to see that Cupitt's assessment of Kierkegaard fits into a wider philosophy of language, which draws heavily on the kind of arguments espoused by Rorty and Putnam, but also structuralism and its heirs. There is no pre-ordained hook up between words and the world for Cupitt.[27] Words are defined contextually and differentially. That is to say, a word only has meaning in terms of its relationship to and difference from other words.[28] There is no way of escaping language entirely, in order to judge whether or not our words match up with a language-independent reality: 'Anti-realism does not say that there is no world at all, but only that we cannot compare our view of the world with the way the world is absolutely, for we have no access to the way the world is absolutely.'[29] All reality comes to us mediated and interpreted – the world is 'a continuous stream of language-formed events'.[30] Indeed, it only gains significant shape at all insofar as we impose patterns upon it.

---

[24] Brian Hebblethwaite, *The Ocean of Truth* (Cambridge: Cambridge University Press, 1988), p. 49. For other arguments against anti-realism in Kierkegaard's thought, see C. Stephen Evans, *Passionate Reason: Making Sense of Kierkegaard's Philosophical Fragments* (Bloomington and Indianapolis: Indiana University Press, 1992) and his earlier article 'Kierkegaard on Subjective Truth: Is God an Ethical Fiction?', *International Journal for Philosophy of Religion* 7 (1976), pp. 288–99. See also Patrick Gardiner's brief discussion in *Kierkegaard* (Oxford: Oxford University Press, 1988), pp. 94ff., in which he argues that it is the paradoxicality of the object of faith which makes it impossible for Kierkegaard to conceive of it as a product of human willing. A similar argument is deployed by George Pattison in his article 'From Kierkegaard to Cupitt: Subjectivity, the Body and Eternal Life', *Heythrop Journal* XXXI (1990), pp. 295–308, though Pattison is more sympathetic to seeing Kierkegaard and Cupitt as complementary on this and other points.

[25] Cupitt, *Sea of Faith*, p. 154.

[26] Don Cupitt, *The World to Come* (London: SCM, 1982), p. 46. It is worth noting that Cupitt has also criticized Kierkegaard for a residual realism which assumes that the various life views can be ranked in only one order. See *The Time Being* (London: SCM, 1993), pp. 114ff.

[27] Cf. Richard Rorty's claim that there is no 'transcendental standpoint outside our present set of representations from which we can inspect the relations between those representations and their object' (*Philosophy and the Mirror of Nature* (Oxford: Blackwell, 1980), p. 293).

[28] Don Cupitt, *The Long-Legged Fly* (London: SCM, 1987), pp. 13–21.

[29] Don Cupitt, *Creation out of Nothing* (London: SCM, 1990), p. 105.

[30] Don Cupitt, *After All* (London: SCM, 1994), p. 63. See Chapter 3 of this work as a whole, 'How It Is', pp. 36–92, for a mature expression of Cupitt's understanding of language and reality.

Whilst Cupitt at times acknowledges that there is an aspect of being which precedes and eludes linguistic grasp,[31] for the most part he is content to offer a radical formulation of the human situation, in which we use our words to shape the world, creating meaning from the meaningless flux of experience.

Notice that, for Cupitt, realism is not a local affair. It is not so much realism about this or that entity that he opposes, but the kind of metaphysical realism that Putnam also attacks.[32] There is a profound connection between realist views of language, and certain interpretations of God as the guarantor of the well-ordered cosmos, in which words successfully copy things. Indeed, even when the reality of God is denied, the old order continues in, for example, the view that philosophy or science will be able to give us the one true theory of everything, stated in a meta-language that eliminates all partial perspectives.[33] Cupitt's self-confessed anti-realism is a religious response to this (as he sees it) false metaphysics. It is meant as a cure for a disease of thinking, which will free us to accept contingency and transience and abandon the insecure, selfish search for some foundational, absolute truth. It is in this religious attack on objectivity that Cupitt feels he has an ally in Kierkegaard. The objective, realist viewpoint is what weighs religion down, turning God into an object that can be known. The very realism which seeks to save God and the cosmos ends by betraying us into idolatry.

Cupitt claims to stand in the tradition of Wittgenstein as well as Kierkegaard in this respect. Another author for whom both figures play an important role is D. Z. Phillips. However, we must acknowledge that whereas Cupitt happily describes himself as anti-realist, Phillips is more circumspect. Nevertheless, his work is of interest because it seeks to avoid founding religious truth on extra-religious facts or evidences, and it concentrates upon an understanding of the way religious language is used.

Phillips characterizes faith in *non-cognitive* terms. That is, he denies that religious faith is a question of *knowing* something about the world. In his view, those who disagree about the truth of religion are not disagreeing about a 'matter of fact',[34] and therefore "Coming to see that there is a God is not like coming to see that an additional being exists ... [It] involves seeing a new meaning in one's life, and being given a new understanding.'[35] For him, Kierkegaard's notion of subjective truth alerts us to the fact that religion is not about accumulating information concerning supernatural beings or events, but about changing the way in which one lives. It involves a shift from a quantitative to a qualitative approach to faith.[36] Faith is not the claim that

---

[31] See Don Cupitt, *The Religion of Being* (London: SCM, 1998), passim.
[32] Don Cupitt, *Creation*, pp. 53–60.
[33] Don Cupitt, *Long-Legged Fly*, pp. 22–35.
[34] D. Z. Phillips, *Faith and Philosophical Enquiry* (London: Routledge, 1970), p. 17.
[35] Ibid., pp. 17–18.
[36] Ibid., p. 206.

certain statements correspond to objective and mind or language-independent states of affairs, but holding certain values to be intrinsically worthwhile. Religious concepts do not refer to transcendent entities, but serve to articulate human discipleship. Hence, for Kierkegaard, 'The God-given ability to give thanks in all things *is* the goodness of God.'[37] The value of faith does not therefore depend on how things go in the world. Kierkegaard is read as saying that 'The love of God is not based on the facts, but is itself the measure by which the Christian assesses the facts.'[38] Belief in external rewards, or an objective survival of the individual after death, is irrelevant to true religion.

In another work, Phillips gives this assessment of Kierkegaard's qualitative interpretation of eternal life:

> Eternity is not an extension of the present life, but a mode of judging it ... Questions about the immortality of the soul are seen not to be questions concerning the extent of a man's life, and in particular whether that life can extend beyond the grave, but questions concerning the kind of life a man is living.[39]

Phillips is close to Wittgenstein here. For the latter too, religious doctrines function in a peculiar way, unlike propositions intended to correspond with a pre-existing, objective reality. They are more like 'rules of life' regulating and guiding the performance of religious discipleship. This suggests an interesting connection with Wittgenstein's application of rules to language use as a whole. Successfully using a language (to refer, for example) depends on following rules. Words in themselves do not refer ('signs do not interpret themselves' as Putnam argues), apart from all context and use. Could the interpretation of religious doctrines as rules of life connect with a reorientation of the metaphysically realist view of language?

A large question mark still hangs over the precise status of such rules of life in Phillips' work. As we shall see, it is far from the case that a reading of religious doctrine in this regulative, 'grammatical' way need entail a strong anti-realist stance. Indeed, the increasing influence of narrative and cultural-linguistic models of interpreting faith is largely due to theologians who would consider themselves 'orthodox' in terms of Christian doctrine. And such models have been influential on recent readings of Kierkegaard's view of doctrine. We will examine this in greater detail in our concluding chapter.

For now, it is enough to note the strains such models place upon the the basic assumptions of metaphysical realism, and its application to religious language. Kierkegaard is seen as a resource for those who want to deny that religious doctrines are primarily cognitive and propositional, and this

---
[37] Ibid., p.209.
[38] Ibid., p.213.
[39] D. Z. Phillips, *Death and Immortality* (London and Basingstoke: Macmillan, 1970), p. 49.

inevitably raises the question of just what *kind* of truth such doctrines possess. And that in turn means that Kierkegaard is an important signpost for those wishing to push the non-cognitive case to what they see as its logical conclusion in anti-realism.

The question of language

Kierkegaard's writings can thus be used to elucidate the peculiar logic of religious beliefs. With their resistance to speculative philosophy, they can be taken to promote a version of Christianity which does not depend for its validity upon the objective truth of supernatural beliefs. However, matters go somewhat deeper than this preliminary sketch allows. Both Cupitt and Phillips are greatly concerned with the nature of language as an integral element of their philosophical theology. For Cupitt, language is the means by which we make the world. The world only comes into being for us as differentiated and defined by our linguistic practices.[40] It makes no sense to ask for a truth which transcends our language, because the only truth we can know is one established by criteria internal to language. 'Transcendence' itself is a metaphor, a linguistic signifier. There is no way of getting outside our language, to check from a neutral vantage point that our statements match up with reality.[41] This interpretation of the role and nature of language thus comes to be a powerful impetus for accepting an anti-realist approach to religious questions.

For his part, Phillips is concerned to emphasize that religion is a distinctive 'language game' in the Wittgensteinian sense.[42] It cannot be justified or discredited on criteria which are fundamentally alien to the logic of the game. Since religion concerns a *way* of looking at the world, rather than a body of information *about* the world, we cannot judge it on the same grounds as we would a scientific hypothesis. Wittgenstein said of religious doctrines: 'Rules of life are dressed up in pictures. And these pictures can only serve to *describe* what we are to do, not *justify* it.'[43] Religious language is not falsifiable as a 'matter of fact', because it is regulative, life-guiding. Insofar as it is religious language it does not refer to states of affairs which are verifiable independently of a religious form of life.

---

[40] See, for example, Don Cupitt, *Creation*, pp. 105–6, 194–5; *Radicals and the Future of the Church* (London: SCM, 1989), p. 55.
[41] Cupitt, *Radicals*, p. 38.
[42] See Phillips, *Faith*, Chapter 5.
[43] Wittgenstein, *Culture and Value*, trans. Winch (Oxford: Blackwell, 1980), p. 29e. See for example, C. Creegan, *Wittgenstein and Kierkegaard* (London and New York: Routledge, 1989); Cook, 'Kierkegaard and Wittgenstein', *Religious Studies* 23 (1987), pp. 199ff., for a comparison of the two figures.

So, whether we consider the constitutive role of language in our knowledge of the world, or whether we pay attention to the internal 'grammar' of religious discourse, a non-cognitive or anti-realist interpretation of Christianity seems to be bound up with the question of language itself. This presents us with a promising opening, because it suggests a new way into Kierkegaard's writings which places his views on the nature and role of language at the centre of our focus. This approach takes seriously the intrinsic importance of attending to the *medium* of communication in any consideration of his work. It also enables us to explore the use of Kierkegaard in recent interpretations of religious language as a form of rhetoric which disputes any cognitively realist position. In exploring the scope of such rhetoric, we will touch upon the connections between Kierkegaard's literary practice and the kind of deconstructive reading practised by Derrida and others,[44] a reading which also calls the representative, truth-asserting role of language itself into question.

Looking further ahead in our argument, we can see how this deepening and complication of the debate about religious truth is also a factor in contemporary narrative theology. In affirming the priority of the Christian story in any theological project, narrative theologians emphasize the total narrative framework of Christian doctrine. They claim that doctrines make sense only in relation to the story out of which they spring, and to which they are related as 'rules for reading'. That is, doctrines are primarily grammatical rather than propositional; they offer the rules for correctly interpreting and performing (living out) the Christian narrative rather than factual descriptions of the divine nature. Narrative theology does not acknowledge any neutral rational vantage point from which stories may be assessed and judged. We are always already embedded in narratives. Moreover, both religious and secular narratives work as total systems, determining what counts as 'rational' within their respective frameworks – frameworks which are essentially incommensurable with one another.[45]

Religious doctrines can thus be understood on cultural-linguistic grounds, as George Lindbeck has proposed. It is an argument which owes much to contemporary structuralist and post-structuralist accounts which view language as an outsideless system of differences. However, it uses such positions to affirm the Christian story, the Christian language, over against what it sees as the nihilist story embraced by secular postmodern thinkers. Thus, it is *Christian* language which becomes outsideless, all-consuming.

---

[44] See Derrida's *Of Grammatology*, trans. Spivak (Baltimore, Md.: Johns Hopkins University Press, 1976).

[45] See Gerard Loughlin, *Telling God's Story: Bible, Church and Narrative Theology* (Cambridge: Cambridge University Press, 1996); George A. Lindbeck, *The Nature of Doctrine: Religion and Theology in a Postliberal Age* (London: SPCK, 1984); John Milbank, *Theology and Social Theory* (Oxford: Blackwell, 1990).

Again, different readings of our contemporary philosophical predicament are rooted in different accounts of the nature of language – and again, these different readings have impacted upon Kierkegaard studies. Kierkegaard has been seen as the forerunner both of poststructuralist claims that truth is in some sense indecipherable and undecidable on any 'rational' ground *and* of a reaffirmation of the orthodox Christian narrative which alone provides a framework for positioning and judging all other narratives. Our basic concern with realism and anti-realism must open out onto these more complex debates as we explore the tensions inherent in Kierkegaard's authorship.

Methods

The focus on language as a central problem of Kierkegaard's thought still requires more justification than is provided by these contemporary agendas. We will also place Kierkegaard's work in a historical-philosophical context, in which language was receiving great attention, and through which issues of truth and representation had already been complicated in unprecedented ways. Our subsequent reading of Kierkegaard's texts will thus be elucidated by questions far from alien to his own context.

The aim, however, will not merely be to accumulate Kierkegaard's scattered observations into a theory or structure; Kierkegaard himself warns that the 'subjective thinker' should not seek for results (*CUP* 73, 78); by extension, the reader should guard against the temptation to distil propositions and conclusions from his work. It will be in the labour of a close reading of his texts that any theory will be discovered, in the interaction between reader and words which creates the possibility of meaningful communication. Moreover, any reading must be sensitive to the form of the communication. The *Concluding Unscientific Postscript* claims that 'The reduplication of the content in the form is essential to all artistry' (*CUP* 297). If this turns out to be less straightforward than it appears, we will avoid crude errors if we let it guide us to begin with. Our intention, in agreement with Mackey,[46] will be to read Kierkegaard well, attentive not just to what he says but to how he says it.

This bears sharply on the status of Kierkegaard's language about God. The Christian's attempt to speak about the Eternal and the Paradox of the God-Man inevitably strains the resources of representation. It must also complicate the question of the *truth* of those representations. What language is appropriate in theological discourse? What counts as a verification of theological statements? Does it even make sense to ask for one? To understand Kierkegaard's theory and praxis of language and communication

---

[46] Louis Mackey, *Kierkegaard: A Kind of Poet* (Philadelphia: University Pennsylvania Press, 1971), pp. x–xi.

is to go some way towards evoking these questions in their full depth and seriousness, both as they shape and rupture Kierkegaard's own writings and as they are implicit in any theology.

It will become clear that I make little interpretative capital out of the various distinctions to be found within the authorship, between signed and pseudonymous works, or between aesthetic, ethical, religious and distinctively Christian writings. The reasons for this will emerge through the argument, but some initial indication of my motives is called for.

I in no way wish to minimize the importance of attending to the differences between strands of the authorship, and the significance of their authorial status. However, my analysis of Kierkegaard's views on language will show that there is a thread binding all the works to a shared recognition of the inescapably indirect nature of communication, particularly as this touches on issues of existential interest. I follow Mark Taylor's view that Kierkegaard's position on indirect communication 'rests upon, and is necessitated by, his conception of language and his understanding of religious truth'.[47] That conception of language and truth is operative, albeit in distinctive ways, in *all* aspects of the authorship, disputing rigid boundary lines between its various categories. Some readings can easily miss these deeper connections through an overly systematic division and separation of the parts of the authorship. It is not enough, for example, to say that Kierkegaard believes in the ultimate desirability of the direct communication of Christianity, if one does not place the object of that communication under scrutiny. It may be that the Paradox of the God-Man only confirms the indirectness of Christian 'proclamation'. Thus, the distinctively 'religious' or 'Christian' writing needs to be seen in the context of problems raised in aesthetic and ethical texts.

Indeed, if form and content are intertwined in Kierkegaard's literary project, then his preoccupation with the opacity of existence to rational comprehension, the peculiar contradictoriness of human spiritual development, the inaccessibility of the eternal to direct gaze and the absurdity of Christian faith must all contribute to depriving us of any straightforward classification of his works. The mere presence of a signature is no guarantee of autobiographical or religious authenticity. Moreover, Christianity itself cannot be approached as a self-contained sphere, like a result whose reality is logically independent of the way in which one gets to it (*PC* 206–11). If this is so, the insights we have into the complex process of communication and fidelity, as we find them in other life-views, will find their echoes, if not their deeper resonances, within paradoxical faith. To read Kierkegaard in this way should not blind us to differences and tensions and indeed ruptures which

---

[47] Mark C. Taylor, 'Language, Truth and Indirect Communication', *Tijdschrift voor Filosofie* 37 (1975), p. 74.

constitute his work, whilst illuminating the basic dynamic of a writing which always skirts the unsayable.

Citing Aage Henriksen and Mark C. Taylor, David Law distinguishes some basic methodological approaches in studying Kierkegaard.[48] Henriksen refers to the literary method, the content method and the psychological method. The literary method focuses on the literary form of the texts, the content method on the thoughts and ideas which are the subject matter of the text and the psychological method on the relation between the texts and the personal life of the author.

As far as the literary and content approaches go, it will be clear from my preceding remarks that I do not believe that form and content can be sharply distinguished in this schematic way. What Kierkegaard writes is affected by the manner in which he writes. Any sharp separation of the two leaves us with either an abstract formalistic view, or a search for the 'essential content' of Kierkegaard from which all the accidental trappings of literary form have been stripped away. Both options contain dubious philosophical assumptions which threaten to split Kierkegaard's texts in artificial ways.

The psychological method has deficiencies of its own. It can lead to another form of reductionism, in which the meaning of Kierkegaard's texts is dominated or exhausted by their reference to the events of his inner and outer life. Such correspondences are notoriously hard to establish, and they can dissolve the wider impact of Kierkegaard's communications into a voyeuristic fascination with the author's life. In fact, Kierkegaard wanted to resist any direct relationship between himself and his works.

That is not to say, however, that the biographical traumas Kierkegaard experienced do not leave their traces within his texts. Clearly, his father's influence, the broken engagement with Regine, the Corsair affair, and so on do figure large in the construction of his writings. Nevertheless, it is not in a reconstruction of Kierkegaard's inner life that the interest should lie, but in the way in which these events are mirrored and refracted to gain a larger significance. Themes of fatherhood, the erotic, the press and the public are insistent in the authorship. In this sense, a renewed and self-critical 'psychological' method can help to reclaim these themes from their marginality in the canon of Kierkegaard interpretation.

Henriksen's psychological method corresponds with the first of Taylor's three categories: the biographical-psychological. His others are the historical-comparative and the descriptive-thematic. The historical-comparative method locates Kierkegaard's thought in relation to his time and to other modern thinkers, whereas the descriptive-thematic approach attempts a fair description of Kierkegaard's thought, whether as a whole or through concentrating on a particular theme. Both contribute to my own approach, which seeks to move beyond the form/content impasse.

---

[48] Law, *Kierkegaard*, pp. 3–4.

Again, it is not a question of either/or; methodological purity risks falling into narrowness. My dominant approach *is* thematic: the question of language will be our guiding thread through the authorship. However, it is important both to recognize how that question was being raised and complicated by Kierkegaard's near contemporaries, and to relate it to more recent philosophical reflection on language. Moreover, I am not aiming to convert Kierkegaard's authorship into a monolithic whole. Whilst language has a privileged place in this exposition, this has more to do with understanding Kierkegaard's practice of communication than any belief that language theory is the essence of Kierkegaard's thought. Language is not an isolated phenomenon for Kierkegaard. It brings into play the dilemmas of immediacy and reflection, self-consciousness, subjectivity and paradox, dilemmas which, for Kierkegaard, admit of no systematic or conceptual resolution.

In taking a predominantly descriptive-thematic approach, I aim to be faithful to both the 'how' and the 'what' of Kierkegaard's texts. The question of realism and anti-realism, as it is bound up with the interpretation of the nature of language, holds these elements together. As we shall see, for Kierkegaard, the articulation of the reality of God in language puts both the form and the content of any utterance under strain. Thus, whilst I will show that these are issues which are highly relevant in Kierkegaard's own philosophical and historical context, this will not preclude him from intervening in an ongoing philosophical debate. Such a hybrid methodology, whilst it cannot avoid giving more weight to certain elements than others, may yet avoid some of the cruder reductions of Kierkegaard's own complex method.

Objectivity and subjectivity

It is appropriate that the methodological issues I have raised connect with the 'substantive' argument of the book. If, for Kierkegaard, form and content in general are inseparably locked together, then the same may be said of his view of religious language. The how of religious language and communication cannot be subtracted from the what. Religious communication is neither contentless rhetoric nor a direct statement of objective truth.

If this is the case, then the ambiguity of Kierkegaard's position in relation to realism and anti-realism becomes more understandable. Kierkegaard does not fit easily into either category. In fact, we will see how Kierkegaard occupies a third position, somewhere between the two, which we will call *ethical realism*. From anti-realism, he might draw the point that religious faith is not a matter of *knowing*, of conceptual cognition. There is no direct or immediate access to God, and faith takes the form of a subjective passion. God is not knowable outside of the forms of life to which faith commits itself in passionate interest and striving.

However, from realism he would adopt the argument that religious faith cannot be reduced without remainder to an expression of human ideals. Language about God still opens us to an otherness which we cannot eliminate or dispose of at will. There is a real constraint operating on our formulation of appropriate practical responses to the religious calling.

To hold such positions together might suggest a dubious philosophical sleight of hand. In fact, although we have said that Kierkegaard occupies a middle position between realism and anti-realism, this does not do justice to the radical nature of his authorship. It is not that Kierkegaard just mixes together a bit of objectivity and a bit of subjectivity to produce the right notion of faith. Rather, he places the boundaries between subjective and objective in dispute, without effacing the difference between them. A comparison might be drawn with Putnam's internal realism, which distances itself from both metaphysical realism and relativism. Putnam, too, remember wants to loosen the grip that the objective–subjective dichotomy has upon us, and so make space for ethical and religious language to breathe again.

Objectivity and subjectivity have many connotations. The 'objectivity' that Kierkegaard resists is that of the neutral and impartial spectator, who is able to judge what the truth is from an elevated vantage point. Objective truth is the correspondence of thought and reality which is valid independently of whether or not we happen to accept it. This model of truth presupposes that it is timeless, universally valid and accessible to intellectual contemplation.

It is virtually a truism that against this kind of objectivity, Kierkegaard advocates the maxim that 'subjectivity is truth'. 'Subjectivity' here means something like inward, passionate faith which has no objective, external guarantee of its validity. The subjective character of truth means that faith is a risk, that faith demands commitment and action rather than the speculative gaze of philosophy. As finite existing beings, we have no vantage point outside existence from which to judge the truth of our conceptions of God. Subjective truth is truth for me.

So far, so familiar. We must add, however, that even such familiar Kierkegaardian themes are easily distorted. Most importantly, proclaiming the 'subjectivity' of truth does not amount to endorsing subjectivism: the idea that our beliefs are nothing more than human inventions or fictions which we project out onto the void of a meaningless universe. One cannot ignore the fact that the famous statement that 'subjectivity is truth' in the *Postscript* is counterbalanced by a recognition that 'subjectivity is untruth' – that is, that human subjectivity is always already answerable to, guilty before, an otherness which precedes it. Kierkegaard, through Climacus his pseudonym, does not license unbridled human subjectivism, for the human will is not deemed to be pure and innocent.

Moreover, Kierkegaard is also able to state in explicit rejection of subjectivism that 'there is a How with the characteristic that when the How is scrupulously rendered the What is also given, that this is the How of "faith." Right here, at its very maximum, inwardness is shown to be objectivity.'[49] The notions of How and What, form and content, rebound upon one another, to transform one another mutually, in ways that promise to elude neat divisions.

The categories of objective and subjective are beginning to look a little shaky. They are neither so self-contained nor so diametrically opposed as we might have thought. Now this might lead us to suggest a compromise. Is Kierkegaard arguing that, although God is a really existing, objective being, we only encounter him through passionate subjective faith? Such a view has much to recommend it. It avoids extreme distortions of Kierkegaard's writings, and it tries to do justice to the whole of what he writes on the nature of faith.

However, just stated in this way, it also remains rather too neat. It is as if adding together the objective existence of God and the subjective faith of the believer solved all our problems. The real question is whether this language of subjective and objective is not placed under unbearable tension by the tasks it is asked to perform: accounting for the nature of human selfhood and divine reality. If we are no longer sure what the objective existence of God or the subjective inwardness of the individual might actually *mean*, then we have to go somewhat deeper than this surface reflection.

This is where the question of language is relevant. Kierkegaard's ethical realism does, in one sense take elements from realism and anti-realism. However, it is not merely a neutral middle point, a no-man's land of philosophy. Rather, it disturbs the whole basis upon which realist and anti-realist conclusions are drawn. Kierkegaard does not just want to take his place along the philosophical spectrum. He wants to wound philosophy from behind, to use its categories against its fundamental presuppositions, to make it tremble with the resonance of the otherness and inwardness which it cannot comprehend even as it tries to incorporate them.

For thinkers since the Enlightenment, through Romanticism and Idealism, and beyond, it is the question of language which has evoked the strangest paradoxes and aporias of thought. Language seems so intertwined with self-consciousness and society, with our attempts to state the truth of who we are, of what the world is and of who God is, that it becomes the locus for a thinking which pushes against the limits of what it is possible to think. Thus, the rhetorical nature of Kierkegaard's texts cannot simply be discounted, even if they resist any dissolution of Christian concepts into aesthetic categories. It is here that we must begin if we are not to reduce Kierkegaard's thought to a result, another philosophical position easily ranged up with the all the rest.

---

[49] JP 4: 4550; Pap. X(2) A 299.

Plan of the book

In order to avoid such reductionism, we need to take a somewhat circuitous route. The aim will be to tease out the implications of Kierkegaard's views on language for the debate about the reality of God. As we will see, however, this debate cannot be separated from philosophical questions about the nature of self-consciousness, knowledge, ethics and paradox – *and* less traditional issues surrounding women, the body, seduction, the erotic and the nature of witnessing.

Chapter 2 provides some of the historical and philosophical context for Kierkegaard's thought which we mentioned earlier. The aim is to provide an overview of philosophical approaches to language – empiricist, romantic and idealist – rather than to specify definite influences on Kierkegaard. However, some authors such as Hamann, Fichte, Schelling, Hegel and the Danes Grundtvig and Heiberg clearly figured large in Kierkegaard's own development.

The chapter explores the intensification of a crisis affecting philosophical understanding of language, truth and representation. Attempts to discover the origin and essence of language end in paradox. There seems to be no pure point of origin, no seamless continuum between prelinguistic nature and the arrival of language. Language seems to inaugurate a break with natural immediacy (a direct and instinctive contact with reality) whilst making self-consciousness possible. The self's quest for truth runs aground against the impossibility of any direct apprehension of truth in language. Language is the condition for any search for truth to be possible, and yet it is a condition which makes the full attainment of its goal unreachable.

In Chapter 3, we examine the ways in which Kierkegaard and his pseudonyms reflect on these issues. In asking whether Kierkegaard provides us with a theory of language, we are led to an initial appreciation of the complex nature of his authorship. Two points emerge. Firstly, language is not a transparent medium. In other words, language does not convey a direct and unmediated access to reality as it is in itself. Language introduces a rupture of the self from direct contact with reality. This leads to the second point: the self is not fully and immediately present to itself. It is not a self-contained whole, which can know itself with perfect knowledge. Rather, self-consciousness is made possible by reflection, and hence by language. Self-consciousness transcends and cancels its own immediate basis. It is thus, to philosophical thought, a kind of contradiction. There is no adequate, objective vantage point from which to give a full description of the self.

Ethical and religious communication must therefore reckon with the philosophical obscurity inherent within the self. They must articulate possibilities for existing, indirectly luring the self into heightened consciousness and commitment. A kind of rhetorical irony characterizes ethical and religious discourse from the outset. That indirectness is seen to characterize even (or especially) talk about Christ. The God-Man is the ultimate sign of contradiction, the fulfilment of language's paradoxical nature. Such discourse goes beyond description and theory; it calls for practical and passionate response.

Chapter 4 explores the risks associated with such a focus on rhetoric and allurement. The character of the seducer in *Either/Or* exposes a permanent possibility of language and communication. Language blocks off the immediacy and certitude we crave. The seducer tries to recapture it precisely by exploiting to the full the deceit and dissimulation which language makes possible. Though his cruelty is self-defeating, the crisis of representation which he intensifies cannot be remedied by any extra knowledge or objective evidence. The way in which the seducer's philosophical prejudices translate into the manipulation of people (and particularly women) signal that the question of language and communication, realism and anti-realism, is an ethico-religious one as much as an epistemological one.

If language is the medium of dissimulation and indirectness, it might seem as if we need to go beyond language to a wordless direct encounter with God. Realism could be justified by an appeal to direct experience. However, as Chapter 5 argues, such silent experience is not self-evident; it always lays itself open to other interpretations. Silence cannot put a stop to the indirectness of language and communication. It can mask demonic defiance as much as faith. However, Kierkegaard's texts use silence as a motif which upsets our confidence in language as a representation of reality. Words cannot express Abraham's absurd faith, which resists any dependence on objective evidence.

Kierkegaard's texts thus seem to deny any simple religious realism. But we are left with a problem. How is religious faith to be distinguished from a self-annihilating irony? Is there *any* extra-human referent to religious language, or is it wholly a projection of human ideals or illusions? Chapter 6 opens with a discussion of Kierkegaard's early critique of Romantic irony. Such irony tried to elevate the human subject to a position of mastery over the world which is no better than its philosophical, speculative counterpart. It seems to dissolve all external reality in the face of the subjective freedom of the ironist. Both irony and speculation, taken to extremes, try to circumvent the ambiguities of existence, to regain a lost immediate unity of thought and being, whether through the artistic expression of the individual or the speculative comprehension of the system.

Against this, Kierkegaard's upbuilding discourses counter with the need for faith – but a faith which takes seriously the inner complexity of the self and the hiddenness of God. The reader/believer is both passive and creative in the act of faith. This has to be so because of the nature of human existence and language, which holds thought and being apart. However, Kierkegaard's texts still argue for a real relationship with God, and we explore how his treatment of the reality of God avoids the one-sidedness of simplistic realism or anti-realism. The reality of God is known indirectly through the transformation of our own existence, a process in which we are wholly receptive and yet also wholly responsible and free. This position we call *ethical realism*.

The fact that God is only negatively present in creation mirrors the author's negative presence in his or her own texts. The reader/believer is faced with ambiguity and responsibility in both cases – so that Kierkegaard's texts invite a response of faith or offence analogous to that which the call of God invites. This leads us, in Chapter 7, to apply to Kierkegaard's texts the idea of *the analogy of communication*. God is known or denied in and through the relationships made possible by human communication. Kierkegaard's texts describe God's relation to the world and the self as being like that of a poet or an author to their text. By withdrawing himself, he opens up a space for genuine freedom and relationship. Thus, God is not knowable from a conceptual, ethically neutral standpoint, but only through the struggles and choices of the passionate and committed life of faith. God must not be proved, but witnessed to.

However, this does not admit the validity of any fundamentalist fanaticism. Witnessing must respect its own limitations – it is not a form of certitude or *self-expression*. The self is intrinsically open to an otherness which has established it. It cannot establish or account for itself, and it cannot control this alterity. Kierkegaard's texts exercise a therapeutic, critical role, exploring the limitations of life-positions, offering a critique of any claim to direct knowledge of God. Such a direct knowledge is dismissed as idolatry. However, the relationship to God is not purely negative. For the Christian, it is given incarnate form in the life of Christ. Christ invites us to embody the truth in our own life. Nevertheless, there is still no evasion of the indirect and paradoxical nature of religious communication. Christianity offers, not a special knowledge or intuition of God, but a pattern of self-emptying and free discipleship.

These threads are drawn together in Chapter 8. Kierkegaard's version of realism is clarified through further discussion of 'postmodern' readings of his texts and narrative theology. Kierkegaard's texts provide no privileged conceptual access to God or the self. Rather, conscious of the nature of language, they are self-deconstructive, exposing their own indirect and paradoxical nature. And yet Kierkegaard does affirm that religious communication can open us to the otherness of God. God is not an object perceptible in the world, but neither is the relationship to God only a human projection. The God-relationship is realized and embodied in concrete ethical, liberating discipleship. On this basis, a possible critique of recent 'orthodox' narrative theology is outlined, a critique which also rebounds upon some of Kierkegaard's own insistence on the exclusive centrality of the Christian story.

CHAPTER TWO

In search of the perfect language

This chapter aims to establish the importance of philosophical reflection on language for thinkers leading up to and contemporary with Kierkegaard.[1] Whilst it cannot claim to be exhaustive, it will draw out themes and tendencies which recur in diverse brands of philosophy. On the one hand, there was from the Enlightenment a conviction that language introduced a split between immediate reality and our representation of it through words and signs. On the other, there was a hope that a language could be found or made which would restore or elevate us to a more perfect comprehension of reality. Such a language should not cut us off from that which it represents. It would be a transparent medium, granting access to things as they really are.

Different philosophers made different assumptions about 'things as they really are'. It might mean returning words to their bedrock significations in the basic sense-impressions which impinge upon us. It might mean seeing in words a means to unveil the rational, universal essence of reality. In either case, issues about the nature of language were bound up with basic attitudes towards the nature of 'reality' as such. And these attitudes had implications which went beyond the 'purely' epistemological into regions of aesthetics, ethics, politics and religion.

The search for the perfect language is no mere academic game. For our purposes, it raises the following question: given that language does seem to be integral to self-consciousness and reflection *and* that it seems to deny us any immediate apprehension of reality, are we not led to a fundamentally anti-realist position on the major concepts in aesthetics, ethics, politics and, perhaps most obviously, religion? In other words, must we admit that such concepts are inevitably human cultural and linguistic products, with no verifiable reference to an external, objective order?

A dilemma arises: the very search for a medium which would reveal reality to us as it is 'in itself' threatens to reveal nothing more than that our very notions of 'reality' are conventional, fictional creations. This line of tension will be our guiding path.

---

[1] The chapter was given its present title as part of my original Ph.D. thesis *The Meaning and Status of Søren Kierkegaard's Language about God* (Cambridge, 1994), and therefore predates my acquaintance with Umberto Eco's book *The Search for the Perfect Language* (London: Fontana, 1997 – first published in English by Blackwell in 1995). Eco's book contains a wealth of material giving more detail on specific attempts to construct an idealized language.

Rationalism and empiricism

Two of the decisive events in the history of modern philosophy were the projects of Cartesian doubt and Kantian transcendental method. Both Descartes and Kant question the basis upon which we can claim to have true knowledge about ourselves and about the world around us. Both highlight the thinking subject's role in constituting that knowledge, so that objective knowledge does not simply impinge upon us from the outside, but is established by criteria internal to the rules governing rational thought. For Descartes, it is the self-evidence of clear and distinct ideas which form the indubitable bedrock of all our thinking; for Kant, it is the necessary a priori validity of the categories of the understanding which compel us to construct experience in the way we do. Both are then left with problems of how we check the self-evidence of our ideas, or the necessity of our conceptual scheme, with reality as it is in itself.

What is missing from these vital episodes in the history of ideas is any consideration of the debt each thinker owes to the *language* which he uses. Descartes, it seems, doubts everything except the adequacy of the language he employs to narrate his passage into doubt and out the other side. Derrida claims that 'Descartes never confronts the question of his own language';[2] Nietzsche exploits this omission, by calling into question whether we know what words like 'I', 'think' and 'exist' really mean.[3] What are supposedly immediate certainties in fact conceal an interpretative framework which is far from self-evident. Similarly, Kant is accused, not of offering any real explanation, but merely of presenting us with a 'repetition of the question'.[4]

Hamann, a contemporary of Kant's, and a significant influence on Kierkegaard,[5] had earlier taken the same line, claiming that Kant failed to give an account of the language he used to articulate the categories of thought. Hamann, on the contrary, affirmed 'the genealogical priority of language and its heraldry over the seven holy functions of logical propositions and inferences'.[6] He ironized Kant's position, claiming that 'Sounds and letters are therefore pure forms *a priori*',[7] because it is they which unite sensibility and understanding,

---

[2] J. Derrida, *Writing and Difference*, trans. Bass (London: Routledge, 1978), p. 53.
[3] F. Nietzsche, *Beyond Good and Evil*, trans. Hollingdale (Harmondsworth: Penguin, 1973), pp. 27f.
[4] Ibid., p. 24.
[5] See R. Gregor-Smith, 'Hamann and Kierkegaard', *Kierkegaardiana* 5 (1964), pp. 52–67. References to Hamann's writings will be to *Sämtliche Werke*, ed. Nadler (Vienna: Herder, 1949–57 (6 vols)), hereafter 'N'; and to *Briefwechsel*, ed. Ziesemer and Henkel (Wiesbaden: Insel-Verlag, 1955 (7 vols)), hereafter 'Z'. Many passages are translated in R. Gregor-Smith, *J. G. Hamann 1730–88: A Study in Christian Existence* (London: Collins, 1960), hereafter 'RGS'.
[6] In his *Metacritique of the Purism of Reason;* N III 286; RGS, p. 216.
[7] Ibid.; RGS, p. 217.

particular and universal. Language comes first, and is presupposed by thought. Thought cannot hope to ignore it, get behind it, or explain it away.

The question of language, left unarticulated in the philosophical elevation of the subject, can thus be employed to complicate the issues of truth and objectivity which arise in its wake. It is a question which was in fact raised with ever greater insistence in philosophical writings from the seventeenth century onwards.[8] This was partly due to a desire for a language which would adequately mirror reality. Bacon advocated a philosophical language 'directly representing things and notions',[9] and various imaginary and philosophical language projects were delineated in the seventeenth century, all aiming at a medium which could correspond exactly to the structure of creation. Pombo[10] links this with the notion of an original Adamic language lost at Babel, a language which was perfect, universal and transparent to reality. It was this original, or something like it, which these projects sought to reconstruct, or which they took as a guiding ideal.

Leibniz was a prime example of this tendency. His metaphysics entailed that the world consisted exclusively of individual substances-with-accidents. This made him both a nominalist (who claimed that abstract, universal values have no real existence) and a proponent of a language which would exactly 'fit' reality and remove all 'equivocations and amphibolies', a language in which 'people will be unable to speak or write about anything except what they understand'.[11] Certain types of propositions (notably of the form 'S is p') were uniquely privileged to depict reality without remainder. A philosophical language, modelled on mathematical calculus, was both something to be recollected in the labour of etymology *and* something to be created anew. It would be a language which conformed exactly to the nature of things and the process of rational thought. Ontology and semiology, being and signs, would no longer be estranged from one another.

However, this ideal had many implications. There was, firstly, an awareness of the present inadequacy of language, of the sort which caused a whole book of Locke's *Essay Concerning Human Understanding*[12] to be devoted to words. Secondly, with the increasing prevalence of historical modes of explanation, and the corresponding search for the *origin* of language, came

---

[8] H. Aarsleff, *From Locke to Saussure* (Minneapolis: University of Minnesota Press, 1982), passim.

[9] Quoted in O. Pombo, *Leibniz and the Problem of a Universal Language* (Münster: Nodus, 1987), pp. 72–3. See also Eco, *Search for the Perfect Language*.

[10] Pombo, *Leibniz*, Chapter 2; cf. Aarsleff, *Locke to Saussure*, pp. 42ff.

[11] Quoted in B. Mates, *The Philosophy of Leibniz: Metaphysics and Language* (New York and Oxford: Oxford University Press, 1986), p. 186.

[12] Quotations taken from Locke, *An Essay Concerning Human Understanding: An Abridgement*, ed. Yolton (London and Rutland: Everyman, 1991). This is based on the fifth edition (1706); the first edition came out in 1690.

an appreciation of the extent to which language was inextricably intertwined with human (individual and societal) self-understanding. The evaluations which are apparent in texts of linguistic 'archaeology' witness to the key place of the interpretation of language in any assessment of the human condition.

Locke's text itself embodies some of the tensions which seem common to writings of otherwise radically differing philosophical perspectives. Despite his empiricism he nevertheless shared with Leibniz a dependency on the Aristotelian theory of words, which saw the purpose of language as 'telementation' – the transportation of ideas from the mind of the speaker to that of the listener;[13] Locke also espoused a kind of nominalism comparable to that of Leibniz. 'All things that exist being particulars' (III/3/1), Locke argues that general ideas are abstractions from particular sensations. Therefore, '*general* and *universal* belong not to the real existence of things, but *are the inventions* and *creatures of the understanding* made for it for its own use and *concern only signs*, whether words or *ideas*' (III/3/15).

Words, however, are themselves secondary to the ideas we form from our sensory data. Following his rejection of innate ideas in 'Book I', Locke describes how the understanding is based on simple ideas drawn from sensory experience (e.g. 'whiteness', 'heat', 'light'). These simple ideas are always adequate to what they represent (II/30–1). However, when more complex ideas are built up out of simple components, the gap between nature and our representations of it becomes apparent. Those ideas which Locke calls 'mixed modes' are complex ideas with no straightforward, observable basis in nature (i.e. human, conventional descriptions such as 'murder', 'gallantry'). The problem is made more acute, because Locke affirms the unknowability of the 'real essences' of things. All our knowledge derives from immediately observed sensory qualities. That which lies at the root of these qualities, causing them to appear just as they do, is beyond the reach of our sensory faculties. This 'beyond' is the real essence, the condition for a thing being what it is – but it is a condition we cannot gain access to.

Words or signs themselves are at yet another remove from nature. Signs are simply annexed to ideas (III/9/2), and therefore 'a man may use whatever signs he pleases to signify his own *ideas* to himself' (ibid.). They have no 'natural connection' with ideas, but function by virtue of a 'voluntary imposition' (III/2/1). Language confirms the fact that real essences are unknown; only nominal essences, abstract ideas created by our convention and for our convenience, can be known (III/3/15–17).

That which can be known best is therefore that which is most distant from natural reality, and most likely to be a purely human creation. As we have seen, 'mixed modes' present us with the clearest instance of this. They are

---

[13] R. Harris and T. Taylor, *Landmarks in Linguistic Thought* (London and New York: Routledge, 1989), p. 113.

altogether arbitrary creations of the understanding. Ideas such as parricide or incest have no foundation in nature (III/5/5–7). The names of mixed modes therefore '*lead our thoughts to the mind and no further*' (III/5/12). They can claim no standard in nature, for they copy no 'really existing' thing (III/9/7).

This presents us with a problem. Language stands at the end of a process in which our representations and concepts become progressively uncoupled from reality. It is only by claiming that our building blocks of simple ideas are always adequate mirrors of reality that Locke can hope to anchor those representations. However, to attribute this status to simple ideas remains an undemonstrated assumption. It is an assumption which is undermined by Locke's own admission that both words *and* ideas are types of sign, and signs of any sort only relate to reality indirectly. They presuppose that we stand at a distance from immediate reality or nature. Besides, Locke admits that many of our most important concepts follow no natural archetype. Mixed modes always haunt Locke's account of words, because they constantly suggest an inversion of his order of things. Rather than conventional and arbitrary words supervening on an original, immediate awareness of nature, it could be that convention, the break with nature, comes *first*, as the condition for any signification, any ideas, to be possible at all. The nature of the names of mixed modes forces Locke to admit the very thing he feared – the lack of a foundation: 'And hence we see that, in the interpretation of laws, whether divine or human, there is no end ...' (III/9/9). Significantly, Locke's assertion that '*morality is capable of demonstration*, as well as mathematics' (III/11/16) was never fulfilled.

Locke cannot specify any wholly 'natural' vantage point from which to judge the adequacy of our representations. Not only are even simple ideas the result of a certain distancing of ourselves from nature, but Locke's insights into mixed modes suggests that language operates in quite different ways than a pure mimicry of the given world. They suggest that our role in defining our concepts and values may play an indispensable role in determining the kind of access we have to that world.

Condillac, who wrote in the wake and spirit of Locke's *Essay*, took a different route to his mentor: a return to the origins of language.[14] His major work on language is the *Essai sur les Origines des Connaissances Humaines* (1746).[15] Here again, we find the link between the questions 'what can we

---

[14] See Aarsleff, *Locke to Saussure*, pp. 146ff. and 278ff.

[15] References are to *Oeuvres Philosophiques*, ed. Le Roy (Paris: Presses Universitaires de France, 1947 (3 vols)), though the *Essai* (OP I 1–118) is referred to by section and paragraph; *An Essay on the Origin of Human Knowledge* (facsimile reprint of Thomas Nugent's translation of 1756), (Gainsville: Scholars' Facsimiles and Reprints, 1971), (this will be referred to as '*Essai*') and *Condillac's Treatise on the Sensations*, trans. Carr (London: Favil, 1930). Other significant passages translated in Harris and Taylor, *Landmarks*, Chapter 10 (pp. 120–35) and Derrida, *The Archeology of the Frivolous*, trans. Leavey (Lincoln and London: University of Nebraska Press, 1980).

know?', 'what kind of things are there?' and 'what are words?'. Condillac sought to show that 'all knowledge arises from sensations',[16] that 'Man is but the sum of his acquirements'.[17] He tries to demonstrate this not only by rational argument, but by a speculative reconstruction of the origin of our ideas, and so of language. The apparent artificiality of this reconstruction will not, Condillac hopes, prevent us from gaining a renewed awareness of our roots in nature.

According to Derrida, Condillac's opposition to Aristotelian metaphysics as the 'first philosophy' depends on another, ultimately metaphysical, move: that of the return to nature. Though Condillac, in *La Langue des Calculs*, echoes Leibniz in his desire for 'the constitution of a rigorously arbitrary, formal and conventional language',[18] it is the speculative reconstruction of *natural* origins which will supply the new language with a grammar. As Derrida asks:

> Isn't that in order to make amends through language for language's misdeeds, to push artifice back to that limit which leads back to nature: 'There is the advantage that algebra will have; it will make us speak like nature, and we will believe we have made a great discovery' (O.P. II, p. 435)?[19]

Condillac's stress on the primacy of feeling is only the first step in a process in which he 'develops sensationalism into a semiotism'.[20] Language is indispensable in forming Condillac's view of human nature. For him, the distinctive character of human existence is freedom of will, defined primarily as freedom from nature. As Harris and Taylor remark, Condillac's distinctive claim is that 'without the use of a language man does not have voluntary control of the faculty of reflection, nor indeed of the other faculties of the mind'.[21]

How can a process rooted in natural sensation lead to a split from nature? When does the break with immediacy occur? In the *Essai*, Condillac imagines two children, survivors of the Deluge, who are to re-enact the founding of language. Language will be part of their growing away from a prior annihilation, from the muteness of a flooded earth. At first, they are determined by instinct alone (II/I/2). They use sounds and gestures in an habitual association with their needs and passions. Condillac continues:

> The more they grew familiar with those signs, the more they were in a capacity of reviving them at pleasure. Their memory began to acquire

---

[16] OP I 313; Carr, p. 236.
[17] OP I 314; Carr, p. 238.
[18] Derrida, *Archeology of the Frivolous*, p. 37.
[19] Ibid.
[20] Ibid., p. 46.
[21] Harris–Taylor, *Landmarks*, pp. 123–4.

some form of habit, they were able to command their imagination as they pleased, and insensibly they learned to do by reflection what they had hitherto done merely by instinct. (II/I/3)

There is a curious twist in this 'explanation'. How can *habit* produce the break with nature? Doesn't this merely repeat the problem in a new form?

As the *Essai* proceeds, its ambiguities mount. Condillac claims that the first language was a language of actions. The use of gesture removed ambiguities, and words were pronounced 'under such particular circumstances, that everyone was obliged to refer them to the same perceptions' (II/I/80). Names of general and simple ideas developed out of sensible data, by extension from the names of complex substances, which would be the first to be derived from the senses (II/I/82). Abstraction and analysis were the key techniques for this extension of language from its core, a development which meant that 'language must, from its first beginnings, have been figurative and metaphorical' (II/I/127n.). Words imitated the language of actions, and these words were available for further adaptation to new contexts.

However, this unavoidable facet of language introduces a problem. For, as language develops, it forgets its origins (II/I/104) and becomes an ambivalent tool. Following Locke, Condillac claims that 'the names of simple terms are the least susceptible of ambiguity' (II/I/112). The problems arise with complex ideas. Condillac argues that many of our disputes concern only the signification of words. Uncertainties arise because of a lack of definition. As for Locke, definition consists of analysis and decomposition of names into their basic elements. But Condillac goes further. In the *Grammaire*, he says that language itself is an 'analytic method', breaking complex thoughts down into their component parts (ideas) and recomposing them at will.[22] However, this model of language, developing analogically from its first origins makes the work of analysis – its *own* work – fraught with difficulties.

The principle of analogy is central for Condillac. He argues in the *Logique* that 'It is analogy that makes up the whole art of language.'[23] This is necessary to keep in check the very arbitrariness which characterizes the higher progression of language. As Derrida argues, this allows him to assert both a real development of language and a limitation of that development to the unfolding of identical propositions, the recollection of language's first content: 'The fact is, production of the new – and imagination – are only productions: by analogical connection and repetition, they bring to light what, without being there, *will have been* there.'[24] The paradoxical formulation captures the ambivalence of the relation between nature and language, instinct

---

[22] Ibid., p. 125.
[23] OP II 398; Harris–Taylor, *Landmarks*, p. 130.
[24] Derrida, *Archeology of the Frivolous*, p. 71.

and freedom. For the original figurative speech, as it forgets itself in the service of human freedom, becomes more and more arbitrary, more and more dissociated from *things*.

A quasi-physical law of inevitable decline sets in. The original state of language – its metaphoricity, the possibility of analogy – has become 'the first and principal cause of the decline of languages' (II/I/141). Words float free from things, and a law of physics is reinstated as a law of semiotics, in which 'motion, the source of life, becomes the principle of destruction' (II/I/158). This leads Condillac to advocate a conscious redesign of language 'without regard to use or custom' (II/II/11). To achieve this, we need to put ourselves into particular circumstances to receive sensible impressions, give them precise names – and then put others in the same circumstances. In this way we can share precise significations of words in relation to their simple, foundational ideas. As Condillac says 'Simple ideas can never occasion any mistake' (II/II/31).

The absurdity of this artifice, its impracticality and the fact that it would surely have to be repeated again and again as language followed the law of its decline, all suggests that the ideality of words cannot be so firmly anchored to reference points as Condillac supposes. The abolition of language according to use or custom would leave us speechless – and how could we found a language out of silence? Condillac, ultimately, only restores the problem with which he began: how does speech arise after the deluge?[25]

Herder and Hamann: disputing the origin

It seems that the very search for a natural origin or perfect archetype for language is intrinsically flawed. It only reveals that the origin or pattern it seeks is an unattainable ideal. None was more aware of the subtlety of these issues than J. G. Herder. His 1772 *Treatise on the Origin of Language*,[26] whilst on the surface a naturalistic riposte to orthodox authors who were asserting the divine origin of language as a gift from God, in fact disputes *any* such reconstruction.[27]

---

[25] Rousseau reproduces, albeit with modifications, the essential logic of Condillac's account. See his *Essai sur l'Origine des Langues*, ed. Porset (Bordeaux: Ducros, 1970), translated in *Rousseau-Herder: On the Origin of Language*, trans. Moran and Gode (New York: Frederick Ungar, 1966). Cf. Derrida, *Of Grammatology*, (Baltimore, Md.: John Hopkins University Press, 1976), pp. 141–268.

[26] References are to *Werke*, ed. Bollacher *et al.* (Frankfurt: Deutscher Klassiker Verlag, 1985 (10 vols)), I: 695–810; Moran and Gode (first part of treatise only); and Barnard, *Herder on Social and Political Culture* (Cambridge: Cambridge University Press, 1969) (selected passages).

[27] Cf. R. Clark, *Herder: His Life and Thought* (Berkeley and Los Angeles: University of California Press, 1955), pp. 130–8, 156–62. Clark argues that the treatise itself is an ironic dismissal of the view that language can have an 'origin'.

Herder begins, naturalistically enough, with the assertion that *'Even as an animal man has a language.'*[28] The wild cries prompted by immediate passion are an animal mode of expression: 'There is then a language of feeling which is – underived – a law of nature.'[29] Each species has its own such language: immediate, accented and understandable only in its natural context. Such a language cannot be reduced to letters. Written language remains a mere shadow ('immer nur Schattern!'[30]) of the voice of present passion. Herder illustrates this by citing Hebrew, in which only the consonants were written, whereas the living part of the language, the vowels, could only be said: 'the dead characters they drew were only the inanimate body, which the act of reading had to animate with the spirit of life'.[31]

However, whilst Herder shows how an account of a divine origin of language can easily be countered by a naturalistic one, his crucial move is to say that language is *not* in fact explained by these immediate cries. These outbursts are not volitional ('willkürlich').[32] They are not used with reason. Here he breaks with Condillac (and Rousseau). In effect, Herder calls into question the whole project of writing a description of the origin of language from a state of nature. Such an account begs the vital question: how can a sign be recognized *as a sign* – as having a meaning and a reference – without prior cognition and use of other signs? Herder thus asserts a breach between nature and language by virtue of which humanity comes into its own as free and rational.

According to Herder, we become human when we are free from the domination of instinct: 'No longer an infallible machine in the hands of nature, he himself becomes a purpose and objective of his own efforts.'[33] Language is linked to a distinctive quality of humanity, which Herder calls 'Besonnenheit'.[34] This capacity for abstraction, recognition and judgement allows us to single out the 'distinguishing characteristics [Merkmale]'[35] of what we encounter, often through the sense of hearing. The sheep, for example, is recognized by its bleating.[36] This simple act encapsulates the possibility of consciousness and freedom, and it manifests itself in the creation of linguistic signs. Herder claims: 'The first indication of this conscious activity of the mind was a word.'[37] In this way, language and reason

---

[28] 697; Barnard p. 117.
[29] 698; Moran–Gode, p. 88.
[30] 704; cf. Moran–Gode, p. 94.
[31] 704; Moran–Gode, p. 95.
[32] 708; Moran–Gode, p. 99.
[33] 717; Moran–Gode, p. 109.
[34] 719; cf. Moran–Gode, p. 172 'reflection'; Pfefferkorn has 'reflective circumspection' in *Novalis: A Romantic's Theory of Language and Poetry* (New Haven and London: Yale University Press, 1988), 'Appendix B', p. 199.
[35] 722; Moran–Gode, p. 116.
[36] 723; Moran–Gode, p. 117.
[37] 723; Barnard, p. 135. Moran–Gode (p. 116) mistakenly has 'work' instead of 'word'.

arise together 'naturally'. The question of the priority of one over the other can only become a vicious circle, which cannot even be halted by the device of a divine communication – for which came first, the revelation or the capacity to receive and understand it?[38]

Much of what Herder goes on to say is an attempt to balance this ambiguity: language is both distinctively human *and* natural. Nature remains 'man's teacher of language and man's muse',[39] but Herder tries to reconcile nature and spirit, through the mediating links of mythology and poetry. The history of language is the history of spirit; the verb is the primal word of power.[40] Language breathes human spirit onto the stuff of nature, in animistic and anthropomorphic fashion. The first dictionary was a 'pantheon', a mythology based on human interests, particularly sexuality ('the genitals of speech are, as it were, the means of its propagation'[41]). Speech is, firstly, eroticized poetry, a poetry which antedates prose:

> For what was the first language of ours other than a collection of elements of poetry? Imitation it was of sounding, acting, stirring nature! ... A dictionary of the soul that was simultaneously mythology and a marvellous epic of the actions and speech of all beings![42]

Language is both mimesis and mythology, submitting to natural paradigms only to incorporate them into the human world. Language is the collective heritage of a nation, the bearer of tradition and culture.[43] The life of a people provides the mediating bond between instinctive nature and the giddy possibilities afforded by our linguistic being. In its poetic and communal character, language is thus able to integrate nature and culture, reason and passion: 'The sense for language has become our central and unifying sense; we are creatures of language [Sprachgeschöpfe].'[44] The expression is – perhaps intentionally – ambiguous. We are products *and* producers of language. To ask for an ultimate order of priority is, once again, nonsensical.

For Herder, to have a language which is more than a sequence of instinctive outbursts is to be awake, to have possibilities. *This* is the true divinity of language. It does not have a divine origin in the crude sense of being handed down from God as an extrinsic addition to our humanity. It witnesses to the dignity of what He has created: 'Thus the origin of language is explained in a truly divine manner only insofar as it is truly human.'[45] It is

---

[38] 727; Moran–Gode, p. 121.
[39] 735; Moran–Gode, p. 130.
[40] 736; Moran–Gode, p. 132.
[41] 739; Moran–Gode, p. 134.
[42] 740; Moran–Gode, p. 135.
[43] 791; Barnard, p. 165.
[44] 747; Moran–Gode, p. 143.
[45] 809; Barnard, p. 177.

an original blessing to which the opposition of nature to revelation does not apply. As such, it hints at our ultimate goal, whilst seemingly eradicating the possibility of any absolute ending:

> We are always growing out of childhood, however old we may be; we are always in motion, restless and dissatisfied. The essence of our life is never fruition [Genuss] but continuous becoming [Progression], and we have never been men until we have lived our life out to the end.[46]

To be 'always growing': both absolute beginning and consummation are obscured by the fact of our existence. Herder points towards the mix of naturalism and irony which characterized the multi-faceted movement of 'Romanticism'.

Hamann, Herder's contemporary, may have been sympathetic to such a vision of the temporality of human life. However, he was far from welcoming to Herder's views on language. According to O'Flaherty, Hamann's view was that 'a consistently rational approach to the great questions of religion and ethics, of theology and philosophy, leads inescapably to nihilism'.[47] Philosophy separates what God had originally joined together. Thus, mind and body, reason and feeling, the theoretical and the erotic are alienated from one another at the hands of an inappropriate rationalism. Hamann, perhaps simplistically, saw Herder's work as an attempt to give language a human origin. As such, it was another example of the presumption of human reason.

What was more serious from Hamann's point of view, however, was that, if Herder was right, our communication with God was broken off – and for Hamann, this communication was more of a communion than a merely external exchange. Language is the key mediating element in Hamann's metaphysics: 'Speech is translation, from the language of angels into the language of men, that is, thoughts into words, things into names, images into signs.'[48] The labour of translation is the mark of creation's coherence, with itself and with its maker. Writing against Herder in *The Knight of Rosencranz's Last Will and Testament about the Divine and Human Origin of Language*, Hamann gave his own account of our original paradisial state:

> Every phenomenon of nature was a word, the sign, image and pledge of a new, mysterious, inexpressible, but for that reason all the more inward union, communication and community of divine energies and ideas. Everything that man in the beginning heard, saw, gazed upon and touched, was a living word. For God was the Word. With this Word in his mouth and in his heart, the origin of language was as natural, as near and easy, as a child's game.[49]

---

[46] 773; Barnard, p. 157.
[47] O'Flaherty, *Johann Georg Hamann* (Boston: Twayne, 1979), p. 150.
[48] N II 199; RGS, p. 197.
[49] N III 32; RGS, p. 73.

Thus, the words we speak derive their meaning and value by analogy with God's Word. Language is portent and partial realization of that incarnation by which the Word is to condescend to the flesh for the divinization of humanity. In a letter to Lindner dated August 1759,[50] Hamann clearly links linguistic and divine mediations:

> The invisible nature of our soul is revealed by means of words – as creation is a speech whose line stretches from one end of heaven to the other ... Between an idea in our soul and a sound produced by the lips lies the distance between spirit and body, heaven and earth. Yet what inconceivable bond unites two things which are so distant from one another? Is it not a humbling of our thoughts that they cannot, so to speak, become visible except in the crude clothing of arbitrary signs? And what a proof of divine omnipotence – and humility – that he was both willing and able to breathe into the babbling and confused tongues of human ideas, with their servant's form, the depths of his mysteries and the treasures of his wisdom. Thus, as man ascends to the throne of heaven, there to rule, so human language is the royal language in the praised fatherland of the Christian.

This incarnational, mediatorial view of language is important for a *Christian* writer. For what is at issue in all speech – the 'inconceivable bond' between thought and word – is perhaps most apparent in the arduous translation of theological discourse, in the communication of the difference between man and God and of its absurd transgression in Christ.

For Hamann, then, nature is already doubled, for 'God repeats himself [wiederholt sich selbst], as in nature, so in Scripture.'[51] Repetition is not identity. There is lack which looks forward to eschatological consummation, a restoration of the presence of the Word among us.[52] Perhaps this encourages an occasional suspicion of language in Hamann's thought: 'Language is the seducer of our understanding, and will always remain so, until we go back to the beginning and origin.'[53] Language is systematically ambiguous, grasping reality and yet doing so by means of abstract, general concepts. Hamann suspects it to be responsible for the decadence of philosophy through 'the misunderstandings of countless words, the posing as real of the most arbitrary abstractions'.[54]

However, it is precisely the arbitrariness of language which is its wonder and promise. Hamann is prepared to see the descent into language and temporality as more than an unfortunate detour or 'fall'. He is well aware that

---

[50] Z I 393-4; RGS, p. 67.
[51] N I 238; translated in W. Alexander, *Johann Georg Hamann: Philosophy and Faith* (The Hague: Martinus Nijhoff, 1966), p. 189.
[52] Cf. RGS, p. 87.
[53] Z VI 173; translated in Alexander, *Hamann*, p. 117.
[54] Z V 272; RGS, p. 250.

'like numbers, words derive their value from the position which they occupy, and their concepts are, like coins, mutable in their definitions and relations, according to time and place'.[55] But it is this very characteristic which enables him, in the *Socratic Memorabilia*, to practise an indirect communication, resisting the hegemony of strict rational proof in the name of Socratic ignorance and the need for faith.[56] The congenital fragmentariness of existence cannot be unified by any conceptual system.[57] This very lack of unity is what calls for faith if we are to assert the meaningfulness of life.

Words are 'indeterminate' and 'only become, by their appointment and meaning in use [Bedeutung des Gebrauchs], determinate objects for the understanding'.[58] Language exceeds rational comprehension by its very nature, and this 'wicked snake in the bosom of ordinary popular language' is what 'gives us the finest parable of the hypostatic union of the two natures of sense and understanding, the mutual commerce in ideas of their powers'.[59] Reason must presuppose the intercourse between sensory data and universal ideas. Hamann's erotic imagery of the 'lovemaking and ravishing' of intuitions and concepts resists the rational control of language which 'purely' discursive argumentation could have succumbed to. For Hamann, language is 'the mother of reason and revelation, their alpha and omega';[60] it is the 'instrument and criterion' of reason.[61] But any word-mysticism is qualified by an emphasis on the arbitrariness of signs and the indispensability of community to establish their meaning in practice. If he speaks of language sometimes in eschatological terms, it is in the context of an ontological relativism of which language is both the medium and the parable:

> Community is the true principle of reason and language ... This and that philosophy separate things which cannot at all be parted: things without relationships, relationships without things. There are no absolute creations, any more than there is absolute certainty.[62]

Hamann admits the systematic ambiguity of language as sign and substance of this relativism. The possibility of a kind of nihilism – that there is no truth, that creation is a meaningless sign – is never finally repulsed. It is the necessary shadow of faith.

---

[55] N II 71; translated by O'Flaherty in *Hamann's Socratic Memorabilia: A Translation and Commentary* (Baltimore, Md.: John Hopkins University Press, 1967), p. 163.

[56] 'Our own existence, and the existence of things outside us must be believed' (N II 73; O'Flaherty, *Johann Georg Hamann*, p. 167).

[57] Cf. the work *Fragments* (1758): 'Here on earth we live in fragments. Our thoughts are fragments. Our knowledge itself is but patchwork.'(N I 299; RGS, p. 161).

[58] N III 288; RGS, p. 219.

[59] N III 287; RGS, p. 218.

[60] Z VI 108; RGS, pp. 252–3.

[61] N III 284; RGS, p. 215.

[62] Z VI 174; RGS, p. 257.

Novalis: poetizing the infinite

It became clear in some romantic writing that, when the ironic art of a text does not hold to such a faith as Hamann's, the play of language in communicating with the infinite is not as straightforward as his paradisial ideal might suggest. It is, significantly, a communication which can be refused. Romanticism is a complex and ill-defined network of movements in art and philosophy, which can be retained as a term of convenience for our purposes, because it raises the question of the nature and limits of the art work in providing an *aesthetic* access to the ideal meaning and coherence of things.[63]

If anyone can be said to touch upon the heart of this approach to art, it is arguably Schelling, the philosophical doyen of the Romantics. According to Schelling, the motivation behind art lies in the satisfaction found in assuaging the contradiction between finite and infinite, conscious and unconscious. Art pacifies our 'endless striving'[64] in an 'infinite harmony'.[65] The true art work does not point *beyond* itself, but realizes this identity and the resolution of riddles *in* itself.[66] Beauty is 'the infinite finitely displayed'.[67] However, this resolution, a perfect coincidence of form and content, seems an unattainable ideal. For the infinite, if it is to remain infinite, must resist all final expression or formulation. The logic of the artistic endeavour demands a continual approach towards and falling back from the ideal it seeks, not only to represent, but to realize.

Thus Romanticism, in its diverse forms, could embody this tension between a desire for reunification with the lost immediacy of nature and a heightened awareness of the creative role of the artist's language. This creativity was indispensable to the desired unity with nature, because only through the art work could the supreme reconciliation of particular and universal come about. As Schlegel puts it, 'Every good poem must be wholly intentional and wholly instinctive. That is how it becomes the ideal'.[68] Schlegel is both a theorist and a practitioner of irony. In his novel *Lucinde*, women are idealized as the bearers of a natural immediacy which calls for

---

[63] According to Andrew Bowie, art became the attempt to 'say the unsayable' – to express a coherence in nature which could not be reduced to legislated, rational rules – after Kant's *Critique of Judgement* and his analysis of sublimity. See *Aesthetics and Subjectivity: From Kant to Nietzsche* (Manchester: Manchester University Press, 1990), p. 40.

[64] *Sämtliche Werke*, ed. K. F. A. Schelling (Stuttgart and Augsburg, 1856–61 (14 vols)) III 617; *System of Transcendental Idealism (1800)*, trans. Heath (Charlottesville: University Press of Virginia, 1978), p. 222.

[65] III 617; Heath, p. 223.

[66] III 615; Heath, p. 221.

[67] III 620; Heath, p. 225.

[68] Schlegel, *Lucinde and the Fragments*, trans. P. Firchow (Minneapolis: University of Minnesota Press, 1971), p. 145.

men's worship. For the author of *Lucinde*, 'the highest, most perfect mode of life would actually be nothing more than *pure vegetating*'.[69] The silence which respects the purity of womanhood leads one to understand 'the beautiful language of nature'.[70] The woman is a divine ideal, a symbol which points beyond the arbitrary nature of words. Through its worship, the soul can come to the point where it 'sees the loving spirit through the delicate veil'.[71]

This idea of a language of nature which is also a divine symbolism is as powerful as it is ambivalent. Novalis, for instance, can write of language in very Hamannian terms: 'Man does not speak alone – the universe *speaks* also – everything speaks – infinite languages/Doctrine of signatures'.[72] The world itself is a '*communication* – revelation of the spirit'.[73] Language expresses the inner spirit of the universe as creation. The reference to Böhme's work *De Signatura Rerum* confirms this impression: language is not arbitrary, but gains its sense from the founding, creative Word of God, manifest in all things.

However, in the poet's attempt to show this ideal, the limits between receptivity and spontaneity are blurred, and this introduces a strain into Novalis' conception of language. Ideally, language in poetical form is a 'translation' of the ideal, in the sense of a creative rendering.[74] It is a product of inspiration, the emotional expression of the idea of a higher being.[75] But this responsiveness to the ideal, infinite being is shot through with both subjective and objective tensions. The poet is no mere imitator, but a creative artist. A translation does not merely imitate an idea, it transforms its content. And when the object of language's concern is infinite being, then the impossibility of any adequate rendering of this ideality can easily lead the poet to forsake the task for the freedom of creativity, the self-referentiality of monologue.

In the short 'Monolog' which Novalis himself wrote, he plays with the tricksterish and capricious nature of language.[76] As author of this ironical piece, he claims to know the nature of language. Language, he claims, does not speak 'for the sake of objects'. However, in a curious way, this non-referentiality serves to reflect the world:

> If one could only explain to people that language behaves like mathematical formulas – they form a world of their own, they play only

---

[69] Ibid., p. 66.
[70] Ibid., p. 129.
[71] Ibid.
[72] *Schriften*, ed. Klucklohn and Samuel, 3rd edn (Stuttgart: Köhlhammer, 1977 (4 vols)), III 267–8; translated in Pfefferkorn, *Novalis*, p. 81.
[73] II 594; Pfefferkorn, *Novalis*, p. 82.
[74] Pfefferkorn, *Novalis*, p.48–9.
[75] II 22; Pfefferkorn, *Novalis*, p.61–2.
[76] II 672; translated in full in J. Neubauer, *Novalis* (Boston: Twayne, 1980), p. 124, used here throughout.

with themselves, express nothing but their own wonderful nature, and for this very reason they are expressive, just because of this they mirror the strange interplay of objects.

But when the author comes to judge his own text, it is found wanting. It is didactic; it fails to speak simply for the sake of speaking: 'a writer is, after all, just somebody who is possessed by language'. What is the status of language in this strange statement? Are its links with the world and the infinite severed in a nihilistic play of signifiers? Does it only mirror nature insofar as it reconstructs it after its own capricious whim, creating nature (and God?[77]) as an effect of writing? According to Neubauer: 'In this view, poetic language is neither a mirror to nature nor a lamp radiating from the mind of a genius, but a set of rules whose application generates texts.'[78] This must entail the unprecedented complication of questions of truth and meaning, in which notions of objective reality and constraint are cast into doubt.

It is as if irony, as the consciousness of the split language introduces between real and ideal, is *both* the enemy *and* the driving force of the creative process. Only in the gap produced in ironic communication can nature be creatively evoked. 'Irony is the clear consciousness of an eternal agility' as Schlegel writes.[79] It is the spur to the whole 'Romantic' project: 'It contains and arouses a feeling of indissoluble antagonism between the absolute and the relative, between the impossibility and the necessity of complete communication.'[80] The price for this may be paid in the threat of a purely negative irony, a nihilistic employment of language to undermine all phenomena. And once we realize that, for Schlegel, it is women who are often on the receiving end of either worship or ironic negation, we understand that this is not only a matter of disinterested theory. The erotic and gendered imagery employed by writers on language is analogous to that employed by religious writers, And it has a similar ambivalence – at once idealizing and yet confining the erotic and the feminine. Clearly, the moves which are made in representing our ideals are more than merely epistemological – they have decisive ethical consequences.

Idealism: language and spirit

This ethical and rational ambiguity, the threat of an all-consuming subjectivism and nihilism, could not satisfy the idealist philosophers. The

---

[77] Cf. Derrida, *Writing and Difference*, p. 108, where he asks, in discussing Levinas, whether the idea of the presence of God is not 'an effect of the trace ... the movement of erasure of the trace in presence?'

[78] Neubauer, *Novalis*, p. 125.

[79] Schlegel, *Lucinde*, p. 247.

[80] Ibid., p. 156.

question of truth and the relation of subjective and objective poles of experience comes to a head in the great systems of speculative idealism. It is intrinsic to their narrative structure. For Schelling, philosophy is '*a constant objectifying-to-itself of the subjective*',[81] an artifice ('Kunst') in which 'one is not simply the object of contemplation, but always at the same time the subject'.[82] As Fichte argues in his 'Second Introduction' to the *Science of Knowledge*,[83] the speculative method demands the ultimate unification of two sequences of thought: that of the philosopher/narrator and that of the ego whose development he describes. Author and content of the system are to become one.

Fichte's own 1795 treatise *Of Language Ability and the Origin of Language*[84] helps us discover how this bears upon the question at hand. In this work, Fichte calls language the '*expression of our thoughts by arbitrary signs*'.[85] He argues that 'the specific drive to realize a language' arises from human rationality.[86] People seek to find rationality outside themselves, to enter into reciprocal exchange with others.

For Fichte, the construction of general concepts, far from being a loss, is a progression to higher rationality. He claims that 'Being expresses the highest character of reason',[87] as abstraction and imagination lead us beyond mere sensory experience. Words derived from sensuous appearances are applied to supersensuous realities metaphorically (Fichte uses the verb 'übertragen').[88] However, there is a kind of deception ('Täuschung') in such metaphors. When reason knows the soul as incorporeal, for example, but the imagination depicts it as corporeal, there results 'an overt conflict of the I with itself'.[89] Seen in the right way, however, from the philosopher's perspective, such conflict is the mature power of speculative reason in its progression from self-estrangement to identity. Language is a necessary detour, sign and medium of the self's predicament *and* its resolution: 'The rendering [Übertragend] of a supersensory concept by a sensory sign is, however, the cause of a deception ... But the deception was unavoidable.'[90] From the idealist's point of view, the deception is justified as the route to rational truth.

---

[81] III 345; Heath, p. 9.
[82] III 350; Heath, p. 13.
[83] I 457–68. References are to *Johann Gottlieb Fichte's Sämmtliche Werke*, ed. I. H. Fichte (Berlin, 1845–6, (8 vols)); *Science of Knowledge*, trans. Heath and Lachs (Cambridge: Cambridge University Press, 1982), pp. 33–42.
[84] VIII 301–41; Pfefferkorn, *Novalis* ('Appendix A') translates some passages from the first part of this two-part work.
[85] VIII 301; Pfefferkorn, *Novalis*, p. 191.
[86] VIII 309; Pfefferkorn *Novalis*, p. 193.
[87] VIII 319*.
[88] VIII 322*.
[89] VIII 323*.
[90] Ibid.*.

The question remains, however: can the philosophical artifice admit the deception and yet retain the rationality of its *own* language?

Hegel believed that the resolution of this dilemma was for language to come into its own proper form, to mediate between reality and ideality in concrete actuality, not merely in theory. In the *Phenomenology of Spirit*,[91] Hegel claims that 'Speech and work are outer expressions in which the individual no longer keeps and possesses himself within himself, but lets the inner get completely outside of him, leaving it to the mercy of something other than himself.'[92] This externalization risks the degeneration of language into 'an external contingent expression, whose *actual* aspect lacked any meaning of its own'.[93] Language is a form of Spirit's estrangement, but it is a negative stage which makes possible a new form of consciousness. For example, in *Sittlichkeit* (the organic, ethical unity of the state), the form and content of language coincide in the authority of the spoken, performative utterance. The individual and the state are reconciled by a language which is itself organic and unified: 'in speech, self-consciousness, *qua independent separate individuality*, comes into existence, so that it exists *for others*'.[94] In any other mode of expression, the self 'is immersed in a reality' from which it can withdraw, 'letting it remain lifeless behind. Language, however, contains it in its purity, it alone expresses the "I", the "I" itself.'[95] Through the alienation of the ego into the mediating form of language, the self is known as both particular and universal. Language is:

> the existence of Spirit [Dasein des Geistes]. Language is self-consciousness existing *for others*, self-consciousness which *as such* is immediately *present*, and as *this* self-consciousness is universal. It is the self that separates itself from itself ... It perceives itself just as it is perceived by others, and the perceiving is just *existence which has become a self*.[96]

The Hegelian dialectic reproduces itself within the movement of linguistic expression.

The mediating role of language is the focus of a section of the third part of the *Encyclopedia* which deals with Spirit's transition from intuition to representation and thought. The movement is away from immediacy towards a unification of subjective and objective experience (Z440).[97] Spirit's goal is

---

[91] References are to *Sämtliche Werke*, Jubiläumsausgabe, ed. Glockner (Stuttgart: Frommann, 1927–30 (20 vols)); *Hegel's Phenomenology of Spirit*, trans. Miller (Oxford: Clarendon, 1977). I will translate 'Geist' by 'Spirit' throughout.
[92] II 242; Miller, p. 187.
[93] II 243; Miller, p. 188.
[94] II 390; Miller, p. 308.
[95] Ibid.
[96] II 499; Miller, p. 395.
[97] References are to paragraph numbers in Hegel's text (found in *Sämtliche Werke* X); translation used is *Hegel's Philosophy of Mind*, trans. Wallace and Miller (Oxford: Clarendon, 1971).

to become '*self-knowing truth*' (ibid.), comprehending objective reality within itself. What is implicit in Spirit must be made explicit, in a progression to a true infinity and eternity which leaves nothing external to itself (Z441).

The word first appears as one aspect of the subjective, theoretical appropriation of an objective content. The word is a preliminary manifestation of Spirit as intelligence, a 'fleeting, vanishing, completely *ideal* realization' (Z444), by which the intelligence 'demonstrates that it is its own end' and points towards the 'unlimited freedom and reconciliation of mind with itself' (ibid.). The true realization of this reconciliation awaits the unification of word and thing, utterance and reality. As yet, language is a form which has not discovered its appropriate content.

The mind must move away from intuition – the inarticulate unity of subject and object in experience – into the articulated sphere of representation, in which Spirit practises ideal mastery over its intuitions. 'Representation is this recollected or inwardised intuition' (Z451) whose goal is both to *inwardize* intuitions and divest itself of the *isolated* 'subjectivity' of a particular inwardness. In other words, it aims 'to be itself in an externality of its own' (ibid.). Language frees Spirit from a merely objective relationship to an external reality and a merely subjective inwardness which turns its back on that reality. Rather, though representation, Spirit unites objective and subjective reality, putting an end to its exile from itself. Through the various stages of representation, this homecoming is enacted, freeing the consciousness from the domination of instinct, universalizing its intuitions by means of signs, and thereby universalizing itself.

At the stage of *recollection*, the content of intuition is given a space and time of its own, in order to create an '*image* or picture, liberated from its original immediacy and abstract singleness amongst other things, and received into the universality of the ego' (Z452). In the *imagination*, voluntary, active possession of these images is attained, alongside a fund of general ideas produced through abstraction (Z455). Spirit seeks to unify the universality and externality of the image in a process described as 'the imagining of the universal and the generalization of the image' (Z456). The intelligence, ultimately, comes to *produce* intuitions, to be 'self-uttering' by 'the imagination which creates signs' (Z457). Spirit must learn to speak itself.

Here, language makes possible a higher realization of the goal. There is a transition from the *symbol*, in which the sensuous material has some correspondence to the universal idea expressed, to the *sign*, in which 'sensuous material receives for its soul a significance foreign to it' (Z457). The sign is arbitrary ('as is especially true of language signs' – ibid.), giving the intelligence 'a definite existence for itself' (Z458). Intuition is *aufgehobt* – 'superseded and sublimated' (ibid.) – in the sign; and as 'speech and, its system, language' (Z459) are further articulated, sensations, intuitions and concepts are raised to a higher existence 'in the ideational realm' (ibid.).

However, Hegel's ultimate goal is not forgotten: a restoration of immediacy – in a higher concrete form, indeed, but immediacy none the less. The idea is not to be authenticated by this limited mediation of the image or sign, but immediately in and for itself alone (Z457). This explains his preference for speech over writing, for only in speech does the intelligence express itself 'immediately and unconditionally' (Z459) in presence to itself. For Hegel, 'the visible language is related to the vocal only as a sign' (ibid.) – the 'sign' here is a necessary estrangement, rather than an end in itself.

The sign enables name and thing to coincide in the stage of *memory*. Name and meaning are permanently united in the 'ideational realm' (Z462). The name becomes 'the externality of intelligence to itself' (ibid.), the means by which we know our thoughts as objective and as our own, possessed *and* produced by us: 'The articulated sound, the *word*, is alone such an inward externality' (ibid.). Hegel denies that it is the 'ineffable' which is the highest, for beyond language is only a formless void. No, 'the word gives to our thoughts their highest and truest existence ... Just as the true *thought* is the very thing itself, so too is the word when it is employed by genuine thinking' (ibid.). Memory, on the threshold of true thought, falls into an inappropriate objectification of language; the ego becomes an otherwise empty container and arranger of words. Only with thought does the true conceptuality emerge, in which form and content, inner and outer, subject and object find their reconciliation in Spirit, in and for itself. Thought 'no longer has a *meaning*, i.e., its objectivity is no longer severed from the subjective, and its inwardness does not need to go outside for its existence' (Z464).

Language and the sign find their meaning in ideality, raising particular intuitions up to be the universal forms in which Spirit may learn to recognize itself. But ideality cannot tolerate absolute otherness; it is 'the reduction of the Idea's otherness to a *moment*, the process of returning – and the accomplished return – into itself of the Idea from its Other' (Z381). In the end, 'Mind is, therefore, in its every act only apprehending itself ... An out-and-out Other simply does not exist for mind' (Z377). Thus, the possibility of the sign and communication is itself reduced to a moment in a greater progression. But can this be done? Through this chapter, we have encountered texts which enlighten us by the tensions they fail to resolve. For Hegel, all these tensions are signposts along the way to a conceptual resolution. However, the ultimate self-referentiality of his conceptual consummation, its closure of the opening between language and actuality, suggests that his, too, is a precarious ending. Can the temporality, labour and other-relatedness which mark the journey of Spirit, and to which Hegel strenuously attempts to give full weight, be stopped up and silenced by such a gesture? Time and existence cannot simply be negated. The question of language can always be reopened, is always already opened as the condition of consciousness being where it is. The system can always be called into question, can always be found to be partial and precarious, because it cannot finally account for the language it must presuppose. Such questions can only be repressed by Spirit's forgetting of itself, of its history and adventure in language. And if this is done, surely the whole process would have to begin again, an endless cycle, realizing and falling away from consummation.

Grundtvig and Heiberg: the inconceivable bond

It may safely be said that the influence of idealism was felt well beyond those philosophers who would have described themselves as followers of one or other of the great system-builders. Some kind of loosely 'idealist' method seems to underlie much Danish thought of the period, albeit in some suitably modified form.[98] To understand how this affects analysis of language and the sign, and how this intersects with Kierkegaard's own work, we shall narrow our focus to consider the terms in which language was discussed in two short texts, written by major figures of the Danish 'Golden Age': Grundtvig and Heiberg. The connections and divergences between these two authors are significant in the context of social, political and economic changes in Denmark at this time.[99]

Changes in land ownership rights, which enriched a section of the peasant class at the expense of those who became landless, created tensions, not only within the peasantry, but also between the rural poor and the relatively affluent bourgeois residents of Copenhagen. This tension between capital and countryside is important for understanding the background of the urban upper bourgeoisie who made up the bulk of the writers and audience for the cultural output of the Golden Age. The pietistic peasant 'awakenings' of this period were particularly suspicious instances of a potential challenge to the absolutist state. Grundtvig stands out as a representative of a populist, reforming movement within the Church, with a strong folk-nationalist outlook. Heiberg, for his part, was a leading light of the cultural circles of Copenhagen, whose support for the political status quo, Kirmmse argues,[100] united them beyond any apparent disagreements in religious or philosophical doctrines.

In the journal passage we quoted earlier,[101] Kierkegaard goes on to praise

---

[98] H. L. Martensen, professor of theology at Copenhagen University during Kierkegaard's days there, and later Primate of the State Church, was frequently mocked by Kierkegaard for his supposed pretensions of 'going beyond' Hegel. See, for example, *FT*, 32–3.

[99] See Bruce Kirmmse, *Kierkegaard in Golden Age Denmark* (Bloomington and Indianapolis: Indiana University Press, 1990), 'Part One'; John Elrod, *Kierkegaard and Christendom* (Princeton, NJ: Princeton University Press, 1981), 'Chapter One'; H. Koch, *Den danske Kirkes Historie*, vol. 6, *Tiden 1800–1848* (Copenhagen: Gyldendal, 1954).

[100] Kirmmse, *Kierkegaard*, pp. 77ff.

[101] See p. 1.

Grundtvig's advocacy of the 'living word'. He claims that it has real merit, perhaps as a portent of the fulfilment of his own dream of the restoration of words. Grundtvig's researches into Norse mythology encouraged him in a love of the Danish language and the oral bardic tradition through which the 'folk-life' of the people was preserved and transmitted. His disdain for Latin was the reverse side of a belief that only the spoken word was truly alive and knitted to the collective memory of a nation. As he declared, 'nothing is more inimical to human life and the mother tongue of the people than a language composed of dead letters and then idolized as a model language'.[102]

Christianity, he argued, should not repress a people's folk-life, the customs and legends which shape its identity. The Word of God is the ally of national consciousness, raising it to new spiritual levels through the mediating link of spoken tradition: 'We all know that it is the Word which raises humanity above animals. It is the Word by which the world of spirit is opened [hvorved Aandens Verden oplader sig]."[103] This opening is the inauguration of distinctively human existence, history and the possibility of faith. Grundtvig affirms that 'the invisible word only becomes alive and strong on the mother tongue'.[104] The word has life in breath, the symbol of spirit. Grundtvig's 'matchless discovery' that the Church is founded not on written scriptures, but on the oral tradition of Christ's own words (baptism and communion) and of the early church (the Apostles' Creed) is of a piece with this identification of life and breath. He wrote: 'the invisible spirit of man as well as of God can demonstrate its life only through that invisible word which can be heard by the ear and felt by the heart'.[105] Human language, our living word, prepares for and is fulfilled by the Word of God.[106]

Om Ordet,[107] written in about 1817, though it was never published, gives an insight into Grundtvig's wider understanding of language. He himself writes that it is necessary to understand the word in general to grasp what he says about the mother tongue. According to Grundtvig, the word is 'the wonderful, mysterious bond between spirit and body, between time and eternity, like a corporeal spirit and a spiritual body, eternal in its ground and temporal in its division' (272). Philosophers and philologists cannot do their work without understanding 'that *in which* human life was, and through which it expressed itself: the word' (273).

---

[102] 'Introduction' to *Norse Mythology* (1832), *Vaerker i Udvalg*, ed. Christensen and Koch (Copenhagen: Gyldendal, 1941 (6 vols)), 4: 29; *A Grundtvig Anthology*, trans. Broadbridge and Jensen (Cambridge: Clarke; Viby: Centrum, 1984), p. 46.
[103] *Folk-life and Christianity* (1847), *Værker* 5: 250–1; *Selected Writings: N. F. S. Grundtvig*, trans. Knudsen (Philadelphia: Fortress, 1976), p. 43.
[104] Ibid.
[105] *Christian Childhood Teachings* (1855–61), *Værker* 6: 92; Knudsen, p. 67.
[106] *Værker* 6: 106–7; Knudsen, pp. 78–9.
[107] Page references are to *Værker* 2: 272–85. All translations are mine.

Unfortunately, the reflection which seeks a human origin of language as a more or less arbitrary system of signs only reduces the word to 'nothing more than a certain articulated sound' (275). At least the scientifically useless theory that language was taught to us by a god does honour to it: 'it is certainly more reasonable that a god, rather than something inarticulate, has been our language-teacher' (276). Neither reflection nor history can explain *how* we begin to speak.

Only revelation gives us the key: in the beginning was the Word and the Word was with God and the Word was God (277). For Grundtvig, this means that 'the word is the highest expression for human life' (278), 'the true Hermes', itself descended from Heaven. Christ is the 'Ground-Word,' of which the human word 'is only a weak and derivative image' (ibid.). The word is thus founded on a mystery we can never truly grasp.

Language is both human and divine: 'The human word in itself is the determinate living thought, the word in its power is the living connection between spirit and body, the word in its activity is the spirit's living means of exchange' (279). But the mediation is most effective in speech: 'The word can only be heard because it cannot unite with anything bodily save the sound in the voice' (ibid.). Writing is merely the sign of speech, secondary and relatively unliving. The opening into spirit provided by language has to be guarded by the presence of the voice. The ultimate criterion of language is 'God's Word, in which spirit and word are one' (280): God's complete self-presence in his Word is the telos of all human words. Paradoxically, this consummation is also the silencing of all words. For when word and spirit are one, communication or expression is superfluous.

Surely, however, if the possibility of language consists in the 'opening' which the word makes into the world of spirit, then the voice, no more than writing, can eradicate this break with immediacy. Grundtvig's insistence on the priority of speech and folk-life does nevertheless contain an important implication: that language only makes sense in *use*, in a communal context. The spiritual exchange of language is not guaranteed. It must be ever made and re-made by its actual users, not *ex nihilo*, but on the basis of life-views articulated in continuity with the heritage of that language.

For Heiberg, language had something of the same significance as it did for Grundtvig. Heiberg's conversion to Hegelianism in 1824 ensured the influence of speculative philosophy among the urban elite of Denmark, the very people who formed Kierkegaard's principal audience. In the 1827 piece, *Om det materialistiske og det idealistiske Princip i Sproget*,[108] something of this background can be glimpsed. Heiberg argues that, just as all philosophical systems can be resolved into either materialism or idealism, so there are two

---

[108] Page references are to *Prosaiske Skrifter* (Copenhagen: Reitzels, 1861 (11 vols)), 8: 381–408. All translations are mine.

comparable approaches to language. He claims that 'In language, *matter* and *form* have always been distinguished' (383). Grammaticians all attempt, in theory, 'to make the formal viewpoint into the highest' (384), but there are two sorts of grammatician. The 'materialist' goes back to the original words of a language, the basic units beyond which there is no real explanation. The 'idealist' claims that language must be resolved into pure form; it presupposes form (syntax) if its words are to have any sense at all (387). Form constitutes language as such; it is logically, if not historically prior, 'as the goal towards which the unconscious matter darkly strives' (ibid.).

Heiberg proposes to examine language with these two viewpoints in mind. He takes a clearly hierarchical approach, working from the material elements, mechanically combined (390), upwards to the achievement of more perfect forms which transcend any etymological justification. As opposed to the unnatural, arbitrary composition of compound words, Heiberg advocates an organic approach, 'by which every new form as it were grows up out of the previous one, much as a tree develops out of itself' (349). The more perfect forms 'change mechanical or chemical composition into a free organic growth' (401). Heiberg is clearly on the side of the 'idealist', for only a 'grammatical atheist' (403) could deny the qualitative superiority of form over matter in language, a form which denies its material origin 'and raises itself to an independent principle' (404). This is the means by which 'the genius of language comes to the light of consciousness' (ibid.). The personification of language is no accident. The development of language is 'a spiritual operation', akin to the awakening of the soul to consciousness, to realize its true form through the material opposition of objectivity: 'This grammatical metamorphosis stands in a remarkable analogy to the awakening of the soul in the organism' (407).

Heiberg is committed to a view of language as both organic and rational. The progression of language towards form reveals the movement of the human soul towards its consummation. In this, language becomes more than mere analogy to spirit, but the very form in which spirit is manifest, awakened and perfected:

> Language is the mirror of the human soul: the two are united with an unmistakable bond, and there cannot be anything in one of them, which is not in the other also. The conditions for the development of the human soul are entirely the same as for human language. (408)

Heiberg too links language with a qualitative transformation of the human spirit. For him, this means a potential unity with the divine form, an organic growth into free self-consciousness, the sublimation of nature in spirit. No doubt Grundtvig would have been very suspicious of the centrality of form and the implied final autonomy of the spirit from objective externalities. Nevertheless, despite their widely differing methods and goals, both men seem to share a surprisingly similar view of the importance of language as a mediating link between body and spirit, and a rejection of mechanical composition and naturalistic accounts of language which obscure its essential connection with the special quality of human existence.

A theme is emerging. Despite the recurrent desire for a perfectly transparent language which would give us immediate access to reality, philosophers of this period increasingly recognize that language itself remains opaque to rational comprehension. And this is not an isolated phenomenon. It is connected with a growing concern with those aspects of our experience which do not seem to be reducible to consciously formulated rational legislation: the erotic, art, mythology, the nature of organisms, peoplehood. This is the other aspect of Kant's legacy, apart from the ideal of an autonomous and self-legislating reason. These practices and phenomena seem to link together the sensuous and the intelligible, the real and the ideal, in ways obscure to reason, and yet no less effective in our experience.

Furthermore, these nonrational (not irrational) ways of relating to the world are analogically linked with one another and with language. Art's ideal is the coherence which nature intimates in the organism and in erotic union; language and peoplehood are not mechanical or accumulations, but spiritual organisms; myth is the collective artwork which binds a people together through shared narratives and a shared language. And in each case, these images hint beyond the parochial towards something universal to our humanity. Even if one takes the view that Hegel aims at a total conceptual resolution of all history, one cannot deny that he too tries to take that history seriously. Philosophy cannot be done without reference to its incomplete precursors in nature, art and religion.

Schelling's later philosophy brings all of this together.[109] He increasingly emphasizes the nonrational reality which reason must presuppose, and which it must seek to raise up to intelligibility. Our selfhood and freedom rests, not on a perfect self-knowledge, but on the dark substratum, the 'Urgrund' of mute Being. Schelling attacks Hegel for vaunting logical concepts above actual existence. Hegel's philosophy is negative, he claims, because it cannot account for actuality – only a positive philosophy like Schelling's can do this.

Taking account of actuality means not reducing it to the operation of rationally transparent laws. No system of existence can be complete, for both the nonrational substrate of Being and the freedom of God elude its grasp. God is free personality, raised above the blind potencies of Being whose separation and conflict inaugurates creation.

Nevertheless there is still hope for existence to be raised up to expression and articulated in art, and, especially in mythology. And this raises the question of language. Language is seen by Schelling as a necessary precondition of

---

[109] See F. W. J. Schelling, *The Ages of the World* (New York: Columbia University Press, 1942).

consciousness, which makes possible a relation between the sensuous and the intelligible. Language can raise up the sensuous to the light of the ideal and the universal. The divine Word – figured in the Christian narrative of the Incarnation – masters Being, and leads it back to reconciliation with God and harmony with itself. Language itself is a 'faded mythology'.

However, mythology must still give way to revelation, in which the dark potencies of Being are brought into living relationship with the freedom of God. The word is powerless in itself to save; only in the concrete utterance of an actually existing person can words be said not only to refer, but to communicate. It is thus to the divine Word, spoken out of the depths of the divine personality in a free dialogue of love, that we must look for healing.

Kierkegaard was of course present at Schelling's lectures in Berlin from November 1841 to February 1842. His initial enthusiasm turned to disdain – but we must not overlook the positive impetus given to Kierkegaard's own thought by Schelling's philosophy of existence. This is merely one of the more obvious links between Kierkegaard and the whole constellation of thinking which emerged out of Kant's third critique. However, before turning to some of Kierkegaard's own texts, let us survey the ground covered so far.

Summary

1. We began with the assertion that *language is something which is presupposed by philosophy*. The development of this chapter suggests that this is far from being accidental. Philosophy cannot detach itself from a dependence upon language which it cannot fully account for.

2. This is due to the fact that *language takes us beyond immediacy and a direct apprehension of reality*. In so doing, it makes self-consciousness possible, by introducing a gap between thought and being, or between particular and universal, real and ideal. Language makes it possible to articulate an ideal of absolute truth, certainty and self-knowledge, whilst making the full attainment of such an ideal unrealizable.

3. This is confirmed by an unresolved tension in the history of linguistic thought we have sketched. *Philosophers oscillate between an ideal of a perfectly transparent language and an acknowledgement of the nonrational, the sensuous basis for thought which thought itself cannot grasp*. There is thus a growing concern with art, myth, the organic, the nation as mediating elements between the sensuous and the intelligible – all of which are inseparably bound up with language. The question of language thus spills over into aesthetics, ethics, politics and religion.

4. This emphasis on artistic creativity, myth and folk traditions suggests that *truth cannot be reduced to propositional truth*. It may be that important

truths of art, ethics, faith and so on cannot be directly stated in the 'S is p' form without distorting their dynamic character. Moreover, irony always plays on the fact that any perspective or expression of the ideal truth is partial, fragmentary and precarious.

5. There is thus an important sense in which *meaning is usage*. That is, language can function as communication only in a determinate context. Its meaning is not fully specifiable either by grammatical rules or by its reference to universal essences – authors as diverse as Leibniz, Locke and Schelling deny the real existence of such essences. Its abstraction and ambiguity can only be countered by being anchored to a practical embodiment in actual life. However, as Hamann is well aware, ambiguity and indirectness can never finally be expunged from language, for no context is fully determinable.

6. Finally, for several of the authors we have looked at, *the divine Word is the archetype for the human word*. The incarnation of God in the Word is the ideal form of communication, which perfectly unites the earthly and the heavenly. Again, however, it remains to be seen how far even this Word is immune to the ambiguities of all human language and testimony.

We are thus ready to engage with Kierkegaard's texts, mindful of the way in which these factors must complicate any naïve realism. If language conditions the very possibility of thought, then there can be no extra-linguistic standpoint from which to judge the accuracy of our representations. And it may be that a correspondence theory of language and truth, centred on propositions, must give way to a more tentative, indirect literary practice in which narrative and irony play a decisive role.

However, before we rush into the easy conclusion that this implies an acceptance of anti-realism, we must pause. The authors we have examined still believed, in different ways, that important issues of truth were at stake in their philosophies – truths which could not be reduced to human projections. Schelling, for instance, does not appeal to art and myth as purely human creations, as fictions with no reference to a reality beyond the human realm. Indeed, it is precisely because art and myth open up a relationship to a reality which exceeds the human subject that they are significant. They do not express 'subjective' feelings which are marginalized by rational, objective science. Rather, they embody irreducible ways of relating to reality which cannot be reduced to conceptual, rule-governed form.

The factors which tell against naïve realism also tell against an anti-realism which would attempt to create our aesthetic, ethical and religious notions *ex nihilo*. Through language, we are related to an otherness which we cannot rationally comprehend. Language revolves around this paradox, a paradox which, whilst it disallows an interpretation of words as crudely representational (words copy reality) *also* resists the conclusion that they are purely instrumental (words create reality). Therefore, since our selfhood arises only out of a nonrational ground, there can be no such fully self-conscious mastery as this form of anti-realism implies. As Judge William might say, we do not create ourselves, we *choose* ourselves. And as the doctoral candidate Kierkegaard was to write in his dissertation, 'actuality (historical actuality) stands in a twofold relation to the subject: partly as a gift that refuses to be rejected, partly as a task that wants to be fulfiled.' (*CI* 276). Perhaps the God-relation too is best seen as both gift and task, demanding both gratitude and creativity.

Whether that is Kierkegaard's view must await a fuller reading of his texts. It is certain, however, that things are not so clear-cut as a cursory glance at the realist/anti-realist dispute might suggest.

CHAPTER THREE

A Kierkegaardian theory of language?

The discussion of Kierkegaard's texts in this chapter has three aspects. Firstly, we will explore the way Kierkegaard takes up the themes and problems we identified in linguistic thought in the previous chapter. This provides the structure for the exposition. Secondly, we will trace the continuity of Kierkegaard's interest in issues surrounding language and words throughout his authorship, from journal entries of 1837 to *Practice in Christianity* (1850) and beyond. Finally, we will show how Kierkegaard approaches the question of language through the 'boundary disputes' between language and various philosophical, aesthetic and dogmatic concepts: immediacy, consciousness, music, sin, ethics and the paradox.[1] This will not only allow us to link the question before us with many, more traditionally recognized, Kierkegaardian themes; it will also help us discover Kierkegaard's approach to theorizing about language in a wide range of contexts.

It will become clear that Kierkegaard shares much of his contemporaries' recognition of the decisive importance of language as a presupposition for philosophy, and, indeed, for self-consciousness in general. Moreover, language has a double aspect for him. It is the medium of spirit, that which makes possible distinctive human selfhood. It is also that which creates the breach between ourselves and nature or immediacy. The language of spirit, the language which aims at self-realization in ethics and before God, must therefore take a new, indirect form, which raises questions about its precise truth status. Understanding the motivation and necessity for this indirect communication helps us to understand the peculiar, hybrid nature of Kierkegaard's texts, and the kind of response they aim to elicit. The substantive questions raised by realism and anti-realism cannot be disengaged from the form of Kierkegaard's communication.

1. Language is presupposed by philosophy

In a journal entry, Kierkegaard criticizes the Kantian philosophy of the 'thing-in-itself' for implying that language concealed thought (JP 2: 1590; Pap. II A 37) – and by 'thought', he seems to mean the capacity to think actuality, to have access to things-in-themselves and not only our own constructions.

---

[1] For Kierkegaard's fascination with 'the boundary disputes in the sciences', see JP 1: 143; Pap. IV C 104.

Instead of this sceptical dualism, he prefers a Hegelian approach: 'Hegel in any case deserves credit for showing that language has thought immanent in itself and that thought is developed in language' (ibid.). Kierkegaard thus seems to take a realist standpoint against Kant. There is no straightforward order of priority between thought and language, but together they do provide an access to reality which Kant had arbitrarily denied.

Matters are not so simple, however. In a passage from the same year, Kierkegaard rejects any seamless continuum between thought and language which would make questions of truth and representation uncomplicated:

> If it were the case that philosophers were presuppositionless, an account would still have to be made of language and its entire importance and relation to speculation, for here speculation does indeed have a medium which it has not provided itself, and what the eternal secret of consciousness is for speculation as a union of a qualification of nature and a qualification of freedom, so also language is [for speculation] partly an original given and partly something freely developing. (JP 3: 3281; Pap. III A 11)

This is precisely Hamann's argument against Kant: philosophy cannot create itself *ex nihilo* because it always presumes upon the adequacy and intelligibility of its own language. Something has always gone before, to which language bears witness. And Kierkegaard is also offering this as a a critique of Hegel.[2] However much Hegel is right in recognizing the interweaving of thought and language, he cannot succeed in using thought to achieve a kind of conceptual mastery of language. Thought presupposes language; it cannot turn it into a wholly transparent medium, developing the ideal language out of its own resources.

Language is thus like the 'eternal secret of consciousness'. That is, it witnesses to the fact that there will always be something in consciousness which eludes manifestation. And this is not simply an interesting fact about consciousness – it is what makes consciousness possible in the first place. For consciousness can only exist where it is already engaged, already interested in its own existence. Consciousness always presupposes its own dynamic, its own self-relatedness – it can never catch its own tail. And that dynamic is expressed through language as a medium of temporality and freedom. Language is an 'original given' whose beginnings cannot be reconstructed. It is also 'something freely developing', opening up a future which no necessity can direct. It comes from an immemorial past and makes possible an unforeseeable future. So, in a curious way, the self-related nature of consciousness is also bound up with its *other*-relatedness, to which language also bears testimony. Language is a means of communication which cannot be

---

[2] See H. Cloeren, 'The Linguistic Turn in Kierkegaard's Attack on Hegel', *International Studies in Philosophy* 17 (1985), pp. 1–13.

recollected or inwardized ('erinnert') by speculation. It is something given (not *created* by individual consciousness) and free (not *controlled* by individual consciousness). It therefore witnesses to an otherness which the system cannot comprehend.

2. Language takes us beyond immediacy and a direct apprehension of reality

We began the previous chapter with a reference to Descartes. His project of doubting everything in order to reach a bedrock foundation on which all knowledge could be built is seminal for modern philosophy. It also leaves a legacy of problems: the split between the certainty of self-knowledge and the dubious reality of the external world; and the lack of any account of the language which the philosopher presupposes. It is significant in this connection that one of Kierkegaard's most important texts on language takes as its starting point precisely that hyperbolic Cartesian doubt which we saw as inaugurating this radical split between consciousness and external reality.

In the unfinished and unpublished work, *De Omnibus Dubitandum Est*,[3] we follow the philosophical trials of a young man, Johannes Climacus, who has decided to take up the great call to doubt everything. If we are to look for any Kierkegaardian 'theory' of language here, it is first vital that we understand the work as a philosophical satire. The narrative context mocks the adoption of the tone and terminology of idealist speculation. This terminology is thus forced to reveal its own limitations.

After finding only discouragement in the writing and conversation of others, the second part of the work begins as Johannes attempts to think for himself. Having 'bade the philosophers farewell forever' (*JC* 165), he embarks on a radical course of questioning: 'WHAT MUST THE NATURE OF EXISTENCE BE IN ORDER FOR DOUBT TO BE POSSIBLE?' (*JC* 166). Johannes takes a Kantian, transcendental approach, seeking 'doubt's ideal possibility in consciousness' (ibid.). In itself this is ironic – Johannes continues to depend upon a philosophical project and language which he has inherited, even as he tries to break free into radical autonomy.

Johannes recognizes that he is not asking how a determinate object in the external world may be known. All such knowledge 'stands in a direct and immanent relation to its object and the knower, not in an inverse and transcendent relation to a third' (ibid.). Doubt and faith alternate in a 'paradoxical dialectic' (ibid.), which cannot be settled by appeal to immanent or internal criteria of truth and falsehood. In other words, there is no self-evident, objective way of deciding between them. As we shall find, this

---

[3] Pap. IV B 1, 103–50; translated in *Philosophical Fragments/Johannes Climacus*, pp. 113–72.

mysterious reference to a transcendent 'third' hints at the very condition for questions of truth and falsehood to arise at all.

Johannes therefore attempts a more imaginative and hypothetical approach to the origin of doubt, asking what consciousness must be like in which doubt does *not* appear. His answer is that it must be *immediate*, like a child's; and '*Immediacy* is precisely *indeterminateness*' (*JC* 167). In other words, in immediacy there is no relation of a determinate knower or subject to a specific object. In this state, everything is at once true and untrue – or, rather, the question of truth itself has not yet been posed. Johannes goes on to ask:

> How does the question of truth arise? By way of untruth, because the moment I ask about truth, I have already asked about untruth. In the question of truth, consciousness is brought into relation with something else, and what makes this relation possible is untruth. (ibid.)

Consciousness is thus divided at its very origin. To the rhetorical question of whether consciousness could remain in immediate unrelatedness, Johannes answers 'This is a foolish question, because if it could, there would be no consciousness at all' (ibid.).

The argument now takes a crucial turn:

> But how then is immediacy cancelled? By mediacy, which cancels immediacy by *pre*-supposing it. What then is immediacy? It is reality itself [Realitet]. What is mediacy? It is the word. How does the one cancel the other? By giving expression to it, for that which is given expression is always *presupposed*.
>
> Immediacy is reality; language is ideality; consciousness is contradiction. The moment I make a statement about reality, contradiction is present, for what I say is ideality.
>
> The possibility of doubt, then lies in consciousness, whose nature is a contradiction that is produced by a duplexity and that itself produces a duplexity. (*JC* 167–8)

We might compare this passage to Hegel's chapter 'Sense-Certainty' in the *Phenomenology*;[4] as we have seen, it is a familiar theme in Kierkegaard's philosophical context. As soon I use language, I transcend the particular thing I am referring to, because language uses ideal terms – that is, terms which apply universally, not just to the particular object before me here and now. We go beyond what is immediately given, just by the fact that we express it in words. The very structure of consciousness transcends brute sensory data.

However, Johannes is saying more than this. Consciousness is not simply a transcendence of immediacy, but a *contradiction*. Reality and ideality,

---

[4] Hegel, *Hegel's Phenomenology of Spirit*, (Oxford: Clarendon, 1977), pp. 58–66.

immediacy and language, do not merge into a harmonious whole. There is a collision. Language is not a transparent medium and truth is not a self-evident category. Truth can only emerge by a primordial division, suppression and cancellation of untruth. Consciousness is doubled from the start, for it always presupposes something which makes it possible, but which it cannot grasp in any straightforward way.

The seemingly banal assertion that words signify more than brute particulars is a key step, because only through this fact can consciousness, freedom and meaning come into being: 'not until the moment that ideality is brought into relation with reality does *possibility* appear' (*JC* 168). Conversely, the earnestness which haunts this satirical text is that with consciousness comes the possibility of doubt and, ultimately, a nihilistic despair of meaning: 'When I use language to express reality, contradiction is present, since I do not express it but produce something else' (ibid.). If consciousness and language cannot make the truth univocally present and self-evident, what is to say that language is not in fact distorting reality, that its truth is mere illusion?

The form of the text itself reveals these contradictions. The passage from the narrator's point of view (Part One) to that of Johannes Climacus (Part Two) might indicate a progression towards the absolute basis for knowledge which the protagonist is seeking in his own thought. Instead, we are led further and further into a labyrinth of reasoning which can never catch its own tail. The text's attempt to make Johannes' reasoning present to us is caught in the same dilemma that Johannes himself faces: language and reflection make any direct apprehension of the foundation of truth and selfhood impossible.

As the text proceeds, it links this dilemma to many of the key themes of the authorship. In Johannes' distinction between reflection and consciousness, for example, there are foreshadowings of the description of the self offered in *The Sickness Unto Death*. He claims that 'Reflection is the *possibility of the relation*; consciousness is *the relation, the first form of which is contradiction*' (*JC* 169). In reflection, ideality and reality do not come into actual collision. Its categories are '*dichotomous*' (ibid.). In other words, reflection is abstract; it contemplates reality and ideality in separation. Johannes goes on:

> The categories of consciousness, however, are *trichotomous*, as language also demonstrates, for when I say, *I am conscious of this sensory impression*, I am expressing a triad. Consciousness is spirit [Aand], and it is remarkable that when one is divided in the world of spirit, there are three, never two. (ibid.*)

In the move to conscious spirit, there is a qualitative transition, a 'coming into existence [Tilbliven]' (ibid.) which cannot be thought. When a person says 'I', the collision between the real and the ideal, the singular and the universal becomes actual and existential. Language exhibits and embodies this transition and collision. There is no primordial foundation of consciousness and language, in which the speaker is fully present to himself in his utterance. As soon as I use language I am divided. In Derrida's words, 'My own presence to myself has been preceded by a language.'[5]

And yet I am not simply split into two separate parts. I still relate to myself; I still recognize myself in this split. Something traverses this contradiction to hold me in being. This is the significance of the reference to the triad or the three. We recall that earlier, Johannes spoke of the knower standing in a transcendent relationship to a third. This third points towards an Other who constitutes me as a self. The self cannot establish itself, cannot create itself from nothing – this is precisely what the dramatic movement of the text is designed to show. As in *Sickness*, the triadic self embodies an irreducible complexity, and is constituted as a conscious 'relation that relates itself to itself' (*SUD* 14) only by a power which transcends all that the self has at its own disposal: 'If the relation that relates itself to itself has been established by another, then the relation is indeed the third, but this relation, the third, is yet again a relation and relates itself to that which established the entire relation' (*SUD* 13). In a sense, the 'third' relates itself to an unnamed 'fourth', which cannot be contained in the system of the self.[6] The self cannot achieve its own realization, just as it did not come to consciousness from an initial moment of self-mastery and self-presence.[7]

Johannes goes on to draw further boundaries between consciousness and reflection:

> Reflection is *disinterested*. Consciousness, however, is the relation and thereby is interest, a duality that is perfectly and with pregnant double meaning expressed in the word 'interest' (*interesse* [being between]). (*JC* 170)

Consciousness stands before the questions of truth, meaning and goodness, not as a disinterested spectator, but as a *participant* in the struggle between doubt and faith. In fact, and this is the double meaning of 'interest',

---

[5] Derrida, *Dissemination*, trans. Johnson (London: Athlone, 1981), p. 340. See Derrida's *Speech and Phenomena*, trans. Allison (Evanston: Northwestern University Press, 1973), in which he analyses the way the linguistic sign functions in the absence of both its speaker and its referent. The sign is thus divided at the outset by the possibility of repetition and absence. The sign and the self are never fully present to themselves in a plenitude of meaning - they are constituted by the movement of difference and deferral of meaning which Derrida calls *différance*. Derrida writes of this that it is 'the operation of differing which at one and the same time both fissures and retards presence, submitting it simultaneously to primordial division and delay' (p. 88).

[6] For Derrida, the idea of a 'fourth' or the image of a splayed square, points to that which exceeds the self-contained trinitarian dialectic of Hegelian speculation. See Derrida, *Dissemination*, p. 352.

[7] See L. Mackey, 'Deconstructing the Self: Kierkegaard's *Sickness Unto Death*', *Anglican Theological Review* 71 (1989), pp. 153–65.

consciousness is constituted by the struggle. Interest is not something external and fortuitous which happens to consciousness by chance. Consciousness is *interest itself*. What Johannes calls 'objective thinking' (ibid.) – disinterested knowledge – is merely the presupposition of doubt. Only an actual subject with a stake in existence can doubt or believe, for 'as long as there is no consciousness, no interest, no consciousness that has an interest in this struggle, there is no doubt' (*JC* 170–1). Doubt inaugurates a higher form of existence, which apathy and objective thought can only partially repress.

How does this consciousness avoid apathy and become aware of the contradiction and collision inherent in its linguistic nature? Here, Johannes draws on another Kierkegaardian motif:

> Immediately there is no collision, but mediately it is present. As soon as the question of a *repetition* arises, the collision is present, for only a repetition of what has been before is conceivable. (*JC* 171)

Repetition is the collision of ideal and real, exactly the collision which language makes possible. In other words, it is that characteristic of language which is able to use universal, iterable terms to refer to particulars. Repetition in this sense is a fundamental characteristic of language, without which it could not operate, but it is also that which undermines all talk of 'foundations' or 'origins'. Even the judgement that something is self-identical is only possible through a mediation. We can see how Kierkegaard's text strongly anticipates Derrida's writing on language at this point. For Derrida too, repetition is intrinsic to the sign:

> For there is no word, nor in general a sign, which is not constituted by the possibility of repeating itself. A sign which does not repeat itself, which is not already divided by repetition in its 'first time', is not a sign. The signifying referral therefore must be ideal – and ideality is but the assured power of repetition – in order to refer to the same thing each time.[8]

Johannes' text is caught in absurdity as soon as he tries to explain this. He writes about 'reality as such', even though his line of thinking has shown that 'reality as such' is inaccessible to language. The only reality we know is mediated by language, and language is inseparable from repetition:

> In reality as such, there is no repetition ... because reality is only in the moment [Moment] ... In ideality alone there is no repetition, for the idea is and remains the same, and as such it cannot be repeated. When ideality and reality touch each other, then repetition occurs. When, for example, I see something in the moment, ideality enters in and will explain that it is a repetition. Here is the contradiction, for that which is, is also in another mode. (*JC* 171)

---

[8] Derrida, *Writing and Difference* (London: Routledge, 1978), p. 246.

The particular, the here and now, is our indispensable access to the idea; and the idea is the indispensable condition for recognizing the particular for what it is. In the collision between reality and ideality, which takes place *within* actual language usage (the application of concepts to reality), human existence is determined as free, temporal and precariously meaningful.[9] Language is not a determinate object which can be known and derived. It is transcendental – the condition of possibility for consciousness and knowledge. Thus the form and content of Johannes' text are interwoven. Absolute doubt is as elusive as the medium which is used to represent it, with the consequence that representation itself is called into question. Form and content do not unite to provide a direct acquaintance with the idea of the text; they work together to frustrate any such acquaintance.

The contradiction inherent in language is not like the affirming of some particular object, 'This both is and is not, in the same respect, circular.' It is rather that any attempt to speak of reality or ideality in itself, in isolation, can only contradict itself; any attempt to discover, in thought, a unitary origin and telos of existence is bound to end in paradox, as Kant had already argued in the 'Antinomy of Pure Reason'.[10] The contradiction is the collision of the unthinkable with thought, or rather, the presence of the unthinkable *within* thought, as its prior condition. Consciousness is always already constituted, situated and differentiated.

Perhaps *De Omnibus Dubitandum Est* remained unused because the radical nature of this thought led further than this text goes. At the end of the work as it stands, recollection and repetition are given virtually equal significance (*JC* 172), something which will later be contested in *Repetition*. Certainly, such a work, which undermines the very philosophical standpoint from which its discourse is possible, is very difficult to write, and impossible without self-contradiction. It is therefore crucial to note that we are dealing primarily, not with metaphysical discourse, but with satire. The comic form witnesses to the strange contradictions which transcendental thinking encounters. The underlying earnestness of the work is reflected in a sketch Kierkegaard wrote for its continuation. Of Johannes it is said 'He came up – cannot come back' (*JC* 'Supplement' 263). Johannes gets lost in doubt, a sign of the failure of philosophy, and the real possibility of perdition.

---

[9] Cf. Mark C. Taylor's *Kierkegaard's Pseudonymous Authorship*, (Princeton, NJ: Princeton University Press, 1975), esp. Chapter 3 'Time and the Structure of Selfhood', pp. 124–5, in which he argues that, for Kierkegaard, 'Time, understood as tensed, emerges only in connection with man's purposeful activity.'

[10] I. Kant, *Critique of Pure Reason*, trans. Kemp-Smith (Basingstoke: Macmillan, 1929), pp. 384–484.

3. Philosophers oscillate between an ideal of a perfectly transparent language and an acknowledgement of the nonrational, the sensuous basis for thought which thought itself cannot grasp

The early journal we quoted earlier saw Kierkegaard hoping for a way beyond the bankruptcy of language. He looks for 'powerfully equipped men' to 'restore the lost power and meaning of words'. In his lament over a language that has spun out of human control, Kierkegaard nostalgically evokes a time when language was subservient to human mastery, when meaning was clear, distinct and forceful.

Kierkegaard's concern was to stop Christian terms being divested of their supernatural content by incorporation into philosophical systems. Stanley Cavell notes Kierkegaard's 'attention to the distinct applicability of concepts'.[11] It is at work defining 'revelation' and 'authority' in *The Book on Adler* (on which Cavell is commenting), 'sin' in *The Concept of Anxiety*, and so on. Kierkegaard wants to draw a line around such concepts to prevent them from being confused with the immanent concepts of philosophical speculation.

As well as this desire to fix and safeguard the original meaning of key words, there is another aspect of Kierkegaard's texts which evinces a dissatisfaction with the ambiguities of language. In his writings on silence, which we will examine in Chapter 5, there is a suggestion that a silent and direct encounter with God is possible, which would do without all the vagaries of words. The idea of being 'transparent' [gjennemsigtig] to God, which is so important in texts such as *The Sickness Unto Death* and *An Occasional Discourse* (or *Purity of Heart*), likewise idealises a relationship to God which is direct and immediate – nothing intervenes to disturb the communion of believer and Lord. One simply sees through the self to God: 'The formula that describes the state of the self when despair is completely rooted out is this: in relating to itself and in willing to be itself, the self rests transparently in the power that established it' (*SUD* 14). The believer must 'win the transparency that is indispensable if a man is to come to understand himself in willing one thing' (*PH* 108).

Sickness aims to challenge the despair which divides a person's selfhood; *Purity* targets the mind's doubleness and ambiguity with its ideal of willing one thing. Both seem to direct us towards a united, self-present self, unambiguous meaning, an end to the obscurity of thought and language. This is undoubtedly an aspect of Kierkegaard's texts which should not be overlooked. It links up with the idea we find in them of faith as a new or second immediacy.[12] Faith is a restoration of the unity of self and God lost at the fall. Such an account also

---

[11] S. Cavell, *Must We Mean What We Say?* (Cambridge: Cambridge University Press, 1969), p. 168.
[12] See *FT* 69 and 82; *SLW* 483–4; *CUP* 347n.

seems to be a realist one, which resists any reduction of the supernatural reference of religious language into immanent terms.

Appearances can be deceptive, however. We know enough even now to suspect that the whole question of language, the real and the ideal, the immediate and the reflected, cannot simply be sidestepped. Texts like *Sickness* and *Purity* are more complex than this interpretation allows. *Sickness* is a pseudonymous work, which thus retains a poetic edge, even as its language satirizes Hegelian psychology.[13] *Purity* is an upbuilding discourse, which uses language of transparency as a tactical ploy against the distractedness and evasions of the reader/listener. We will examine these textual factors in more detail in Chapters 6 and 5 respectively.

The very fact that faith is described as a *new* immediacy is telling. A new immediacy is not the same as the first. Repetition is not identity. The immediacy of faith cannot be understood without an account of the way that leads to faith, with all its paradoxical collisions. So to focus on Kierkegaard's ideal of a perfect transparent language or silent faith would be only part of the story. Like other thinkers we have looked at, he is more subtle than that.

In this context, it may therefore help to look at a text which brings together some of these themes in the aesthetic context. The essay 'The Immediate Erotic Stages' in *Either/Or Part One* touches on issues of immediacy, language, transparency, form and content. The writer, the aesthete known only as 'A', argues that Mozart's opera *Don Giovanni* is a classic, because it expresses its content – the sensuous immediacy of Don Juan – in its perfect form: music.

Kierkegaard once formulated a project to categorize, through representative figures, various life-tendencies which fell outside Christianity, but which facilitated a clearer grasp of the need to integrate the self beyond aesthetic parameters (JP 1: 795; Pap. 1 A 150). The figures are described as 'ideas', suggesting that they are ideal possibilities for human life and as such bear some essential relationship to the individual's self-development. Moreover, Kierkegaard positions each idea in relation to its appropriate aesthetic expression, in accordance with Heiberg's classification: 'It must not be forgotten, either, that Don Juan must be interpreted lyrically (therefore with music), the Wandering Jew epically and Faust dramatically' (JP 2: 1179; Pap. 1 C 58). This idealistic aesthetic, fixing the relation of form to content, was of paramount importance. For the cultural circles centred on Heiberg, the correct allocation of these correspondences was tantamount to the exercise of good taste.[14]

---

[13] For a valuable reading of the satirical nature of *Sickness* and other Kierkegaardian texts, see Roger Poole, *Kierkegaard: The Indirect Communication* (Charlottesville and London: University of Virginia Press, 1993).

[14] See George Pattison, *Kierkegaard: The Aesthetic and the Religious* (Basingstoke and London: Macmillan, 1992), pp. 15ff., for an analysis of Heiberg's aesthetics.

Kierkegaard insists that 'The Don Juanian life is really musical' (JP 5: 5226; Pap. 2 A 598), because he represents the immediacy of sensual life in all its immanence.[15] 'A' uses this to justify his evaluation of Mozart's opera. In the 'classic' work, he argues, there is an 'absolute correlation' of the subject matter and the form of its expression (*EO* 49). However, this intrinsic conjunction means that the artist conditions the kind of access we have to the subject. We have no idea of Homer's epic material, for example, without 'the transubstantiation due to Homer' (ibid.) – an argument which echoes Novalis in disputing the immediacy of any work of art. If all art consists of this transformative translation of the idea, any direct access to its content is rendered impossible.

Nevertheless, 'A' believes that, in the classic work, a determinate form is transparent to the idea which is its subject matter ('Only where the idea is brought to rest and transparency in a definite form can there be any question of a classic work' – *EO* 54). This makes any straightforward ranking of classics difficult, because all are, in theory, equally perfect. 'A' therefore decides on an accidental criterion:

> The more abstract and thus the more impoverished the idea is, the more abstract and thus more impoverished the medium is; hence the greater is the probability that no repetition can be imagined and the greater is the probability that when the idea has acquired its expression it has acquired it once and for all. On the other hand, the more concrete and thus richer the idea and likewise the medium, the greater is the probability of a repetition. (ibid.)

What does this mean? 'A' claims that an idea becomes more concrete when it is 'permeated by the historical' (*EO* 55). This concreteness is measured by how nearly the the expression approximates to language, 'for language is the most concrete of all media' (ibid.).

The point is something like this: aesthetic media are ranged along a spectrum from the most abstract to the most concrete, which is also the most historical. Language stands at one end of this spectrum, because it is the most historical medium. Presumably, this means that only in language is it possible to make utterances which have a definite context and a definite tense. Language expresses the idea in connection with a specific time and place. Other media – such as sculpture – can only express an abstract, atemporal idea. Language is thus mediation of the idea, making it available to us in temporal, articulated form.

Music, for its part, cannot be reduced to linguistic expression. It is an abstract medium which does not have such an intrinsic relation to linear time. It is well suited to express ideas which language's very concreteness would obscure.

---

[15] Cf. JP 1: 133; Pap. 2 A 180.

'A' thus identifies the absolutely musical subject matter: 'The most abstract idea conceivable is the sensuous in its elemental originality [Genialitet]' (*EO* 56). The original sensuous is appropriately rendered through music alone because it is both inward *and* consists, not of a coherent historical development, nor of a static moment, but of a mere succession of moments. Since the musical idea is abstract and immediate, it can only find one absolute expression, whilst an historical idea could be multifariously expressed in language, as is the case with the Faust legend (*EO* 57). The possibility of repetition is essential to language.

This points to a strange tension in language. On the one hand, it is concrete and historical. It enables the expression of ideas by particular speakers at determinate spatio-temporal locations. It has a context. On the other hand, however, language can only work if it contains the possibility of repetition within its very structure. A word can only have meaning if it can be repeated beyond its original context. This is what Johannes Climacus found, and what Derrida argues.

This is where the ironic, self-defeating form of the text comes into operation. Remember that the whole structure of *Either/Or* denies us any final conclusion as to which of its two parts – aesthetic or ethical – is ultimately superior. Moreover, within the first part, the texts are internally riven. They are torn between the idealization of total self-presence and mastery ('The Unhappiest One', 'The Seducer's Diary') and the celebration of a nihilistic dispersal of meaning, from the initial aphorisms, through the speeches given to the Symparanekromenoi (fellowship of the dead), the review of 'The First Love' and the seducer's own dissimulation.

We explore this structure more closely in Chapter 4. For now, it is enough to realize that the aesthete's account of language and music is far from being neutral or stable. 'A' wants to set up a rigid distinction between language and music which cannot hold, for aspects of each one contaminate the other's purity. For instance, sensuous immediacy, in the sense in which 'A' is interested in it, is itself a dialectically qualified category. In other words, it only appears as such when it is excluded by the principle of spirit proclaimed by Christianity: 'Sensuality is posited as a principle, as a power, as an independent system first by Christianity, and to that extent Christianity brought sensuality into the world' (*EO* 61). Prior to this, the sensuous is only a psychical phenomenon, in harmony with the rest of existence. With Christianity, the pleasure of the senses is conceived of as an enemy to the spiritual life – but this gives it a higher status as a definite, threatening force. The individual who can represent this idea is the counterpart to the Christian incarnation of the Word (*EO* 64). However, this representation can only take place in music, and hence music becomes the medium Christianity excludes: 'In other words, music is the demonic. In elemental sensuous-erotic originality, music has its absolute theme' (*EO* 65).

Music is more complex than 'A's quest for a purely sensuous and abstract medium demands. How then are language and music related? 'A' uses the image of two kingdoms, one of which is familiar, the other unknown and impossible to visit. The kingdoms border one another, and one can go to this border and look into unknown territory. Language is the familiar land, music the enigma. Their close proximity is due to the fact that both are spiritually determined, music by its exclusion from spirit. This is also their essential difference, for language *expresses* spirit:

> Language, regarded as a medium, is the medium absolutely qualified by spirit, and it is therefore the authentic medium of the idea ... In language, the sensuous as a medium is reduced to a mere instrument and is continually negated. (*EO* 67)

Language uses a sensual vehicle – sound, or visible words – not for its own sake, but solely for the expression of ideas. Language is bound up with reflection:

> Reflection is implicit in language, and therefore language cannot express the immediate. Reflection is fatal to the immediate, and therefore it is impossible for language to express the musical, but this apparent poverty in language is precisely its wealth. In other words, the immediate is the indeterminate, and therefore language cannot grasp it; but its indeterminacy is not its perfection but rather a defect in it. (*EO* 70)

So language, temporality and reflection seem to depend upon an original exclusion and negation of the immediate. There is no 'innocent' language, no language which straightforwardly depicts things and thoughts as they 'really' are; for the idea of 'reality' and the possibility of its expression emerge from the struggle and complicity of language with its demonic other.

However, this implies that pure 'immediacy' is thus a tactical category; it can nowhere appear as such without negation and repetition entering in. Music itself involves a creative transformation of its material. Consider the following:

> Language has its element in time; all other media have space as their element. Only music also occurs in time. But its occurrence in time is in turn a negation of the feelings dependent upon the senses. (*EO* 68)

Music too involves negation; it is a rendering of an idea, an interpretation and a translation. There is no ideal purity, no unspotted presence, innocent of the duplexity of reflection. This is not to suggest that music can be reduced without remainder to a linguistic substitute, or replaced by a commentary. Rather, it is to hint at the irreducible excess which conditions *all* media of representation, that which, though it cannot be thought or represented within reflection, provides the possibility for any reflection at all. As 'A' pushes his thought to 'venture the ultimate', he enters into a laborious oscillation in which the capacity of language and reflection to represent reality are continually called into question: 'It [Thought] laboured in vain; egged on by me, it was continually going beyond itself and continually collapsing back into itself' (*EO* 58).

Music, though an autonomous kingdom in its own right, is no Eden. 'A's denigration of music which is not accompanied by a libretto harms his case more than he realizes, for it suggests more of a dependency upon a linguistic parallel than he would like to admit. In any case, it is important to recognize that the immediate erotic is itself differentiated into stages of development. Through the figures of the Page, Papageno and Don Juan, 'A' traces a movement away from undifferentiated desire and narcissism to a greater degree of separation from, and determination of, the object of desire (*EO* 84–5). There is an awakening and maturation, a separation from the maternal breast, which is surely conditional on the possibility of such a breach being there from the start; and where there is possibility, immediacy is, and always has been, transgressed.

The image of thought going beyond itself and collapsing back again is an ironical synechdoche. That is, it is a part of the text which stands for the status of the whole text. The essay is unable to articulate the presuppositions on which it depends. A's entire effort to separate music from language founders. Music is not purely abstract and immediate. Language cannot dispense with the sensuous, immediate basis it presupposes even as it cancels it. The border between the two kingdoms begins to look permeable.

Now this is not to collapse the difference between language and music. Andrew Bowie argues that 'The failure to take music seriously is often the index to why key positions in modern philosophy are questionable.'[16] This is because it is a non-representational medium, which articulates aspects of our experience in ways which are not reducible to language. This is fair enough. Our point is twofold: firstly, music is still an articulated and mediated expression – it is not purely transparent; secondly, language should not be reduced to a solely representational model, in which the only truth is the objective correspondence of words to things. Language is capable of a 'musical' indirectness. It cannot shed all relation to the immediacy which it presupposes but is incapable of representing.

It is important to see how this view of art can be correlated neither with simple realism nor with simple anti-realism. The best art is not that which merely 'copies' an external object. There is indirectness, transubstantiation involved in creative art. But nor is art the result of wholly 'subjective' human expression. It labours to express ideas which are not our creation, which touch

---

[16] A. Bowie, *Aesthetics and Subjectivity: from Kant to Nietzsche* (Manchester University Press, 1990), p. 10.

on a greater reality to which we can relate.[17] If this is so for aesthetic expression, may it not also be relevant to ethical and religious communication? For ethics and religion also defy reduction to a representational model, as we shall find. They both endeavour to upbuild and awaken us to new possibilities for living.

4. Truth cannot be reduced to propositional truth

The concern with music links with the interest philosophers were showing for mythology and art generally, which we identified in the previous chapter. Romantic and idealist writers hoped that such media could attain a realization of truth which went beyond a proposition-centred, correspondence theory of truth. This propositional approach was trapped within a subject-object ('S is p') schema offering no ultimate reconciliation of inner and outer reality.

Kierkegaard is not so optimistic about art. The aesthetic essays in Part One of *Either/Or*, for example, reveal the internal contradictions of any attempt to regain a lost immediacy through art. Such a quest cannot rid itself of the very language and reflection it seeks to transcend. It risks negating the concrete life-world to dwell in an abstraction which obscures rather than reconciles our divided nature. Time after time, the initial words of *Either/Or*, which dispute any attempt to merge inner and outer reality, are confirmed by the contradictions between the aims and achievements of the text. Artistic yearning for the ultimate idea ends up as unhappy love, boredom, resignation or seduction.

However, just because Kierkegaard is not sold on the idea of the redemptive function of art, this does not entail that he cannot use aesthetic forms to articulate the divisions and contradictions within us, and so contribute to a process of healing. *Either/Or* may be seen as a late Romantic or post-Romantic novel, a text split between various genres which are linked, but which do not trace the satisfying development [*Bildung*] of a character into spiritual wholeness. The fragmentariness of the text points beyond itself, not to an as yet unexpressed aesthetic ideal, but to the self-defeating nature of Romantic aesthetics. It is a dilemma far from unknown to writers like Schlegel: the twin ideals of aesthetic spontaneity or immediacy and a developed sense of irony always threaten to tear one another apart.

So Kierkegaard's use of aesthetic form is indirect, playful, and yet earnest about the real issues of life-view and truth which are at stake, and which cannot be resolved by internal aesthetic criteria. So does he go beyond such forms to a more directly dogmatic approach, which would reveal the Christian answers to the human dilemma in all their authoritative force?

---

[17] See George Pattison, 'Non-realism in Art and Religion' in C. Crowder, *God and Reality: Essays on Christian Non-Realism* (London: Mowbray, 1997), pp. 160–74.

One text which might seem promising on this score is *The Concept of Anxiety*. It seeks to give an account of the dogmatic concept of sin, to preserve it from translation into aesthetic categories. Perhaps here, Kierkegaard will come to a proper, propositional description of Christian categories which can lead us to salvation. However, the pseudonymous form of the book should put us on our guard, and we find that, where the text touches on issues of language and immediacy, pure dogmatics is as elusive as pure art.

In this work, the pseudonym Vigilius Haufniensis attempts a psychological examination of anxiety whilst keeping the doctrine of hereditary sin in mind (*CA* 14). He cannot deal with sin directly, because 'Sin does not properly belong to any science' (*CA* 16); it is a qualitative category which dogmatics itself can only presuppose and never explain. Neither psychology nor ethics can account for sin's coming into existence ('Tilblivelse') (*CA* 21–2). Sin ruptures the Aristotelian metaphysical project of the 'first philosophy', 'whose essence is immanence' (*CA* 21), and Haufniensis heralds the invention of a 'second philosophy', 'whose essence is transcendence or repetition' (ibid.). On these categories, and on that of 'interest', 'immanence runs aground and actuality for the first time properly comes into view' (*CA* 21n.).

Sin cannot be assimilated by the immanent movement of logic, spuriously invented by speculative philosophy in order to comprehend all actuality (*CA* 12–13). Commenting on *Fear and Trembling*, Haufniensis argues that 'the religious ideality breaks forth in the dialectical leap' (*CA* 17n.), that existence can be renewed only 'through a transcendence' (ibid.), separating the repetition from the former existence. No logic can comprehend this temporal, paradoxical, passionate leap. Dogmatics cannot stop with immediacy. It presupposes 'an earlier beginning' (*CA* 10), which seems to be bound up with the possibility of language. As Haufniensis says, 'the immediate is annulled at the very moment it is mentioned' (ibid.) – a clear echo of *De Omnibus Dubitandum Est*.

Several of our earlier themes come into view once more. Speculative thought cannot account for its own possibility. It always presupposes something which thought cannot think. What is presupposed must be connected with language. The key ideas of repetition, transcendence, interest and the cancellation of immediacy are those which linked language to consciousness in *De Omnibus Dubitandum Est*. A rigorous account of sin destabilizes the correspondence theory of truth embedded in simple realism. Something altogether more indirect will be needed if Haufniensis' text is to communicate. Again, this indirectness is connected to the nature of human consciousness, or spirit, and language.

The concept of the 'leap' is at the heart of Haufniensis' work: 'The new quality appears with the first [sin], with the leap, with the suddenness of the enigmatic' (*CA* 30). What is not so obvious, perhaps, is the key role of language in making that leap possible. The text focuses on what makes for the characteristically human quality of our existence. Even before the 'fall', before the leap into sin, humans and animals are decisively different:

> Man is a synthesis of the psychical and the physical; however, a synthesis is unthinkable if the two are not united in a third. This third is spirit. In innocence, man is not merely animal, *for if he were at any moment of his life merely animal he would never become man.* (CA 43; my italics)

This ambiguous, slumbering spirit 'relates itself [to itself] as anxiety' (*CA* 44). This self is not a substantial, self-present ego, but is riven by anxiety and ignorance. Here, 'Innocence still is, but only a word is required and then ignorance is concentrated' (ibid.). This word – God's prohibition to Adam – cannot be understood by innocence, but it arouses a yet deeper anxiety: 'the anxious possibility of *being able*' (ibid.). And, in turn, this arousal of the burden of freedom can only take place because spirit is always there, presupposed as the condition of human existence.

Haufniensis then engages on an extraordinary piece of demythologizing. He recognizes that many thinkers have been disturbed by the fact that in the Biblical story of the fall, the voice of prohibition and punishment comes from an external source:

> But the difficulty is merely one to smile at. Innocence can indeed speak, inasmuch as in language it possesses the expression for everything spiritual. Accordingly, one need merely assume that Adam talked to himself. (*CA* 45)

The casual tone belies the crucial move: here, it is *language itself* which does not merely evoke freedom and consciousness, but is their presupposition. There can be no account of the origin of language, because such a thing must presuppose what it sets out to explain. A state without language is unspiritual, inhuman, and, for us, inconceivable. Adam speaks to himself; and this is not a symbol of Paradise, of the speaker's immediate self-presence in the fullness of God's manifest creative Word. Rather, in the disruptive power of language is the inauguration of the fall. Language cancels our immediate innocence. However, language does not come upon humanity from the outside; it is intrinsic to its very structure.

In the following pages, Haufniensis develops this point of view. He dismisses the story of Adam naming the animals as an 'imperfect' instance of language 'similar to that of children who learn by identifying animals on an A B C board' (*CA* 46). Such a simplistic realist account of reference cannot do justice to the nature of language. Moreover, he repeats that the objection that Adam could not understand the words God spoke to him 'is eliminated if we bear in mind that the speaker is language, and that it is Adam himself who speaks' (*CA* 47). In a footnote, the search for an origin of language is rejected:

'it will not do to represent man himself as the inventor of language' (*CA* 47n.). In denying the validity of any naturalistic derivation of language, Haufniensis does not fall back on the mythological motif that it is a gift of the gods. Language is not derived from an external source. Rather, Haufniensis proposes a radical hypothesis: language is so constitutive of human spirit that it is impossible to say whether Adam or language is the speaker. Any idea of a transcendent God literally addressing Adam is left out. Haufniensis realizes that such an unexamined anthropomorphism simply begs the question of how Adam could have understood God.

Kierkegaard seems to have toyed with the idea of identifying language with the serpent, an indication perhaps of its potentially demonic consequences (Pap. V B 53: 11). Nevertheless, the text contains no such one-sided equation of language with good or evil. Language is the presupposition of sin, not sin itself. Haufniensis will not allow any *explanation* of the leap into sin from its presuppositions: 'the fall is the qualitative leap' (*CA* 48). However, we can say that the fall does not impinge upon an undifferentiated perfection. As *Sickness* elucidates, spirit is an original relation, a differing and synthesis within itself, *and* a relation to an otherness which establishes it, and which it presupposes.

The ironic self-negation of the book lies in the collision of its psychological form, which aims to lead up to dogmatics, and a content which evades any direct comprehension by any discipline. 'Every science lies either in a logical movement in immanence, or in an immanence within a transcendence that it is unable to explain' (*CA* 50). As we have seen, that goes for dogmatics as much as for speculative thought. *The Concept of Anxiety* satirizes its own inability to do what it declares speculative reason cannot do, and thus casts further doubt on the adequacy of realist assumptions about religious discourse. It communicates through its own necessary failure to represent directly the object of its language.

Haufniensis, by denying the explanatory power of scientific reason, has cleared a space for a different sort of discourse to emerge. As the journal states in the same year that *Anxiety* was published: 'Basic principles can be demonstrated only indirectly (negatively) ... It is significant to me for the leap, and to show that the ultimate can be reached only as a limit' (JP 2: 2341; Pap. V A 74). Concepts like 'sin', 'despair', 'revelation', and so on may function more as limit concepts than descriptive representations. In other words, Kierkegaard's texts may attempt to secure them against reduction into the terms of speculative philosophy without thereby giving them a direct or positive content. If this is so, they may work less as positive referents than as negative concepts which point beyond semantics to the need for a practical, existential response. In other words, they are rhetorically employed to regulate religious discourse, preventing it from being wholly translated into immanent logic or direct, objective language. It should be clear by now that this does not commit Kierkegaard to anti-realism. The ultimate which we reach as a limit is not our creation. The use of negative, limit-concepts guards against any such subjectivist reduction and mastery.

So how is discourse to be reshaped if it is to avoid the pitfalls of one-sided theories of truth? This is hinted at in the early journals, where Kierkegaard reflects on the significance of the indicative and subjunctive moods in language. He writes that 'everything depends upon how something is thought, consequently how thinking in its absoluteness supersedes an apparent reality' (JP 3: 2309; Pap. II A 155). This idealization of reality in thought and language is familiar to us. Here, however, Kierkegaard is claiming that there is more than one way in which this can be done. The various moods of language give him the hint that what matters is *how* thought supersedes reality, a realization which informs much later writing, particularly in the *Postscript*.

At this stage, however, the subjunctive, rather than epitomizing an attitude of existential interest, seems instead to represent the pretensions of pure thought held by speculative philosophy. *Cogito ergo sum* is the life principle of the subjunctive (JP 3: 2313; Pap. II A 159), a point spelled out more clearly in another passage: 'The indicative thinks something as actuality [Virkeligt] (the identity of thinking and actuality). The subjunctive thinks something as thinkable' (JP 3: 2310; Pap. II A 156). The subjunctive remains within possibility, and its user thus courts the danger of absconding from reality altogether. However, it does suggest that the relation of thought to actuality in language is not as straightforward as the indicative implies, pointing towards Kierkegaard's later exploitation of this to present his reader with *existential* possibilities.

In the *Postscript*, Climacus argues that communication about existence can only take the form of possibility (*CUP* 320). What he means, however, is not that ethics and religion should be transformed into *mere* possibility, but that they should constitute a challenge and a claim upon the reader or listener: 'A communication in the form of a possibility compels the recipient to face the problem of existing in it, so far as this is possible between man and man' (ibid.). The subjunctive lays bare this idealizing force of language and thought, and presents us with the dilemma of *how* we think reality. The subjunctive

> is a dramatic retort in which the narrator steps aside as it were and makes the remark true of the individuality (that is, poetically true), not as factually so and not even as if it may be that, but it is presented under the illumination of subjectivity. (JP 2: 2315; Pap. II A 167)

What Kierkegaard says of the subjunctive in fact corresponds closely to the dramatic technique of parabasis. Parabasis is a concept which is itself the subject of much disputed interpretation. In the sense in which it interests us, however, parabasis can be seen as the part sung by the chorus in Greek drama, representing the dramatist's own commentary on the action. This dramatic concept gained a heightened significance in the hands of the Romantics. According to Schlegel, 'Die Ironie ist eine permanente Parekbase';[18] the suspension of the illusory spatio-temporal world of the narrative or action by authorial intervention hints at the fictive quality attending all speech and writing. Pure mimesis and pure fantasy are confused[19] in what amounts to 'a destruction of the illusion of either a temporal actuality or a temporal causality or linearity'.[20] *Permanent parabasis* is an effort to display the impossibility of perfectly uniting language and reality, because there is no moment in which the act of writing or speaking exactly coincides with what is written or spoken about.

This connects with Kierkegaard's view of the structure of language and consciousness, and suggests that irony may play a large role in forming his practice of communication. Language's connection with consciousness means that the latter is never fully self-present. It always presupposes something which makes it possible. Therefore, the ideal of a pure, indicative, self-evident meaning is placed under strain. The subjunctive could thus be seen to characterize *all* language to some degree. This has clear implications for a postmodern reading of Kierkegaard, which would see his literary practice as one of destabilizing the referentiality of language per se. Newmark claims that 'Kierkegaard's special theory of indirect communication, then, is also a general theory of language as irony.'[21] Irony is no longer a distinct domain or embellishment of language, but defines its very structure.

The link with Kierkegaard's mature thought on this issue will become more evident through an examination of his proposals, written in 1847, for a course of 'Lectures on Communication'.[22] Though they were never given, they offer important insights into the way he perceived the dialectic of communication. In these outlines, he attempts to clarify the distinctive features of ethical and religious communication by setting them in contrast with the means by which knowledge ('Viden') is conveyed. He begins by berating the modern age, because 'what it means to be a human being has been forgotten' (649; 81/3). He complains of our loss of 'naïveté' (ibid./1), arguing that

---

[18] Quoted in M. Finlay, *The Romantic Irony of Semiotics: Friedrich Schlegel and the Crisis of Representation* (Berlin etc.: Gruyter, 1988), p. 107.

[19] 'Die Parekbase kann eben so wohl *absolut* Mim[isch] als absolut Fant[astisch] sein; eigentlich beides aber ganz rein zusammen, also die höchste Antiform und Naturpoesie' (*Friedrich Schlegel's Literary Notebooks 1797–1801*, ed. Eichner (Toronto: University of Toronto Press, 1957), no. 395).

[20] Finlay, *Romantic Irony*, p. 108.

[21] 'Introduction' to S. Agacinski, *Aparté: Deaths and Conceptions of Søren Kierkegaard* (Tallahassee: University of Florida Press, 1988), p. 20.

[22] JP 1: 649ff.; Pap. VIII B 81ff. References in the text are to JP and Pap. respectively and where appropriate, after the slash, to the numbered section of the entry in which the passage occurs.

> The powers of the human world have been fantastically extracted and a book world has been produced (one now becomes an author simply and solely by becoming a reader – instead of by primitivity, just as one becomes a man simply and solely by aping 'the others', instead of by primitivity), a public of fantastic abstractions. (ibid./4)

Writing and reading exemplify a kind of disease of the spirit, in which it becomes merely a passive recipient of externally produced communications. This malaise is a symptom of relating to ethical requirements in the same indifferent way as one would to any communication of knowledge which has no essential connection with the way one lives.

Instead of this misunderstanding, Kierkegaard argues, we should realize that 'The ethical is indifferently related to knowledge; that is, it assumes that every human being knows it' (ibid./5). In other words, 'The ethical does not begin with ignorance which is to be changed to knowledge but begins with a knowledge and demands a realization' (ibid./10). What kind of knowledge does ethics presuppose? Certainly Kierkegaard does not give a list of ethical dictums which he believes are innate within us. His emphasis is not so much on the *content* of ethics as its *form*. He regrets the fact that 'men are preoccupied with the WHAT which is to be communicated' (657; 89), a clear echo of the *Postscript*, where Climacus writes '*Objectively the emphasis is on what is said; subjectively the emphasis is on how it is said*' (*CUP* 202). The reference to subjectivity recalls the importance of the subjunctive in illuminating ideal possibilities to which the criteria for assessing factual truth claims do not apply.

If ethics is not a body of objective, factual truths, what is it? Kierkegaard's answer is that it is an 'art [Kunst]' (649; 81/13) or a 'capability [Kunnen]' (651; 83), and 'in regard to the communication of a capability it holds that there is no object' (ibid.). It must therefore be communicated in a very different way from that in which science is taught: 'The communication here implies luring the ethical out of the individual, because it is *in* the individual' (649; 81/5). To lure out (in Danish 'at lokke ud') suggests overtones of enticement and seduction, as if the communicator must beguile the learner into the truth. And indeed, this is precisely what Kierkegaard expects. The form of ethical communication must be indirect and maieutic (i.e. like assisting at a birth), and this requires a certain disillusionment to take place in the recipient:

> All indirect communication is different from direct communication in that indirect communication first of all involves a deception – simply because an attempt to communicate the ethical directly would mean to deceive. (ibid./22)

It is in this context that Kierkegaard may say that irony is 'the highest earnestness' (ibid./23). No human being may claim authority over another in ethics, 'because, ethically, God is the master-teacher and every man is an apprentice' (ibid./16). The ironist may help a person relate to God as an individual by stripping away all direct modes of appropriating the ethical.

This conception of ethical communication, offered as a corrective, involves Kierkegaard's text in difficulties of its own. Part of his intention is to complicate the process of communication by focusing on the relation between giver and receiver, and on the medium in which it takes place. He distinguishes between the medium of imagination and the medium of actuality (649; 81/26–7). In the former, the communication remains at the level of fantasy merely as an object for scientific appraisal, so that 'All communication of knowledge is in the medium of imagination (possibility)' (651; 83). Conversely, actuality is the proper medium for conveying capability. However, this medium must itself be divided three ways, between aesthetic, ethical and religious spheres (ibid.). Only the ethical is unconditionally communicated in actuality, since it involves no objective knowledge *and* it demands a realization in the way one lives. Aesthetic competence 'is not to be realized in the existential of the everyday' (653; 85/15). Religious edification, on the other hand 'must first of all communicate a knowledge' (650; 82/13). In other words, religion presupposes some objective content of revelation as the basis for the way of life which it proclaims. Though Kierkegaard says that this knowledge 'is only a preliminary' (653; 85/29), he clearly thinks that it is enough to distinguish religion (and particularly Christianity) from ethics.

For ethics, then, realization is the key. This is why Kierkegaard associates it with actuality, for '"Actuality" [Virkelighed] is the existential reduplication of what is said' (ibid./17). And this is also where the issue relates to our earlier discussion of language and consciousness in *De Omnibus Dubitandum Est*. There, we recall, the repetitive structure of language made any access to pure reality or ideality impossible for consciousness. The word Kierkegaard used for reality was 'Realitet'. Actuality – 'Virkelighed' – is a different matter entirely. It is not immediate reality. It is the realisation of possibility, and it therefore presupposes an original division between the real and the ideal. It presupposes language. It can only be communicated indirectly, for its essential realization depends upon the way the recipient responds to it.

Of course, Kierkegaard is well aware of the irony of choosing the seemingly direct form of the lecture to talk about ethics, but he justifies it as a '*necessary concession*' (656; 88) to foster awareness: 'I am going to use direct communication to make you aware of indirect communication' (ibid.). In fact, the irony of the lecture-form in this context can serve Kierkegaard well, in a way similar to his use of pseudonyms:

> Therefore I regard it as my service that by bringing poetized personalities who say *I* (my pseudonyms) into the center of life's actuality I have

contributed, if possible, to familiarizing the contemporary age again to hearing an *I*, a personal *I* speak (not that fantastic pure *I* and its ventriloquism). (ibid.)

The lectures involve a kind of parabasis, in which Kierkegaard steps aside from his ironic masks to speak directly to his audience – only for us to realize that this is itself an ironic, deceptive gesture. In a sense, Kierkegaard is only practising his own theory of ethical communication. For the point is not to communicate knowledge, nor to make the recipient dependent in any way. It is rather to help the other 'stand alone' (650; 82/15), to be a free individual. To this end, the communicator must be an ironist, one who repulses people and turns them back to rely on their own resources. Using pseudonyms instead of speaking for oneself – and then admitting that this is what you are doing – is just such an ironical ploy.

5. Meaning is usage

The oscillation between irony and the desire for a return to direct immediacy haunts these lectures too, however. Kierkegaard criticizes the ephemeral and secondary literature of his day, and hankers after a 'primitivity' and naïveté which his age is sadly lacking (650; 82/3, 6). He bemoans the superficial nature of society as it is 'squeezed together in the big cities' (655; 87).

The danger of nostalgia is especially great for Kierkegaard. Because he sees language as ideality, as a *negation* of immediacy, there is always a temptation to seek out a moment of originary unity and foundational meaning which language cannot supply. But if there is no such site beyond language (and on Kierkegaard's grounds, it would be hard to see how humans could have access to it even if there were), how can the volatilization of concepts and nihilism of values be resisted?

In 1854, another journal passage finds Kierkegaard again deriding 'ventriloquism', a speaking which is essentially detached from the speaker's personality (JP 4: 4056; Pap. XI(2) A 106). This comes about, he claims, because 'language is an abstraction'; what gives it point and meaning is the existential setting in which it is used:

> The situation determines decisively whether or not the speaker is in character with what he says, or the situation determines whether or not the words are spoken at random, a talking which is unattached. (ibid.)

The situation is what gives concretion to language usage. Seen as a system, language is necessarily abstract and general. It is in use – when someone says *I* in a particular situation – that their actual character may be revealed.

Now this passage must be held together with the earlier one we quoted, in which Kierkegaard refers to his pseudonyms as 'poetized personalities who say *I*'. In the case of the pseudonyms, of course, there is a tension between this personalized communication, and the fact that the I who speaks in them is a fictional, literary device. The pseudonyms seem at once to establish and to deconstruct the I-Thou context for communication.

This is no less the case in Kierkegaard's signed texts. The upbuilding and religious discourses take as their context the fictional situation of a speaker and a listener in one another's presence. They are also very conscious of the fact that this is a fiction, that the speaker is absent, and that an enormous responsibility lies with the reader in establishing how the discourses are to be read. We will examine this further in Chapter 7.

The very forms of Kierkegaard's texts thus make an essential point. Meaning is not a static content transported from the mind of the giver to that of the receiver in any act of communication. There is a creative interaction, which depends as much on the repellent, ironical, seductive aspects of the text as it does on any transferal of objective information.

The very fact that ethics and religion are primarily arts or capabilities intensifies this necessity for a rhetorical, pragmatic approach to communication. Again, however, we must insist that this does not amount to anti-realism. Ethics is universal and binding, and religion appeals to a notion of revelation. However indirectly they are communicated, neither are reduced to being human creations, or explained by any emotivist theory. As we saw above, religion in particular demands the communication of a piece of preliminary knowledge which is not produced by us.

The complexity of Kierkegaard's writings is thus encountered pre-eminently in his texts on the paradox of God incarnate. The Word made flesh might promise to be the most direct revelation of God possible – God present to us in person. However, we soon find that, especially in this case, direct communication and any model of revelation which depends upon it, are strained to breaking point by the impossibility of representing this paradox. The preliminary knowledge is not just a neutral bit of objective information which we can digest. It is the challenge to faith or offence.

6. The divine Word is the archetype for the human word

Practice in Christianity devotes a section to the idea of the God-Man as a sign. It begins from the now familiar premise that the sign is 'the denied immediacy or the second being that is different from the first being' (*PC* 124). The sign is certainly an immediate 'something' – a post or lamp (in the case of a navigation mark), or, we might add, black marks on a page (in the case of writing). That the sign qua sign is something other than and beyond this immediacy is the precondition for both communication and deceit:

> This underlies all the mystification by means of signs, for the sign is only for the one who knows that it is a sign and in the strictest sense only for the one who knows what it means; for everyone else the sign is that which it immediately is. (ibid.)

The fact that the sign is a negated immediacy makes disingenuity and irony possible. As we read, we are made aware that we only understand the meaning of something if we presuppose that it can be 'meaningful'. This is the work of reflection:

> The striking thing is the immediate, but my regarding it as a sign (which is a reflection, something I in a certain sense take from myself) indeed expresses that I think that it is supposed to mean something. But that it is supposed to *mean* something is its being something different from what it immediately is. (ibid.)

Reflection holds the signifier and the signified apart. This semiotic gap is the necessary condition for truth, error, lying and irony to be possible. It is also at the root of a kind of unease about the meaning of what we see around us. We cannot 'know definitely' that something is a sign (ibid.), let alone what it might mean. We must remember that Anti-Climacus' concern is guided by the aim he has in mind: of giving some kind of account of the ultimately ambiguous sign, that of the Word made flesh.

He begins by introducing the phenomenon of the '*sign of contradiction* ... a sign that intrinsically contains a contradiction in itself' (*PC* 124–5). He gives the example of a communication which is a unity of jest and earnest. It is not *directly* one or the other, its significance does not lie in a didactic transference of some objective, preformed meaning to the recipient. Rather, its objective ambiguity means that its real earnestness is found elsewhere – in making the reader 'self-active [selvvirksom]' (*PC* 125). The recipient becomes explicitly responsible for the task of interpreting the communication and translating it into an existential task. This type of discourse raises the stakes in the game of interpretation, implicitly challenging the reader by making him or her attentive to the relationship between sign and reality:

> A sign is not what it is in immediacy, because in its immediacy no sign *is*, inasmuch as 'sign' is a term based on reflection. A sign of contradiction is that which draws attention to itself and, once attention is directed to it, shows itself to contain a contradiction. (ibid.)

Anti-Climacus now makes the crucial leap into a consideration of the God-Man as a sign. The transition itself is vital, because the sign is now a living human being. What is more, of course, this is no ordinary human being. Christ contains in himself the absolute qualitative contradiction between 'being God and being an individual human being' (ibid.). The miracles and Christ's occasional direct statements about his status can only draw attention to the enormity of the contradiction involved; the nature of the paradox means that there cannot really be direct communication. However, it is crucial that they *do* at least make the paradox noticeable, because a sign that 'exists for no one' (*PC* 126) is not a sign at all. There must be a communication if there is to be salvation, and this premise, implicit in much of this passage, seems to be the key antidote to nihilism and despair over the adequacy of signs. God wishes to communicate with us, however difficult and impenetrable the resulting form this takes.

It is a consideration of language *in the abstract* which appears to lead us to doubt the possibility of communication. But, as Kierkegaard argued, the significance of communication depends upon the particular situation in which it is made. The connection between signs and actuality is made by the good will and sincerity of the communicator and the actively attentive receptivity of the listener.[23] It is therefore important to note that Anti-Climacus here launches into an attack on the idealist philosophical notion of the 'speculative unity of God and man' (ibid.) which dissolves the qualitative distinction between the two. The didactic approach of the systematic paragraph writers misses the whole point about the dialectic of indirect communication, making everything as direct as 'putting one's foot in a sock' (ibid.). The God-Man is a stimulant to decision, but also a *mirror*; for in the way one construes or judges this sign, the disposition of one's heart is revealed: 'as he is forming a judgement, what dwells within him must be disclosed' (*PC* 127).

This is the crux of the matter. The emphasis on the recipient's own part in establishing the meaning of any sign was a preparation for this sting in the tail: how we choose to interpret some signs is not just a question for epistemology or semantics, but for ethics and faith. Some riddles are not mere intellectual curiosities, but questions posed to our whole way of thinking and living. But how can we tell if we are being confronted by such a demand? There is one sign: 'the possibility of offense ... [which] is the negative mark of the God-Man' (*PC* 143). The essential paradoxicality of the incarnation is the greatest insanity to our reason, and yet the most radical challenge to its self-sufficiency. It is in the passionate collision of the two that the possibility of our encountering the salvific communication of God may be realized.

---

[23] Cf. the discussion of reference and realism in J. M. Soskice's *Metaphor and Religious Language* (Oxford: Clarendon, 1985), Chapter VII, in which she describes Hilary Putnam's view with the words 'It is not words which refer, but speakers using words who refer' (p. 136). She quotes Putnam as follows: 'The realist explanation, in a nutshell, is not that language mirrors the world but that *speakers* mirror the world; i.e. their environment – in the sense of *constructing a symbolic representation of that environment*' (ibid.). Kierkegaard's writing on the abstraction and ideality of language and the need for a concrete situation of communication provides a point of contact with modern defences of referential realism. However, note that this quotation predates Putnam's move to 'internal realism' and his consequent questioning of the objective/subjective split, a move which itself echoes the subtler complexities of Kierkegaard's resistance to direct communication.

The relation between the Word and words in general is not a straightforward hierarchy or order of priority. The Word made flesh intensifies the paradoxical unity of real and ideal, particular and universal, temporal and eternal, which is characteristic of all language usage. It does not anchor language (particularly language about God) in a self-evident instance of absolute meaning, which closes the gap between signifier and signified. Christ, as sign of contradiction holds the two apart to a radical degree. There is no opting out of the ambiguity of language, no encounter with a truth that is clear and fully present.

The meaning of the incarnation thus seems to lie in the impact it makes on our life. And this eludes capture by either realist or anti-realist accounts. The truth of the story of the incarnation cannot be reduced to propositions which can be verified by objective evidence. Relating to it in this way misses the decisive ethico-religious importance of it. However, nor is the truth of the story something constructed and put there wholly by us as its recipients. The paradoxicality of the incarnation is not an intellectual conundrum, but involves an intrinsic rebuff to such mastery on our part. We do not create the meaning of the incarnation, but that meaning only emerges in the practical effect it has on our whole life-view. Faith in the incarnation is not of the order of knowing, but neither is it a subjective creation. It is *witness*. *Practice* culminates in the contrast between admiration and imitation – the truth lies in treading the way of Christ, not contemplating him as an ideal, or holding his teachings to be objective descriptions of the truth. We will return to the nature of witnessing in Chapter 7.

Again, the form of the text is important here. The initial representation of the attractive invitation to follow Christ is interrupted; a passage entitled 'The Halt' [Standsningen] signifies the leap to reflecting on the paradoxical nature of the one who issues the invitation. The 'philosophical' reflections we have principally quoted from here give way to a more edifying form of religious discourse. The whole is presided over by Anti-Climacus – a Christian of extraordinary degree, a slightly unreal character, whose forays into speculation and poetry compromise his own purity. And even with his stature, he can do no more than expose the indirect, subversive nature of this paradox.

Summary

We have found significant points of contact between the themes of Kierkegaard's contemporaries and his own texts when it comes to the question of language. However, it is the differences and tensions he introduces which mark out his distinctive contribution to this field – a contribution which serves more to disturb fixed boundaries between 'objective' and 'subjective' truth than to add to our store of such truths.

1. Kierkegaard agrees with Hamann and others that language is presupposed by philosophy. However, this does not entail (any more than it did for Hamann) a belief that we are trapped in language, or that we only have access to the reality dictated to us by our internal conceptual categories. Language is gift and task, pointing to the grace and creativity which it enables us to encounter.

2. Kierkegaard explores the way in which language cancels immediacy. He shows how any absolute beginning is impossible for philosophy. Language makes consciousness possible, but debars us from direct acquaintance with immediate reality. Language is bound up with themes of temporality, repetition, contradiction. It cannot be tied down to an ideal of meaning as self-presence or timeless identity. It makes possible the pathos and interest which allow consciousness to relate to actuality in ways other than those of objective cognition.

3. Nevertheless, we may see how Kierkegaard's texts themselves swing between the acceptance of the inevitably indirect nature of our relationship to truth and to God, and the ideal of a transparent encounter with God through words or silence. Without wishing to reduce this tension, we have shown how it is to some extent embedded in texts whose form subverts any direct encounter with God. The complex relationship between music and language is suggestive: music is not a pure representation of immediacy; nor can language dispense with its immediate, sensuous basis. A more subtle interweaving of immediacy and spirit is called for, one which will resist such rigid boundary lines.

4. It is evident, therefore, that Kierkegaard does not equate truth with the truth of direct propositions, which can be objectively verified. Ethical and religious truth is about awakening capabilities in us; it cannot be reduced to a matter of cognition. Religion does demand communication of a preliminary knowledge, but we have already discovered that neither the form nor the content of such knowledge is conformable to a straightforward correspondence theory of truth.

5. Thus, Kierkegaard is led to advocate that meaning is tied to usage. Meaning is established by pragmatic criteria of context and situation, and in the interaction between giver and receiver of communication. It is not preformed and self-contained. Nevertheless, his textual strategy points to the fact that contexts are indeterminate. It is basic ethical-religious dispositions which will determine how the recipient construes a communication, though an author can use literary effects which resist the reduction of meaning to objective correspondence with perceptible or cognisable objects.

6. Finally, Kierkegaard does play on the link between Word and words. The divine Word is in one sense a paradigm for language in general; but it does not provide an ultimate foundation for meaning. It is paradoxical, indirect and existential in its impact. It thus points to a relationship to truth which is characterized by faith, passion, imitation and witness, rather than correct credal belief.

Throughout this chapter, we have emphasized that Kierkgeaard's texts cannot be equated with either realism or anti-realism as we have defined them. They dispute the priority of a correspondence theory of truth or a representational model of language, but they also challenge Romantic and speculative notions of self-creation. They open the reader to a relationship with 'reality' which is mediated and ruptured by all the indirectness and pathos of language, as it is inextricably linked to self-consciousness. This relationship is not primarily one of knowing, but of ethico-religious commitment.

In a journal entry from 1842–3, Kierkegaard claims that Descartes' 'rescue of the finite world' from the nadir of radical doubt was a *'pathos-filled transition'* (JP 3: 2338–9; Pap. IV C 11): a qualitative leap unassimilable to rational thought (an idea of such importance in *The Concept of Anxiety*). Reason alone cannot escape from doubt, for the *cogito*, he argues, is derivative: freedom, the will, action – these are primordial, and they resist dialectical thought. Writing of Plato's use of such a concept of pathos-filled transition in his account of 'God's uniting of the idea with matter', he remarks 'Strangely enough he [Plato] denied it with respect to the origin of language' (ibid.). Language has a transcendental, creative, *incarnational* character of its own, uniting ideal and material. For Kierkegaard, the origin of language cannot be explained in 'theory': it is coextensive with human existence as spirit, and it is the organ of temporality.

The problem for us becomes one of how actual language usage is to be evaluated and validated. A hint has been found in that 'sign of contradiction' which is Christ: in the light of how we are invited to appropriate the narrative which gives the communication its context, its situation, it may be judged whether or not it comes to set us free or to enslave us. It is in terms of the concrete act of communication itself, of how it is given and received, that the test of its authenticity must be made – for there is no site beyond language from which to judge.

Again and again, we have seen the importance of attending to the form of Kierkegaard's communication. That form might now be seen as primarily performative. His texts do not serve to communicate objective information, but by engaging the reader in their own dilemmas of indirectness and representation, they can perform a therapeutic role, interrupting the monologue of a self-contained reason. However, this in turn involves relating the reader to an otherness which the self does not create or comprehend. The inevitable failure of Kierkegaard and his pseudonyms to represent this other reality perhaps places their texts in that strange borderland *between* performative and constative, realist and anti-realist, where communication is not assured. It is also a borderland between the irreducible singularity of the reader who is addressed, and the necessary universality of the address – a tension embodied in the 'intimate impersonality' characteristic of Kierkegaard's discourses.

Such tensions and lack of assurances of course leave language open to a nihilism which denies any relationship between language and a truth which is not wholly fictional. It also leaves it open to the ethical abuses of dissimulation and deceit. In examining the role of the seducer in *Either/Or*, we will gain a greater insight into what is at stake ethically in the question of language, and why faith cannot evade the risky passage through nihilism which shakes the representational model of language to its foundations.

CHAPTER FOUR

The seduction of language

With the texts examined so far, it has proved impossible to ignore the literary form in which they are presented. This interlacing of form and content is given heightened importance by the conclusion of the last chapter: if the nature of truth cannot be comprehended on a basic correspondence model, then Kierkegaard is forced to invent new strategies of literary *performance*, in which the link between philosophy and poesis is made explicit. In 'The Seducer's Diary' from *Either/Or*, for example, ethical questions are only implicit in a narrative which exhibits the potential for cruelty and deception inherent in our linguistic nature. Through the fictional, pseudo-confessional form, Kierkegaard shows us one way in which language, as the negation of immediacy, can be exploited.

This is crucial to the question of realism and anti-realism. The story of the seducer offers a critique of a certain form of poetic self-creation, but, together with other texts from the first part of *Either/Or*, the challenge it poses to a realist view of language cannot be evaded. In some ways, the seducer and his co-authors anticipate the affirmation of philosophical nihilism which Nietzsche made the spur for the abolition of realism and the re-creation of values *ex nihilo*. Nietzsche's atheism was entwined with his fictionalist account of truth in general. It is a peculiarly modern and radical atheism.

The character of the seducer itself is unmistakeably modern. It combines a number of roles specific to the milieu of the early nineteenth-century urban scene. He is the romantic poet, the ironist, the gentleman of leisure – roles made possible by cultural and economic upheavals which had left their mark on the nascent bourgeoisie of the Danish capital. Urbanization brought with it the promise or risk of a richly varied public space inhabited by different social strata, and by men and women alike. The seducer himself shares some characteristics with the semi-mythological *flâneur*, described by Elizabeth Wilson as 'a new kind of public person with the leisure to wander, watch and browse ... an archetypal occupant and observer of the public sphere in the rapidly changing and growing great cities of nineteenth-century Europe'.[1]

The *flâneur* is a key figure in some of the literature of modernity, typifying the freedom of the bourgeois male to explore the new environment.[2] Wilson cites an anonymous pamphlet from the Paris of 1806, detailing the life of one

---

[1] E. Wilson 'The Invisible Flâneur', *New Left Review* 191 (Jan./Feb. 1992) pp. 90–110 (quote from p. 93).

[2] For example, Walter Benjamin, *Charles Baudelaire*, trans. Zohn (London: NLB, 1973).

'M. Bonhomme,' whose 'predominantly aesthetic' interests involve him in visits to cafés, salons and exhibitions, and in 'simply looking at the urban spectacle'.[3] Though M. Bonhomme appears to take little interest in women, he does share one telling trait with Kierkegaard's creation:

> In his resolution 'to keep a little diary recording all the most curious things he had seen or heard during the course of his wanderings, to fill the void of his nocturnal hours of insomnia' is the germ of the *flâneur's* future role as a writer; it also hints at the boredom and ennui which seem inescapably linked to the curiosity and voyeurism that are so characteristic.[4]

It may seem odd to link the diary of a vacuous Parisian with that of the super-confident seducer, but it will be shown that both share a kind of anxiety about their own self-sufficient status as voyeurs. The seducer's own diary is itself an attempt to gain control over the multifarious appearances and threats of the life of the city.

The idea of a diary appears first in *Either/Or* in the 'Diapsalmata', where 'A' looks for a way to refresh his memory of his past motivations:

> It frequently happens that with the passage of time I have completely forgotten the reasons that moved me to this or that, with regard not only to trivialities but also to the most crucial steps. If the reason occurs to me, it can sometimes be so strange that I cannot even believe that it was the reason. This doubt would be removed if I had something written to refer to. (*EO* 32).

He has faith in the power of written words faithfully to record and preserve one's reasons for acting, and assumes that it is only the passage of time which deprives our motives of their clarity. But as 'A' himself declares, 'a reason is a curious thing' (ibid.), and there is no necessarily clear and rational link between act and motive. The grounds for our choices may remain in obscurity. This may be something that 'A' can affirm in some moods ('One ought to be a riddle not only to others but also to oneself' (*EO* 26)), but it also initiates a kind of depressed cynicism which defers one from taking any sort of decisive step. As the 'Ecstatic Discourse' claims, you may do anything, but whatever you do you will regret it – so the solution is to live suspended above all choosing: 'the true eternity does not lie behind either/or but before it' (*EO* 39).

'A's inability to step out into the public realm of communication becomes a consciously chosen *method* for the seducer. The distinction between the inner and the outer, which stands at the head of *Either/Or* (*EO* 3), is sharpened when set against the background of the recently manufactured and thus fluid divide between public and private realms in the nineteenth-century city. The

---

[3] Wilson, 'Invisible Flâneur', p. 94.
[4] Ibid., p. 95.

promise of writing, as a sure testimony to what has been, cannot be sustained in the multiple ambiguities of this scene of interpretation. Writing can offer no escape from a public realm, which is becoming ever more inundated by the arrival of competing perspectives on reality. Can nihilism be resisted in this strange modern context?

The poet and his recollection

'A's prefatory remarks to 'The Seducer's Diary' give his own assessment of the character of its writer: 'His life has been an attempt to accomplish the task of living poetically ... Therefore, his diary is not historically accurate or strictly narrative; it is not indicative but subjunctive' (*EO* 304). As we found in the last chapter, the subjunctive represents both language's capacity to transcend the mere givenness of the facts, and the danger that this capacity could be abused so as to lose all contact with actuality. The poet tries to relate his experiences to the idea, to the essential determinant of their reality and value. However, in the seducer's case, this is not an attempt to communicate those insights to others, but to heighten his own enjoyment. Poetry is not a matter of writing verse, it is a way of living and of transfiguring what one lives through in retrospect, such that even the moment of actual experience is always already enjoyed to a heightened degree:

> The poetic was the plus he himself brought along ... In the first case, he continually needed actuality as the occasion [Anledning], as an element [Moment]; in the second case, actuality was drowned in the poetic. (*EO* 305)

Actuality is merely the occasion ('Anledning' – meaning 'leading to' something other than itself[5]), bearing within itself the seeds of its own sublimation. The word 'Moment' carries Hegelian overtones of the process of *Aufhebung*, whereby a concept is both cancelled out and preserved in a higher synthesis, driven by the contradictions to which it gives rise.[6] Here, however, the actual appears to be completely overwhelmed by the waters of the poetic, compelled to serve the idiosyncrasies of the poet rather than the self-unfolding of Spirit.

The diary is not, therefore, an authentic record of the facts. 'A' suggests that the diary absolves itself from questions of historical veracity, because 'it came so close to being idea that specifications of time became unimportant' (*EO* 310–11); it does not have its primary purpose in *remembering* but in *recollecting*.[7] To recollect something, whatever else it may entail, is not

---

[5] See the discussion of the 'occasion' in the review of *The First Love* (EO 236).
[6] See *Hegel's Science of Logic*, trans. Miller (New York: Humanities Press, 1969), pp. 105–7.
[7] Cf. *SLW* 9ff.

merely to store it away, as the seducer himself says: 'Recollection [Erindring] is a means not only of conserving but also of augmenting something; something that is permeated by recollection has a double-effect' (*EO* 343). Recollection is also internalization ('Er*in*dring'); it is a way of taking possession of what lies outside of you so that it may be performed again before the imagination. The seducer must maintain his control over the way in which he experiences actuality. Despite his reliance on fortune, his own manipulation must ensure that experience is only allowed to trespass upon his enjoyment once it has been duplicated in reflection and enhanced by recollection.

The diary presents us only with the triumphant self-certainty of this approach. To discover its more ambiguous façade we must turn to the 'Diapsalmata'. The very first aphorism of this section suggests that the poet's transfiguration of what he experiences can be a symptom of a deep alienation from the public realm, and a source of misunderstanding between the poet and those who read him only superficially: 'What is a poet? An unhappy person who conceals profound anguish in his heart but whose lips are so formed that as sighs and cries pass over them they sound like beautiful music' (*EO* 19). To be sure, the poet can be in love with the recollection which relates him to the idea and is the basis of his own creativity. We are told that 'Real enjoyment consists not in what one enjoys but in the idea' (*EO* 31) and that 'only recollection's love is happy' (*EO* 41). But the images the poet uses are ambivalent. In the last passage quoted, the poet complains that an angel of death walks by his side, which, in unbiblical fashion, *enters* the homes of the chosen ones rather than passing them by. Further on, the poet sees himself in fairytale terms, swooping down from his castle of sorrow to snatch his prey from actuality and weave it into his tapestries: 'Everything I have experienced I immerse in a baptism of oblivion unto an eternity of recollection' (*EO* 42).

This association of the height of creativity with death is brought out in an explicitly erotic reference: 'There are, as is known, insects that die at the moment of fertilization. So it is with all joy: life's highest, most splendid moment of enjoyment is accompanied by death' (*EO* 20). This witnesses to a profound disquiet at the heart of the poetic venture. The poet cannot help but find satisfaction in his imaginative production, whilst recognizing that it bars him from a real relationship with other people or with the temporal world in which he lives. The recollected relationship is 'more richly satisfying than all actuality' and yet 'for me nothing is more dangerous than to recollect ... A recollected life relationship has already passed into eternity and has no temporal interest anymore' (*EO* 32).

The poet's words take leave of their anchor in actuality. In his own poetic practice, he experiences a crisis of representation, for he cannot fulfil the role of the one who gives voice to the sentiments of others: 'I can describe hope so vividly that every hoping individual will recognize my description as his own; and yet it is forgery, for even as I am describing it I am thinking of recollection' (*EO* 36). This apparent admission of anxiety seems foreign to the vocabulary of the seducer. For he is, surely, more than a mere observer or *flâneur*. He is an active force, a manipulator of people and not merely of ideas. However, if we examine his views on the category of people he takes most interest in, these traces of ambiguity and anxiety may be taken as hints in discovering what really is at stake in the work of seduction.

Woman and immediacy

It is clearly of central importance for the seducer that women are seen to embody very definite characteristics, and the way in which he describes the girls who occupy his attention reveals much of his underlying motivations. The girl he observes while she is shopping is said to have 'a Madonna head' with no 'delineation of the powers of understanding' (*EO* 316). Cordelia, the one who is the object of his seduction, is not 'subjectively reflected' (343), not able to distinguish dream from actuality, possessing 'purely immediate womanliness' (*EO* 345). She is to be brought to the point where she is able to 'confuse poetry and actuality, truth and fiction, to frolic in infinity' (*EO* 392). She does not move into a sphere of greater reflective or conceptual clarity, but descends deeper into immediacy and the time of dreaming infancy:

> A young girl does not develop in the sense that a boy does; she does not grow, she is born ... the moment she is born, she is full grown ... She does not awaken gradually, but at once; on the other hand, she dreams that much longer ... But this dreaming is an infinite richness. (*EO* 331–2).

The seducer concentrates his attention on teenagers because they are supposedly free from the taint of awakening. Women are meant to be essentially full-grown at birth, and yet the seducer fears that they are under threat of being woken up out of this dreaming innocence. The use of organic images binds this conception of women to a romantic vision of nature.[8] Like a beech tree, Cordelia is 'a unity that has no parts', 'hidden in herself'; but she is also 'an enigma that enigmatically possessed its own solution, a secret' (*EO* 330). The female's organic unity is something unreachable, a riddle to the male's reflective gaze, but one which the seducer hopes will be solved [løst] by a loosened [løst] tongue (ibid.). The seducer has the power of intellect and spirit (the Danish 'Aand' carries both connotations), and these are his weapons in the game of manipulation. The woman's poetic slumber is

---

[8] Cf. F. W. J. Schelling, *Ideas for a Philosophy of Nature*, trans. Harris and Heath (Cambridge: Cambridge University Press, 1988), p. 51: the organism is 'the perfect mirror-image of the absolute in Nature and for Nature'.

neutralized by the numbing prose of common sense and by the intellect (*EO* 346): 'What does a young girl fear? Intellect [Aand]. Why? Because intellect constitutes the negation of her entire womanly existence' (*EO* 362). The seducer is the cavorting power of the Zephyr, the wind which robs the young girls of the power of language in the dangerous open spaces of the city streets: 'How they laugh and talk – and the wind carries the words away; is there really anything to talk about?' (*EO* 357). Exposing and resisting, the wind draws out the immediate richness of the girls' extra-linguistic appeal.

The woman's closeness to nature is linked to this suggestion of her muteness in a passage describing a visit to Cordelia's house. She is referred to as a 'freshly picked blossom' (*EO* 373): 'She looked so young and yet so fully developed, as if nature like a tender and luxuriant mother, had this very moment released her from her hand' (ibid.). Released from her mother/nature, Cordelia is not left without defence in the world. Nature speaks to her, saying '"Take now this kiss as a seal upon your lips. It is a seal that guards the sanctuary; it cannot be broken by anyone if you yourself do not want it to be ..."' (*EO* 374). The girl's virginity is a symbol of her unbroken immediacy and continuity with her mother. Her difference from the male is linked with a profound difference in their means of communication: 'Wonderful nature, how profound and enigmatic you are! To man you give words, and to the girl the eloquence of the kiss!' (ibid.). The man has been separated from the physical contact of the mother's kiss, and compensated with the power of speech; only men have the minds to grasp the abstractions of language needed to bring concepts and ideas to expression.

The seducer proceeds to use this gift to unsettle the girl and close his grip upon her imagination. He seeks at once revenge and satisfaction for his own sense of lack, for having been woken up too soon into male adulthood. The nature which is Cordelia's mother *is his mother also* – but the linguistic gifts she has given him are second hand abstractions compared to the girl's plenitude. The enigma of nature and the riddle of the girl are questions posed to the heart of the male's sense of who he is, and his insecurity in feeling cut off, disconnected from the nature which gave birth to him and his fellow human beings. His game is a risky one; it depends heavily on the actual women he meets conforming to his preconceived ideas. He is adamant that 'a young girl should not be interesting either, for the interesting always involves reflecting on oneself ...' (*EO* 339). The interesting woman has 'surrendered her womanliness' and the men she pleases are 'unmasculine'; her self-sufficiency is illusory (*EO* 340). There must be no confusion of genders if the one-sidedness of seduction is to remain a possibility. The reference to 'unmasculine' men is revealing, for it shows how much of the seducer's own identity *as a man* is at stake.

These associations are far from marginal to our interest. Women are associated with those aspects of reality – dreams, myth, poetry – which

Romantic authors took to articulate truths which could not be captured by propositional language. By seeking to negate the immediacy they represent, the seducer pushes to an extreme the dilemma of representation which faces the Romantic poet. His view of spirit and language is one-sided and undialectical. It fails to preserve a relationship between spirit and the immediacy it transcends, because it has a negative, poverty-stricken notion of spirit. If language, as the expression of spirit, is seen as a pure negation of the sensual and immediate, this will lead to a total nihilism. And what goes for immediacy also goes for the ethical and religious ideals which cannot be reduced to propositional language or direct communication. Whilst the Romantics attempted to evoke a relation to that which exceeded rational grasp by using forms of communication which were conscious of the inadequacy of propositions and representations, the seducer takes a wholly destructive attitude towards spirit's other even as he tries to recapture it. His use of language is bound up with negative ethical attitudes towards the women who signify a relationship with nature and embodiment.

Many of the themes we have touched on are concentrated in a long passage near the end of the diary, when the seducer gives a kind of philosophical analysis of woman in her essential being. Woman is defined as 'being-for-other', a designation which points through woman to nature as her mother and paradigm, since:

> the whole of nature is for-other – is for spirit ... likewise, an enigma, a charade, a secret, a vowel, etc. are merely being-for-other. This explains why God, when he created Eve, had a deep sleep fall upon Adam, for woman is man's dream ... She became flesh and blood, but precisely thereby she falls within the category of nature, which essentially is being-for-other. Not until she is touched by erotic love does she awaken; before that time she is a dream. (*EO* 430).

Nature is an enigma or secret, even a charade, but the connotations of duplicity and dissimulation associated with these ideas threaten the separateness of the seducer's reflection. Both nature and spirit are indispensable aspects of a whole, just as vowels and consonants are equally essential components of the Danish language. Moreover, even this idea of complementarity is undermined by the realisation that the differences between male and female may not be as 'natural' as the seducer supposes. It is unclear who is supposed to be asleep; woman is *man's* dream, but *she* is the one whom erotic love awakens. If this is so, if both man and woman can be said to be in some sense awake and asleep, conscious and unconscious, who is to say that the woman may not awaken to more than an immediate devotion to self-conscious male desire?

To avoid this possibility, the seducer must place severe constraints on the woman's potential growth, in the guise of preserving her purity: 'As being-for-other, woman is characterized by pure virginity' (*EO* 430). She is the unattainable ideal, like the virgin mother to whom she is compared; she is made for man's pleasure, yet she remains a dream. To enjoy her is to destroy her proper meaning as the unbroken vessel of immediacy. Her virginity is an 'abstraction' (ibid.), a negative reality which is only made apparent by the *possibility* of its loss, by the approach of a suitor. Thus, 'that which is for-other is not, and, so to speak, first becomes visible through the other' (*EO* 431). The woman becomes free through the man (to propose = 'at frie'), but, ironically, she appears dominant in this situation. The choice is hers; the man must make his request and await her decision.

The ambivalence of all this does not escape the seducer, when he notes that 'In a certain sense, man is more than woman, in another sense infinitely less' (*EO* 431–2). The man is more dependent on woman than would at first seem to be the case, and Johannes' anxiety becomes obvious when he scorns those women who take the initiative towards men. If this happens, the woman's devotedness becomes 'coyness [Knibskhed]' and ultimately 'abstract cruelty' (*EO* 432). Such a fear of women is inscribed in fairy tales, myths and legends. Women are the representatives of the ruthlessness of nature devoid of spiritual control, revelling in 'cruelty for the sake of cruelty alone' (ibid.). The seducer must seek the woman out as the bearer of a pure immediacy he lacks, but he must also fear the total eclipse of *his* being by the fullness of her presence: 'I still always approach a young girl with a certain anxiety; my heart pounds, for I sense the eternal power that is in her nature' (*EO* 435).

The clue to his dilemma lies in that image of womanhood which he deems more honourable than that of the young girl: the mother holding a child in her arms. The figure is an ideal representation, 'it is a nature myth, which therefore may be seen only in artistic portrayal, not in actuality' (*EO* 435). No other figures should be present in this scene; if the father is included, he 'cancels the myth, the charm' (ibid.). This suggests that Johannes is harking back to a time when he wished to be held in his mother's arms, undisturbed by the father's unsettling interventions which would exile him from intimacy into the borderlands of maturity. The picture recalls a childhood time of myths, a time the seducer wishes at once to recapture and to despoil for others.

The seducer is thus torn between two myths, or two versions of the same myth: woman as tender mother and as cruel goddess, both perhaps subsumed under the heading of woman as nature. From his point of view, his anxiety is not necessarily a negative feeling, for fear 'makes love interesting', 'this anxiety captivates the most' (*EO* 424). Nevertheless, he wishes to control a fear and desire which is continually escaping his domination, to the extent that *he* becomes the one who is being led astray. He says of Cordelia that 'She will herself become the temptress who seduces me into going beyond the universal' (*EO* 425). Ultimately, when he has enjoyed his prey, he must annul her continuing significance with the statement that 'in man innocence is a negative element, but in woman it is the substance of her being' (*EO* 445). She has lost all – all, that is, that she could be for the seducer. Now she must be neutralized, as if the loss of virginity were also a loss of womanhood. The seducer fantasizes a final expression of his triumph: 'If I were a god, I would do for her what Neptune did for a nymph: transform her into a man' (ibid.).

Cordelia's only meaningful future is as a man. But doesn't this imply that even she, the naïve 16-year-old, has reached a point of disillusioned reflectivity; that she, *as a woman*, always had the potential for intellect and spirituality which the seducer tries to reserve for men? If this possibility cannot be ruled out, then all the seducer's conceptions of control and all the seductive power of his communications do not have the final word. The reality of language and the distinctions and hierarchies with which it is bound up, especially at such a time of fluidity as the growth of the European cities and their bourgeois economy, is far harder to dominate – even within the confines of one's own poesis.

In fact, the woman represents the bodily and substantial being which eludes the male. Victor Eremita, in *Stages on Life's Way*, expresses the seducer's situation thus:

> The seducer wants to assert himself by deceiving, but that he deceives, that he wants to deceive, and that he takes the trouble to deceive are also manifestations of his dependence on woman, and the same holds true for the experimenting male. (*SLW* 64)

In their various ways, all the speeches at the fictive banquet which forms the backdrop for the first part of *Stages* ('In Vino Veritas') repeat this dependency. The Young Man flees the uncertainties of the erotic for the self-contained world of thought (*SLW* 45f.); Constantin tries to reduce the significance of woman to a jest which cannot be taken seriously (*SLW* 48). Both attempt to suppress a relation to an other which cannot be constructed after their own image or defined on terms they have set in advance. The Fashion Designer derives sadistic enjoyment from women's enslavement to fashion (*SLW* 70), reflecting the dehumanizing nature of bourgeois commodification of reality. The seducer's idolization of women has been treated before. All these witness to forces beyond their comprehension or control, which they feel must be tamed, manipulated or avoided without any threat to their self-repose.

Victor Eremita delivers perhaps the most revealing speech. He gives thanks that he is not a woman, declaring that 'Woman's meaning is negative' (*SLW* 61). She is an 'abstraction' (*SLW* 59) with no determinate meaning. However, she has a crucial role to play, because 'ideality came into life because of a woman' (ibid.). It was she who caused poetry and longing to exist, as men sought, through her, to satisfy their lack. Unfortunately, ideality could only be aroused as long as this lack persisted, for 'As long as man does not have her, she inspires him' (ibid.). As soon as man possesses her and settles down to domestic bliss, superficial mundanity rules. Woman is nothing as a possession; she signifies an absence, an opening of desire. She is not a plenitude to be enjoyed, but a sounding board for man's striving, an ever-deferred promise of plenitude. She is an immediacy which must be negated if man is to achieve his own ideality:

> man has his ideality only in a reduplication. Every immediate existence must be annihilated and the annihilation constantly safeguarded by a false expression. Woman cannot grasp a reduplication such as that; it makes it impossible for her to state man's nature [Væsen]. (*SLW* 65)

Woman cannot 'state man's nature'; she is robbed of language, unable to manage its ideality. It follows that 'If she is really going to awaken ideality in her husband, she must die' (*SLW* 61). However, this ideality is a dubious gain; it manifests itself as an ironic play which knows that all the currency of communication has only an arbitrary value: 'It makes no difference whether someone uses gold or silver or paper currency, but the person who does not pay out even a farthing unless it is false, he knows what I mean' (ibid.). The man must become one for whom 'every immediate expression is a forgery' (ibid.). In annihilating the woman, man seems cut adrift in an arbitrary circulation of forged papers, ever unable to consummate his relationship to her who was the reason for his ideality coming to birth.

Man is thus caught in a self-contradiction. He attempts to achieve fulfilment, but by this very movement finds himself trapped in the duplicity of existence, in the nexus of language, reduplication and forgery. He cannot become totally free and transcendent. Just as language is nothing without its sensuous vehicle, so he is nothing without some element of material givenness, of embodiment. The attempt to negate women – like the description of language as an ideal negation of immediacy – is a reflection of a bourgeois dream of freedom from all constraints, of a self-contained mastery over all phenomena. It is a dream which dissolves into futility, because every self must have a sensuous basis, and must, in a sense, be 'being-for-other'.

Breaking silence

'All love is secretive' (*EO* 336) claims the diary; and there is a sense in which its public profession and legitimization in engagement and marriage is a distortion of its essence. To break silence is to profane the sanctuary of erotic love, subjecting it to all the petty moralizing distinctions of social discourse.[9]

---

[9] K. Pfefferkorn in *Novalis: A Romantic's Theory of Language and Poetry* (New Haven, Conn. and London: Yale University Press, 1988) describes the poet's dilemma: either to control language by irony, or to yield to his own lack of power, to 'cultivate a mood of receptive stillness and acquiesce to accept the words of the higher power that may speak through him. The poet's paradox, then, is that silence is his proper mode'. (p. 73).

As a letter to Cordelia affirms, 'Erotic love loves secrecy – an engagement is disclosure; it loves silence – an engagement is a public announcement' (*EO* 388). The silence of the erotic has an eloquence of its own, more suited to the unlimited content of its passion. Words are inadequate, because what seeks expression lacks the kind of *conceptual* content which propositions can reproduce: 'erotic situations [are] much too significant to be filled with chatter. They are silent, still, definitely outlined, and yet eloquent, like the music of Memnon's statue' (*EO* 418). The Egyptian statue of the goddess of the dawn made music when touched by the rays of the morning sun; it has no language of its own.

As we saw in 'The Immediate Erotic Stages', language negates the sensuous as the mere instrument of spirit and reflection, whilst music takes the sensuous and immediate, excluded by spirit, as its absolute theme. Silence and music are related by their indeterminacy, by a lack of conceptual definition. If the silence of the immediate is to be broken, the only medium which can do so, and yet retain its sensuous potency, is music.

The seducer attempts in his own way to evoke the full expression of immediacy in the girl's devotion to him. His intellectual negation of her immediacy is designed to provoke it out into the open. Her womanly being is caught up in a kind of musical harmony with his, but he retains control of the situation, not by his bodily presence, but by being the means by which her whole essence is articulated:

> It is as if I were not present, and yet it is my very presence that is the condition for this contemplative wonder of hers. My being is in harmony with hers. In a state such as this, a girl is adored and worshipped, just as some deities are, by silence. (*EO* 379)

In this articulation, mood and setting are key elements. Language must play a subservient role, teasing out her interest in him; but the goal is an almost pictorial state of repose, in which her contemplation of him displays her essential devotedness, the purity and divinity of the idea of womanhood. The final tryst is itself dependent on the romantic power of the surroundings and interior of the house; it is, as we shall see, a moment when history is suspended and language is resolved into mythology.

Even myths intrude upon the purity of the immediate, however. The seducer wishes to step out of his own highly reflective nature; all his tactics are merely means to an end which no language can account for, for it resides in a space beyond language: 'public information is irrelevant to the mysteries of love ... I for my part am not looking for stories – I certainly have enough of them; I am seeking immediacy' (*EO* 381). Narratives come after the moment of reflection in which the immediacy of being is negated. Even as the poet seeks to give voice to it, the immediate is cancelled, erotic love is delivered over into the differentiated public realm of concepts and dialectics.

To publish poetry is self-defeating folly: the true and original 'poetry' of the feminine does not require mediation through reflection to be found in its full essence (*EO* 443).

However, the seducer's love of silence conceals a guilty secret. He tells his stories, if only to himself; he manipulates Cordelia for his own gratification, using all his reflective powers. In enjoying her, he knows that she will lose her immediacy. The moment of possession is also the moment of irretrievable loss. In a letter to Cordelia, he claims that she has understood him fully, 'literally' (*EO* 398). But the seducer could never be *literally* understood; his is a duplicitous text. His admonition to her to keep silence represents not a sincere regard for the purity of their love, but a guilty secretiveness which knows itself as the destroyer of that which it claims to treasure: 'Will you keep this secret? Dare I depend upon you? Tales are told of people who by dreadful crimes initiated each other in to mutual silence' (ibid.). This silence is anything but 'mutual', if that is to mean a full sharing of its intention and significance. The seducer uses his reflection and his poetry as weapons rather than as means of communication. He wants to possess immediacy by imposing silence on the woman, by, in effect, *defining* her as silent, unspiritual, sensuous, devoted. His inability to enter into a relationship of mutuality denotes both his fear of the feminine awakened to reflection, able to speak on equal terms with him, and his fear of an immediacy from which he feels forever excluded. His identification of woman and immediacy serves his desire to subdue both; his unmusical mediations ensure that he really encounters neither.

The two worlds: myth, symbol and representation

The preface to the diary, giving 'A's rather guilty account of how he came about the work, gives some important insights into the figure of the seducer. These gain in significance when we recall Victor Eremita's belief that the diary is in fact 'A's own poetic creation. He argues that 'A's claim that the work is that of another person is:

> an old literary device to which I would not have much to object if it did not further complicate my own position, since one author becomes enclosed within the other like the boxes in a Chinese puzzle ...
>
> It really seems as if A himself had become afraid of his fiction, which, like a troubled dream, continued to make him feel uneasy, even in the telling. (*EO* 9)

Of course, Eremita himself is a literary fiction, and the Chinese puzzle gains in absurd complexity when we consider what all this has to do with the signature 'Kierkegaard'. These formal conundrums reflect the 'theme' of the work in all its disparateness: that the inner and the outer do not correspond to one another; that there are depths which reflection does not penetrate to, excesses which it cannot illuminate and dispose of as it will. The ambiguity of the author's identity and of the relation of narrative to truth and fiction is all part of Kierkegaard's enactment of this motif.

With this in mind, we can understand the intimations of mythological and fairy-tale themes within the text as invocations of a discourse which resists philosophical appropriation.[10] When 'A' first read the diary, he claims he was close to fainting, so awestruck was he by the impression it produced. He prides himself on a well-developed reflection, which, like 'a passport officer checking foreign travellers', has a familiarity with 'the most fabulous [eventyrligste] characters' (*EO* 304). However, even he is overcome by the character of the seducer, because he exemplifies in an extreme form this terrifying disjunction of inner and outer lives, a disjunction which is described, significantly, in quasi-mythological terms:

> Behind the world in which we live, far in the background, lies another world, and the two have about the same relation to each other as do the stage proper and the stage one sometimes sees behind it in the theater. Through a hanging of fine gauze, one sees, as it were, a world of gauze, lighter, more ethereal, with a quality different from that of the actual world. Many people who appear physically in the actual world are not at home in it but are at home in that other world. But a person's fading away in this manner, indeed, almost vanishing from actuality, can have its basis either in health or in sickness. (*EO* 306)

This other world encompasses all that is spiritual and ideal. It is, presumably, the realm of fantasy and illusion – but also the realm of the eternal, of the idea. The 'world of gauze' makes such distinctions difficult to make. Nevertheless, there is a difference – all the difference in the world, perhaps – between health and sickness of the spirit.

The seducer's 'journey through life was undetectable', because he had 'infinite reflectedness into himself'; he retained his footprint under his sole (*EO* 307). He causes a person 'to go astray within himself', into 'a circle from which he cannot find an exit', a state of 'conscious madness' (*EO* 308). He is a 'matchless instrument', the quintessence of all moods in harmony, a music at once beautiful in its evocation, yet arousing a 'cryptic' anxiety (*EO* 309–10). The music only hides a linguistic ferment of ideas, observations, strategies and poetry. Such is the alluring nature of this contradiction that 'A' feels himself 'carried along into that kingdom of mist, into that dreamland where one is frightened by one's own shadow at every moment' (*EO* 310).

---

[10] Cf. Schlegel's advocation of the creation of a 'new mythology' as a 'hieroglyphic expression of surrounding nature in this transfigured form of imagination and love' in *Dialogue on Poetry and Literary Aphorisms*, trans. Behler and Struc (University Park and London: Pennsylvania State University Press, 1968), pp. 81 and 83 respectively.

This fantasy world threatens the dissolution of all criteria of truth and falsehood, a crisis of representation and authenticity. The seducer is the shadow the author fears, the one who visits us in dreams; he is the power of spirit and creative reflection loosed from all constraints of fidelity to truth, morality and the social order. As we have seen, he seeks to bring about a confusion of 'poetry and actuality, truth and fiction' in Cordelia (*EO* 392).[11] He uses what he calls 'amphibolies', a 'loan word from Greek, meaning equivocality, ambiguity':[12] 'My art is to use amphibolies so that the listeners understand one thing from what is said and then suddenly perceive that the words can be interpreted another way' (*EO* 370). This lack of definite meaning serves the seducer's purposes of dissimulation, but he can only take advantage of it because a certain indeterminacy is inherent in language from the outset. The threat he poses to true representation is developed from the resources of representative language itself.

Language, as 'A' puts it, negates what is immediately given, making it subservient to the articulation of spirit. Two things follow from this: firstly, much of reality remains inexpressible, beyond the borders of language in the regions of silence and music; secondly, language itself is an expression of the freedom of spirit from the constraints of what is given in nature, from the sensuous substratum of human existence. This freedom can challenge straightforward mimetic or correspondence notions of truth and representation, something which can be exploited to the full in the borderland between the spiritual and the sensuous occupied by myth.

The seducer feeds Cordelia on a diet of mythology and fairy tales (*EO* 412). This is a preparation for his own gospel of the mythicization of all reality in the light of love. In a letter to Cordelia, he writes: 'Love is everything; therefore, for one who loves everything ceases to have intrinsic meaning and has meaning only through the interpretation love gives to it' (*EO* 407). All of life, he writes, becomes 'a myth about you' (ibid.). The world is drained of essential meaning in this eulogy of love. The literal is entirely subsumed by the figurative: 'For love, everything is a symbol [Billede]; in recompense, the symbol in turn is actuality' (*EO* 418). Language becomes pictorial and time is negated by this recreation of a mythical world of allegorical meaning. Nothing has worth for its own sake, but only in the service of passion, as illustrations and ciphers for the dramatization of an inner reality. Cordelia will belong to him 'when history is over and the myths begin' (*EO* 441). On the night of the tryst itself, the seducer is almost dissolved into his own fantasy. The seducer's discourse becomes self-referential; it creates its own victim and its own fulfilment, and all reference

---

[11] Cf. Schlegel, ibid., p. 100: Romantic poetry does not distinguish 'appearance and truth, play and seriousness'.

[12] *EO* 'Notes' p. 628.

to an 'objective' world is thrown aside: 'Everything is a metaphor [Billede]; I myself am a myth about myself, for is it not as a myth that I hasten to this tryst? ... How vigorous, sound, and happy is my soul, as present as a god' (*EO* 444). He is divinized by his own narrative, at the point where that narrative must fall silent. The culmination of this seduction is not described, for stories cannot capture its timeless immediacy. Whether it happened, whether anything 'actually' happened, is impossible to decide.

The seducer's fantasy will go on recurring, because the pleasure he seeks is momentary and evanescent. The seducer's narrative poetry betrays an ambiguity of its own. It can neither attain to a depiction of the immediacy which is its theme, nor really dispense with the feminine as a bearer of spiritual meaning. At one point the seducer says that he is body to Cordelia's spirit, the 'humble narrator who follows your triumphs' (*EO* 406). No doubt this is a deceitful phrase, but it neatly depicts his real dependency on Cordelia as an ideal. He is enslaved to a deluded narcissism. It is a symptom of his own search for embodiment, for an end to the division in which 'woman is substance, man is reflection' (*EO* 431). Cordelia represents not only the freedom of the immediate from language, but the freedom of the spirit *within* language, the freedom of which language can be the incarnation, if it is not made to serve the idolatrous myth of self-divinization at the expense of faithful communication.

The metaphor of writing

An examination of the use of language and writing as metaphors in the diary provides a telling commentary on the issues underlying the work. The process of seduction, though it supposedly leads up to a climax beyond words, is told through a mass of narratives, which, far from being superfluous, indicate something essential about the nature of seduction: 'For most people, to seduce a young girl means to seduce a young girl, period – and yet a whole language is concealed in this thought' (*EO* 363). Seduction has a complexity of its own. Its language hints at the infinite content of erotic love, whilst drawing the victim into a private world of meaning divorced from all public criteria. Indeed, the objectivity of the public realm, symbolized by the ethical reality of engagement, is dismissed as prosaic (*EO* 368). Poetry and prose represent radically different views of language and communication, inextricably bound up with different evaluations of ethics.

The seducer's tactic is to make the beginning of the affair 'as nebulous as possible; it must be an omnipossibility' (*EO* 372). This theme of radical ambiguity is taken up again in terms which reflect upon the nature of writing:

> A person who talks like a book is extremely boring to listen to, but sometimes it is rather expedient to talk that way. That is, a book can be interpreted as one pleases ... Her expression was multifarious – indeed,

just about like the still unpublished but announced commentary on my book, a commentary that contains the possibility of any and every interpretation. (*EO* 374)

The seducer is himself a literary fragment, a figment of creative imagination. He represents the undecidability of interpretation, the absence of any final authoritative decision on the meaning of any text. He feels free to read as he pleases, and implicitly challenges us as readers to decide how we wish to interpret him.

In a letter to Cordelia, the writing motif recurs in a deeply ironic way:

There are manuscripts in which the fortunate eye quickly sees faintly an older writing that in the course of time has been supplanted [fortrængt] by trivial inanities. With caustic substances, the later writing is erased, and now the older writing is distinct and clear. In the same way, your eye has taught me to find myself in myself. I allow forgetfulness to consume everything that does not touch on you, and then I discover a pristine, a divinely young, primitive text; then I discover that my love for you is just as old as I myself. (*EO* 401)

Of course, there is no question of the seducer really finding himself in himself, in some pure and primordial sense. Rather, we must note that between the lines of the writing which is clearly visible on the page there lies, not some clear and immediate meaning, but one of the forger's 'specimens of handwriting' to which 'A' likens the diary as a whole (*EO* 303). Irony, rather than forgetfulness, is the true caustic substance. It reveals no divine text of unequivocal meaning, but the duplicity of endless interpretation.[13]

This is not to say that writing cannot have its function in seduction's play of powers; it is rather that communication is deprived of any role besides that of a power-play of competing interpretations. The seducer's art is to use language consciously in this way, as a means of persuasion and ultimate domination:

the dead letter of writing often has much more influence than the living word. A letter is a secretive communication; one is master of the situation, feels no pressure from anyone's actual presence, and I do believe a young girl would prefer to be alone with her ideal ... In the ideal there is a vastness that the actuality does not have. (*EO* 415)

The seducer does not need to be personally present for his writing to have its effects. Indeed, it is better to exploit the special characteristics of writing so

---

[13] M. Finlay in *The Romantic Irony of Semiotics: Friedrich Schlegel and the Crisis of Representation* (Berlin: Gruyter, 1988) argues that Schlegel's practice of ironic writing, especially in the essay 'Über die Unverständlichkeit', shows 'the impossibility of positing any fixed centres at all' (p. 265). Mimesis is only perfected when nothing is represented but the act of representation (p. 116).

that the capacity of language to express ideal realities can be utilized to its full extent. The link with actuality is not broken; rather, the letters give Cordelia the opportunity to enjoy 'festivals of atonement', from which she returns refreshed to actuality:

> In this, letters are an aid; they help one to be invisibly and mentally present in these moments of sacred dedication, while the idea that the actual person is the author of the letter forms a natural and easy transition to the actuality. (*EO* 415-16).

Writing embodies to a special degree the essential nature of language in linking the particularity of actual entities with an ideal or abstract form of expression. The author, as the guarantor of meaning and authenticity, is both present and absent. The seducer's absence is eloquent; in it, he is at once idealized and rendered inaccessible to his reader.

In a passage excluded from the final work, Kierkegaard wrote 'Therefore, the person who is unable to write letters and notes never becomes a dangerous seducer.'[14] That this passage was not included should be a warning to us: it is not the physical use of script per se which holds this seductive capacity. All language rests on an intrinsic duplicity of which writing is only the clearest instance. We have only to remember the seducer's similar use of the voice to confirm this: 'I, unlike Jehovah, become not more and more visible in the voice, but less and less' (*EO* 363).

A passage from 'Silhouettes' takes up the imagery of the letter. The writer is describing Marie Beaumarchais as an instance of what he calls 'reflective sorrow' (*EO* 170). He claims that: 'the subject for artistic portrayal must have a quiet transparency so that the interior rests in the corresponding exterior' (*EO* 169). Art therefore cannot represent reflective sorrow:

> Joy is communicative [meddelsom], sociable, open, wishes to express itself. Sorrow is inclosingly reserved [indesluttet], silent, solitary, and seeks to return into itself ... reflective sorrow ... cannot be depicted artistically, for the interior and the exterior are out of balance and thus it does not lie within spatial categories. (*EO* 170)

A person's exterior, even their face, the 'mirror of the soul', takes on an 'ambiguity' (*EO* 174–5) in this condition. The observer must look out for a fleeting 'telegraphic report' (ibid.) of the turmoil within.

This turmoil is the consequence of being deceived in love, the unassimilable fact of infidelity. The forsaken lover cannot be sure she has interpreted the deception correctly: was she really betrayed? What actually happened? The answers are as elusive as trying to decipher a person's sorrow. Both lover and writer are trying to read a language which eludes any certain meaning:

---

[14] Pap. III B 161:1; *EO* Supplement p. 582.

> If a person possessed a letter that he knew or believed contained information about what he had to consider his life's happiness, but the characters were thin and faint and the handwriting almost illegible, then, presumably with anxiety and agitation, he would read it most passionately again and again and at one moment derive one meaning, at the next moment another, according to how he would explain everything by a word he believed that he had deciphered with certainty, but he would never progress beyond the same uncertainty with which he had begun. He would stare, more and more anxiously, but the more he stared, the less he would see. His eyes would sometimes be filled with tears, but the more frequently this happened to him, the less he would see. In the course of time, the writing would become fainter and less legible; finally the paper itself would crumble away, and he would have nothing left but tear-filled eyes. (*EO* 190)

If there is a way through this grief, it has to be of a different quality to the grief itself. That is, it cannot be resolved by gaining more information, by searching harder for a sure foundation on which to base a reading of one's own existence. None is to be found. The new beginning which is required must be of a different order: 'The will must be altogether impartial, must begin in the power of its own willing; only then can there be any question of a beginning' (*EO* 188). When this happens in a person's life, she can no longer interest the poet who is caught in this endless circle of interpretations – then 'she falls outside our concern entirely' (ibid.).

The abyss – infinite jest

'An engagement is nothing but a comic predicament' (*EO* 328), the contradiction between the infinite inwardness of erotic passion and the outer forms which try to contain and channel it. The 'Diapsalmata' often return to this theme of the comic nature of existence. There is the well-known story of the man who rushes on stage to warn everyone of a fire in the theatre, only for the audience to mistake him for part of the show and carry on laughing (*EO* 30). This dissolution of everything into jest engenders a fundamental mistrust of existence, making the poet despair of ever being able to understand existence: 'What if everything in the world were a misunderstanding; what if laughter really were weeping!' (*EO* 21).

The review essay on Scribe's 'The First Love' provides the clearest expression of this comic nihilism. All the absurdities of mistaken identity in the play reveal the utter vacuity of the characters' (particularly Emmeline's) claims to believe in anything as foundational and fundamental as the belief that one only truly loves once. 'A' argues that 'The play is not moralizing in a finite sense but witty in an infinite sense; it has no finite purpose but is an infinite jest with Emmeline' (*EO* 258). It is arbitrary for the play to end where it does. There is 'an infinite possibility for confusion'; it may be 'the poet's intention that the play be endless' (*EO* 259) – there is no 'explanation' [Forklaring – a word related to the Danish for 'transfiguration', that is, a qualitative transformation which escapes this all-consuming jest, cf. *EO* 251, 274]. The metaphor of language links this with our the previous discussion:

> When the curtain falls, everything is forgotten, nothing but nothing remains [kun Intet bliver tilbage], and that is the only thing one sees; and the only thing one hears is a laughter, like a sound of nature, that does not issue from any one person but is the language of a world force, and this force is irony. (*EO* 273)

This ironic 'world force' resurfaces in 'Silhouettes', a discourse addressed to the 'fellowship of the dead', which celebrates the 'universal law' of 'the downfall of everything' (*EO* 167). The society rejoices in the 'vortex, which is the world's core principle' (*EO* 168) and the toast is offered to 'you, silent night, eternal mother of everything! ... in eternal oblivion you shorten everything' (ibid.). The triumphalist tone of this nihilism is the reverse side of the despair to which it also gives rise. In either case, the ultimate pointlessness of everything seems inescapable. We are left to face 'the nothing that interlaces existence' (*EO* 291). All sense is lost, as the essay 'The Unhappiest One' echoes:

> See, language breaks down [brister], and thought is confused, for who indeed is the happiest but the unhappiest and who the unhappiest but the happiest, and what is life but madness, and faith but foolishness, and hope but a staving off of the evil day, and love but vinegar in the wound. (*EO* 230)

Language, as it were, bursts its banks, unable to contain this infinite confusion save in a total cynicism towards anything which could be said to have value.

There is little doubt that these literary sighs mark the prevalence of late Romantic nihilism in Danish and German intellectual circles, which formed the backdrop for Kierkegaard's early writing, and the work of his mentor P. M. Møller.[15] The seducer is parasitic upon a threatening dissolution of all stable, fixed meanings, all societal norms, a dissolution which Karl Marx was to associate with the peculiar characteristics of bourgeois society itself:

> Constant revolutionising of production, uninterrupted disturbance of all social conditions, everlasting uncertainty and agitation distinguish the bourgeois epoch from all earlier ones. All fixed, fast-frozen relationships, with their train of ancient and venerable prejudices and opinions, are swept away, all new-formed ones become antiquated before they can ossify. All that is solid melts into air, all that is holy is profaned, and man

---

[15] G. Pattison, *Kierkegaard: The Aesthetic and Religious* (London: Macmillan, 1992), pp. 26ff.

is at last compelled to face with sober senses his real conditions of life and his relations with his kind.[16]

For Kierkegaard too, the forces of economic, social and cultural uncertainty could not be staved off by an attempt to recapture a lost panacea of cohesion. Innocence, once lost, is never regained. And once we have fallen, we see that we have always been fallen – that our 'innocence' itself hid a potential for fragmentation. However, the fall opens a space for our own responsibility for our construction of reality to emerge, a space in which our view of language takes on paramount importance. For the state of language is not merely epiphenomenal, a secondary by-product of material structures. As Condillac suggested a more complex interplay between language and societal change, so Kierkegaard seems to hint at the crucial link between the use we make of language and the evaluation of human existence we make. Is the repetitive and idealistic structure of language to encourage us in a rhetoric devoid of ethical shape, or a cultivation of meaningless variety, as the essay 'The Rotation of Crops' recommends?[17] Or are we to eschew monotony, seduction and a futile return to immediacy for a commitment to gratuitous liberating reciprocity – in short, to opt for real communication?

The tragic dilemma

The shadow of the ethical cannot be expunged from *Either/Or Part One* (any more than the second part finally escapes from the ironic endlessness of the text). There is always an implicit demand upon the reader to pass judgement upon the life-views presented. Though 'The Seducer's Diary' represents an extreme form of nihilistic abstract cruelty, all the texts seem to display the dilemma of modernity in some form, bringing us to the very limits of the 'aesthetic' viewpoint. The speech on 'The Tragic in Ancient Drama', for instance, recapitulates in condensed form many of the themes we have touched upon. Again, it is delivered before the 'fellowship of the dead', whose credo undermines the universality of interpretations and the systematic construal of the world. For them, it is 'a characteristic of all human endeavour in its truth that it is fragmentary' (*EO* 151); the pleasure of creativity is focused in its 'glinting transiency' (*EO* 152): '[we acknowledge that] an individual's wealth consists specifically in his capacity for fragmentary prodigality and what is the producing individual's enjoyment is the receiving individual's also ...' (*EO* 151–2). Any 'tedious' presumption of completeness is a literary Tower of Babel over which the shadow of God lurks as a

---

[16] K. Marx, *Manifesto of the Communist Party*, in *Marx and Engels: Basic Writings on Politics and Philosophy*, ed. Feuer (London: Fontana, 1984), p. 52.
[17] *EO* 281ff.

subliminal threat of retribution (*EO* 151). And yet, creativity *does* afford a 'glimpse of the idea' (*EO* 152), whose 'fulguration' stimulates the productivity of the recipient. Creation and reception constitute a game of mutual stimulation, an ironic and inexhaustible circulation of poetic productions and readings.

The orator argues that modern subjectivity is the acid which has corroded the substantial bonds of life – state, family, religion – which formed the seemingly inviolable horizon for the enactment of Greek tragedy. Modernity is thus the inauguration of nihilism. But 'A' sees that this has a laughable aspect: the modern subject becomes comical because he wants to act as if the 'objective' world moral order of the ancients can be replaced by an almighty (theatrical) act of self-affirmation. In itself, this is comical:

> Every individual, however original he is, is still a child of God, of his age, of his family, of his friends, and only in them does he have his truth. If he wants to be the absolute in all this, his relativity, then he becomes ludicrous. (*EO* 145)

He grasps neither the sadness and healing in the tragic, nor his own givenness and dependency. He is content with an ethics whose self-sufficient hubris prevents him from pushing through to the decisive realization of the need for grace and mercy. The 'profound discrepancy [dybe Modsaetning]' (*EO* 146) of sin breaks the 'motherly' (*EO* 145) embrace of the immanent tragic and propels the individual into the reflective father-love of the religious, which 'is the expression for fatherly love, for it embraces the ethical, but is mitigated, and by what means – by the very same means that give the tragic its gentleness, by means of its continuity' (*EO* 146).

As we saw in the 'Diary', the feminization of immanence means that the move into maturity is always a move *away* from the mother and the erotic disdain for boundaries, towards the articulated, bounded separateness of individual *male* subjectivity. However, the feminine is not simply displaced, but is retained as that which informs the father's love with gentleness and continuity; the self is separate, but still *related* to the divine, no longer the self-legislating subject of the ethical. The father is only what he is as the full realization of the mother's love, not as its denial. The identification of motherly/immediate and fatherly/religious cannot be sustained in its purity, for the anxiety of the male subject demonstrates the illusoriness of his self-sufficiency. Anxiety implies a repressed relation to one's unavoidable other – an antipathetic sympathy and a sympathetic antipathy.[18]

To repress this anxiety is to deny the fundamental relatedness of one's life. The idea that one is one's own creator is the death of compassion:

---

[18] See *CA* 42.

> Our age has lost all the substantial categories of family, state, kindred; it must turn the individual over to himself completely in such a way that, strictly speaking, he becomes his own creator. Consequently his guilt is sin, his pain repentance, but thereby the tragic is cancelled ... the spectator shouts: Help yourself, and heaven will help you – in other words, the spectator has lost compassion. (*EO* 149)[19]

Ethical and religious communication can challenge this individual self-creation by evoking an irreducible otherness which demands our response. However, ethics and religion cannot simply contradict modern nihilism by an appeal to objective authority or evidence. It must choose a different approach.

Christ resists aesthetic representation, because his life is supposed to combine absolute action and absolute suffering (*EO* 150). He is clearly introduced as a limit figure, one who calls into question the means and motivations of all representation. His 'absoluteness' reveals something about the opacity of all actuality to the systematic view. We have no godlike vantage point – our production is something 'left behind', our authorial lives a continual dying into communication.[20] This sensitivity to the givenness of our own tradition, and the forsakenness of our once-given utterances, encourages a sort of quietism, a deadness which hinders action. It is an ambiguous mix of receptivity, submission to fate and conscious manipulation of one's impressions. 'A' does not know whether he leads his Antigone, or she leads him. There is an eroticism in creativity, a passive-activity which borders violation and fulfilment:

> She is my creation, her thoughts are my thoughts, and yet it is as if in a night of love I had rested with her, as if she in my embrace had confided a deep secret to me, had breathed it out together with her soul, as if she had then instantly changed before me, had disappeared, so that the only trace of her actuality was the mood that remained behind, instead of the reverse situation that she is brought forth by my mood to ever greater actuality. (*EO* 153)

Who seduces whom in this literary game? Who *needs* whom? The author's control over the subject of his discourse is as open to doubt as the omnipotence of the seducer's charms.

Our modern Antigone is beyond the fateful necessity of Greek substantiality, ennobled by anxiety and the inner pain of her secret (*EO*

---

[19] Cf. *EO* 145: 'the vigor, the courage, that wants to be the creator of its own good fortune in this way, indeed, its own creator, is an illusion, and when the age loses the tragic, it gains despair.'

[20] 'Let us, then, designate our intention as a venture in fragmentary endeavour or the art of writing posthumous [efterladt = left behind] papers' (*EO* 152). Cf. *EO* 153: 'I also assume it to be a feature of all authentic human production in its truth, as we have interpreted it, that it is property left behind, since it is not granted human beings to live with an eternal view like the gods.'

157). She cannot communicate and yet this is somehow her glory, her transcendence of the world: she is saved from 'all futile consideration of the surrounding world' (ibid.). Despite trying to conceive her as a virgin mother (again, compare the seducer's search for madonnas), 'A' is forced to admit that she is above nature, beyond the immediacy that women are meant to represent: 'Precisely because she is secretive, she is silence, but this turning back into oneself implicit in silence gives her a preternatural [overnaturlig] bearing' (*EO* 158). She wants no confidant. Her language becomes a figurative play which none can penetrate. Still, she is connected by pious familial ties, to her own facticity, the givenness of family and grief. This is the ambiguous nexus of the tragic, a microcosm of the ambiguities of communication. When Antigone falls in love, the possibility of a real erotic union threatens the inviolability of her spirit (*EO* 162). The dilemma of authentic communication is posed: love seems to require an openness that cannot be given without self-betrayal, without a kind of dying.[21]

As it stands, the essay – like *Either/Or* as a whole – only poses the problem. Any conclusion would seem to distort the situation it seeks to portray. For the essay is not only *about* the undecidability of Antigone's dilemma; it is also, as was suggested, a *performance of* the undecidability of distinctions such as immediacy/reflection, masculine/feminine, ancient/modern, and of the hierarchies implicit in such polarities. Nevertheless, such a performance invites our own construal of modernity: which ideal are we to embody? To understand the problem of communication as one of *embodiment* in this way is justified by the seducer's own desire to be both the body to Cordelia's spirit and the spirit which negates her existence as a woman (and therefore as bodily). The seducer's problem is partly an inability to reconcile body and spirit in his own existence. And as long as language is seen *only* as a negation of immediacy, the problem persists. For language is thus seen to be working against the material basis which is its indispensable possibility, to be seeking a wholly spiritual form of communication. Language conceived as ideality, remember, is not itself the defining characteristic of human existence, but language in use, in consciousness, where ideal and real touch one another. Only then is there repetition, paradox, incarnation; only then is there the possibility of self-involving decision, of ethics and a respect for persons which does not negate them as means to an abstract and unattainable end of pure, immediate spirituality.

---

[21] 'To take her secret away - this is what the lover must struggle to do, and yet it is also her certain death' (*EO* 164).

Summary

The seducer's diary connects with a certain form of post-Romantic nihilism, in which the impossibility of equating truth and representation was pushed to its limit. In the seducer's own case, we find the following:

1. A radical split between language as the expression of (male) spirit and (female) immediacy, which meant that the former is bound to destroy the latter even as it tries to capture it.
2. An obsession with aspects of experience such as myths, dreams, poetry and organic nature, which point beyond the supremacy of a prosaic, propositional model of truth.
3. A desire to master and control that 'beyond' through intellectual and poetic superiority – a desire which is undermined by evidence that the seducer lacks any such control, is anxious and dependent before that which eludes his grasp.
4. The risk of an all-corroding nihilism which leaves no stable reference points intact for knowledge, ethics or faith – a despairing anti-realism.
5. The limits of any realist response to such nihilism. Tragedy cannot be resolved conceptually, or only through accumulating objective knowledge; it demands existential resolve and commitment.

This examination of the figure of the seducer may seem marginal to the issue of realism and anti-realism. The reader might wish to evade the literary execution of Kierkegaard's texts to focus on his 'mainstream' philosophical opinions. It should be clear by now that such a view would grossly misconstrue the nature of Kierkegaard's texts, as they explore their own limits and the limits of the kind of reasoning which would reduce all truth to propositional truth.

If the text is ultimately self-defeating, it nevertheless points beyond itself and, for us, beyond the rigid separation of realism and anti-realism. The seducer's manipulations only reveal his lack of control, and they reopen the possibility of affirming ethical and religious ideals which resist the corrosive nihilism the seducer articulates. However, such affirmation must take stock of the twin perils which afflict the seducer: on the one hand, an extreme idealization of language and creativity to the point where any constraint on subjective self-creation is abolished; on the other hand, an extreme idealization of a lost immediacy, when reality was transparently knowable. The seducer reflects a truth about the indirectness of language, but by splitting spirit from immediacy in this total way, he reifies them and only ensures that his life must be self-destructive and destructive of others.

CHAPTER FIVE

Significant silences

If language is intrinsically tainted by the risk of dissimulation, if it is inevitably inadequate for representing the ethical and the religious, should we not dispense with it altogether? Words may be useful for a time, but ultimately, should we not transcend their indirectness and learn to obey duty immediately, or meet God face to face? The wordless unknowing which mystics have evoked as the culmination of the spiritual path might encourage us to tread a linguistic *via negativa*. Religious language will always be open to this or that interpretation; only silent, direct encounter can be satisfying to the spiritual quest.

Such sentiments seem to accord well with several of Kierkegaard's texts, in which the cultivation of silence is given religious prominence. Is this the relation with God which we are seeking – a relation which goes beyond the order of discursive, propositional knowledge into a direct 'knowledge' by acquaintance? However promising this seems, we will show that it cannot evade the questions about truth status which are raised by the realism/anti-realism debate. And silence occurs as a motif in those of Kierkegaard's texts which either betray an unwelcome similarity to that of the seducer or place silence in a self-consciously ironic context. The art of cultivating silence is as open to interpretation as its linguistic counterpart.

The disguises of language

The seducer appears to be a necessarily marginal figure, who insinuates himself into the tissue of respectable social relationships. However, his very marginality witnesses to a potential for deceit inherent in the heart of bourgeois propriety. Dispossessing it of its aura of cohesion, Johannes destabilizes his society from within.

Kierkegaard does not have a high opinion of his age's ascendant 'bourgeois-philistine' culture. In *A Literary Review*, a discussion of Gyllembourg's novel *Two Ages*, he differentiates between the past age of revolution and passion, and the present one, with its exaggerated capacity for reflection and its superficial confusion of the categories of thought and existence. In his criticism of the state of society, Kierkegaard is drawn to the curative power of silence. He isolates the devaluation of language as one of the principal symptoms of the impersonality of Danish life: 'What is it to *chatter*? It is the annulment of the passionate distinction between being silent and speaking. Only the person who can remain essentially silent can speak essentially, can act essentially' (*TA* 97). 'Essential' speech and action, require a deep inwardness as their prior condition, and 'Silence is inwardness' (ibid.). The modern bourgeois subject risks dispersal into the media-created flux of the public drama, in which the only values are commodity values and where individuality becomes an abstract template upon which the changing fashions of the age are inscribed. Silence reveals the fundamental hollowness of such a system, for 'chatter cringes before the moment of silence, which would reveal its emptiness' (*TA* 98*). The age has become 'extensive' rather than 'intensive' (*TA* 97). The press has aided in the creation of 'the public' (*TA* 90), a phantom abstraction, which has the only advantage that, once it is seen through, the individual is turned back on his or her own resources.

Kierkegaard wishes to preserve the individual from this intrusion of the public realm. He claims that 'authentic intensive actions spring from an individual and from silence' (JP 4: 3986; Pap. X(4) A 16). If language becomes a situationless abstraction, then it is a debased currency. As we saw, this lies at the root of the 'bankruptcy' of words, which deprives religious categories of their power over life. In this context, the appeal to silence is a tactical ploy, to escape the abstraction and evasions of language. Silence *signifies* – it alerts us to that in our experience which cannot be assimilated by the system, the order of knowledge.

In 1841, Kierkegaard proposes the foundation of a Trappist-like aesthetic order to shut up the chatter of the day (JP 4: 3977; Pap. III A 100). By 1854, he seems convinced that 'Language, the gift of speech, engulfs the human race in such a cloud of drivel and twaddle that it becomes its ruination' (JP 3: 2337; Pap. XI(2) A 222). In the Christian context, language usage has become fraudulent, a masking of the authentically Christian which negates its disturbing contradiction of materialist accumulation: 'Let God proclaim "joy" and human speech comes along and immediately takes the word "joy" and makes out that Christianity means "Enjoy life"' (JP 2:1935; Pap. XI(1) A 550).

The fact that people use words without meaning anything by them is a constant complaint of Kierkegaard's throughout his adult life.[1] What is worse, however, is that words come to signify the opposite of their real meaning. When this happens, simply proclaiming 'true' Christian values only serves to bolster the edifice it seeks to undermine. In the last year of his life, Kierkegaard seems to despair of any return to an authentic usage of language, preferring the comical alternative of revealing the embarrassment of the academic fraternity in an exhibition of intellectual nudity:

---

[1] See, for example, the passage about the 'bankruptcy' of concepts (p. 1 above) (1836–7), a complaint about the lack of meaning of words in sermons (JP 3: 3467; Pap. 6 A 150) (1845) and his polemic against the Danish Church (JP 3: 2329; Pap. 10(1) A 80) (1854).

> The police thoroughly frisk suspicious persons. If the mobs of speakers, teachers, professors, etc., were to be thoroughly frisked in the same way, it would no doubt become a complicated criminal affair. To give them a thorough frisking – yes, to strip them of the clothing, the changes of clothing, and the disguises of language, to frisk them by ordering them to be silent, saying: Shut up, and let us see what your life expresses, for once let this be the speaker who says who you are. (JP 3: 2334; Pap. XI(2) A 128)

This appeal to an existential justification of one's life's values – letting one's life be the speaker – is more than a response to the decadence of the age. It is linked to the impossibility of direct teaching of ethics and religion which we examined earlier. Indeed, in some moods Kierkegaard sees *any* communication about faith as a depletion and erosion of one's inward resolve:

> Silence in the relationship to God is invigorating; absolute silence would be like a jack or the point outside the world of which Archimedes speaks. Talking about one's God-relationship is an emptying that weakens. (JP 4: 3988; Pap. XI(2) A 143)

He seeks a space beyond language and its messy ambiguities, to secure a proper interiority, for 'every thought (when truth is defined as inwardness) is most true in the person in whom it first arose, and by continual communication it steadily becomes less and less true' (JP 2: 1644; Pap. X(1) A 415). The contemporary dissolution of authorities has deprived us of any centre from which language could be defined and kept in order. The Bible, the Church and religious experience are subject to the relativizing reflection of scholarship, which never delivers any certain result.[2] If we are to escape the realm of mere approximation, then Christianity would seem to demand a withdrawal from language usage into an interior ideality. As Kierkegaard says of God: 'He does not want this drivelling to other men about one's relationship to God. It may well be conceit to do this – and this is displeasing to God' (JP 4: 3987; Pap. I (2) A 142).

Does Kierkegaard give up on the possibility of articulating faith?[3] The religious believer seems to seek an Archimedean point of identity beyond discourse, which will protect him from intercourse with a dissipated external world. The problem is that, as the believer pulls up the drawbridge and retreats inwards, so the possibility of specifying a cognitively real, extra-human referent for religious language is placed in jeopardy. Any return to a supposed extra-temporal immediacy actually undercuts the conditions upon

---

[2] See, for example, 'Part One: The Objective Issue of the Truth of Christianity' (*CUP* 19–57).

[3] For useful discussions of silence in Kierkegaard's texts, see A. Hannay, *Kierkegaard* (London: Routledge, 1982), Chapter 3; Pat Bigelow, *Kierkegaard and the Problem of Writing* (Tallahassee: Florida State University Press, 1987), Chapter 2; Mark C. Taylor, *Altarity* (Chicago: University of Chicago Press, 1987), pp. 331ff.

which language depends for its referentiality. If the seducer's desire for immediacy is in fact an unattainable fantasy, does the same hold true for the believer's direct, silent relation to God? Indeed, is there not a troubling link between the two in their idealization of silence?

The silent feminine

Kierkegaard routinely couples silence and the feminine. In *The Concept of Anxiety*, Haufniensis discusses the different conceptions of beauty which are appropriate to men and women (*CA* 66). Whilst, in romanticism, man makes a 'distinct and noble' impression, his countenance stamped by the 'history of spirit', the woman 'will make her effect as a whole in a different way', which her face must show: 'The expression must be that of a totality with no history. Therefore, silence is not only woman's greatest wisdom, but also her highest beauty' (ibid.). Woman has no distinct face, no history and no voice. Her lack of language is bound up with her spiritual inferiority. She is a sensuous and bodily being, whose essence, ethically speaking, is to procreate (ibid.).

In *Sickness Unto Death*, we are told that the woman lacks 'in a decisive sense, intellectuality' (*SUD* 49n.), that she is characterized by 'devotedness' (*SUD* 50n.). The peculiarly feminine form of despair is her need to relate to the male in order to have any spirituality: 'in most cases the woman actually relates to God only through the man' (ibid.). This clearly represents a familiar enough patriarchal ideology. What is more surprising, perhaps, is Kierkegaard's use of this theme to hold woman up as an ideal for man to copy. Her silence is her *wisdom*: she bypasses the corrosive negative reflection of the male subject.

In *For Self-Examination* (1851), silence is further associated with a woman's relation to her faith (*FSE* 46–51). Whilst man cultivates his character in worldly dealings, woman's virtue lies in her domesticity ('Huslighed'). One aspect of this is her ability to keep silence over the most profound things. She does not talk about what she hears in church: 'No let her be silent; let her treasure the Word in silence; let her silence express that she treasures it deeply' (*FSE* 46). Kierkegaard exclaims 'oh, the power of silence!' (ibid.), a power which lies in its ability to remove a person from all noisy cleverness (*FSE* 47–8). Silence is not merely an absence of speaking; it provides a context for becoming aware of God. As Kierkegaard writes:

> Silence! Silence – it is not a specific something, because it does not consist simply in the absence of speaking ... it is not something one talks about, but it is there and it exercises its beneficent power. Silence is like the tone, the fundamental tone [Grund-Stemningen], which is not given prominence and is called the fundamental tone precisely because it lies at the base. (*FSE* 49)

This 'fundamental tone' makes possible a relation to the divine. It is not an absence of meaning ('she is silent. Yet she is not absent-minded, far off in other worlds' (*FSE* 47)), but a deep interiorization of the Word which is addressed to us. A woman's silence is thus eloquent: 'And you, O woman, even if you are quite speechless in charming silence – if your life expresses what you heard, your eloquence is more powerful, more true, more persuasive than the art of orators' (*FSE* 11).

This connection of silence with power is key, since 'it is precisely this silence we need if God's Word is to gain a little power over people' (*FSE* 47). Silence witnesses to the woman's special power, the way in which she presides over the domestic scene. This contains an implicit challenge to patriarchy. The motherly benevolence of the woman provides a surer model for a proper relation to the divine than all of man's busyness – 'silence brought into a house – that is eternity's art of making a house a home [Evighedens Huslighed]' (*FSE* 50). It is as if the eternal itself were to mother us, to make us at home in the world.[4] This snug domesticity is not what we might expect from Kierkegaard, until we realize (in the following discourse, 'Christ Is the Way') that what the believer is called to witness to in silence is the fact that the truth is always persecuted in the world. Suffering, not domestic bliss, is the mark of faith. What is really at issue is the degree of self-collection and self-presence which the believer enjoys in the face of this, for 'You must see to it that you take time every day to collect yourself in the impression of the divine' (*FSE* 50). Here, too, Kierkegaard associates speech with dissipation: 'You know, of course, the one who fell in love – and became talkative – oh well! But to become silent – that is a surer sign!' (*FSE* 51).

In *Either/Or Part One*, this idealization of self-presence is most clearly delineated in 'The Unhappiest One':

> The unhappy one is the person who, in one way or another has his ideal, the substance of his life, the plenitude of his consciousness, his essential nature, outside of himself. The unhappy one is the person who is always absent from himself, never present to himself. (*EO* 222)

The passages we are considering suggest that woman is the model for a recapturing of such presence and fullness. However, Kierkegaard chooses to identify with motherly virtues and feminine passivity in a way which only apparently subverts patriarchy. For the woman who is silent about what she hears in church is still silent about *something*. Language is not absent – rather,

---

[4] In the essay 'The Tragic in Ancient Drama' in *Either/Or Part One*, 'A' writes of the tragic as an aesthetic analogy to 'divine grace and compassion' (*EO* 145), and goes on to say 'it is even more benign, and therefore I say that it is a motherly love that lulls the troubled one'. This unexpected association of divine grace and the mother (though the true religious is reserved for father-love in hierarchical fashion) undermines an exclusive connection of God's love with the father in Kierkegaard's texts.

the terms on which she shall live and the role she is to play are dictated to her by the Word of God. The woman, like Cordelia, is still subject to the whim of a male narrator who will expound her significance for her.

A clearer instance of this comes in the discourse 'The Woman That Was a Sinner', one of the *Three Discourses at the Communion on Fridays* (1849). The subject of the discourse is the gospel passage in which a sinful woman shows her contrition and her love for Jesus in the act of anointing and washing his feet and head. The emphasis is on the woman's passivity: 'she is able to do literally nothing, He everything – she loved much' (*CD* 382). She forgets herself in wordless devotion. She is 'like a picture – she has forgotten speech and language and the restlessness of thoughts and (what is more restless) the self' (*CD* 383). Her silence is eloquent in a way that Jesus makes use of by turning her into 'a picture, a parable' (ibid.). He does not speak to her, but of her. He provides her static image with a narrative meaning: 'It is almost like a story, a sacred story' (ibid.). This situation must be replicated in the believer's life. There must be no self-will, no consciousness of a 'self' that is merely a superficial, restless association of social roles and inchoate yearnings. The inner and outer significance of one's life must coalesce in a state of utter simplicity and dependency. The believer must become as the woman is.

These discourses articulate a tension. On the one hand, they challenge the self-sufficiency of patriarchal bourgeois society, challenging it to learn from those who are marginalized within it. To attend to the woman's silence is to subvert the propositional relation of language to truth by pointing to another way of being addressed by the divine Word. On the other hand, such tactics risk confirming the very bourgeois institutions which keep women marginalized and deny them a voice. The point is that silence is not self-interpreting. There is no self-evident good in silence, as we shall see.

Silence is thus a tactical motif which is not without its associated perils. In itself, it cannot decide the realist/anti-realist debate, for it can raise no question about the status of its faith. If silence points to an alterity which we cannot master, it also risks being a contentless abstraction which can be filled by any humanly constructed content.

The unnameable eternal

One of the *Eighteen Upbuilding Discourses* from 1843, says that we should be like

> the person who is quick to listen to the divine Word – which sounds now, as formerly, when one is silent, when the Pharisees and the scribes have gone away or are silenced, when the crowd has dispersed and gone. (*ED* 138)

The motion of the spiritual life is to listen and to receive the gifts that God gives 'from above'. The idea that God speaks in silence is also found in a journal entry of 1846, which contains a prayer to the Father who speaks in many ways:

> You speak with him also in your silence, for he also speaks who is silent in order to examine the pupil; he also speaks who is silent in order to test the beloved; he also speaks who is silent in order that the hour of understanding, when it comes, might be all the more inward ... Father in heaven, is it not true that this is merely the moment of silence in the intimacy of conversation? (JP 3: 3404; Pap. VII(1) A 131)

In silence, a communication deeper than words can occur, in relation to One who judges, examines and loves the one who prays. Silence is not just nothing, as God makes clear in rebuking Moses: '"Why are you shouting so loudly?" – and Moses was being silent. Silence can be that heaven-scaling' (JP 4: 3948; Pap. X(1) A 394). The profundity of silence is that it can bring to light the question of one's ultimate source and goal, obscured in the superficiality of human discourse: 'Every human being who knows how to keep silent becomes a divine child, for in silence there is concentration upon his divine origin; he who speaks remains a human being' (JP 4: 3978; Pap. IV A 28).

In prayer, one finds oneself in relation to Another, who demands obedience. The silence of prayer enables one to relate appropriately to God, as one who is nothing before him. Prayer then takes on its true aspect – not demanding things of God, nor telling him things, but *listening*:

> the true prayer-relationship does not exist when God hears what is being prayed about, but when the *pray-er* continues to pray until he is the one who hears, who hears what God wills. The immediate spontaneous person uses a lot of words and therefore is actually demanding when he prays. The true pray-er is simply obedient [hørig]. (JP 3: 3403; Pap. VIII(1) A 56)

The ideal state of affairs is achieved when one attains a relationship to God in which words are not necessary, because one simply obeys/listens. This is

> the moment when the whole language is superfluous, when it makes no difference if every single word in the language has been forgotten, since a person has no use for it, because there is nothing more to add than 'Amen'. (JP 3: 3425; Pap. IX A 24)

The themes of passivity and self-presence are strikingly evident in the first of the *Upbuilding Discourses in Various Spirits* (1847), popularly known as *Purity of Heart*. Kierkegaard writes of the need for stillness if one is to achieve unity of will, and in this unity to become aware of a reality beyond words:

> But he that in truth becomes at one with himself, he is in the silence [Stilhed]. And this is indeed like a changing of raiment: to strip oneself of all that is as full of noise as it is empty, in order to be hidden in the silence, to become open [aabenbar]. The silence is the simple festivity of the holy act of confession ... When the wanderer comes away from the much-traveled noisy highway into places of quiet, then it seems to him (for stillness is impressive) as if he must examine himself, as if he must speak out what lies hidden in the depths of his soul. It seems to him, according to the poet's explanation, as if something inexpressible [noget Unævneligt] thrusts itself forward from his innermost being, the unspeakable, for which indeed language has no vessel of expression ... what silence means, what the surroundings will say in this stillness, is just the unspeakable. (*PH* 47–8)

The wanderer is in the grip of that which has no name ('noget Unævneligt'), that which essentially *cannot* be named.

If this is to be more than a passing mood, it has to be placed in the context of the believer's relation to the eternal. Unlike the wanderer, the believer does not come upon the stillness by accident; he cultivates it in earnestness, preparing for the time of confession which is the occasion for this discourse. In repentance, there is an awareness of the presence of One who is omniscient. Before this One, silence itself is confessional, for nothing can be hidden from him (*PH* 50). Inwardness and passivity are intimately connected; only after serious preparation can the believer achieve the state of single-minded collectedness and simplicity which is the condition for willing the Good and relating to the unchanging Eternal, a relation in which 'The prayer does not change God, but changes the one who offers it' (*PH* 51). Indeed, to will one thing, to be one with oneself, simply *is* to will the Good, for

> The person who wills one thing that is not the Good, he does not truly will one thing. It is a delusion, an illusion, a deception, a self-deception that he wills only one thing. For in his innermost being he is, he is bound to be, double-minded. (*PH* 55)

To will anything worldly is to be divided from oneself, because 'the worldly is not one in its essence, because it is the inessential; its so-called unity is essentially nothing but an emptiness which is covered up by the manifold' (*PH* 59–60*). The world is empty, devoid of substance, like the emptiness which lies beneath the chatter of the age: '*In truth to will one thing, then, can only mean to will the Good*, because every other object is not a unity' (*PH* 66). Unity, self-presence and immutability are the characteristics of essential reality, and, as we noted in Chapter 3, it is this reality to which the believer must become *transparent*. The believer must 'win the transparency that is indispensable if a man is to come to understand himself in willing one thing' (*PH* 108).

However, such transparency is not an easy thing to attain in an unreal, divided world. As Kierkegaard admits, 'the temporal order cannot be the transparent medium of the Eternal' (*PH* 136). If it could, the degree to which one carried out the will of the Eternal would be measured by how much one achieved (*PH* 135). But Christ shows that the good suffer in the world, achieving no measurable result. Temporality is in fact 'det Eviges *Brydning*' (*PH* 138), the 'refraction' or 'breaking-up' of eternity. And this reminds us of why the discourse and the confession are necessary in the first place. Purity demands singleness, but 'Something has come in between. The separation of sin lies in between' (*PH* 31). Repentance is a new 'interruption [Afbrydelse – literally a 'breaking-off']' (ibid.) which must intervene in the busyness of the fragmented world to restore a point of contact with the Eternal. Silence interrupts the world and reveals the breach with eternity which is the inviolable horizon of time.

This implies that no restoration of simple presence can be attained, at least in this life. All that can be won is an interior unity of will, which has no external guarantee of its eternal validity. In fact, the only external mark of a good will is a negative one, that of suffering. We find confirmation of this in the *Two Minor Ethico-Religious Treatises* of 1849. Recalling the journal passage quoted above, Kierkegaard argues that 'silence and the power to act correspond to one another completely' (*SV* 15: 18*), and that 'to be resolved is precisely to be silent' (19*). However, when we realize that the question of this discourse is whether a person has the right to allow others to put him to death, we can see that what passes for 'action' and 'resolve' in Kierkegaard's eyes can also be viewed as the greatest passivity to suffering. As 'The Gospel of Sufferings' in *Upbuilding Discourses in Various Spirits*: puts it:

> Only suffering shapes one for eternity; for eternity exists in faith, but faith exists in obedience, and obedience exists in suffering. Obedience is nothing apart from suffering, faith nothing apart from obedience, eternity nothing apart from faith. (*GS* 64*)[5]

So is eternity anything other than an internal ideal of our faith, which itself is nothing but a pure passivity? That which justifies the believer's will – the presence of the Eternal – cannot be present in time in any straightforward way. The believer is thus at once radically dependent and utterly cast upon his or her own resources.[6] It is unclear how we could have any cognitive grounds

---

[5] See also, amongst many other instances: 'religious existence is suffering, and not as a transient element but as a continual accompaniment' (*CUP* 288); 'in this world the truth is victorious only by suffering' (*PC* 194); 'The disciple has amongst other marks also this: to suffer for the doctrine' (*FSE* 207); 'you can love him [Christ] only by suffering' (*KAUC* 245*); 'The Christianity of the New Testament is to love God in opposition to men, to *suffer* at the hands of men for one's faith' (*KAUC* 277).

[6] Cf. S. Sponheim's analysis of the rhythms of 'diastasis' and 'synthesis' in the God/human relationship in *Kierkegaard on Christ and Christian Coherence* (London: SCM, 1968), p. 9 and passim.

to use language about the Eternal. If the Eternal is known only in an unattainable unity of presence and silent passivity, it appears to be forever beyond the fragmented powers of cognition. For us to exist at all, we must already be separated from the Eternal. In the situation of existence, an awareness of the Eternal becomes indistinguishable from an awareness of this founding absence at the heart of our existence, and the emptiness underlying all phenomena. There can be no immediate, spontaneous intuition of the divine. As Kierkegaard remarks, our immediate feeling may well be the wellspring of our life ('Livskraften' – *PH* 113), but it is split, egotistical and impure from the start; it is 'in the discord [Splid] of double-mindedness' (ibid.). That which makes existence possible also makes the cognitive status of language about the Eternal indeterminable.

However, this is to ignore the indirect form of the discourse. It creates a fictional environment for the reader, who is invited to cultivate the stillness required for confession. This repentance is an interruption of the busyness of life – and the text itself is an interruption of the monologue of self-contained reason. It presents the reader with the possibility of a relation to the Eternal, to that which cannot be reduced to an aspect of the believer's self-projection. Though the discourse 'wholly abandons itself' to the reader, the reader is nevertheless only reading faithfully 'in the distance of the separation', that is, 'if he retains for himself both the distance and the understanding in the inwardness of appropriation' (*PH* 27). Comparing the text to a sacred cloth, Kierkegaard insists that one forget the author/weaver. Its meaning 'really lies in the beholder and in the beholder's understanding, if he, in the endless distance of the separation, above himself and above his own self has completely forgotten the needlewoman and what it was hers to do' (*PH* 28).

This is the tension which the reader is called to embody: on the one hand to be active in the process of giving the text a meaning; on the other hand, to do this whilst recognizing the distance that separates human readers from the Eternal. The meaning is both internal to the beholder, and yet *above* the self. The text is thus ironic and multi-levelled. The ideals it presents – single-mindedness and transparency – are regulative rather than descriptive. They serve to disturb the reader out of complacency, but they cannot be realized in any absolute way in temporal existence, any more than language and mediation can finally be abolished. They cannot be appropriated directly, but only by means of an ironic earnestness such as Kierkegaard's text evokes. The form and content of the discourse must be held together in creative tension.

There is an artistry in Kierkegaard's idealization of silence, femininity and nature which resists assimilation to escapist bourgeois prejudices. This is not to claim, however, that Kierkegaard is immune to nostalgia and escapism himself, nor to evade the fact that his texts, read in a certain way, can serve to confirm the marginalization of those who represent a threat to self-sufficient male spirituality. He still betrays a kind of essentialism when it comes to defining womanhood. Nevertheless, the poetic distance he maintains from his texts points us to different ways of reading them than that of direct appropriation of an essential content. Read in this way, they can subvert even the author's intentions and articulate a way of communicating which neither metaphysical realism nor anti-realism can fully contain.

Natural resources: the lily and the bird

A key example of this comes in the second part of *Edifying Discourses in Various Spirits*, 'What We Learn From The Lilies In The Field And The Birds Of The Air', which takes Matthew 6: 24 – end as its text, in order to address 'the anxious' (*GS* 14). The truly anxious are those whom human consolation fails to help. They are directed to the lily and the bird, teachers who ask for no payment, who do not misunderstand the unfortunate 'for they keep silence' (*GS* 14). This seems like a fairly banal way of avoiding misunderstanding, until we see why human speech is so prone to it:

> all misunderstanding does arise from speech, or, more precisely, speech, especially conversation, holds within it a comparison, as when the happy one says to the anxious: Be glad – the expression implies the addition: As I am. (*GS* 14*)

The problem lies in the essentially comparative nature of our social relationships and ways of speaking. Even the mere presence of other people with the one who suffers is overshadowed by implicit comparisons, as Job found in the company of his friends:

> The silent friends did not compare Job with themselves ... Yet their presence caused Job to compare himself with himself. The case is thus, that nobody can be present in such a way, even though he keep silence, that his presence will not give any occasion for comparison. (*GS* 15)

Language and society exact a price which the lily and bird, by their very nature, cannot exact. Human intercourse is always reflective. It magnifies the perceived gap between the sufferer's actual situation and the ideal for which he longs. The initial remedy for this is a form of self-forgetfulness: the anxious one is led to contemplate images of nature which seem to float free from the conventional, comparative, reflective human world. Where the lily and the bird are – in the textual space created for them as the opposite pole to busy human chatter – silence is unbroken, no one is present (*GS* 15). The sufferer is called to give them his full attention, a deep contemplation rather than a fleeting glance (*GS* 16). His immersion in a purely ideal 'natural' life becomes the means by which he learns contentment and self-acceptance:

> Look at them, that is to say, take particular heed of them ... It is in this sense that one must, not with divided mind and thoughts distracted, but with attention fixed, in meditation, if possible in wonder, take particular heed of the birds. (*GS* 26)

The virtues necessary to pay attention to the birds are integral to the consolation and healing which such a meditation seeks to promote.

These 1847 discourses stand in continuity with those published in 1849. In 'The Anxieties Of The Heathen' (Part One of *Christian Discourses*), the lilies are praised for their efficacy as teachers. This is because they are not involved in the struggles for supremacy of competing human interpretations of reality:

> Paganism stands in opposition to Christianity, but the lilies and the birds stand in no opposition to any of these contending parties; if one may say so, they play apart by themselves, keep shrewdly aloof from all oppositions. (*CD* 13)

Their playfulness is not frivolity, but an essential part of their teaching, an expression of its freedom from the dogmatism of human disputation. If we give them our full attention, we find in them a paradigm for Christian communication:

> Surely one can learn from them in the very first instance what it is to teach, what it is to teach in a Christian sense, can learn from them the great art of teaching, namely to be careless about it, to care for oneself, and yet to do this in such an arousing way ... that it is impossible not to learn something from it. (*CD* 14)

Their immediacy means for us that the teacher/learner relationship is not one of reproach, impatience or dependency. They are merely faithful to themselves, and silence is their medium.

In *The Lily of the Field and the Bird of the Air*, also published in 1849, Jesus' parable is the starting point for a prolonged eulogy of nature, whose silence expresses absolute contentment and obedience to the will of God. Although it may seem as if nature were in noisy tumult:

> when day is vibrating with a thousand notes and all is like a sea of sound, there still is silence out there; each one in particular does its part so well that no one of them breaks the solemn silence and not all of them together (*CD* 324).

Though the forests whisper and the sea rages, they are still silent 'for after all uniformity also is silence' (*CD* 325). As Kierkegaard says of the bird, 'its silence is eloquent' (ibid.), but such an eloquence cannot have a self-evident meaning. For the religious discourse, the fundamental passivity of nature witnesses to *God*:

> But what does this silence express? It expresses reverence before God ... And just because this silence is reverence before God, it is (so far as it can be in nature) worship. Just for this reason is the silence so solemn. And because this silence is solemn, therefore it is that one senses God in nature ... Even if *He* does not speak, the fact that everything keeps silence in reverence before Him affects one as if He were speaking. (*CD* 328)

Moreover, the order of nature is due to the fact that it unconditionally represents the will of God. Kierkegaard praises nature according to the maxim that 'In nature all is obedience, unconditional obedience' (*CD* 336–7). Nature simply *is* assent to its Author's will, its apparent self-sufficiency entirely contingent upon that fact: 'For nature so understood is all of it naught, it is nothing else but unconditionally God's will; the very instant it is not unconditionally God's will it has ceased to exist' (*CD* 338). Nature is the immediate expression of God's eternal will. This is what the wanderer, confronted by nature as an alien entity, failed to recognize. Our alienation from nature can only be resolved by awakening to the fact that it is the creation of the One to whom we owe our existence and therefore our worship.

In 'The Anxieties Of The Heathen', the lilies and birds suffer no alienation or anxiety. Outwardly, the bird is poor, but it has no inkling of this comparative judgement, so it is free from the anxiety of poverty (*CD* 17–19). It is precisely the bird's lack of relative thought which minimizes its capacity to suffer. *The Lily of the Field* confirms the idea that human reflection, especially as manifested in language, only worsens suffering. Whilst the bird 'is *silent* and *suffers*' (*CD* 326), enduring suffering as 'neither more nor less than it is' (*CD* 328), language-users are burdened by the misapprehending sympathy of others, and by their own impatience and melancholy. The universal terms of language make the pain so much harder to isolate:

> But when it becomes indefinite, however great the suffering really is, the indefiniteness increases the suffering endlessly. And this indefiniteness emerges precisely with man's ambiguous advantage of being able to talk. (ibid.)

For the lily and bird, silence signifies acceptance that everything happens in its due season. In silence they wait for the moment, for 'as one talks, though one says only a word, one misses the moment' (*CD* 325–6*) in which time and eternity touch, and in which the self can truly be itself. Silence is not merely the absence of words, it is presence to self, uniformity and simplicity; language represents dispersal, comparison and difference. Indeed, 'Only in silence does the moment exist' (*CD* 326*[7]). This silence relativizes human plans and reveals the absolute demands of God (*CD* 333–4). The lily becomes itself in its whole possibility by giving itself unconditionally to his will (*CD*

---

[7] This sentence is untranslated in Lowrie. See SV 14: 138.

340). To learn from the lilies and birds is to follow this simplicity and unity of will without ambiguity, for 'if thou art absolutely obedient to God, then there is no ambiguity [intet Tvetydigt] in thee, and if there is no ambiguity in thee, then art thou mere simplicity before God' (*CD* 344). In this simplicity, one finds unconditional joy, unconcerned for the morrow. The silencing of our plans and projects enables us to see that there is only *this* day: 'Joy is the present tense, with the whole emphasis upon the *present*' (*CD* 350).

Kierkegaard is, however, aware of the irony of this evocation of presence. He expends many words extolling the abandonment of words; after berating the poet for his unrealizable wishes, he proceeds to paint a highly idealized portrait of nature. He is aware that appointing the lily and bird to be our teachers is like a jest. Amidst the seriousness of the religious discourse, 'the birds and the lilies are in the company – it sounds almost as if it were turning the thing into a jest that they come along ... playfully' (*CD* 13). There is no way that we can simply return to a state of undifferentiated immediacy and continuity with nature.

In 'Anxieties' he praises the bird, which simply is what it is (*CD* 43), whilst doubting that the bird can really be said to be alive in any meaningful sense (*CD* 19). Unlike the Christian, the bird cannot pray for his daily bread – he simply receives it:

> How poor not to be able to pray, how poor not to be able to give thanks, how poor to have to receive everything with ingratitude, how poor to be as it were non-existent for its Benefactor to whom it owes life! For to be able to pray and to give thanks is precisely to be existent for God [and to do this is to *live*]. (*CD* 20[8])

To be truly alive, I must be more than the immediate expression of God's will. To exist in this sense implies a degree of autonomy over against the Creator. If nature becomes nothing but the expression of God's will, to become as nature is blurs the distinction between man and God – or at least removes any awareness of such a distinction.

Of the bird, Kierkegaard says 'In order to be, in order to have joy in being, it does not have to take the long road of learning first to know something about the others in order thereby to learn to know what it is itself' (*CD* 40). For us, however, this detour is unavoidable. Reflection cannot be wished away, but this also implies that our potential for life is much greater than any natural immediacy. If the bird 'simply is what it is', the Christian's task is to be 'doubly himself [i Fordobelse at være sig selv]' (*CD* 43).

We are unavoidably reflected, doubled, immersed in the differentiations of language. Unaware of all this, the bird can be described as light-minded relative to the Christian faith (whereas it is carefree in comparison with heathen

---

[8] Words in brackets not translated by Lowrie. See SV 13: 23.

melancholy) (*CD* 25). The bird's immediacy only means anything in relation to my situation as a reader, from which I abstracted in order to contemplate the bird. We can see the bird's riches, but the bird itself is ignorant of them (*CD* 27). The key difference is that what the bird *is* in its immediacy represents a task for the person who accepts it as an ideal. This is the art of faith:

> For it requires no art to be ignorant, but to *become* ignorant, and by becoming so, to be ignorant, that is the art. To this extent the Christian is different from the bird, for the bird *is* ignorant, but the Christian becomes ignorant. (*CD* 29)

Similarly, in *The Lily of the Field*, the silence of nature must be cultivated, even though language is the mark of human uniqueness in creation:

> For no doubt it is speech which distinguishes man above the beasts ... [But] just because a man is able to speak, it is an art to be able to keep silent; and just because this advantage of man is so easily a temptation to him, it is a great art to be able to keep silent. (*CD* 322)

Language is not evil per se, it is the concomitant of our humanity. How could Kierkegaard denigrate language entirely – in a text? He must suppose language is adequate to describe its own deficiencies and present a corrective. Rather, it is in the ironical recommendation of silence in words which creates new possibilities of self-knowledge by calling our whole reflective standpoint into question. These texts are tactical and indirect, even though they are published under Kierkegaard's own name. Their evocations of nature are in fact artfully contrived depictions of an idealized order which are used to undermine the self-sufficiency of the craving ego, and to foster a joyful acceptance of life based on patience and humility.

However, a problem persists. Kierkegaard says of the birds that they 'live without temporal anticipation, with no sense of time, simply in the moment' (*GS* 27). Temporality, language and reflection are inseparable, as we have seen. Strictly speaking, the bird cannot come to be anything – it just *is*. But this makes the bird a deeply ambiguous ideal: 'Why has the bird no material care? Because it lives only in the moment, because, therefore, there is nothing of the eternal in the bird; but is this to be called a perfection?' (*GS* 51). That the human self is constituted by a dialectic between time and eternity, real and ideal is the very condition for life to have any meaning at all. As for the bird, if it knows no such dialectic, then it is fated to remain merely an object for our gaze – it can never become the subject of its own history: 'the worry of the next day the bird does not have – because it lives but one day, which we might also express in another way, by saying that it has no self' (*CD* 74).

In the end, Kierkegaard does not wish to move beyond the contradiction that the bird is a teacher left far behind by its disciple, to whom it has a curious inverse relation:

> The bird's highness is a symbol [Sindbillede] of the Christian's highness, which is in turn a counterpart of the bird's highness, the one corresponding to the other with perfect understanding, though with endless difference. (*CD* 61).

Only in the difference made possible by reflection can the lily and bird have meaning for us. They have their sense only in relation to a temporal narrative of our spiritual maturation. Once you have learned and internalized their meaning, these fictions have done their job. They lose their pedagogic dynamism. They become static images, signposts or markers along the way the self has travelled, but now entirely subsidiary to the narrative of actual life, their message subsumed in the Christian's submission to God:

> But if you can become unconditionally obedient like the lily and the bird, then you have learned what you should have learned, and you have learned this from the lily and the bird (and if you have learned it fully, you have thus become more perfect'than them, so that the lily and the bird, instead of being teachers, become an image [Billedet]) you have learned to serve one Master, to love him alone and to hold to him unconditionally in all. (*CD* 345*)

The unconditionality of commitment is evoked through the narrative movement of the text, as it undermines its own tendency to express a static essence or meaning. The text resists its own idolization, through the correspondence within endless difference which characterizes its technique, and which points to the 'eternal and essential difference of infinity' between God and humanity (*CD* 66*). The Eternal is not to be reduced to the status of heuristic fiction as the lily and bird are. That would be to close the infinite distance, the separation which is both the what and the how of religious communication.

Inclosure

Kierkegaard's nuanced approach to silence aids him in this task. He is undoubtedly aware of the dangers of elevating the silent cultivation of immediacy to normative status in the religious life. On one level, silence can be a cowardly form of evasion, as both the discourse 'Against Cowardice' (*ED* 371) and *Purity of Heart* (213–4) claim. Kierkegaard is particularly scathing about the sentimental aestheticism associated with 'quiet hours' for meditation in the State Church.[9] The silence of the clergy and of Bishop Martensen was met with sarcastic attacks on their status as witnesses to the truth during Kierkegaard's attack on the Church (*KAUC* 47ff. and 67ff.).

---

[9] See JP 4: 4051 and 5048, Pap. X(4) A 306 and XI(2) A 35 respectively.

According to Kierkegaard, Martensen's silence is a comical revelation of the fact that he is in a fix, and that of the clergy only demonstrates that they are a mercantile class with no interest in Christianity.

In this way, silence only lends implicit support to the commodification of religion and the abandonment of questions of truth and falsity. Silence can also cloak more insidious evils. As we saw, the seducer's love of silence formed part of a well-defined plan of manipulation, whilst intimating an unreachable condition of pure immediacy. Another example of this comes in *Repetition*, when Constantin discusses the young man whose inability to consummate his relationship with a girl leads him to despair. The young man disappears, but continues to correspond with Constantin by letter, addressing him as 'My Silent Confidant' (*R* 188). Constantin recommends that the young man should deceive his erstwhile lover into thinking that he is a bad character, in order to alienate her and thus be rid of her. When the young man fails to carry out the plan, Constantin observes 'He had not the strength to make irony's vow of silence, had not the strength to keep it. Only he who is silent will amount to anything' (*R* 145). In this silence, one gains mastery over moods. This silence has a complexity of its own which makes it almost linguistic, for 'He who knows how to keep silent discovers an alphabet that has just as many letters as the ordinary one' (ibid.). He learns a 'jargon' ['Tyvesprog'- lit. a 'thieves' language'] in which he can know and manipulate all contrary moods, a stolen language of permanent dissimulation. One who learns this will experience an appalling moment when it seems 'as if he were losing his mind' (*R* 145), when irony threatens to rob one of all meaning. Constantin declares: 'If one lasts out that moment of madness, one will surely triumph' (ibid.).

This victory seeks complete control over one's communications and emissions, dominance over the sensual material of one's life (and therefore superiority over those who represent a lower sensual level, women especially). However, it is a most duplicitous triumph, which opens up the prospect of a dissolution of all norms of behaviour and the enjoyment of manipulation and wilful transgression. Such a step is a risk to sanity, as the young man seems to sense while he compulsively fantasizes about the experience of Job's perdition:

> Then suddenly I am mute; I no longer hear anything, no longer see anything, and have only an intimation in dim outline of Job sitting at the hearth and of his friends, but no one says a word. Yet this silence hides all horrors within itself as a secret no one dares to name [Ingen tør nævne] (*R* 205–6).

What the believer knows as the moment of presence before the Eternal, others may know as an unnameable anxiety.

In his doctoral dissertation *The Concept of Irony*, Kierkegaard dwells at length on the dissolution of stable frameworks of truth and value, from which irony takes its force. Whatever the ironic status of the dissertation itself,[10] its overtly Hegelian pretensions do appear to be subverted by other currents within the text. Kierkegaard tries to justify Socratic irony as a necessary, if negative, stage in the development of world history. Socrates, he argues, stood in opposition to the false positivity of the Sophists, who attempted to control and master the reflection they had awakened, to lull corrosive doubt to sleep by means of a turn to rhetoric. Pursuing finite concerns (money and political prestige), they would hold reflection at bay in a way analogous to the chatter of the present age. As against this false positivity and limited reflection, Socrates' ignorance prepared the way for an infinite ideal: 'Truth demands silence before it will raise its voice, and Socrates was to bring about this silence. For this reason, he was purely negative' (*CI* 210).

However, if, as Hegel himself says, irony is purely negative, can it be relied upon to function as a 'controlled element' in a meaningful whole (*CI* 324ff.)? Irony in its strictest sense 'maintains the contradiction between essence and phenomenon, between the internal and the external' (*CI* 257) and 'is directed not against this or that particular existing entity but against the entire given actuality at a certain time and under certain conditions' (*CI* 254). This last clause seems to relativize irony to specific contexts, but when Kierkegaard says that irony views 'the totality of existence' (ibid.) ironically, it is difficult to see what positive truth can emerge from it. For, unlike doubt, irony is not primarily a conceptual dilemma, but an 'essentially practical' (*CI* 257) act of subjective will:

> In doubt, the subject continually wants to enter into the object, and his unhappiness is that the object continually eludes him. In irony, the subject continually wants to get outside the object, and he achieves this by realizing at every moment that the object has no reality. (ibid.)

In this way, 'the subject becomes free' (*CI* 258), in an affirmation of the nothingness of everything. But this nothingness is not compensated for by a conceptual resolution or extra-linguistic presence:

> For irony, everything becomes nothing, but nothing can be taken in several ways. The speculative nothing is the vanishing at every moment with regard to concretion, since it is itself the craving of the concrete ... the mystic nothing is a nothing with regard to representation, a nothing that nevertheless is just as full of content as the silence of the night is full of sounds for someone who has ears to hear. Finally, the ironic silence is the dead silence [Dødestilhed] in which irony walks again and haunts (the latter word taken altogether ambiguously [at spøge = to haunt or to jest]). (ibid.)

---

[10] See Lee Capel, 'Historical Introduction' to *The Concept of Irony* (London: Collins, 1966) for a summary of the arguments.

Irony's silence is a threat to all plenitude, even more so because it is wilfully adopted. The speculative philosopher seems condemned to chase a concretion which is always eluding him, whilst the mystic's interpretation of wordless presence is itself relativized by another, ironic, reading of silence as emptiness.

The *complicity* between this irony and Kierkegaard's own view of the contradictory nature of consciousness, torn between poles of immediate reality and linguistic ideality, raises the possibility of an ironic reading of his own recommendations of silence, which seem to promise a self-presence and simplicity which ever eludes the human individual. Certainly, Kierkegaard's religious discourses cannot be understood without an appreciation of the irony at work within them. These texts ironically deconstruct themselves, betraying the impossibility of their ideal by the contradictions inherent in trying to present it.

However, Kierkegaard does not simply give in to the free play of irony. The duplicity of silence awakens us to the possibility of its abuse, of its masking a potentially evil interior which is unable to bear the risk of openness to an alterity which is not under the self's control. The *Concept of Anxiety* culminates in a description of the category of anxiety about the good, or the demonic. The demonic person is closed up in himself, refusing the salvation which would take away the basis of his existence: 'The demonic is *inclosing reserve and the unfreely disclosed*' (*CA* 123). It is the muteness of the demonic which is the mark of bondage:

> Freedom is always *communicerende* [communicating] (it does no harm to take into consideration the religious significance of the word); unfreedom becomes more and more inclosed and does not want communication. (*CA* 124)

In this context, it is precisely a saving word which is required, a point of contact with one who seeks to control all his communications: 'Language, the word, is precisely what saves, what saves the individual from the empty abstraction of inclosing reserve' (ibid.). Anxiety implies an irreducible relation to others, or to an Other. Defined as '*a sympathetic antipathy* and *an antipathetic sympathy*' (*CA* 42), anxiety is ambiguously related to an object which is 'a something that is nothing' (*CA* 43). It is afraid of its own freedom to act, of the abyss or leap between possibility and actuality, and of the responsibility it will incur in the eyes of others for taking this leap. As we saw, anxiety results from the original split in the conscious subject in which it is bound up with language. The contradiction of the demonic is that it seeks to cancel the basis for its existence in mute, unrelated, reserve. But 'language does indeed imply communication' (*CA* 124), and the demonic is unable to fully contain his dilemma, suddenly betraying himself in an involuntary word or gesture (*CA* 125ff.).

What can call the demonic person out of reserve? Clearly, this is not a question of getting the inclosed person to adopt certain credally correct beliefs. The demonic, with all its attendant irony cannot be addressed on these terms. Kierkegaard's approach seems to be to explore the demonic, the ironic and the seductive from within, to push them to their limits where they founder on internal contradictions. That is fine as far as it goes – but does Kierkegaard have an alternative to offer? Such an alternative must itself be presented indirectly, through narratives which offer different possibilities for living, and which, if they are to be religious, reflect on their own inability to represent their content matter. It must recognize the need for its own 'inclosure' and reserve as a condition for respecting the otherness of author, reader and God.

In this way, the debate between realism and anti-realism is shifted on to different ground. Rather than concentrating on the truth status of propositions based on a split between correspondence and expressive models of truth, an indirect approach centres on narratives whose truth status is much harder to pinpoint. This is because they are narratives which to some extent define truth and falsity by criteria which cannot be abstracted away from the narrative structure itself. There is no external, unmediated vantage point which is not already part of some narrative, some poetic transubstantiation. But equally, there is no narrative which does not contain within itself an irreducible reference to that which it cannot represent. This will become clearer if we try to read one of Kierkegaard's most difficult texts.

The sacrifice of language

In *Fear and Trembling*, published in 1843 (under the pseudonym, significantly, of Johannes de *Silentio*), the story of God's command to Abraham to sacrifice his son Isaac is used as the basis for an idea of paradoxical faith, a faith by virtue of the absurd. God's call sets Abraham outside the universal domain of ethical duties, all that binds him to human society and makes his life intelligible to others. He is initiated into an absolute relation to God, which suspends his identity as an ethical agent. One like Abraham is called to 'lose one's understanding and along with it everything finite, for which it is the stockbroker, and then to win the very same finitude again by virtue of the absurd' (*FT* 36). This step can have no rational basis apart from his absurd faith in God.

Ethically speaking, this cannot be justified, for 'The ethical as such is the universal; as the universal it is in turn the disclosed [det Aabenbare]' (*FT* 82). The ethical individual must work himself out of his hiddenness, for to remain obstinately silent or inclosed is to trespass against the moral order. The Hegelian philosophy, like ethics, 'assumes no justified hiddenness, no justified incommensurability' (ibid.). It cannot really come to terms with Abraham, for, on ethical grounds, he must be considered a would-be murderer. Abraham thus becomes a cipher for all that exceeds conceptual, abstract comprehension. Faith is the 'paradox that the single individual is higher than the universal' (*FT* 55); it invokes 'an interiority that is incommensurable with an exteriority, an interiority that is not identical, please note, with the first, but is a new interiority' (*FT* 69). We are not called to recapture a lost immediacy, for 'faith is not the first immediacy, but a later immediacy' (*FT* 82).

Faith does not bypass or repress the original complexity of the self, or attempt to take up an eternal standpoint. But the example of Abraham does make us aware of the unarticulable, unspeakable ground of our existence, an existence which, as we saw, is constituted as interest, not as a neutral, blank tablet on which our experience is inscribed:

> Abraham cannot be mediated; in other words, he cannot speak. As soon as I speak, I express the universal, and if I do not do so, no one can understand me. As soon as Abraham wants to express himself in the universal, he must declare that his situation is a spiritual trial [Anfægtelse], for he has no higher expression of the universal that ranks above the universal he violates. (*FT* 60)

Speech is a kind of mediation or translation into an ideality which all can comprehend. But Abraham represents, not an unmediated reality, but an ideality which eludes such mediation – a 'later immediacy'.

De Silentio wants to make us aware of the duplicity of a silence which ethics cannot comprehend, and which is absolutely different to the silence which aesthetics demands for the creation of interesting situations. He insists that 'secrecy and silence make a man great because they are qualifications of inwardness' (*FT* 88). However, to go beyond aesthetics and ethics is to risk falling prey to monstrous evil:

> If I go further, I always run up against the paradox, the divine and the demonic, for silence is both. Silence is the demon's trap, and the more that is silenced, the more terrible the demon, but silence is also divinity's mutual understanding with the single individual. (ibid.)

The finite and temporal must be utterly given up, in order to be regained from God; what is an impossible ideal for the poet, who conceals his naked misery with the 'leafage of language' (*FT* 61), becomes a certainty for faith, but only for the faith which is purified from all selfish clinging to this life and brought out of the self-inclosed world of ethical duty. In this movement, the individual becomes an enigma to those around him: 'the single individual simply cannot make himself understandable to anyone' (*FT* 71). The result of Abraham's faith is that he falls silent. He cannot fulfil the ethical demand for self-disclosure:

> Abraham remains silent – but he *cannot* speak ... The relief provided by speaking is that it translates me into the universal ... Speak he cannot; he speaks no human language. And even if he understood all the languages

of the world, even if those he loved understood them, he still could not speak – he speaks in a divine language, he speaks in tongues. (*FT* 113–14)

Abraham becomes an unreadable text, for 'his life is like a book under divine confiscation and never becomes *publice juris* [public property]' (*FT* 77), unlike the one who 'translates himself into the universal, the one who, so to speak, personally produces a trim, clean, and, as far as possible, faultless edition of himself' (*FT* 76). Like irony and humour, faith owes its special character to the 'individual's incommensurability with actuality' (*FT* 51); but unlike them, faith moves beyond resignation and the renunciation of finitude to re-establish the individual's relationship to the world on another level. Individuality, finitude and temporality are no longer annulled for the sake of an abstract, timeless ideal, but are affirmed as gratuitous gifts.

However, this affirmation comes at a price. There is, firstly, the ever-present threat of madness: to others, Abraham must appear mad (*FT* 76). Indeed, his is a 'divine madness' (*FT* 23), which merits only a 'demented [afsindig]' admiration (*FT* 57). The 'Exordium' which precedes the development of the themes and arguments of the work gives four alternative readings of the Abraham story, in which he is far from being the father of faith. In each, despair and loss of faith in God haunt the characters, and in each, the poetic rendition cannot capture the movement of faith (*FT* 9–14). So what reassurance is there that Abraham is obeying the voice of God? None – certainly none that can be spoken in words. But neither can there be any intuitive certainty that one's faith is true, for this is what de Silentio rejects when he rejects the idea that faith is the same as immediacy. Precisely this lack of reasons, from any human point of view, is the distressing mark of true faith. The movement of faith is not merely *beyond* reason – it is *against* reason, subverting and overthrowing it.

Derrida reads in this text 'a narrative development of the paradox constituting the concept of duty and absolute responsibility'.[11] The paradox is that responsibility, on the one hand, must respect the other in his or her absolute singularity, and yet, on the other, is only responsible if it acts in accordance with universal ethical norms. Responsibility implies at once being able to account for one's actions in terms of such laws, but also going beyond the order of reasons, knowledge or the application of rules. To be responsible or to act justly on the basis of rational and prudential calculation is not to be responsible or just at all, because it suppresses the singularity of the other.[12]

---

[11] J. Derrida, *The Gift of Death*, trans. D. Willis (Chicago and London: University of Chicago Press, 1995), p. 66.
[12] See also Derrida's 'Force of Law: The "Mystical Foundation of Authority"' in D. Cornell, M. Rosenfeld and D. G. Carlson (eds), *Deconstruction and the Possibility of Justice* (London and New York: Routledge, 1992), pp. 3–67; and Mark Dooley, 'Repetition and Justice: A Derridean/Kierkegaardian Reading of the Subject' in George Pattison and Steven Shakespeare (eds), *Kierkegaard on Self and Society* (London: Macmillan, 1998).

One might compare Derrida's analysis of Bataille's 'concept' of sovereignty.[13] Unlike the Hegelian dialectic, whose negative movement only apparently takes the risk of a loss of all meaning, sovereignty is a movement of transgression which expects no return, an unmeaning which does not serve to establish meaning. It is a 'heedless sacrifice of presence and meaning',[14] for to move towards sovereignty is to sacrifice reason in a movement of negation without reserve. Sovereignty is a 'nonprinciple and a nonfoundation, it definitively eludes any expectation of a reassuring *archia*, a condition of possibility or transcendental discourse'.[15] It demands a movement beyond significant discourse, to 'find a speech which maintains silence',[16] a speech which does not serve meaning. Sovereignty, in its own way, repeats the dream of absolute freedom, in a sacrifice which serves no purpose or end. It requires an indirect form of communication, which 'risks *making sense*, risks agreeing to the reasonableness of reason'.[17] Therefore 'we must redouble language and have recourse to ruses, stratagems, to simulacra ... In so speaking "at the limit of silence," we must organize a strategy and "find [words] which reintroduce – at a point – the sovereign silence which interrupts language."'[18]

Kierkegaard too interrupts language through the call to silence and the figure of the sacrifice, in which reason or language itself is as much the victim as Isaac. Mark C. Taylor uses some of Derrida's words from another context to claim that *Fear and Trembling* 'remains a story without an event in the traditional sense of the word, the story of language and writing as the inscription of the thing itself as other'.[19] Silence makes explicit language's inability to make reality present to us, as it is in itself. Kierkegaard practises a communication disciplined in silence, as we shall see. This is necessary, in disputing the validity of Hegel's philosophy, if the objection is not itself to be incorporated within the system. The movement of faith must be excessive. However, it is *faith* Kierkegaard talks about, not a play of unmeaning. For the problem with Bataille's sovereignty is that it is by definition pointless, that it serves no purpose; however, being so empty of content, it risks an unwitting servitude to egoism and cruelty. The seducer's ironic play provides a convenient mask for a servile repetition of his compulsive search for immediacy, at whatever cost to his victims. The denial of reason, that one should have to 'make sense', can leave one impotent to resist when the forces of irrational violence and terror are

---

[13] J. Derrida, *Writing and Difference* (London: Routledge, 1978) pp. 251–277.
[14] Ibid., p. 257.
[15] Ibid., p. 262.
[16] Ibid.
[17] J. Derrida, *The Archeology of the Frivolous* (Lincoln and London: University of Nebraska Press, 1980), p. 263.
[18] Ibid.
[19] From *Signéponge/Signsponge*, quoted in Taylor, *Alterity*, p. 350.

unleashed on the world, or to criticize the subtler forms of violence endemic in bourgeois social and economic systems.

Faith *is*, however, inherently transgressive of speculative reason. As Derrida recognizes, 'Our faith is not assured, because faith never can be, it must never be a certainty.'[20] If it does not wish a return to primordial immediacy, neither does it desire the speculative goal in which all alienation and estrangement of self from other is overcome in conceptual terms. It wills the creation of a new immediacy, in which the self maintains its separateness. It relates to others through a faith which does not claim to comprehend them.

This is why the narrative form is important for Kierkegaard here. It is able to communicate without translating the absurd, secretive faith of Abraham into a determinate content. The narrative is open-ended, or rather, it cannot constitute a seamless whole which is self-evident or self-interpreting. It contains within itself a paradox which resists any narration, but which requires a narrative context to appear as such (and here 'to appear as such' means precisely not to be made manifest or intelligible, but to be respected in its hiddenness and paradoxicality).

The story of Abraham is told and re-told through the work. It circles around the paradox which cannot be brought to the light of conceptual knowledge. At the end of each of the four initial renditions of the Abraham story, there is a reference to the ways in which a mother weans a child from her breast (*FT* 11–14). This moment of separation is the necessary condition for maturity. The implication seems to be that only by embracing and affirming this primordial wounding and separation, and extending it to the whole of one's finite relationships and concerns, will one win the kind of self that can bear the strain of knowing that existence has no clear, universally accessible, sayable meaning. As Bigelow remarks, 'in holding open the relation to the absolutely other, thinking breaks with language',[21] resulting in a silence which resists the assimilation of all recalcitrant mystery. On this basis, there is hope for re-establishing one's relationships and concerns as purely gratuitous passions, not supported by any justifying rationale, nor given meaning only as parts of a greater whole, as means towards an overarching telos.

However, the risk of such a strategy cannot be evaded. Kierkegaard's retelling of the Abraham tale can be read in several ways.[22] Most commonly it is taken as a reflection of Kierkegaard's belief that he had to sacrifice his love for Regina (and thus in a sense sacrifice her) to be true to his calling. It has also been read as a narrative of the father sacrificing the son – much as Kierkegaard believed his childhood had been sacrificed to his father's all-

---

[20] Derrida, *Gift of Death*, p. 80.
[21] Bigelow, *Kierkegaard*, p. 101.
[22] See Taylor, *Alterity*, p. 155f.

pervasive, melancholic, religious guilt. Much can fruitfully be said on these themes. However, when the step is taken from Isaac, Regina or the child Søren to the categories of 'the finite', 'immediacy', 'temporal hope' or whatever these figures are taken to represent, then it must be acknowledged that an enormous act of abstraction has taken place. Instead of a concrete individual, a child bound on a rock with a knife at its throat, we have a parable of the movement of faith *within* the individual, in which all reference to exterior relations is erased, or at least rendered insignificant. Child and woman become ciphers for aspects of one's own (presumably male) self which must be violently sacrificed, and only received back from the hands of an absolute Father, who thus provides the justification for one's act. Of course, it does not matter if the sacrifice *is* actually restored, only that one has faith that it will be. The form of one's inner faith is the only criterion for its truth. Faith is a passion (*FT* 67), and 'the conclusions of passion are the only dependable ones – that is, the only convincing ones' (*FT* 100). However, it is far from clear that this approach contains any real safeguards against the deceit of a seducer, for deceit and love can look very similar. Indeed, the risk of cruelty is heightened if others are viewed only as adjuncts to one's own spiritual development.

It is becoming clear why the issue of realism and anti-realism is so much harder to resolve in reading Kierkegaard's texts. On the one hand, the point seems to be that one makes the correct movements internally, not that any correspondence with external matters of fact should be established. Moreover, this internalization of the drama of faith affects its ethical expression too. When de Silentio seeks to describe the knight of faith, the one who has made the movements of resignation and absurd belief, he is shocked to discover that this knight looks outwardly exactly the same as any bourgeois-philistine tax collector (*FT* 38–40). Faith makes no outward difference, the drama is played out solely on the interior stage.

On the other hand, however, the narrative opens us to an absolute otherness, the possibility of an infinite, redeeming love, which disturbs the order of sacrifice on the internal stage, and demands a response which does not stay within the interior castle of the self. The response demanded is that of communication.

In *Fear and Trembling*, Kierkegaard goes as far as he ever did towards embracing a form of hidden inwardness which would render all communication null and void. But such an extreme is self-cancelling and, without an awareness of its inherent paradox, can become the vehicle for quietism or even collusion in cruelty. To pull back from this extreme is not to water down Kierkegaard's notion of the absurd, but to accentuate its ethical and religious challenge. Hidden inwardness, adopted without irony, only blunts the salvific potency of the paradox.

We are justified in resisting this extreme, because after all, Kierkegaard wishes to *communicate*, however indirectly, precisely through his discipline of poetic silence. In his narratives, Abraham's silence speaks, it signifies. But it speaks of an order of responsibility, address, love and gift which goes beyond anything speech can translate into universal concepts. It signifies the One who escapes all signification, who puts signification into play. This is indeed a transformed notion of communication, which does not play down the paradoxes of language and faith. It calls for a new form of poet, whose discourses on the absolutely other still hold passage open to the universality of language and ethics.

The poet's silence

In *Stages on Life's Way*, the anonymous writer of the diary in 'Guilty – Not Guilty?' has this to say about inclosing reserve: 'Inclosing reserve, silence (the teleological suspension of the duty to speak the truth), is a strictly formal qualification and therefore can just as well be the form for good as for evil' (*SLW* 230). This has important implications:

> every individuality who solely by himself has a relation to the idea without any middle term (here is the silence toward all others) is demonic; if the idea is God, then the individual is religious; if the idea is that of evil, then he is in the stricter sense demonic. (*SLW* 231)

Kierkegaard is aware that silence is a purely formal phenomenon, with no essential relation to a corresponding content. It therefore has no intrinsic value. What is more, *both* good and evil forms of silence are demonic. Both reject any mediating term (language, duty, reason) and thus represent an absurd, contradictory self-assertion on the part of the individual. Like the demonic, the believer rejects the very language which makes his position possible, and ends by merely supporting the status quo of hierarchies and definitions inherent in the concrete forms of language of his time and place.

De Silentio claims 'I am not a poet' (*FT* 90); but he *is* a poetized personality, and says of himself that he is '*poetice et eleganter* [in a poetic and refined way] a supplementary writer' (*FT* 7). Like Kierkegaard, his religiosity creates a tension with his poetry, for he wants to be 'more than "the poet"' (JP 6: 6718; Pap. X(3) A 789). This tension means that Kierkegaard cannot himself become the knight of faith. He is too passionately committed to communication. He takes the risk of writing, of involvement in the duplicitous world of language and interpretation. And yet this venture demands its own discipline of silence for the sake of the communication. Writing to his brother Peter in 1847, Kierkegaard says:

> Silence is necessary for my life, and precisely through silence it gains its

power. Even if I wanted to speak, I would have to keep silence about that which is most important to me and most deeply determines my life. (*LD* 167)

When Kierkegaard agonizes about his use of indirect communication in 1848–9, we learn that this silence is intimately related to his activity as a writer:

> What troubles me most is whether or not I have the right to do this, whether in relation to God this silence is permissible, whether it is permissible to let a productivity which is so infinitely indebted to Him for its ingenuity remain an enigma and for many somewhat odd. (JP 6: 6345; Pap. X(1) A 115)

In the end, Kierkegaard did maintain an indirectness in his production, as we shall see. His reasons for doing are in fact foreshadowed in the 1846 work *A Literary Review*. Here, he argues that the 'law of poetic production' (*TA* 98–9) involves an essential silence:

> Anyone who experiences anything primitively also experiences in ideality the possibilities of the same thing and the possibility of the opposite. These possibilities are his legitimate literary property. His own personal actuality, however, is not. His speaking and his producing are, in fact, born of silence. The ideal perfection of what he says and what he produces will correspond to his silence. (ibid.)

To allow one's own personal life to intrude upon one's poetry is to 'trespass against the holy modesty of ideality' (ibid.) with the first word one speaks.[23] Like Bataille, the poet must practise 'a speech which maintains silence'. As the *Postscript* says, 'only doubly reflected subjective thinking has secrets; that is, all its essential content is essentially a secret, because it cannot be communicated directly' (*CUP* 79). The very form of the communication is disciplined by this secrecy, which is not an accidental act of hiding, but an internal necessity of the nature of truth itself.[24]

This suggests that silence, poetically speaking, is only justified in the service of a transformed communication. Like the ironical form of his works, a certain 'silence' is necessary in communicating ideals of the eternal. Like silent prayer to God, this becomes 'the moment of silence in the intimacy of the conversation'. The poet's silence resists any attempt to dominate or merge with the otherness of the reader. He writes so that the reader becomes more

---

[23] See *From The Papers Of One Still Living*, in which H. C. Andersen's works are accused of being more like amputations than productions, because he puts so much of his own personal life into them (*EPW* 83–4).

[24] Cf. Derrida's writing on the secret in 'Passions: "An Oblique Offering"' in *On the Name* (Stanford, Calif.: Stanford University Press, 1995), pp. 3–31.

than an object, or a passive consumer in the bourgeois economy; so that the reader can act for him or herself, become a subject in her own right, rather than a spectator. Something similar holds true of the ethicist, for, as we saw, Kierkegaard rejects the idea that ethics can be communicated directly. It requires an awakening of a capability, an artistry translated into existence: 'To that extent, all communication ends in a kind of silence; for when I existentially express it, it is not necessary for my speaking to be audible' (JP 1: 653; Pap. VIII(2) B 85). It is in this sense that the idea of silence can perhaps show a way beyond stereotypes of female passivity, or the dispiriting quietism which can be read in *Fear and Trembling*, towards an ideal of creative action and mutual reciprocity, of a communication which sets its recipients free. Indeed, in the early work *From The Papers of One Still Living*, Kierkegaard rejects the idea that true genius should fall prey to either an 'abortive activity' or an 'original passivity', characterized respectively as 'broken manliness' and 'consistent womanliness' (*EPW* 81). Notwithstanding the identification of the feminine with passivity, this at least suggests that a worthwhile 'life-view' (*EPW* 75ff.) must transfigure both of these extremes.

The question of realism and anti-realism admits no easy solution. The texts we have looked at do not necessarily provide us with the resources to specify what the reality of 'God' consists of beyond its function as a cipher for absolute otherness. However, the fact that Kierkegaard's religious language is orienting us towards an otherness which exceeds every concept and every objectification suggests that it may still be able to destabilize the closed economy of any immanent religiosity. Nevertheless, if ironic dissemblance does not have the last word, its challenge cannot simply be dismissed. Nihilism and the crisis of representation cannot be staved off by an appeal to objective evidences in nature or experience, because it is the very status of 'evidences' and 'objectivity' which is at issue.

Indeed, Kierkegaard is willing to go some of the way with a nihilistic appraisal of the insubstantial emptiness of the temporal world, of its barrenness or superficiality. What he tries to do, as in *Purity of Heart*, is use this meaninglessness as a way of making us aware of our irreducible relation to an Other, an Eternal One. This is what makes the position of the religious author and his reader so precarious – for in the absence of any assured objective constraints, what is to prevent *any* projection of human will or imagination from occupying the place of the Eternal? However, we might see Kierkegaard's texts as exercises in resisting such arbitrary idolatry through the discipline that the paradox imposes, and the intimation of an infinite love which inaugurates a communication beyond the orders of knowledge, representation and sacrifice.

Summary

We can see how different aspects of silence thus co-exist in tension and inter-relation in Kierkegaard's texts:

1. Silence is a means of escaping from the ambiguity of language to a more direct, immediate and authentic relationship to oneself and to God – a relationship often presented as the natural preserve of women.
2. Silence is nevertheless used as an ironic or strategic figure in Kierkegaard's texts, which emphasize the artistry of silence. Silence is not pure and self-evident, it has a meaning which differs in different contexts. Ideals of immediacy are thus deconstructed.
3. Kierkegaard uses motifs of silence to bring the reader into a relationship to that which exceeds the order of objective knowledge and representation.
4. However, Kierkegaard also recognizes the risks in making silence so central, risks which emerge most clearly in Haufniensis' portrayal of the demonic, inclosed person, whose silence masks despair and defiance.
5. The promise and risk of silence are brought together in Johannes de Silentio's re-telling of the story of Abraham. The narrative explores the paradoxes of responsibility, ethics and communication, paradoxes which the poet must respect in his or her own literary practice. Narrative is one form in which such complexities can be brought into play without diminishing or obscuring them.

The importance of narrative and communication is the importance of a *certain form* of narrative and a *certain form* of communication. This is why the issue of realism and anti-realism cannot be addressed in Kierkegaard's writings without attention to the form they take. That form is, in a certain sense, ethical and liberating, respecting the otherness of reader as it respects the otherness of God – in their intrinsic absence.

CHAPTER SIX

Kierkegaard's ethical realism

Derrida recognizes that *Fear and Trembling* is a narrative which invokes the possibility of a disymmetrical infinite love, a movement of grace which establishes the alterity of the other:

> On what condition does goodness exist beyond all calculation? On the condition that goodness forget itself, that the movement be a movement of the gift that renounces itself, hence a movement of infinite love. Only infinite love can renounce itself and, in order to *become finite*, become incarnated in order to love the other, to love the other as a finite other.[1]

Derrida interprets this, however, in a way that seems congenial to anti-realism. He suggests that the monotheistic critique of idolatry could be extended to undermine the very idea of God as an external, supernatural being:

> We should stop thinking about God as someone, over there, way up there, transcendent, and, what is more – into the bargain, precisely – capable, more than any satellite orbiting in space, of seeing into the most secret of the most interior places. It is perhaps necessary, if we are to follow the traditional Judeo-Christiano-Islamic injunction, but also at the risk of turning it against that tradition, to think of God and of the name of God without such idolatrous stereotyping or representation. Then we might say: God is the name of the possibility I have of keeping a secret that is visible from the interior but not from the exterior.[2]

In other words, 'God' refers to the inviolable subjectivity of the self, and thus to the irreducible otherness of people and things to one another, for 'God, as the wholly other, is to be found everywhere there is something of the wholly other'.[3]

How far Derrida is committed to this position is unclear. However, it is fraught with tension. If God is met as infinite alterity, how can 'God' name a possibility that 'I' have? At this point, Derrida seems to fall back on a reductionist option which is as open to challenge as the crude realism which he rejects as idolatrous. Surely whatever God names eludes any control or possession on my part; and if that is so, it cannot be equated with a characteristic of human subjectivity without further ado. We are driven to ask, in the spirit of the first quotation from Derrida: what is the condition for this

---

[1] J. Derrida, *The Gift of Death*, (Chicago and London: University of Chicago Press, 1995), p. 51.
[2] Ibid., p. 108.
[3] Ibid., p. 78.

ethical relationship to others as others to be possible? How do others become bearers of an infinite otherness, signalling an infinite love?

For Levinas, it is the idea of infinity which breaks apart self-contained philosophical reason and human subjectivity. It is an idea which thought cannot think, cannot contain. It opens a way to the 'metaphysical' other, which is 'prior to every initiative, to all imperialism of the same. It is other with an alterity constitutive of the very content of the other.'[4] He later adds that 'We name this calling into question of my spontaneity by the presence of the Other ethics.'[5]

The relation to God is structured by this disruptive effect of infinite ethical otherness. God is transcendence who defies representation, and thus defies reduction to being a cipher for the ethical relationship to the other person. God is 'other than the other, other otherwise'.[6] The idea of infinity breaks through the orders of objective knowledge and representation, and suggests another dynamic:

> The idea of infinity is *revealed*, in the strong sense of the term. There is no natural religion. But this exceptional knowledge is thus no longer objective. Infinity is not the 'object' of a cognition (which would be to reduce it to the measure of the gaze that contemplates), but is the desirable, that which arouses Desire, that is, that which is approachable by a thought that at each instant *thinks more than it thinks*. The infinite is not thereby an immense object exceeding the horizons of the look. It is Desire that measures the infinity of the infinite, for it is a measure through the very impossibility of measure.[7]

What Levinas is saying cannot be straightforwardly equated with realism or anti-realism. He denies that God can be known through objective knowledge, but he does not thereby turn God into a creation of our subjective wills (whether individually or collectively). God is known in the meeting of our passion and his movement towards us in revelation.

This, I would suggest, is instructive for Kierkegaard's position, and for what I propose to call his 'ethical realism'. By this I do not mean that he takes a realist attitude to ethical norms, that is, that he believes ethical values to correspond to objectively existing realities or essences, in Platonic fashion. Rather, I am claiming that Kierkegaard can be described as a realist about religious language, but a realist of a very particular sort.

For Kierkegaard, as we shall see over the next two chapters, anti-realism would represent a kind of one-sided, undialectical view. Despite its apparent

---

[4] E. Levinas, *Totality and* Infinity, trans. A. Lingis (Pittsburgh: Duquesne University Press, 1969), p. 39.
[5] Ibid., p. 43.
[6] E. Levinas, *Collected Philosophical Papers*, trans. A Lingis (Dordrecht: Nijhoff, 1987), pp. 165–6.
[7] Levinas, *Totality*, p. 62.

agnosticism, it holds to a totalizing philosophical standpoint which believes it can fully determine the origin and meaning of religious language. Kierkegaard would not accept that language about God is an indirect way of talking about humanly created ideals.

However, for all this, Kierkegaard would accept that religious faith cannot be a matter of objective knowledge, and that religious language is inextricably tied to existential possibilities which the believer is called to live out. He is not a metaphysical realist, in Putnam's terms. Language about God can only ever be indirect, aiming to upbuild and awaken, to arouse a passion for the infinite. It is embodied in patterns of communication and significant action which are primarily ethical rather than descriptive. Nevertheless, it is the God-relationship (whether objectively thematized or not) which is the irreducible condition for such communication and action to be possible.

We have seen that, for Kierkegaard, the ethical is a category under dispute. The phrase 'ethical realism' invokes this tension. On the one hand, the ethical is the indispensable system of universal norms which constitute our duty. On the other hand, the ethical is the respect for the absolute individuality and otherness of each person, a relationship which cannot be encompassed or determined by rules. Ethical realism holds out the universal possibility of relating to God through patterns of liberating communication and action. God is known in and through ethical relationships. However, those very patterns of communication and action call to account the totalising illusions of a system of ethics that would try to be self-sufficient. Such systems smother the relationship to the other in his or her singularity – and thus to the infinite love of God which makes that relationship possible. Ethical realism unites both the unavoidable responsibility and creativity of the believer with his or her radical dependency upon the measure beyond measure which is passionate faith in God. I believe that this is akin to what Michael Weston is describing when he writes of 'Kierkegaard's *ethical* critique of philosophy, and thus the actuality of a non-philosophical site from which philosophy can be criticized'.[8]

Kierkegaard must tread a tightrope between faith's lack of objective assurances and its resistance to dreams of subjective mastery. How does this work itself out in the progression of his texts?

Irony: reflection without content

To follow this question through the authorship, we need to return to *The Concept of Irony*. In that work, Kierkegaard follows Hegel in tracing the modern concept of irony back to its philosophical roots in Fichte's idealism.

---

[8] Michael Weston, *Kierkegaard and Modern Continental Philosophy: An Introduction* (London and New York: Routledge, 1994), p. 9.

According to Fichte, philosophy could comprehend all reality as the product of the absolute Ego, in which the division between subject and object in experience is shown to be merely apparent. In his *The Vocation of Man*, of which the young Kierkegaard had been an avid reader, he argues that 'My consciousness of the object is merely an unrecognized *consciousness of my production of a presentation of an object*.'[9] The 'I' is described as '*subject-objectivity*, this return of knowledge upon itself',[10] and Fichte assures his reader that 'You yourself are the thing ... all that you perceive beyond yourself is still yourself alone.'[11] This charade of an extra-subjective reality serves only to awaken our own ethical striving, in which 'The sole end of reason is pure activity, absolutely by itself alone, having no need of any instrument outside of itself – independence of everything which is not reason, absolutely unconditioned.'[12] This represented a radical extension of the Kantian critique of our unexamined, dogmatic tendency to divide the world up into subjective and objective poles, and to see our thinking as constrained to copy real structures and events outside of itself. It was a vision of the power and freedom of the self in its absolute form which could have repercussions unforeseen in Fichtean philosophy.

By the time he came to write his dissertation, Kierkegaard seemed convinced that the effects of Fichte's idealism were largely pernicious. He based his assessment, not so much on Fichte's results, as on his philosophical *method*: 'Because reflection was continually reflecting about reflection, thinking went astray, and every step it advanced led further and further, of course, from any content' (*CI* 272). Fichte, according to Kierkegaard, 'infinitized the *I* in *I-I*' (*CI* 273), but this was 'an infinity without any content' (ibid.) which resulted in 'acosmism' (ibid.). Without any external reality or order to constrain it, the self became an indeterminate abstraction. The very way in which Fichte philosophized guaranteed that his system could only amount to empty tautologies. What is lacking is any encounter with the substantial presuppositions for human life:

> The starting point for the problem of philosophy is hereby brought to consciousness. It is the presuppositionless with which it must begin, but the prodigious energy of this beginning goes no further. In other words, in order for thought, subjectivity, to acquire fullness and truth, it must let itself be born; it must immerse itself in the deeps of substantial life, let itself hide there as the congregation is hidden in Christ; half fearfully and half sympathetically, half shrinking back and half yielding, it must let the waves of the substantial sea close over it, just as in the moment of

---

[9] J. G. Fichte, *The Vocation of Man*, trans. Chisholm, (Indianapolis and New York: Liberal Arts Press, 1956), p. 56.
[10] Ibid., p. 60.
[11] Ibid., p. 64.
[12] Ibid., p. 124.

inspiration the subject almost disappears from himself, abandons himself to that which inspires him, and yet feels a slight shudder, for it is a matter of life and death. (*CI* 274)

The religious analogy is significant; for Kierkegaard in this text, the idealist claim to have no presuppositions amounts to a presumptuous denial of the sheer givenness of life. To be sure, recognizing that one is merely derivative is experienced as a threatening moment of loss, an abandonment to that which cannot be comprehended in thought alone. It is a moment in which madness and the ultimate dispossession of death are invoked. Without this yielding, however, the self can only go astray; and one can hardly fail to notice that this represents an implicit rebuff to Hegel's own project, despite the overt deference paid to him. The religious moment escapes the economy of self-contained reason.

To the romantic ironists, however, Fichte offered the prospect of an absolute freedom of the self, which would rise above the apparent distinctions and evaluations of the phenomenal world, whilst at the same time making explicit the aesthetic heart of Fichte's idealism, in which intuition took precedence over discursive thought. In *Irony*, Kierkegaard rejects their stance. He argues that Schlegel and Tieck were guilty, firstly of confusing the empirical, finite *I* with the eternal *I* and, secondly, of confusing metaphysical actuality with historical actuality (*CI* 275). In other words, they tried to translate idealist metaphysics into a way of everyday life, in which they, individual men, claimed to have the viewpoint of the absolute. In this situation, irony claimed 'the absolute power to do everything' (ibid.). Presumption knew no bounds. Caught in the contradiction between their theoretical standpoint and their actual finitude, the ironists risked putting themselves above all limited moral codes.[13]

For Kierkegaard, actuality cannot be dismissed so lightly. It constitutes a claim upon the individual, for 'actuality (historical actuality) stands in a twofold relation to the subject: partly as a gift that refuses to be rejected, partly as a task that wants to be fulfilled' (*CI* 276). In both gift ('Gave') and task ('Opgave'), there is an irreducible givenness. Neither thought nor poesis can begin from a state of presuppositionless abstraction. Expanding on what Kierkegaard says, we might argue that something always precedes them and renders them derivative, because even to formulate thought or art as a task to be achieved by the self alone presupposes a whole language in which such a task ('Opgave') can be articulated. As we have already seen, Kierkegaard argues that all philosophy is dependent upon a language it cannot account for.

Irony goes on to dispute the romantic claim to a higher conception of poetry. The true art does not claim mastery over all phenomena in aesthetic production; it is rather a style of living humbly:

---

[13] See George Pattison, 'Friedrich Schlegel's Lucinde', *Scottish Journal of Theology* 38 (1986), pp. 545–64, esp. 556ff.

> In other words, it is indeed one thing to compose oneself poetically; it is something else to be composed poetically. The Christian lets himself be poetically composed, and in this respect a simple Christian lives far more poetically than many a brilliant intellectual. (*CI* 280–1)

The implication is that art requires the recalcitrance of its material, that it is a yielding to constraints as well as an active manipulation of one's environment and language. Art is inescapably dialogical. Indeed, Kierkegaard turns the tables on the Romantics by claiming that it is the Christian, who receives the shape and goal of his or her life from without, who is the true artist. That the Christian should be seen as living poetically is significant, for it implies that there is an aesthetic aspect to the religious life, a relation of ideality and reality which bears comparison to that effected by poetic language (and, indeed, to some extent by all language). The ironist, however, comes to resemble the debasement of poetry and language:

> An individual who lets himself be poetically composed does have a definite given context into which he has to fit and thus does not become a word without a meaning because it is wrenched out of its associations. But for the ironist, this context, which he would call a demanding appendix, has no validity, and since it is not his concern to form himself in such a way that he fits into his environment, then the environment must be formed to fit him – in other words, he poetically composes not only himself but he poetically composes his environment also. The ironist stands proudly, inclosed within himself, and just as Adam had the animals pass by, he lets people pass before him and finds no fellowship for himself. (*CI* 283)

In effect, the ironist attempts to create his or her own private language, an absurd venture which can only issue in meaninglessness and consequent isolation. The ironist is located on the primal scene of naming, that of Adam with the animals, for a language of mere reference does not inaugurate any deeper communion between namer and named. It remains an external and abstract collection of ciphers. The ironist 'lives in this totally hypothetical and subjunctive way' (*CI* 284), recalling those early journal entries we examined previously. The poetical and ethical power of language seems bound up with a subjunctive mood that, at every moment, threatens to be debased into mere indifferent possibility.

It is important to realize just how close the extremes of the demonic and the believer can lie. The moment of faith is one of loss, shadowed by madness and death. However, faith is not an escape from the relativities and ambiguities of language. In fact, it represents a deeper relation to the communicational world in which all our thinking and believing is made possible. The Christian does not so much leave poetry behind as translate it into an obedient way of life which alone can make the ideal or the good actual. This venture, which at once incorporates and rejects the poetic ideal is a risky and ambiguous one, but it does hold out the possibility of breaking through the illusion of subjective mastery towards a genuine relation to the other. Indeed, it is a venture which implies a critique, not only of irony, but also of a certain form of ethics itself.

Choosing the absolute

Judge William, in *Either/Or Part Two*, attempts to show that the purely aesthetic life, left to itself, ends in despair, at odds with the temporality of existence. Ethical commitment, on the other hand, gives the self a concrete identity which gives meaning to time, and earnestness to one's personal relationships and to one's social duty. It does this, however, not at the expense of aesthetics, but as its fulfilment. Ethics directs us to ennoble beauty and sensuality by freeing them of their arbitrary and transitory appearance, and locating them within the concrete and yet universal structures of public life, of which marriage is the prime example. It is an argument which bears some relation to Kierkegaard's critique of pure irony.

In the course of his argument, the Judge gives an account of the nature of the fundamental ethical choice by which a person is freed from the dissipation of mere sensuality. This choice, however, is not a choice between this or that particular course of action. It is a choice which will save the whole personality from ruin, and therefore it must be absolute. That is, it must provide a person with an entirely new framework by which life must be evaluated. As the Judge puts it, 'Rather than designating the choice between good and evil, my Either/Or designates the choice by which one chooses good and evil or rules them out' (*EO2* 169). With this choice, the fundamental division between good and evil first emerges. One chooses whether or not one will live in these categories – not whether one will choose the good. There is no framework for evaluating the choice at the moment of decision, because only with the decision does such a framework come into being. Thus, 'the point is not the reality [Realiteten] of that which is chosen but the reality of choosing' (*EO2* 176).

So what, exactly, is chosen? Judge William goes on to suggest that the choice is entirely self-referential, indeed, that only as such could it be an *absolute* choice:

> I choose the absolute, and what is the absolute? It is myself in my eternal validity. Something other than myself I can never choose as the absolute, for if I choose something else, I choose it as something finite and consequently do not choose absolutely. Even the Jew who chose God did not choose absolutely, for he did indeed choose the absolute, but he did not choose it absolutely, and thereby it ceased to be the absolute and became something finite. (*EO2* 214)

The absolute choice cannot rely on any relation to a reality external to itself. Not even God can intrude upon this action of the self, because that would introduce a factor of heteronomy inconsistent with the subject's positing of good and evil. The idea of God, it would seem, is secondary to a moment when the self posits itself *ex nihilo*. It is an idea which has a meaning only within the total framework which the subject provided for itself.

This moment of choice parallels two moments which we came across in *Irony*, and which, for all their apparent difference, seem to display a disturbing similarity. The moment of religious faith, we recall, was one in which all certainties seem to have disappeared, in which death and madness threatened, before the substantial life of Christ was reasserted within the individual. That of ironical creation, however, consisted of the ironist's free creation of his entire environment out of nothing, an act of self-assertion by which he provided himself with his own values and reality. These two phenomena seem to be entirely at odds with one another, but only because we have the benefit of a third person report and evaluation of them. *In the moment of choice itself*, both are subject to an inspiration which lets go of all previously held systems of belief, and which undertakes an absolute risk of meaning which has no external guarantees that it will be justified. Judge William's choice is of the same sort: if it is really absolute, then it must be entirely undecidable, in the moment of choosing, whether the self is composing its own values from its own resources or whether it is yielding to 'objective' values which have a universal validity apart from the self's act of choice.

The ambiguity is well expressed in the Judge's text. Having claimed that the self cannot choose anything external to itself – that it is itself the absolute – he goes on to qualify this radically:

> if what I chose did not exist but came into existence absolutely through the choice, then I did not choose – then I created. But I do not create myself – I choose myself. Therefore, whereas nature is created from nothing, whereas I myself as immediate personality am created from nothing, I as free spirit am born out of the principle of contradiction or am born through my choosing myself. (*EO2* 215–16)

If choice is not to be confused with creation, then what is chosen must already be in existence. But does this make sense? Good and evil do not exist without the self's choice: 'The good is because I will it, and otherwise it is not at all' (*EO2* 224). At issue is not the existence of some object or other, but the existence of an absolute framework of values by which life is given meaning. Unlike an empirically discoverable object, these values have the characteristic that they only come into being through an act of choice. Good and evil, it seems, are evaluations, not facts which can be justified through observation; and the choice by which they are brought to bear on reality appears to be one of unconstrained freedom: 'this absolute choice of myself is my freedom, and only when I have absolutely chosen myself have I posited an absolute difference: namely, the difference between good and evil' (*EO2* 223–4).

However, to talk like this is to risk resembling the ironist, whose pretensions to absolute creativity leave him like a word torn from its context, without meaning and coherence with the world. The Judge's choice, therefore, must necessarily be ambiguous. Spirit is 'born out of the principle of contradiction', in which meaning and value are at once created and received. The absolute difference posited in freedom seems rather to signify the self's paradoxical difference from itself, as both free spirit and product. On the one hand, the Judge can write 'if there were something in me that I could not choose absolutely, then I would not be choosing myself absolutely at all, then I myself would not be the absolute but only a product' (*EO2* 224). On the other hand, it is only by recognizing himself as a particular, conditioned individual, that the Judge could articulate such a choice:

> the person who chooses himself ethically chooses himself concretely as this specific individual ... And this choice is freedom's choice in such a way that in choosing himself as product he can just as well be said to produce himself. (*EO2* 251)

The Judge tries to resolve this by appealing to the religious nature of the choice. The unity of freedom and passivity is found in an act of repentance, whereby the individual takes responsibility both for his own past, and that of all humanity. One who chooses 'repents himself back into himself, back into the family, back into the race, until he finds himself in God' (*EO2* 216). In this way, the individual is preserved from ironical hubris, by acknowledging the imperfection of his humanity when placed under absolute categories of good and evil, for 'only when I choose myself as guilty do I absolutely choose myself, if I am at all to choose myself absolutely in such a way that it is not identical with creating myself' (*EO2* 216–17). God is recognised in his nature as 'the almighty source of everything' (*EO2* 20), to whom one must relate as a passive recipient of one's own being: 'His [the chooser's] self is, so to speak, outside him, and it has to be acquired, and repentance is his love for it, because he chooses it absolutely from the hand of the eternal God' (*EO2* 217). However, the role of God in this is not straightforward. There is little sense of an ongoing relationship to God; rather, the relation to God seems to function as a cipher for the imaginative, retrogressive repentance whereby a person accepts the fact that he is not his own creator: 'But there is also a love with which I love God, and this love has only one expression in language – it is "repentance"' (*EO2* 216). This 'love of God' expresses the awareness that, even at the moment of choice, the self is fundamentally derivative. The self is at once the absolute source of value and the guilty penitent. The appeal to a religious basis for the self does not really resolve the dilemma, it merely renders the fissure in the self in a different way.

The Judge is at pains to minimize the destabilizing potential of this choice. The individual has to be fitted into an order:

> The true concrete choice is the one by which I choose myself back into the world the very same moment I choose myself out of the world. That is, when repenting I choose myself, I collect myself in all my finite concretion, and when I have thus chosen myself out of all the finite in this way, I am in the most absolute continuity with it. (*EO2* 249)

In other words, on the far side of this fundamental, absolute choice, as far as society is concerned, things go on exactly as they did before, save that one person's detached dalliances are eliminated, and he is incorporated into the well-ordered state. As both product and producer, the self re-enacts bourgeois dependency upon, and freedom over, the material constraints of existence. In fact, the Judge's choice plays out its role in a carefully managed economy, in which the risk of loss is minimized:

> even though a person chose the wrong thing, he nevertheless, by virtue of the energy with which he chose, will discover that he chose the wrong thing. In other words, since the choice has been made with all the inwardness of his personality, his inner being is purified and he himself is brought into an immediate relationship with the eternal power that omnipresently pervades all existence. (*EO2* 167)

Indeed, the Judge is bold enough to deny the possibility of going wrong at all, for 'As soon as a person can be brought to stand at the crossroads in such a way that there is no way out for him except to choose, he will choose the right thing' (*EO2* 168). However, it is far from clear where the Judge gets this certainty. This immediate relationship to the eternal hardly fits with his belief that the immediate spirit sickens to despair and must be transfigured (*EO2* 188); or his disparagement of the mystic's 'immediate rapport with the eternal' (*EO2* 246). It only works if the self's choice of a framework of values makes it infallible, because there remains no standpoint from which to judge the self to be in error. In other words, the self cannot be wrong, since it decides what counts as right and wrong. In this case, the self would only agree with its own 'eternal power', and not with any divinity outside itself.

This reveals the paradoxicality of the attempt to transform everything into the self's free act. Either the self denies its givenness and dependency, in which case its ideals would seem to be arbitrary self-creations; or it embraces its dependency, with the result that any absolute choice of itself becomes impossible, and it ends by passively accepting its values from the society around it, which may be equally arbitrary. In effect, the Judge chooses the latter course, but his text reveals the strains of his position. The ethical individual is at once 'his own editor [Redacteur]' and 'responsible to the order of things in which he lives, responsible to God' (*EO2* 260). In a remarkable erotic metaphor, the Judge seems to show a yearning for total independence: 'Through the individual's intercourse with himself the individual is made pregnant by himself and gives birth to himself' (*EO2* 259). The individual wants to become his own mother and father – the ultimate symbol of self-contained autonomy. In the Judge's unwitting admission of his own narcissism, we find a dream of Godlike power: 'When the personality is the absolute, then it is itself the Archimedean point from which one can lift the world' (*EO2* 265). To the young journal writer's question as to what is the Archimedean point, the idea for which he can live and die,[14] the Judge answers: it is yourself. Truth should not be a cold, foreign body, but should coincide with your own existence, should be wholly embodied in you, without debt to others.

However, in this order of things, there is a resistant element which must be assimilated: immediacy is the cipher for sensuality, eroticism and therefore for woman. The woman must be kept in her secondary place, if the man's self-control is to be kept. The power of eros cannot be denied, but must be tamed of its excesses. The woman threatens man, both as the mother to whom he seems to owe his existence, and as the object of his unfulfilled desire. Therefore, she must be assigned her role in the symbolic order, in a text every bit as insidious as the language of seduction:

> A woman comprehends the finite; she understands it from the ground up ... she is in harmony with existence as no man can or ought to be ... She is more perfect than man, for surely the one who explains something is more perfect than the one who is hunting for an explanation. Woman explains the finite; man pursues the infinite ... woman is not supposed to know the anxiety of doubt or the agony of despair. She does not stand outside the idea, but she has it at second hand. But because woman explains the finite in this way, she is man's deepest life, but a life that is supposed to be hidden and secret, as the life of the root always is. (*EO2* 311)

The Judge praises the woman: 'she is humble, she is much closer to God than is man' (*EO2* 53); 'as surely as corruption comes from man, salvation comes from woman' (*EO2* 207), and thus admits his dependency even as he tries to nullify her status as free spirit. This is why the Judge expresses so much anger and hatred at the prospect of female emancipation (*EO2* 311–13). The woman is without the reflection necessary for doubt or despair; she can have no first hand relation to the idea. She is concerned with the finite, the bodily, the sensual, 'She is nature's mistress' (*EO2* 313). Man needs her to anchor his idealistic flights. But even as he needs her, he must seek to give birth to himself, to create his own perfect body, free from the unstable, pierced body which the woman represents.

---

[14] JP 5: 5100; Pap. I A 75.

Issues of power and control intersect once more with philosophical concerns about freedom, the self and God. But if the Judge is a flawed character, Kierkegaard is surely aware of this. In the *Postscript*, Climacus rejects the idea that, having despaired to the point at which the absolute choice emerges as a possibility, the self has the resources to restore meaning to everything: 'In despairing, I use myself to despair, and therefore I can indeed despair of everything by myself, but if I do this I cannot come back by myself' (*CUP* 258). This recalls the fate of an earlier Climacus, who doubted everything only to find despair and perdition. So must the individual reject an ethic which is complicit with the presumption of modern irony? And if so, is a way opened up to a religiosity which is not attendant upon a self-contained ethics, but which really opens the self out to utter dependency upon the Creator? As is well known, *Either/Or* ends with a sermon from a Jutland priest, who declares that **'in Relation to God We Are Always in the Wrong'** (*EO2* 339), a thought which challenges the pretensions of irony and ethics. Again, the form of the text reveals the limits of the internal point of view expressed within that text and points the way to some of the themes of Kierkegaard's edifying discourses.

The jest of faith

Some of the tensions within the discourse material have already been suggested. At the forefront of our interest here is the relationship between the action of God and the freedom of the believer. In 'Every Good and Every Perfect Gift is From Above' (1843), we are told that God is the 'the almighty Creator of heaven and earth' (*ED* 36), 'the almighty God who can crush every arrogant thought' (*ED* 38), 'the constant who remains the same' (*ED* 40), who 'penetrates everything with his eternal clarity' (*ED* 39). Over against such a one, we quickly gather, a human being must be submissive and humble. If we receive all things from his hand, without any presumption that we can contribute ourselves, then God 'makes everything a good and perfect gift for everyone who has heart enough to be humble' (*ED* 40–1). Even the idea that our faith and confession are our own work becomes laughable:

> In repentance, you receive everything from God, even the thanksgiving that you bring to him, so that even this is what the child's gift is to the eyes of the parents, a jest, a receiving of something that one has oneself given. (*ED* 46)

If the changing temporal order is to become transparent to eternity, then, as we saw in the later discourses, it must submit to the almighty will of God.

'To Need God Is A Human Being's Highest Perfection' (1844) is perhaps the most sustained exposition of this viewpoint. Kierkegaard aims to show that, far from being a sign of imperfection and regrettable weakness, need has its proper place in faith as the most ennobling factor in human life. The person accustomed to hearing that one should be contented with God's grace must be confronted with the reality of this statement, needs to hear 'the little magic formula that transformed everything' (*ED* 300), the 'momentous word ... that wounds unto death in order to save life' (ibid.). A person must overcome 'the language difference between God's eternal trustworthiness and his childish little faith' (*ED* 302). The relation to God is the inverse of the relation to earthly things, of which it is true that 'to the degree that one needs less, the more perfect one is' (*ED* 303). Ultimately, the highest is 'that a person is fully convinced that he himself is capable of nothing, nothing at all' (*ED* 307). This is intimately bound up with one's awareness of God, for 'Insofar as a person does know himself in such a way that he knows that he himself is capable of nothing at all, he does not actually become conscious in the deeper sense that God *is*' (*ED* 321).

God is given definite characteristics, as we have seen. He is the unchanging, omnipotent Creator. Nevertheless, we must ask what function such ideas play in the discourses in which they are found. In the case of 'Every Good and Every Perfect Gift', interest is quickly drawn away from God's role as Creator of the world to 'something even more marvellous – from your impatient and inconstant heart he created the imperishable substance of a quiet spirit' (*ED* 36). God's ability to do this depends upon the receptivity of the believer/reader. Indeed, the very virtues of patience and constancy which God is said to create are the conditions for reading the discourses and appropriating their message.[15] The issue is brought out most explicitly in the first 'Love Will Hide A Multitude of Sins' (1843), where Kierkegaard states 'what one sees depends upon how one sees; all observation is not just a receiving, a discovering, but also a bringing forth, and insofar as it is that, how the observer is himself constituted is indeed decisive' (*ED* 59). In the case of religious truths, this factor applies even more strictly:

> the more the object of observation belongs to the world of spirit, the more important is the way he himself is constituted in his innermost nature, because everything spiritual is appropriated only in freedom; but what is appropriated in freedom is also brought forth. (*ED* 60)

The meaning of one's spiritual existence is therefore entirely dependent upon the way in which one interprets and evaluates it. It is not decided by any appeal to matters of fact, to decidable propositions, or observable phenomena; it is a question of *how* the particular circumstances of life are valued in the context of a subject's life-view.

---

[15] For the key role of patience in the discourses, see especially 'To Gain One's Soul In Patience' (*ED* 159ff.) and 'To Preserve One's Soul In Patience'(*ED* 181ff.).

In this situation, the passivity of the believer is balanced by a necessary creative responsibility. Kierkegaard tells us that 'patience is always just as active as it is passive' (*ED* 196), and it is within this tension that the life of faith is lived. Although the highest is to confess our impotence, Kierkegaard refers (in 'Strengthening') to 'a human being's exalted destiny – to be God's co-worker' (*ED* 86); and he goes on to talk about the way in which a person craves an explanation of life's meaning:

> Not until the moment when there awakens in his soul a concern about what meaning the world has for him and he for the world, about what meaning everything within him by which he himself belongs to the world has for him and he therein for the world – only then does the inner being announce its presence in this *concern*. (ibid.)

Such concern 'is not calmed by a more detailed or more comprehensive knowledge'; it craves 'a knowledge ... that is transformed into an action the moment it is possessed' (ibid.). It signifies a lack within the self, and a need to be related to the world on other terms than through the indifferent medium of pure knowledge. It is through a 'deeper reflection that makes him *older* than the moment and lets him grasp the eternal' that a person 'assures himself that he has an actual relation to the world' (ibid.).

No event in the world can give objective evidence of the presence or will of God, for 'Any external witness from God, if such a thing could be thought of, can just as well be a deception' (*ED* 88). Concern 'craves an explanation, a witness, but of another kind' (*ED* 86). Objective knowledge is incommensurate with the interest of a free spirit in existence. The believer seems cast on his or her own resources to bring this faith to bear upon the circumstances of life. However, we are also told that 'nobody can provide this strengthening for himself; indeed, the one who receives a witness is not the one who gives it' (*ED* 98). This is crucial, for '*the witness itself is a gift from God*' (ibid.). The very creativity of the believer as a unique 'I' is conditioned by this gift of love from God, expressed in the witness. To witness is not to give objective proofs, but it is to bear testimony to the actuality of that which cannot be philosophically grounded. We will examine the nature of witnessing further in Chapter 7.

This quality of faith is well brought out in 'The Expectancy Of Faith' (1843). This text dwells upon the distinctive way in which human beings relate to time:

> this is precisely the greatness of human beings, the demonstration of their divine origin, that they are able to be occupied with this; because if there were no future nor past, then a human being would be in bondage like an animal, his head bowed to the earth, his soul captive to the service of the moment. (*ED* 17)

Again, it is the 'moment' which humans should transcend. In this context, the moment is the sign of a life dispersed into discrete points of time, an unthinking life unable to transcend the particularity of here and now. Note that the divinity of human existence signifies its consciously *temporal* nature, a startling subversion of the discourses' constant appeal to the eternal as the true basis for human life.

We are told of the risks to which this temporal consciousness exposes us. Time gives our life an intrinsic and disturbing impermanence and uncertainty. What is most striking, however, is that time is so disturbing, not because it is an objective something over against us, but because it is constitutive of our very being:

> He who battles with the future has a more dangerous enemy; he cannot remain ignorant of himself, since he is battling with himself. The future is not; it borrows its power from him himself, and when it has tricked him out of that it presents itself externally as the enemy he has to encounter. (*ED* 18)

The objective, external nature of the future is an illusion, created out of our own anxious projection. The 'future' really seems to signify an openness of the self to possibility, which cannot be closed however much knowledge or power we acquire, because it is inherent in the self's nature. So what can we do? Kierkegaard advocates casting one's cares upon the eternal: 'By the eternal, one can conquer the future, because the eternal is the ground of the future, and therefore through it the future can be fathomed' (*ED* 19). One who expects an eternal victory cannot be defeated by any possibility which life in time may throw at him. Eternity is a wholly different quality, through faith in which one gains an unshakeable perspective on human life.

However, eternity is not a state which any existing person can attain, Indeed, the divinity of being human depends on its time-bound freedom. And this is why it is not the *attainment* of eternity which is decisive, but the *expectation* of it. Expectation itself is the victory (*ED* 24). Nothing that actually happens can prove or deny faith (*ED* 26). As Kierkegaard puts it, 'Time can neither substantiate nor refute it, because faith expects an eternity' (*ED* 27).

The expectation of eternity is of a wholly other order than that of knowing. In this life, freed from servility to momentary immediacy, we are left with the witness of another moment, in which time and eternity meet as lovers at a tryst: 'Now we are separated; we do not see each other every day, but we meet secretly in the victorious moment of faithful expectancy' (*ED* 26). There is no escaping the moment; it must, however, be transfigured beyond its immediate givenness. It is the presence of eternity, but it is a *secret* presence within an overarching separation and absence. It seems to transcend human temporality, by taking us out of ourselves, so to speak; but it simultaneously reaffirms the inescapability of time, for it is a moment which passes.

This discourse recalls passages in the *Postscript*. Climacus is well aware that a human being cannot claim an eternal standpoint. This lies at the basis of his attack on systematic method in philosophy. However, this causes him to make a revealing statement: 'For an existing person, is not eternity not eternity but the future, whereas eternity is eternity only for the Eternal, who is not in a process of becoming?' (*CUP* 306). If eternity is not eternity, then how can it be recognized as such? If its appearance in time is thoroughly temporal, then is there any more to eternity than a particular way of facing the future, which is valid on grounds wholly internal to human religious faith? But notice the way in which Climacus expresses the same thought slightly later:

> But where everything is in a process of becoming, where only so much of the eternal is present that it can have a constraining effect in the passionate decision, where the *eternal* relates itself as the *future* to the *person in a process of becoming* – there the absolute disjunction lies. (*CUP* 307)

This 'absolute disjunction' is what resists all attempts to comprehend the eternal as no more than an aspect of time, and points to the 'difference of language' between God and humanity. Climacus wishes to preserve the interest and pathos of faith; just when we think we may have a viable immanent reading of his transcendent concepts, he slips in a warning: that we must above all respect the absolute difference between time and eternity, God and humanity. As the discourse seeks to keep us from the presumption of having understood the eternal, so Climacus protests against the transcendental perspective which would assign time and eternity to their respective places *within* human consciousness.

This rhetorical resistance to closure or systematization derives from an analysis of the irreducible complexity and other-relatedness of consciousness as it comes to birth in language. In *De Omnibus Dubitandum Est*, we found that consciousness is a contradiction, structured by the collision of real and ideal in language. The discourse 'To Gain One's Soul In Patience' (1843) links up with this by examining the peculiar dialectic of the self's appropriation of its own nature.

The soul, Kierkegaard claims, must be acquired; it is not an immediately given presupposition of human life. However, in order for anything to be acquired at all, then the soul must be possessed as a presupposition (*ED* 162–3). The soul cannot grasp itself in a total self-reflection. Consciousness (for which the soul seems to stand) appears to presuppose itself – and this, according to Kierkegaard, is a 'self-contradiction' (*ED* 163). This contradiction lies in the relation between time and eternity (real and ideal). As language is presupposed by philosophy, so this time–eternity relationship is presupposed by any notion of selfhood. The soul is derivative, opened out onto an actuality which it cannot grasp. The eternal is wholly other, for 'In the eternal there is no such self-contradiction, but not because it, like the temporal, either is or is not, but because it is' (ibid.). The eternal simply 'is' – an order of actuality which we cannot comprehend or represent, but which is constitutive of our very selfhood: 'The soul is the contradiction of the temporal and the eternal, and here, therefore, the same thing can be possessed and the same thing gained and at the same time' (ibid.).

If one wishes to gain one's soul, one must face the resistance of worldly values, which centre on the possession of things external to oneself. In this struggle, the significance of the soul is revealed in its starkest form:

> However, if he wants to gain his soul, he must let this resistance become more and more pronounced and in so doing gain his soul, for his soul was this very difference: it was the infinity in the life of the world in its difference from itself. (*ED* 165)

The soul, human existence in its spiritual expression, is *difference itself*. Not only that, but, in almost Fichtean terms, Kierkegaard names the soul as the site wherein the infinite differs from itself. Here, the division between time and eternity is both within the dialectic of the self and that which forever ruptures the self's autonomy and completeness. The task is not to become eternal, but to express the contradiction which is the inescapable condition of human life. For the soul, 'wanting to express the contradiction within itself is precisely what makes it what it is' (*ED* 166). Kierkegaard speaks of God being the true possessor of the soul (ibid.), for neither the world nor the individual can truly be said to possess it. God, 'the eternal being' (ibid.), is possessor by default; but this God is not encountered through objective knowledge, but as the self-differing source of all difference, the irreducible, unobjectifiable negativity which opens temporality to an immeasurable standard of judgement.

Any external good is a dubious possession, Kierkegaard argues, because it is imperfect and unreliable. Any means to an external end is just as dubious, because it bears only an accidental relation to that end. The stick the walker carries serves a purpose only as long as it aids his walking. If it ceases to do so, it can be thrown away and the purpose is served by another means. With the soul it is different, for 'the condition that made possible the gaining of the soul was precisely the possession of the soul' (*ED* 168). Patience, the virtue by which one gains the soul, is not a means to an end, but the end itself, and thus Kierkegaard can say 'The perfect, however, can be gained with full certainty, because it can be gained only by coming into existence within its own presupposition' (*ED* 169).

The logic of acquiring one's soul follows the contradictory course mapped out for it at the start of the discourse. The phrase 'to gain one's soul in patience' is revealed as 'a redoubling repetition [en fordoblende Gjentagelse]' (ibid.).

Repetition, we might recall, is the true transcendence (*CA* 21), not the illusory claim to have direct access to the supernatural, or an eternal viewpoint over world history. It is a transcendence that is part of the fabric of human existence and language. Kierkegaard says of gaining one's soul that 'it takes place much as the words proceed with their communication – that is, it is all a repetition' (*ED* 170). Repetition, in the sense we came across in *Johannes Climacus*, is intrinsic to the sign and to language (see Chapter 3 above). It renders the full presence of the sign to its meaning impossible. Human existence, and its religious appropriation as a thing of ultimate value, runs in the same groove. Its goal is not an eternity of pure presence, but a patient expression – a repetition – of the contradictions of time and eternity which will free it from selfish craving and enslavement to external goods. Only in *this* sense does the act of enunciation coincide with what is enunciated, because the religious communication reduplicates the soul's struggle to express the eternal in time. The locus of the God-relationship is the soul's existential striving, a striving solicited by the indirect appeal of the discourse.

The discourse thus repeats the fragmentary and ambiguous nature of all communication. It can be ignored or misunderstood, it can remain impotent to move its reader to action. One of the keys to understanding the role of the discourses is an awareness of this inevitably tense complicity between their aim and the linguistic medium which they must employ. Kierkegaard shows his awareness of this issue in the prefaces to the various collections of discourses. Here, the reader is oriented in his or her mode of reading in such a way that the prefaces do not stand in an arbitrary, external relationship to the following text, but are part of the intrinsic nature of the communication.[16] In fact, Kierkegaard uses the prefaces to dramatize his *loss* of authorial control. The book is sent out on a journey, subject to all the chances and caprices of the world (*ED* 5). It is a messenger that never returns home; and Kierkegaard himself 'continually comes to his reader only to bid him farewell' (*ED* 295). He wishes 'to be as one absent on a journey' (*ED* 179), he 'continually desires only to be forgotten' (*ED* 231). The author is absent, and the text must make its own way.

Where does it go? Here Kierkegaard gives his directions, specifying his ideal of a happy rendezvous with a sympathetic reader. The book travels:

> until it finds what it is seeking, that favorably disposed person who reads aloud to himself what I write in stillness, who with his voice breaks the spell on the letters. with his voice summons forth what the mute letters have on their lips. (*ED* 53)

---

[16] Kierkegaard anticipates in literary practice Derrida's famous argument that prefaces insinuate themselves into the main body of a text, occupying a curious border territory in which the author asserts his control over his text, whilst implicitly admitting that it cannot stand by itself. See Derrida, *Dissemination*, trans. Johnson (London: Athlone, 1981), 'Outwork', pp. 1–59.

The reader must give life and breath to the dead letter of writing. Kierkegaard wishes to place his reader in the concrete situation of a listener at an oration. Speech, it seems, has a power and authority which writing cannot have. So the reader must read aloud; but she reads aloud to *herself*. The reader animates the text, because only in the act of giving one's interest and attention to it can the act of communication be consummated. And this transfers a tremendous responsibility to the reader. The fiction of the spoken word only seals this, for it simply heightens one's awareness that no author or speaker is really present. The reader it is who 'sanctifies the gift, gives it meaning, and transforms it into much' (*ED* 107). The book does not stand by itself, it invites a creative rendering through the reader's self-activity. The book, like the mute demonic, is 'inclosed in itself [indesluttet i sig selv]' (*ED* 231). It is the reader who 'transforms the discourse [Talen] into a conversation [Samtalen]' (ibid.) and 'accomplishes the great work of letting the perishability of the discourse arise in imperishability' (ibid.).

The text cannot impose a preordained meaning upon the reader. The author must renounce such dreams of control, and allow the recipient to interpret his words. These words can have no systematic finality. To be sure, Kierkegaard's preference for the spoken word seems to indicate a mistrust of writing; but the irony is that speech itself is no greater guarantee of the final, definitive meaning of any utterance. Meaning is made in the relation of reader to words, and through the unspecifiable contexts in which the two may meet. The discourses are revealed as being, in this sense, every bit as 'indirect' as their pseudonymous siblings.

It should come as no surprise that Kierkegaard uses his prefaces in this way, since he once wrote a book consisting of nothing but prefaces as a humorous antidote to systematizing pretensions. In the 1844 work *Prefaces*, by Nicolaus Notabene, he examines the question of the preface itself: 'In relation to the book, the preface is an insignificance', he says. (SV 5: 197).[17] Such is its apparently accidental character that prefaces have taken many different forms over the centuries. However:

> In recent scholarship [Videnskab] the preface has received its mortal wound ... for when one begins the book with its subject matter [Sagen] and the system with nothing, it is thought that there is nothing left to say in a preface. (198)

Notabene, however, welcomes this situation as an opportunity. He himself could never get to finish a book. Now there is a 'bill of divorce', a 'breach [Brud]' (ibid.) between preface and book, and 'the emancipated preface' (159)

---

[17] All translations from *Prefaces* are my own. This work lends itself to the kind of deconstructive reading practised by S. Agacinski in *Aparté: Deaths and Conceptions of Søren Kierkegaard* (Tallahassee: Florida University Press, 1988), pp. 218ff.

can go its own way. Notabene dryly remarks that 'here is a phenomenon which points to a deeper ground' (198).

This deeper ground is no less than the impossibility of the system's ridiculous pretension, and thus the impossibility of the book itself as the closed repository of a fixed meaning.[18] The ironic celebration of the preface is an affirmation of what resists closure. Writing a preface, says Notabene, is, amongst many other things, like spitting out of a window (199): a kind of arbitrary, hit-and-miss production. It points to the rupture and breach at the heart of all textual production. It is an open space, a window which opens out the possibility of a creative relationship between reader and text. Its own deeper ground is the breach which makes language and selfhood possible at all, which resists comprehension and demands repetition.

The spacing of existence

Kierkegaard's various texts thus constitute a critique of totalizing visions, be they ironic, ethical or religious. They reject a certain form of reflection which annuls the otherness of God – and that means certain forms of realism as well as anti-realism. The realism which makes God a knowable object has also reduced his otherness. This kind of realism has a shadow side – the idealism which makes God into a product of the objectifying thought which knows him. The presentation of God as object can easily be interpreted as the invention of God by imaginative projection.

Reflection, as we saw previously, is thought conceived as a disinterested combination of possibilities, as opposed to the tensed, committed nature of consciousness. It is the over-emphasis on thought as reflection at the expense of actual existence which leads the systematic philosopher astray. As Climacus puts it in the *Postscript*, the problem is that reflection abrogates the contradictory poles of existence, because it cannot think the specifically *temporal* nature of human life: 'since all thinking is eternal, the difficulty is for the existing person. Existence, like motion, is a very difficult matter to handle. If I think it, I cancel it, and then I do not think it' (*CUP* 309). In fact, this is the very contradiction which lies at the root of human consciousness, between the ideality of thought (and, indeed, language) and the reality or particularity of the individual. Both are indispensable for human freedom to emerge, because only through the contradiction is a transcendence of unthinking immediacy possible.

The danger is that the contradiction is given an illusory resolution in thought alone. Climacus argues that 'Existence is always the particular; the

---

[18] See J. Derrida, *Writing and Difference* (London: Routledge, 1978), 'Edmund Jabès and the Question of the Book', pp. 64–78.

abstract does not *exist*. To conclude from this that the abstract does not have reality [Realitet] is a misunderstanding' (*CUP* 330). Like Locke and Schelling before him, Climacus asserts the irreducible particularity of existence, which cannot be comprehended by abstract essences and universals. It is not that abstraction does not have its proper reality, but that it must not be confused with actuality, in which the real (particular) and the ideal (essence) hold together in a precarious and partial union.

Existence remains stubbornly particular, finite, temporal, differentiated; so any claim to transcend it by means of pure thought is cut off from the very conditions which make such a claim possible. Indeed, 'the idea that pure thinking is supposed to be the positive truth for an existing person is scepticism, because this positivity is chimerical' (*CUP* 310). This is closely related to Kierkegaard's earlier attacks on Fichte and the ironists. Thought thinking itself is a narcissistic play divorced from that engagement with otherness which existence presupposes:

> When thinking turns toward itself in order to think about itself, there emerges, as we know, a scepticism ... of which the source is that thinking selfishly wants to think itself instead of serving by thinking something. (*CUP* 335)

Climacus goes as far as to say that 'All scepticism is a kind of idealism' (*CUP* 352). Idealism's claim to begin without presuppositions and to comprehend everything immanently, as the self-development of spirit, actually leads one to distrust all external constraints upon thought. When it becomes clear that idealism fails to account for its own starting point, not least the language it uses, a thoroughgoing scepticism about objective truth can arise.

The construction of a system of thought cannot, therefore, proceed without presuppositions. But this means that no system is possible at all, because it will never be brought to a conclusion. Something – the possibility of its own origin – will always elude it, and this is fatal to pure systematic endeavour:

> if the conclusion is lacking at the end, it is also lacking at the beginning. This should therefore have been said at the beginning. But if the conclusion is lacking at the beginning, this means that there is no system. (*CUP* 13)

Climacus parodies the scholar caught in 'the parenthesis of his labor', who forgets 'the decisive dialectical *claudatur* [let it be closed]' (*CUP* 28). Closure is at once the indispensable condition and the unattainable dream of the system.

It is this which leads Climacus to his well-known contention that '*(a) a logical system can be given; (b) but a system of existence cannot be given*' (*CUP* 109). Logic corresponds to the 'eternal' nature of thought, to its timeless formal rules.[19] It has an analytic and classificatory task; it cannot be called upon to yield new information about the world, to add to our store of facts. We might compare the relation it has to reality to that between the grammar of a language and the utterances made in that language. The difference is that logic has a universal validity which a particular grammar does not, but it is nevertheless similar in being a set of rules rather than a set of propositions. Thus, any system created out of the self-evident resources of logic alone cannot begin to comprehend the givenness of actuality, because it will be merely tautologous. Its application to reality is brought about by an unaccountable leap, for 'The beginning of the system that begins with the immediate *is then itself achieved through reflection*' (*CUP* 112). The system of logic must try to begin with immediacy, that presuppositionless state of self-evident certainty, because only then can it stave off questions as to the arbitrariness of its procedure. Unfortunately, pure immediacy cannot be had; it is abrogated even as it is thought, and our concept of immediacy is itself a product of reflection. Climacus declares that 'a logical system must not boast of an absolute beginning, because such a beginning is just like pure being, a pure chimera' (ibid.). Reflection can pretend to absoluteness, only if the thinker forgets that there is no pure reflection apart from consciousness. Reflection can neither account for itself nor bring itself to a conclusion: 'Reflection has the notable quality of being infinite. But being infinite must in any case mean that it cannot stop of its own accord, because in stopping itself it indeed uses itself' (ibid.). As *De Omnibus* made clear, reflection's inability to engage with reality is the source of a corrosive, nihilistic doubt, which cannot be resolved by reflection itself.

In fact, reflection and doubt have an interesting and ambiguous relationship to faith. In the edifying discourse 'Every Good Gift And Every Perfect Gift Is From Above' (1843), doubt is that which disturbs the state of Paradise, in which, had it lasted, 'the blessedness of heaven would have enveloped everything' (*ED* 126). Then, 'heaven would be earth, and everything would be fulfilled' (ibid.). All would be perfect peace; words would have their true meaning 'for Adam did indeed give the proper name to everything as it truly is' (ibid.). But this is also a curiously inhuman vision. The distinction between good and evil would not exist, and 'no one would have asked *where* everything came *from*' (ibid.). All would go on in unthinking banality, for 'the gift offered itself in such a way that receiving it did not arouse questions about the giver' (ibid.). Into this context knowledge intrudes, and with it doubt. Word and thing, gift and giver could be set apart by reflection, their immediate connection severed. Paradise was closed to humanity, and a new life of toil and distress opened up.

---

[19] Kierkegaard's rejection of Hegelian logic was influenced by his reading of Trendlenburg. See the latter's *Logische Untersuchungen*, I–II, (Berlin, 1840).

The ambiguity lies in the fact that, without reflection, distinctive human existence, goodness, truth and faith would not be possible. Only through the separation is the relationship to God made possible; only then is language really made possible, for Adam's direct naming of the essence of things could not function as a language unless iterability and therefore the separation of sign and signified were always inherent within it. This suggests that Kierkegaard's vision of Eden is no more than a rhetorical device to make us appreciate the nature of human existence as it must be. But it also alerts us to the fact that reflection alone cannot free itself from the doubt that attends it. There must be a relation to something other: 'Doubt cannot be fought with its own weapons. Thought cannot find its way to the good, 'since there is no way to it, but every good and every perfect gift comes *down* from above' (*ED* 135). Reflection fuels doubt, and can be settled only by some form of faithful resolution, rather than any process of reasoning: 'If the demonstration could be made in the way that doubt demands, then doubt could not be halted any more than sickness can be arrested by the remedy the sickness itself requests' (ibid.). The condition for overcoming doubt must be given by God himself (*ED* 136).

We can follow a clear line of argument in Kierkegaard's texts. Reflection goes astray if it attempts to encompass everything, to resolve all doubt and attain an absolute standpoint, because reflection is derivative and conditioned. The problems thrown up by reflection can only be resolved in an existential way, and not by greater amounts of knowledge. As Climacus states, 'reflection can be stopped only by a leap' (*CUP* 115), by an incommensurable resolve: 'the leap is the most decisive protest against the inverse operation of the method' (*CUP* 105). The system is the denial of the leap, and thus the denial of faith: 'every system must be pantheistic simply because of the conclusiveness' (*CUP* 122).

Ultimately, the system denies any real alterity, and Climacus characterizes it in terms very reminiscent of Fichte: 'The systematic idea is subject-object, the unity of thinking and being; existence, on the other hand, is precisely the separation ... existence does space and has spaced subject from object, thought from being' (*CUP* 123). Existence is a spacing and must not be subject to illusory conclusions; in a similar fashion, a text can only have meaning if the spacing between words and things, and between words and words is respected. The text is inevitably fragmentary, differentiated, irreducible to summarizing propositions.[20] In his 'First and Last Declaration', appended to the *Postscript*, Kierkegaard refers to 'the original text [Urskrift] of individual human-existence relationships' (*CUP* 630), and this form of words is not accidental. Existence can be understood through the analogy of

---

[20] Note Climacus' indignation at a German review of *Fragments*, whose 'didactic' summary of the book misses entirely the significance of its indirect form (*CUP* 274ff.n.).

linguistic productions, not least because *human* existence is made possible in and through language's role in consciousness. A fragmentary text can use language to subvert the pretensions of the scholar, whose aim seems to be 'to become a book or an objective something' (*CUP* 93). The 'book' corresponds to closure, to the self-contained exposition of truth; but language will not tolerate such an intrinsically questionable undertaking.

Actuality, like consciousness, has its being only in the space opened up by a relation between different qualities:

> Actuality is an *inter-esse* between thinking and being in the hypothetical unity of abstraction ... Actuality, existence, is the dialectical element in a trilogy, the beginning and end of which cannot be for an existing person, who *qua* existing person is in the dialectical element. Abstraction merges [slutter ... sammen] the trilogy. (*CUP* 314–15)

Abstract thought imposes a false closure upon the triadic, relational structure of actuality. Existence holds the gap between thought and being open. And this inevitably has consequences for Climacus' idea of truth. At the start of the *Postscript*, he states that 'the issue is not about the truth of Christianity but about the individual's relation to Christianity' (*CUP* 15); but as the work proceeds, we come to suspect that this is not an accidental self-limitation on Climacus' part, but an essential aspect of his interpretation of Christian truth. As he develops his attack on the system, he declares:

> Christianity therefore protests against all objectivity; it wants the subject to be infinitely concerned about himself. What it asks about is the subjectivity; the truth of Christianity, if it is at all, is only in this; objectively, it is not at all. (*CUP* 130)

In other words, the truth of Christianity is only a question for the concerned individual, and it is not susceptible to 'objective' methods.

It is here that the individual is called to a responsibility which is ethical of a kind. This ethics exceeds the boundaries of the Judge's absolute choice, because it witnesses to an irreducible alterity and lack of self-mastery: 'ethics looks with a suspicious eye at all world-historical knowledge' (*CUP* 134). Such knowledge is quantitative, it eliminates subjectivity and passion. The 'truly enthusiastic ethical individuality, moved in earnestness, elevated in the holy jest of divine madness' unites the urgency and objective uncertainty of this responsibility, which no external result or outcome can underwrite (*CUP* 136). There can be no reduction of this responsibility through objective reflection. But this responsibility is not that of creating the idea of God from 'subjective' ideals. Kierkegaard does not advocate anti-realism because it is as totalizing as its idealist counterpart. To appreciate why this is so, we must examine further the ways in which objectivity and subjectivity are used in the *Postscript*.

Subjectivity and objectivity: horns of a dilemma

Climacus discusses the issue at most length in the chapter entitled 'Subjective Truth, Inwardness: Truth is Subjectivity'. He begins with a consideration of the classical definition of truth as a correspondence between thought and reality:

> Whether truth is defined more empirically as the agreement of thinking with being or more idealistically as the agreement of being with thinking, the point in each case is to pay scrupulous attention to what is understood by being ... If, in the two definitions given, being is understood as empirical being, then truth itself is transformed into a *desideratum* and everything is placed in the process of becoming, because the empirical object is not finished, and the existing knowing spirit is itself in the process of becoming. (*CUP* 189)

The point is familiar enough to us now. As existence necessarily resists all final conceptualization, so absolute truth must be ever elusive. There is simply no standpoint from which an absolute truth could be proclaimed, and no language in which it could self-evidently be communicated. Doubt is always possible, because the act of enunciating a *cognitive* truth is always distinguishable from the truth itself. The only way in which self-evidence can be produced, as we have pointed out, is when truth is made abstract. Abstract truth is finished, because it is a tautology – 'thinking and being signify one and the same' (*CUP* 190).

For an existing individual, truth must be subjective in Climacus' sense. If any truth which is not abstract lacks self-evidence, the onus is upon the recipient of that truth to resolve to accept it:

> When for the existing spirit *qua* existing there is a question about truth, that abstract reduplication of truth recurs; but existence itself ... holds the two factors [Momenter] apart, one from the other, and reflection shows two relations. To objective reflection, truth becomes something objective, an object, and the point is to disregard the subject. To subjective reflection, truth becomes appropriation, inwardness, subjectivity, and the point is to immerse oneself, existing, in subjectivity. (*CUP* 191–2)

Abstract reduplication – the tautology of the logical system – gives way to another form of reduplication, in which the truth at issue has to be *made true* for the individual. In determining the truth of anything which is not tautologous, the subject's role in constituting it as the truth cannot be ignored:

> *When the question about truth is asked subjectively, the individual's relation is reflected upon subjectively. If only the how of this relation is in truth, the individual is in truth, even if he in this way were to relate himself to untruth.* (*CUP* 199)

The truth is a relation in which the subject's role is not a contingent externality, but an indispensable condition. As Climacus puts it, '*Objectively the emphasis is on **what** is said; subjectively the emphasis is on **how** it is said*' (*CUP* 202).

Is truth then simply reduced to rhetoric, or made to serve the whim of the subject? Climacus talks of relating to 'untruth' (however 'truly' one might relate to it) in a way which implies that there is some ultimate standpoint from which it can be judged that some statements about reality are truer than others. However, no such standpoint seems to be available to us – so how can Climacus justify his language? With regard to Christianity, belief in God seems to be entirely identical with a quality of the believer's inward attitude: 'Objectively, what is reflected upon is that this is the true God; subjectively, that the individual relates himself to a something *in such a way* that his relation is in truth a God-relation' (*CUP* 199). There does not appear to be any need for further reference to extra-subjective matters of fact to justify the believer's position. Religious truth in particular seems to elude any empirical confirmation or disconfirmation.

Does this amount to religious subjectivism? Those commentators who think not[21] point out that, in principle, it is possible to relate oneself to the (objectively) true God, but that one must go about this subjectively, that is, one must appropriate one's beliefs in an inward way, on the basis of a passionate decision of faith rather than on objective evidences. The underlying argument is that the subjectivity of the method or the way does not preclude the objectivity of the goal, that is, the extra-human reality of God. This argument has much to commend it. After all, if truth is relational, as we have suggested, subjectivism or anti-realism would seem to represent another form of closure. That is, they would identify the 'truth' of religious language with the sincerity or degree of passion with which it is held, and would thus cut it off from the relation to the irreducible otherness of God which gives it its pathos. As C. S. Evans says, if faith is a risk for Kierkegaard, then its disconfirmation must be possible; if it cannot be 'objectively' wrong (as subjectivism seems to hold) then it cannot be a risk.[22] Consider Climacus'

---

[21] For examples of this kind of argument, see Patrick Gardiner, *Kierkegaard* (Oxford: Oxford University Press, 1988), pp. 91ff.; Gregor Malantschuk, *Kierkegaard's Thought* (Princeton, NJ: Princeton University Press, 1971), p. 306; Stephen Crites, *In the Twilight of Christendom* (Chambersburg, Pa.: AAR, 1972), pp. 24ff.; L. Mackey, *Kierkegaard: A Kind of Poet* (Philadelphia: University of Pennsylvania Press, 1971), p. 173; C. S. Evans, 'Kierkegaard on Subjective Truth. Is God an Ethical Fiction?', *International Journal for Philosophy of Religion* 7 (1976), pp. 288–99; Mark C. Taylor, *Kierkegaard's Pseudonymous Authorship: A Study of Time and Self* (Princeton, NJ: Princeton University Press, 1975), pp. 46ff; Louis Dupré, *Kierkegaard as Theologian* (London and New York: Sheed and Ward, 1963), pp. 124ff. Dupré argues that it is precisely God's objective transcendence which requires a subjective response: 'Only by the abandonment of all objectivity does our relationship with God become truly objective' (p. 130).

[22] Evans, *Kierkegaard*, pp. 293–4.

definition of truth: '*An objective uncertainty, held fast through appropriation with the most passionate inwardness, is the truth*, the highest truth there is for an *existing* person' (*CUP* 203). He goes on to say that 'Faith is the contradiction between the infinite passion of inwardness and the objective uncertainty' (*CUP* 204). Certainly, there is a world of difference between a subjective invention and an 'objective uncertainty', and without the resistance of the object to subjective comprehension, the passion of faith would not exist.

This position also seems to make sense of the famous parable of the idol-worshipper:

> If someone who lives in the midst of Christianity enters, with knowledge of the true idea of god, the house of God, the house of the true God, and prays, but prays in untruth, and if someone lives in an idolatrous land but prays with all the passion of infinity, although his eyes are resting on the image of an idol – where, then, is there more truth? The one prays in truth to God although he is worshipping an idol, the other prays in untruth to the true God and is therefore in truth worshipping an idol. (*CUP* 201)

It is not that God is not 'objective' (extra-human), but that he cannot be attained or comprehended by objective (idealist) reflection. Climacus can distinguish between the true God and the idol, whilst maintaining that only a proper subjective, inward passion will really establish one in a relation to the former. Interest makes the relation to God possible,[23] it does not supplant it with a projection of its own making:

> With the infinite, passionate interest in his eternal happiness, the subjective individual is at the extreme point of his exertion, at the extreme point, not where there is no object, (an imperfect and undialectical distinction) but where God is negatively present in the subjectivity that with this interest is the form of the eternal happiness. (*CUP* 53)

This appears to be clear evidence that the *Postscript* does not advocate subjectivism, or any view which implies that God's reality is *dependent* upon human belief. Anti-realism would seem to represent an 'undialectical' closure of the subject from the ultimate relation to a God who remains other than human.

Nevertheless, it remains possible for an anti-realist interpretation of Climacus' position to be put forward. As we have pointed out, it is difficult to see what grounds Climacus could claim for distinguishing the true God from the false. The only criterion he gives is subjective: the quality of the believer's inward passion. He talks of 'the passion of infinity', as if this passion could only

---

[23] Cf. E. McClane, 'Kierkegaard and Subjectivity', *International Journal for Philosophy of Religion* 8 (1977): 'Kierkegaard felt it was not primarily cognition ... but *interest* ... that finally establishes the relation to the "other"' (214).

be appropriate to one object; indeed, he claims that to take any other object for faith than the infinite God is an absurd fanaticism: 'To be infinitely interested in relation to that which at its maximum always remains only an approximation is a self contradiction and thus is comical. If passion is posited nevertheless, zealotism ensues' (*CUP* 31). Objectively, however, all the claims of Christianity can be given no more than the status of approximations. No evidence can fully justify a religious claim, because no finite evidence is commensurable with the eternal happiness which religion promises. What is more, Climacus seems to call on wholly different criteria for the validity of faith: 'Since the questioner specifically emphasizes that he is an existing person, the way to be commended is naturally the one that especially accentuates what it means to exist' (*CUP* 193). So if the only apparent justification of religious belief and language lies in its capacity to intensify the individual's passionate interest in existence, does it stand in any need of any further underpinning with a realist doctrine of God?

Consider the ultimate intensification of faith – the 'absurd' belief that, in Christ, God has become an existing human being:

> Subjectivity is truth. The paradox came into existence through the relating of the eternal, essential truth to the existing person. Let us now go further; let us assume that the eternal, essential truth is itself the paradox. How does the paradox emerge? By placing the eternal, essential truth together with the existing ... The eternal truth has come into existence in time. That is the paradox. (*CUP* 209)

Here, the 'passion of infinity' is given a specific form. It is no longer the relation of the individual in time to eternal truth; it is the paradoxical faith in the incarnation of eternal truth in time. But Climacus goes on to say that 'Existence cannot be accentuated more sharply than it has been here' (ibid.). The implication is that Christianity is to be commended on the basis of its intensification of the fundamental dialectic. Its proclamation of the paradox could be no more than a reflection, in its most extreme form, of the paradoxical contradiction involved in all existing, between reality and ideality, immediate givenness and transcendent freedom. The validity of Christian belief could be argued for purely on the grounds that it heightens our appreciation of the precarious nature of existence in time.[24]

---

[24] Indeed, L. Pojman, in 'Kierkegaard on Justification of Belief', *International Journal for Philosophy of Religion* 8 (1977), has contended precisely that there *is* a rational argument for the truth of Christianity in the *Postscript*, in which Christian faith in the absurd fits the criteria for the most passionate interest in existence which objective uncertainty about the meaning of life requires. However, he goes on to maintain that, for Kierkegaard, the truth is objective, and that there is a 'harmonious fit between the objective truth and the way of appropriating that truth, without which the truth cannot really be experienced' (89). Absurdity becomes the only 'logical' option. Unfortunately, as Pojman points out, once this is accepted, it becomes absurd to *reject* Christianity, so Anti-Christianity becomes the highest truth, and so on *ad infinitum*. This hints at the aporias in Kierkegaard's texts which we are exploring more fully.

The problem with this anti-realist interpretation is that it fails to recognize that the passion of infinity – like Levinas' idea of infinity – opens the self out of its inclosed 'subjectivity'. It inaugurates a different form of subjectivity that is constituted by a passionate relationship to an Other who is not contained or produced within it. From the fact that Climacus denies any objective knowledge or evidence of God, it does not follow that 'God' is an idea produced by the human psyche.

As a token of this, we need to keep in mind the distinction between the 'paradox' that an existing individual is related in time to the eternal truth, and the Absolute Paradox of the God-Man in time[25] – and that the latter can in no way be equated with any aspect of ordinary human existence. However much Christianity emphasizes subjective appropriation, the Christian 'how' of faith cannot be the appropriation of *any* content: 'Being a Christian is defined not by the "what" of Christianity but by the "how" of the Christian. The "how" can fit only one thing, the absolute paradox' (*CUP* 610). Commenting on this passage in the journal of 1849, Kierkegaard writes that Climacus should not be misunderstood when he advocates a subjective approach, since:

> there is a How with the characteristic that when the How is scrupulously rendered, the What is also given, that this is the How of 'faith'. Right here, at its very maximum, inwardness is shown to be objectivity. (JP 4: 4550; Pap. X(2) A 299)

It seems, then, that 'only the Truth can be the object of that kind of belief which we call "faith"'[26] and that Kierkegaard is at great pains to distance himself from any subjectivist reduction of faith or its object.

Of course, the situation is far from simple. Read differently, for instance, even this remark in the journal could amount to saying that the objectivity of the 'what' is *produced* by the subject in his or her maximum passion of intensity.[27] But I would hold that this does violence to Kierkegaard's words and the subtlety of what he is trying to say. It seems incontrovertible that anti-realism in its strongest form – that we *create* all order and meaning through our conceptual schemes – would be an undialectical form of totalizing reflection for Kierkegaard. The difficulty arises, of course, when we try to specify just how the self does then relate to God. It is not as though we could settle the question by appeal to accepted norms of what constitutes the 'reality' or 'objectivity' of God, because it is precisely these concepts and judgements which are at issue in Kierkegaard's own texts.

Notice how Climacus writes of the way in which, in the freedom of the believer's act of worship and commitment, God *comes into existence*: 'But

---

[25] As Heywood-Thomas makes clear in *Subjectivity and Paradox* (Oxford: Blackwell, 1957).
[26] Jeremy Walker, 'Kierkegaard's Concept of Truthfulness', *Inquiry* 12 (1969), p. 213.
[27] This is how Don Cupitt interprets it in *The World to Come* (London: SCM, 1982), p. 47.

freedom, that is the wonderful lamp. When a person rubs it with ethical passion, God comes into existence for him' (*CUP* 138). On the surface, this looks like a potentially anti-realist statement. However, to interpret it in this way would ignore two things. Firstly, Climacus has already exclaimed 'How highly embarrassing to be Creator if it turned out that God came to need the creature' (*CUP* 136). Secondly, Climacus says that the spirit invoked by the lamp is not the servant of the believer, but his or her Lord. And it is precisely 'God's freedom' which resists philosophical construal of the immanent necessity of world-history (*CUP* 157). The freedom of God breaches a speculative system of necessity *and* any interpretation of faith which would make it no more than a human creation.

What is at issue in Climacus' statement is the *mode* in which God is encountered. That mode is ethical, passionate, interested. The eternal God must come into existence for the believer – a paradoxical event which is possible only because human existence and language already presuppose the collision of real and ideal, time and eternity. Human existence and language are made possible by a prior paradoxical relationship which ruptures self-contained reason and creates the possibility for relating to the transcendent reality of God. That reality is encountered only ethically, because it is a relationship to a God who is hidden, free and creative. The 'how' of faith must answer to the 'how' of God's manifestation. Thus, Kierkegaard can write in the *Journals*:

> God himself is this: *how* one involves oneself with Him. As far as physical and external objects are concerned, the object is something else than the mode: there are many modes. In respect to *God*, the *how* is the what. He who does not involve himself with God in the mode of absolute devotion does not become involved with God. (JP 1405)

Ethical realism refuses to reduce the reality of God to that of a brute object among objects in the universe, but it also refuses to reduce God to the status of a subjective fiction – God demands absolute devotion. God is related to otherwise, and only in this relationship is the nature of his 'reality' communicated.

The question thus remains whether the inextricable interdependence of 'how' and 'what' might not fundamentally alter the nature of both, in ways which binary oppositions between 'subjectivity' and 'objectivity', 'reality' and 'fiction' cannot capture. What *kind* of 'objectivity' can only be met and recognized in a corresponding 'subjectivity'? We recall that Climacus resists any undialectical closure of the subject's existence which would leave out the object of faith (*CUP* 53). But this does not mean that God can simply be classified as an 'object', for God is not an object among other objects in the world. Indeed, 'God is a subject and hence only for subjectivity in inwardness' (*CUP* 200). Not only this, but his presence has the peculiar characteristic that it is *negative*. It is not as the simple presence of an object to a subject, nor even of a subject to a subject, that God is recognized. It is this indirect and ambiguous presence in absence which we must explore.

Negative presence

God is negatively present in the faith of the believer (*CUP* 53). This faith has its own proper certitude, which is not that of objective evidences. Climacus speaks of 'the certitude of faith (which at every moment has within itself the infinite dialectic of uncertainty)' (*CUP* 55). This dialectic of uncertainty within certainty resists the notion that faith can appeal to some immediately evident authority. There is no such unsurpassable, self-validating limit available to human beings, for the very concept of the limit itself is a dialectical one, arrived at through the necessary detour of reflection and appropriation:

> Whether it is a word, a sentence, a book, a man, a society, whatever it is, as soon as it is supposed to be a boundary, so that the boundary itself is not dialectical, it is superstition and narrow-mindedness. In a human being there is always a desire, at once comfortable and concerned, to have something really firm and fixed that can exclude the dialectical, but this is cowardliness and fraudulence toward the divine. Even the most certain of all, a revelation, *eo ipso* becomes dialectical when I am to appropriate it; even the most fixed of all, an infinite negative resolution, which is the individuality's infinite form of God being within him, promptly becomes dialectical. (*CUP* 35n.)

God is not present as a positive authority within the world. Indeed, he is only negatively present in the believer's own resolution, in the self-emptying and self-annihilation of faith.

As Climacus says in the *Fragments*, 'the god cannot be known directly' (*PF* 63). There is no way, whether through intuition or discursive reasoning, in which finite phenomena can become the grounds for faith. Anything that seems to bear witness to God's reality could just as well be a deception. In a significant analogy, the *Postscript* likens our interpretation of nature to the reading of a text. As with the discourse prefaces, we find that it is the reader's self-activity which determines the meaning of what is read:

> Nature, the totality of creation, is God's work, and yet God is not there, but within the individual human being there is a possibility (he is spirit according to his possibility) that in inwardness is awakened to a God-relationship, and then it is possible to see God everywhere ... Is it not as if an author wrote 166 folio volumes and the reader read and read, just as when someone observes and observes nature but does not discover the meaning of this enormous work lies in himself. (*CUP* 246–7)

A text can remain an abstraction, a product of the ideality of language. Meaning can only be established through the active interpretation of a reader, who wishes to apply and practise what is learned. What is learned was really within the reader all the time, as a possibility which is awakened in the act of reading.

God's creative activity is thus like the writing of a text:

> No anonymous author can more slyly hide himself, and no maieutic can more carefully recede from a direct relation than God can. He is in the creation, everywhere in the creation, but he is not there directly, and only when the single individual turns inward into himself (consequently only in the inwardness of self-activity) does he become aware and capable of seeing God.
>
> The direct relationship to God is simply paganism, and only when the break has taken place, only then can there be a God-relationship. (*CUP* 243)

Language, the open-ended text rather than the closed book, works within this break. The author is absent from his work, so that the reader may be free to determine the meaning of the work. To believe in God as Creator has everything to do with the way one evaluates and acts in the world, and nothing to do with objective evidences that the world is the product of a design. Even revelation itself, 'the most certain of all', does not provide us with new information on which to base our faith, for 'the mystery expresses that the revelation is revelation in the stricter sense, that the mystery is the one and only mark by which it can be known' (*CUP* 245). Revelation does not so much dispel darkness as deepen the shadows. God, as the creative author, is characterized by 'divine cunning', by elusiveness, and by an invisibility which *is* his omnipresence (ibid.). Mystery is not accidental to his being; it is his very mode of presence in existence.

This has important implications for the subject's relation to God. The self is fissured, articulated by language, freed from brute necessity and reality in the consciousness of ideality and freedom which language makes possible; and the presence of God within the self is inevitably determined by this fact. God is like the author of a text: absent, unavailable to objective observation, but enabling the reader to enjoy his or her own free creativity. There can be no systematic comprehension of the self, and thus no timeless union of the subject with God: 'Since a human being is a synthesis of the temporal and the eternal, the speculative happiness that a speculator can enjoy will be an illusion, because he wants to be exclusively eternal within time' (*CUP* 56). Thus, God's negative presence does not consist in the repression of the self's temporality and linguisticality. Indeed, it is in the very instability of the textual, temporal world that this presence becomes possible. Climacus writes of 'the god, who is present just as soon as the uncertainty of everything is thought infinitely' (*CUP* 87). This negativity is an aspect of existence itself, of its irreducible uncertainty and precariousness. To think of God or the eternal is, for an existing human being, to express the contradiction of existence in explicit form:

> The negativity that is in existence, or rather the negativity of the existing subject (which his thinking must render essentially in an adequate form), is grounded in the subject's synthesis, in his being an infinite existing spirit. The infinite and eternal are the only certainty, but since it is in the subject, it is in existence, and the first expression for it is its illusiveness and the prodigious contradiction that the eternal becomes, that it comes into existence. (*CUP* 82)

Neither an acosmic, speculative closure, nor an empirical relation to an objective existent can comprehend the peculiar reality of the self. This reflects the self-contradictory nature of the soul, which we examined in the *Edifying Discourses*. It is akin to a wound, which cannot be healed by an appeal to the objective presence of God. The believer, Climacus says:

> is cognizant of the negativity of the infinite in existence; he always keeps open the wound of negativity, which at times is a saving factor (the others let the wound close and become positive – deceived); in his communication he expresses the same thing. (*CUP* 85)

In fact, the wound is the condition for a liberating communication, which neither represses freedom through an unjustifiable authoritarianism, nor represses our relatedness through the closure of the system, or of any arbitrary subjectivism. Indeed, Climacus makes the explicit claim that 'the secret of communication specifically hinges on setting the other free' (*CUP* 73n.), and that it is therefore 'irreligious' for someone to 'communicate himself directly' (ibid.). This is absolutely crucial, for it locates a practical, ethical concern for liberating communication at the heart of Climacus' theoretical dispute with the system.

It might be thought, however, that Climacus is nevertheless guilty of an individualism which denies any real relatedness of self to other. Surely to claim that the meaning of the text/world lies entirely within the reader/believer is to invite a subjectivist if not anti-realist interpretation? Moreover, Climacus claims at one point that 'The only actuality there is for an existing person is his own ethical actuality; concerning all other actuality he has only knowledge about it, but genuine knowledge is a translation into possibility' (*CUP* 316). If the individual's own selfhood is his or her only actuality, then the rug is pulled from beneath any realist epistemology about God or anything else for that matter.

However, this misunderstands Climacus' fundamental ideas about communication, and the putting into practice of those ideas in *Postscript*.

Climacus' idea of the self, as we have seen, is far from the isolated, cognitive subject of Cartesianism. It is precisely his point that the real self is the 'ethical existing subjectivity' (ibid.), the self which is always already differentiated and located within the text of existence. The self is irreducibly finite and particular; but these qualities emerge only out of its originary wounding, its difference from itself which establishes the possibility for relating to others and, ultimately, to God. His point is that relating to others and to God in the mode of an impersonal objective knowledge actually prevents one from relating to them at all. It is the objective standpoint of speculation which is closed, undialectical, self-contained – and thus, ironically, subjectivist. And the text of *Postscript* satirizes and performs this deficiency of speculative knowledge in its parodic structure. On its own premises, it cannot present God descriptively; but it aims to make a God-relationship possible by wounding the reader's self-contained reason from behind.

We might compare the *Postscript* in this respect to *The Sickness Unto Death*, which claims that 'The human self is such a derived, established relation, a relation that relates itself to itself and in relating itself to itself relates itself to another' (*SUD* 13–14). The self does not establish itself. It is a relation made possible by the originary division between time and eternity which no finite spirit can realize for itself. Thus, Anti-Climacus writes 'The formula that describes the state of the self when despair is completely rooted out is this: in relating itself to itself and in willing to be itself, the self rests transparently in the power that established it' (*SUD* 14). The self is inevitably related to a power beyond itself. However, as we have seen, this power cannot be conceptualized as an objective presence. So how does this ideal transparency come about? What must the self do to allow God to be negatively present?

This is the crux of the matter. The concept of transparency is, as we have seen, a problematic one. The ideal it presents seems to be unattainable for an existing individual. This tension within *Sickness* means that not only is the ideal of transparency called into question, but so is the very reality of God. As with the *Postscript*, however, we must avoid hasty conclusions, particularly ones which neglect the satirical-poetic form of the book itself, as it formally mimics works of Hegelian psychology. Let us explore this a little further.

Anti-Climacus describes various forms of despair, including that which follows from a inability to accept the self's finitude. In this context, he refers to the imagination. The imagination ('Phantasien') 'is infinitizing reflection ... is the rendition [Gjengivelse] of the self as the self's possibility. The imagination is the possibility of any and all reflection' (*SUD* 31). The imagination is here the name for the constitutive factor in the self, that which makes knowing, willing and feeling possible. It is the capacity for idealization; only in the transcendence of the here and now can the categories of human consciousness come to be. What interests us is that it renders the self as its own possibility, and in so doing rends and repeats the self in ideal form. The self is projected in its infinite aspect, free from all constraints of finitude.

This description may be compared with Anti-Climacus' account of the God-relationship. He distinguishes the believer from the fatalist, who is in bondage to necessity:

> The fatalist ... has no God, or, what amounts to the same thing, his God is necessity; since everything is possible for God, then God is this – that everything is possible ... For prayer there must be a God, a self – and possibility – or a self and possibility in a pregnant sense, because the being of God means that everything is possible, or that everything is possible means the being of God; only he whose being has been so shaken that he has become spirit by understanding that everything is possible, only he has anything to do with God. That God's will is the possible makes me able to pray; if there is nothing but necessity, man is essentially as inarticulate as the animals. (*SUD* 40–1)

If God 'is' that all things are possible, does 'God' then simply refer to the self in its ideal, infinite form, as envisaged by the imagination? God is not a being apart from the self, but the self's own possibility, its freedom from immediate necessity. More particularly, God is the possibility of *speech*, that which distinguishes human from beast. Anti-Climacus says of the fatalist's worship that 'essentially it is a muteness' (*SUD* 40). The fatalist lacks language, which is the medium of possibility and repetition. God appears to be demythologized as the power of language, thanks to which the self can re-make itself according to an ideal pattern. Bigelow delineates such a non-cognitive reading of this passage:

> So to say, as does Anti-Climacus, that God is that everything is possible and that everything is possible is God is simply to say that God is the *presence* of one's own *infinite future*; God *is* the inbreaking of infinite possibility ... God is that the existing individual steadfastly refuses to foreclose on any possibility by taking existence upon himself again and anew.[28]

However, Bigelow overstates his case. By failing to recognize that the reality of God could only ever be presented indirectly and negatively in a text, by means of poetic, existential possibilities, Bigelow draws a straightforward conclusion that 'God' must refer only to 'one's own' future, which one must take upon oneself repeatedly. But this is a one-sided reading. The self is not it's own; it is derivative, established by an irreducible relation to an otherness which is not its own. The 'infinite future' referred to by Bigelow recalls

---

[28] P. Bigelow, *Kierkegaard and the Problem of Writing* (Tallahassee: Florida University Press, 1987), p. 174. Cupitt, in *Taking Leave of God* (London: SCM, 1980), p. 64f. concurs in giving this passage a non-realist interpretation, comparing Kierkegaard to Feuerbach at this point.

Climacus' words that the future is the incognito of the eternal. The inbreaking of future possibility is a mode of the eternal's paradoxical presence; but to say that the eternal is *nothing but* the individual's futurity is an inadmissible leap.

We must bear in mind that Anti-Climacus elsewhere writes of the infinite self that it

> is really only the most abstract form, the most abstract possibility of the self. And this is the self that a person in despair wills to be, severing the self from any relation to a power that has established it, or severing it from the idea that there is such a power. With the help of this infinite form, the self in despair wants to be master of itself or to create itself, to make his self into the self he wants it to be, to determine what he will have or will not have in his concrete self. (*SUD* 68)

Bigelow's anti-realist reading repeats this desire for mastery, because at this point, it reads the text of *Sickness* in too direct a way.

As we mentioned earlier in connection with *Practice in Christianity*, Anti-Climacus is a complex pseudonym, part ideal Christian, part poet. In fact, his poetic nature undermines the supposedly superior vantage point he enjoys. *Sickness* is one of the texts of which Kierkegaard wrote in the journal that they must be 'kept poetic as poetic awakening' (JP VI 6337; Pap. X (1) A 95). This means that he presents the religious ideal, but has no more direct access to the religious object than any one else. The reality of God must be communicated indirectly via an examination of the limits of human existential possibilities.

This lends the text a certain ambiguity. There is an odd logic involved: at the moment when God appears most transcendent, and thus most unattainable, the self is cast back upon its own resources. However, the dialectic of this process cannot easily be resolved into either simple realist or anti-realist form. That would be reductionist, making the reality of God either an object of knowledge, or a projected ideal. Both options reduce God to something conformable to our way of knowing or shaping the world. Both therefore fall prey to an idolatrous tendency to confuse our representation of God with the reality represented. Kierkegaard's ethical realism breaks open such pretensions, because it relies neither on a logic of representation nor on one of projection. It relies on a form of communication which is liberating and yet mindful of the ultimate power that makes it possible. That this affects the surface consistency and 'good sense' of Kierkegaard's texts is an unavoidable consequence. Again, the *Postscript* is a case in point.

Climacus' system

The system is refuted by the actual practice of religious communication. Climacus claims that 'Double reflection is already implicit in the idea of communication itself' (*CUP* 73n.). Truth is not a content specifiable independently of the form in which it is presented. It requires a reduplication which defies direct presentation: 'Existing in what one understands cannot be directly communicated to an existing spirit, not even by God, still less by a human being' (*CUP* 274). Not even God can communicate directly, we are told. However, Climacus also claims that indirectness is appropriate *unless* the communicator is 'God himself' or one who has 'the miraculous authority of an apostle' (*CUP* 74).

Why the apparent contradiction? The ideals of direct authority from God and a relation to him which requires no mediation shadow the pages of the *Postscript*. Climacus claims that 'an apostle's *direct* relation to God is paradoxical-dialectical' (*CUP* 605n.). But this does not make sense. The apostle's relation to God *cannot* be direct if it is the result of a paradoxical dialectic. If Climacus were to counter that a paradox is not *supposed* to make sense, we are justified in requesting a distinction between paradox and plain nonsense. The description of the apostle simply seems to use the word 'direct' in a confused and nonsensical way.

The ideal of a communication which will evade the necessity of indirectness is connected to Climacus' apparent belief that it is only in this life that faith is necessary and the claims of the system absurd. He goes so far as to envisage an 'absolutely perfect world' in which faith will become superfluous: 'In such a world, faith is indeed inconceivable. Therefore it is also taught that faith is abolished in eternity' (*CUP* 30), Faith, constituted as existential interest and striving, is subordinated to a final restoration of direct presence to God.

This is made explicit in those very places where Climacus distances himself from the systematic approach:

> Existence itself is a system – for God, but it cannot be a system for any existing spirit. System and conclusiveness correspond to each other, but existence is the very opposite ... Existence is the spacing that holds apart; the systematic is the conclusiveness that combines. (*CUP* 118)

The point that existence is a spacing which resists the closure of the system is familiar. But Climacus establishes this only to reintroduce closure at a higher, divine level. If existence really is a system from the eternal viewpoint, then is existence merely an illusion of our finite perspective? Surely, if existence is what Climacus says it is, then the fact that it eludes systematic comprehension is not an accidental limitation on the part of the observer, but is intrinsic to any understanding of it. To understand existence requires a consciousness that is itself ruptured and 'interested' – between being and thought.[29]

---

[29] See R. Edwards, 'Is an Existential System Possible?', *International Journal for Philosophy of Religion* 17 (1985), pp. 201–8.

Climacus maintains that God 'in his eternal co-knowledge ... possesses the medium that is the commensurability of the outer and the inner' (*CUP* 141). God is the 'only spectator' (*CUP* 158) of world history, the fulfilment of what the systematizer would like to be. He can be this because, in fact, he transcends existence altogether: 'God does not think, he creates; God does not exist, he is eternal. A human being thinks and exists, and existence separates thinking and being, holds them apart from each other in succession' (*CUP* 332). It is difficult to see what prevents this God from being an empty abstraction, who can hardly be said to possess knowledge, freedom and love.

However, Climacus is surely claiming for himself a vantage point which his own argument claims to be impossible. He is giving us an overview, a description of God. In a sense, it is a self-cancelling description, one which presents God in categories inconceivable to our reason. The interest lies, not in the correspondence of this description to the reality of God's essence, but the way the text oscillates between the unavoidable indirectness of religious communication, and an idealization of apostolic and divine ability to cut through such indirectness – a tendency we have previously noted in connection with Kierkegaard's writings on language.

This tension is what sets the book in motion, what gives it its impossible task to say the unsayable. Consider the following:

> For an existing person, the goal of motion is decision and repetition. The eternal is the continuity of motion, but an abstract eternity is outside motion, and a concrete eternity in the existing person is the maximum of passion. That is, all idealizing passion is an anticipation of the eternal in existence in order for an existing person to exist; the eternity of abstraction is gained by disregarding existence. (*CUP* 312–13)

The concrete eternity is realized in time, whereas the eternity which remains beyond time is altogether abstract and indeterminate. Existence requires a repetition, an act of free transcendence, in which the eternal element of our contradictory soul is allowed to interrupt our sensual immediacy and self-centred possessiveness. Recollection of an eternal past ideal is not enough. As Constantius says in *Repetition*, 'Modern philosophy makes no movement ... and if it makes any movement at all, it is always within immanence, whereas repetition is and remains a transcendence' (*R* 186). Recollection remains in immanence, because it presupposes that the individual has access to the eternal truth as a completed whole. Repetition is a risky, paradoxical venture, by which 'actuality, which has been, now comes into existence' (*R* 149). It is a kind of 'κινησις' (ibid.), an existential movement by which an ideal is realized in time. It is essentially connected to the constitutive interest of human existence which resists systematization. Thus, 'repetition is the *interest* of metaphysics and also the interest upon which metaphysics comes to grief' (ibid.).

Repetition is a creative act, which Constantius associates with the action of God himself, for 'If God himself had not willed repetition, the world would not have come into existence' (*R* 133). This is a crucial point, left unexamined in *Repetition* itself. It calls into question the abstract, eternal simplicity which Climacus attributes to God. If God is truly Creator, then there must be *within the divine nature itself*, a moment of rupturing and of self-differing. The divine creativity is analogous to that of the writer; it is a creativity which hides itself in revealing itself, and which thus opens a space for freedom. God is intrinsically opaque to rational or intuitive vision. The tension in Climacus' text opens up a new way of drawing on a practical analogy to the divine nature, one which does not compromise the indirectness of our relationship with God.

Derrida, in his essay on Jabès and the book, touches on the same point. Commenting on Jabès' texts, he says 'God separated himself from himself in order to let us speak, in order to astonish and to interrogate us.'[30] He continues: 'If God opens the question in God, if he is the very opening of the Question, there can be no *simplicity* of God.'[31] To create existing selves, which are contradictions to themselves, could be said to be God's way of opening the question. And it leads us to ask, what is the condition for this creation to be possible? How could such a thing arise if God were simple, self-contained, abstract eternity? This is why the very moment of creation is necessarily the moment of God's veiling, of his absence – an absence which is bound up with the questionability of the 'book' and of all final meanings:

> If absence is the heart of the question, if separation can only emerge in the rupture of God – with God – if the infinite distance of the Other is *respected* only within the sands of a book in which wandering and mirages are always possible, then *Le livre des questions* [Jabès' work] is simultaneously the interminable song of absence and a book on the book. Absence attempts to produce itself in the book and is lost in being pronounced; it knows itself as disappearing and lost, and to this extent it remains inaccessible and impenetrable.[32]

Is the *Postscript* 'a book on the book' – on the system – which, however, tries to foreclose the separation and hang on to a promise of pure presence? Climacus' own estimation of his work is suggestive: 'the book is superfluous ... everything is to be understood in such a way that it is revoked, that the book not only has an end but a revocation to boot' (*CUP* 618–19). How much of Climacus' statements are due to irony, how much to the limitations of his humouristic position, is hard to determine. But, certainly, the tensions in his

---

[30] Derrida, *Writing and Difference*, p. 67.
[31] Ibid., p. 68.
[32] Ibid., p. 69.

text determine its interest for us, because it raises the question of whether any writing about God can avoid these strange contradictions, and of what resources we can call upon if talk about God is still to be meaningful.

Summary

We have once more seen the interconnection between form and content in Kierkegaard's works. That interconnection makes possible a critique of totalizing systems which resists falling into the same traps it sets out to expose. It is a critique evident in different ways throughout the authorship.

1. Kierkegaard rejects the 'pure' irony which results in an affirmation of subjective mastery over self and world. Such an irony negates the relation to the other and to God which Kierkegaard's communication presupposes.

2. Kierkegaard's texts also criticize a self-contained ethics, which risks becoming a doctrine of self-creation. The relation to God is irreducible to such a one-sided dialectic.

3. However, the God-relationship cannot be presented directly, or in the mode of objective knowledge. The *Edifying Discourses* point to the reader/believer's double role – as an active creator of meaning, and yet as entirely dependent on a transcendent God. God's otherness is performed rather than described, because it is in the active participation of the reader in the communication that the citadel of the self is opened up to an absolute alterity.

4. This relationship to God is adequately described by neither crude realism nor anti-realism. Both represent a desire for comprehension or mastery which the very nature of human existence disqualifies. There is a separation of thought from being in human existence which cannot be surmounted in thought, intuition or poetic creativity. God's presence in the world is negative and indirect.

5. Climacus' words on subjectivity and objectivity are thus seen in all their complexity. Both realism and anti-realism threaten to short-circuit the dialectic of Kierkegaard's writing, reading it in too direct a manner. What we have called ethical realism seeks to respect the tensions and indirectness which are built into these texts. God is known in and through the paradoxes of thought and the practice of liberating communication which the texts enact. God is known in the way of discipleship which faith in him makes possible – a circle which is only closed to totalising reflection, but which can be entered by the passion for infinity which resolves to seek an eternal happiness.

6. Kierkegaard's texts elicit a dynamic of creativity and humility. In their respect for the otherness of the reader and the hiddenness of the author in what is communicated, they provide a practical analogy for the creativity of God. The God who makes possible this complex communicational world cannot be an abstract and static being, an unmoved mover available to objective contemplation. If more positive images of God can be used, they can only be licensed by a kind of analogy which is oriented towards practice and which undermines its own pretensions to direct presentation of God's nature.

The next chapter explores the possibility of such an analogy.

CHAPTER SEVEN

The analogy of communication

Kierkegaard's writings tremble in the space between silence and objective certainty, between being able to say nothing of God at all and being able to describe God as he is in himself. All theology finds itself in this difficult place. Nicholas Lash, quoting David Burrell, poses the following question in an essay on metaphor and analogy: 'if "we cannot pretend to offer a description of a transcendent object without betraying its transcendence", does it follow that there is nothing which we can truly say of God?'[1] Kierkegaard is clearly sensitive to the betrayal of transcendence which objective, descriptive language about God seems to entail. The indirect form of his texts and his stress on the otherness of a God who is only negatively present in the world witness to as much. But is Kierkegaard in danger of depriving us of anything to say about God at all? Is his rejection of objective knowledge and evidence in a religious context so all-encompassing that it reduces 'God' to a cipher for an utterly unknowable 'beyond'?

The conclusion of the last chapter suggested an alternative to such an unhappy impasse. It has to do with what I shall call the 'analogy of communication'. This is a notion which builds on the classical concept of analogy along with modern linguistic and narrative philosophy, to suggest a dynamic interrelation between, on the one hand, God's creativity and revelation and, on the other, the forms of communication and practical discipleship in which God is known. It thus attempts to articulate a mode of 'knowing' God which is not reducible to objective knowledge in Kierkegaard's sense, but which is all the richer for that. After all, to equate all knowledge with theoretical knowledge would be a travesty.

It is here that I must tread very carefully. I am using language which is foreign to Kierkegaard in order to elucidate what I believe to be a fundamental dynamic of his writings. In so doing, I risk taming them, or turning them into the very thing they actively resist: speculative comprehension of God in himself. However, by taking this risk, I hope to show that the continuities and differences between Kierkegaard and the classical Thomist idea of analogy actually serve to clarify the traditional *and* radical nature of Kierkegaard's project.

Aquinas appeals to analogy as a middle way for religious language between the extremes of equivocation and univocity. If words used about God are entirely equivocal, this means that their meaning when predicated of God

---

[1] Nicholas Lash, *Theology on the Way to Emmaus* (London: SCM, 1986), pp. 109–10.

is entirely disconnected from their meaning in any other context. In a sense, they tell us nothing at all about God. On this view, God becomes so transcendent as to be utterly unknowable, and we can say nothing about God which has any cognitive content. If, however, our language about God is univocal, then this means that words used about God have just the same meaning as they do in other, natural contexts. We are able to describe God accurately – with the unwelcome result that a crude anthropomorphic deity, stripped of his infinite otherness, becomes our God. Whereas equivocation reduces us to impotent silence, univocity presumes to comprehend God but ends by distorting God's divinity.

Analogy is a middle way because it consists of judgements or propositions which can accurately be applied to God without specifying *how* they so apply. The significance of words like 'good', 'wise' and so on cannot be exhausted by their use in the natural or human context. Such concepts are open-ended, because they are perfections, which no particular mundane instance can fully encompass. It is therefore appropriate to apply them to God, who is the possessor of all perfections. However, Aquinas maintains his agnosticism about the possibility of comprehending God in himself by denying that we can know the way in which God possesses or exercises these perfections.

Analogy thus preserves the transcendence of God whilst affirming the possibility of nonequivocal communication about God. It has the further twist that, since God is the author of all perfection, it is God who is by right the subject of whom all such perfections are predicated. As creatures, we only possess perfections in a secondary, imperfect, derivative way. So although it appears that we are taking words out of their primary human context and stretching them to apply to God, faith sees that such perfections must have their original context in the nature of God. And as this original context is transcendent and mysterious to us, our words about God must be irreducibly indirect and metaphorical.

Two forms of analogy were distinguished by later scholastics, those of attribution (or proportion) and proportionality:

> According to the first (the analogy of attribution or proportion) the predicate actually (or formally) belongs to one (but not the other) of the objects. According to the second (the analogy of proportionality) both objects actually possess the predicate.[2]

On the first model, I can say that 'God is good' because God is the cause of all goodness in creatures. However, this makes the analogical predicate external to God, and risks falling into equivocation. If there is only a causal

---

[2] H. P. Owen, *The Christian Knowledge of God* (London: Athlone, 1969), p. 209. A third alternative, where neither object possesses the predicate, but where both stand in a relation to a third object which does possess it, is a species of the analogy of attribution.

relationship between God and goodness, what sense does it make to say that God *himself* is good?

The analogy of proportionality goes beyond this, claiming that certain predicates inhere in the very essence of God. They do so in a manner incomprehensible to us, but they are nevertheless not mere projections on to the blank screen of God's invisible nature. In some way, they correspond to his nature.

Aquinas would clearly want to resist the presumption that arguably characterizes the analogy of proportionality, because he is careful not to claim too much for our knowledge of God as he is in himself. However, if it is the case that Aquinas' position is closer to the analogy of attribution, we should be careful to set this in context. Aquinas' view of causation was Aristotelian. The term 'cause' could have several different senses. The cause of something is not only that which actuates or produces something. It may also be the substance out of which a thing is made; the form or pattern that makes it what it is; or the goal or end for the sake of which the thing exists. In other words, saying that 'God is good' means that 'God is the cause of all goodness' does not lead to the conclusion that God is an utterly unknown x which stands in a purely external relationship to goodness and good things. On the Aristotelian view, a cause can be much more intimately related to its effect, as that which gives it substance, form and purpose. Causation in this sense is much more holistic that that envisaged by the model of two billiard balls hitting one another – a purely external instance of causation.

On the one hand, then, analogical terms are available to us only as creatures, as derivative beings; God is the source of all perfection, and we must not presume to intrude on the workings of God's inner being. The analogy of proportionality may threaten to err on the side of univocality, to claim an insight into God's essence which is unavailable for existing creatures. However, as we noted, for Aquinas, analogical terms have their original sense in their application to God. Despite our profound agnosis in relation to God, analogy can provide a patterning and direction to talk of God. And that talk cannot remain mere talk; it is untrue if it does not form the life of faith dynamically as an expression of being in relation to God.

This has two corollaries. Firstly, it shows that, as Burrell and Lash claim, Aquinas is not interested in building up a doctrine or theory of analogy. Such a theory would presume that the way we use language in different contexts is open to theoretical comprehension. But, as Lash remarks, 'Linguistic usage is an art, not a science. And, if we *were* able theoretically to formulate the way in which the contexts in which we use such terms are related, then we would be unable to use them of "a God who transcends all our contexts."'[3] Aquinas' concern is thus more accurately described as grammatical – that of clarifying

---

[3] Lash, *The Way to Emmaus*, p. 111, quoting Burrell.

what cannot be said of God. His philosophical theology has this critical, purgative role, of guarding against an inappropriate and even idolatrous literalism with regard to speaking about God.

The second corollary is closely related to this. Grammar has a regulative, elucidating function. It cannot substitute for the actual art of linguistic communication. Similarly, the strictures of Aquinas' investigations into analogy are parasitic upon the concrete practice of Christian faith. As Lash remarks, 'The way of analogy serves neither as a substitute for nor, in any direct sense, as a confirmation of the way of discipleship.'[4] What it does do is expose the limitations of a theoretical understanding of God whilst holding open the possibility that God may yet be 'known' otherwise. The disciple knows God in the practice of faith hope and love, as he or she actualizes that possibility held open by grace, and mediated through the narratives of redemption which are at the heart of Christian proclamation and liturgy.

The idea of the analogy of communication is a tentative attempt to relate Kierkegaard's religious communication to this tradition, as it has engaged with modern reflections on the grammar, narrative and witness of lived faith. For Aquinas, it was not so much isolated words which could be used analogically, but judgements and propositions which were embedded in the life of faith. I hold that, whilst Kierkegaard does not dispense with propositional language about God, it is the actual practice of religious communication which provides the analogical model for knowing God (in a sense irreducible to the theoretical or objective). Kierkegaard thus places the practice of discipleship and witness even more firmly at the centre of any elucidation of the content of Christian faith. He is not interested in a theory of communication in the abstract, any more than he articulates a doctrine of God in the abstract.

Rather than concentrating upon predicates or propositions derived from the idea of communication, therefore, it is the concrete practice of communication which is analogous to divine communication, in a sense which embraces creation *and* revelation. The religious author remains hidden in the work, presenting possibilities for the reader to awaken. The author's communication is not that of information, but of capabilities. It is indirect, alluring and ambiguous. It requires that the reader is elevated to a level of freedom and creativity which is not under the dominance of the author. But it does require a response and therefore a responsibility, as it explores the limits of any project of self-mastery or self-creation. The ethic of reading suggested here involves a recognition of the reader's autonomy *and* dependency.

The divine communication is analogous to the extent that God too is hidden in the 'text' of creation, a creation which nevertheless contains within itself the possibility of a God-relationship, of passion and faith. But God is

---

[4] Ibid., p. 112.

never directly or positively present in creation; God is 'known' only in the infinite passion which keeps open the wound of negativity, that is, in the renunciation of all self-mastery, of all ideals of self-presence, and in the practice of an infinite responsibility.

This indirectness is not cancelled by revelation. Revelation and creation thus form a continuity, though revelation retains its singularity, its focus in particular indirect embodiments of paradoxical faith. This revelation is not a package of new information sent down from above, but as in the voices which called to Adam or Abraham, or the voice which invites us to follow Christ, a testing of the limits of rational comprehension and ethical self-creation, a call to absurd faith. The light of revelation does not so much dispel the shadows as reveal their depth; what is revealed remains mysterious to the understanding, but may be sought by passion.

So the practice of religious communication is analogous to divine communication because the discourse of communication, creation and revelation cannot be exhausted by its practice in human contexts. It is an open-ended discourse. Moreover, the claim of faith is that such a discourse and such a practice has its primary sense with reference to God. God makes language, communication and creativity possible; his Word calls forth our words. This analogy of communication is thus of a form which Aquinas might have recognized. It names God as the original Author, without claiming to know *how* God is that. It does not claim to know what inheres in God's essence, since that essence remains mysterious. God is 'known' in his effects, effects which are indirect, and known only in our passionate appropriation of them.

This is where Kierkegaard even more than Aquinas, puts the emphasis on the primacy of discipleship in any articulation of Christian faith. His analogical discourse about God is structured by the 'how' of God's communication to us, as this is met and answered in the 'how' of witness and discipleship. The analogy of communication is not a theory about how to talk about God or describe God, but a formula which derives from and guides Christian practice. It is not 'merely' linguistic, because, for Kierkegaard, language usage is shot through with these urgent issues of how to relate real and ideal, of how to resist seduction and demonic despair, of how to witness without betraying. The analogy of communication attempts to evoke these ethical and religious questions at the heart of language usage, and at the heart of the particular language-usage which is Christianity.

Kierkegaard's ethical realism is thus intrinsically related to the 'how' of witnessing faith as it meets the 'how' of God's revelation. It is self-critical and dialogical, in ways which offer to us a possible critique of some of Kierkegaard's own positions, as well as those of more recent nuanced versions of narrative realism – possibilities which will be taken up in the Conclusion. The analogy of communication is as subversive as it is suggestive.

Where Kierkegaard's conception is more demanding that that of Aquinas is in taking account of the shift of conceptual and social context that has occurred since the scholastic age. The givenness of a body of revelation and the authority of Church and Bible cannot be taken for granted – indeed, they may become stumbling blocks for faith. It is no surprise to find Kierkegaard drawing on romantic and idealist resources even as he twists them into new shapes to meet a new historical situation.

Lash suggests that the primary form of Christian discourse is narrative. It is structured by the remembrance and performance of irreducible Scriptural and liturgical narratives. The philosophical theologian has a role in offering a critique of such narratives, which attempts to guard them from idolatry and ideological abuse. Analogy is a grammatical tool which helps elucidate the limits and pitfalls of the narrative form. However, such a critique will itself employ irreducible narratives, whether historical or literary-critical. There is no beatific vantage point from which we could escape the temporality and relatedness which call for narration. This complex dialectic must always be self-critical without ever finding an absolute point of rest which would help it evade the ambiguities and risks of faith.

Kierkegaard knows something of this dilemma. In renouncing the objective, eternal viewpoint, he cannot avoid narrating manifold alternative points of view. These points of view embody a self-critical exploration of their own limitations, be they aesthetic, ethical or religious. Christian faith is not immune from distortion, as Kierkegaard's texts bear witness. His attention to exploring limit-concepts, concepts which cannot be brought under objective philosophical control, is grammatical in the sense we are using here. It is regulative and critical, rather than objective and descriptive.

Nevertheless, Kierkegaard does not escape the need for narratives. This is true, not only of the frequent stories which punctuate his texts, but of the structure of those texts themselves. They are not systematic 'summas'. They employ a mode of narration which indirectly calls the reader to embody or reject the existential possibilities which are put forward.

If narrative is irreducible it is nevertheless not innocent. Kierkegaard's narratives demand a response, they intervene in the monologue of reason with new possibilities. They also risk falling into the idolatry and ideology they unmask. The analogy of communication guards against this by divesting the author of authority and objective mastery, and fostering a communication which is liberating and self-renouncing. But this analogy of communication, as I have described it, itself depends upon certain narratives about divine creativity. Communication has its primary sense with reference to God, who is its primary practitioner. But by recalling us to the inevitability of narrative, Kierkegaard's indirect communication nevertheless does not pretend to exhaust the full meaning of communication. If God is the original author, then no human author can claim to master the art of communication. Narrative is not a seamless whole, which we can look down upon as something complete and at our disposal. It contests our identity and calls us to the risky venture of witnessing faith. A narrative theology which forgets that is just another idolatry.

This chapter explores the way in which Kierkegaard's texts can be seen as practising such an analogy, through his reflections on religious language, his treatment of specific practices and doctrines, and his late concern with the nature of witnessing.

A difference of language

Kierkegaard does not give any sustained attention to a doctrine of analogy or the general problem of religious language, though it will have become clear that I hold the question of language itself to be intimately bound up with the central issues of his texts. This in itself may be significant: like Aquinas, Kierkegaard does not develop a 'theory' of analogy which would betray the transcendence of God, but he is nevertheless committed to a communication which makes a relationship to that transcendence possible. Religious language is not so much a fenced-off area of special terminology as a particular 'how' of communication. Kierkegaard's occasional references to the 'grammatical' nature of such language throw further light on this basic position.

Climacus argues that a dialectical religious communication is a negative presentation of the object of faith. God's negative presence must be reduplicated in the form of the communication, which ends, not in the appropriation of a present content, but in the differentiating act of worship: 'Dialectic itself does not see the absolute, but it leads, as it were, the individual to it and says: here it must be, that I can vouch for; if you worship here, you worship God' (*CUP* 491). In the same way, religious language can have a regulative, rather than a descriptive function. The absolute is not an object available for inspection. Indeed, it frustrates all idolatrous attempts to make it present and cognizable, since it is that which makes all presence and cognition possible. Climacus can therefore say on the one hand that one should be 'using analogy [Analogien] in order by it to define the paradox' (*CUP* 580), but on the other that 'the absolute paradox is indeed distinguishable in such a way that every analogy [Analogon] is a deception' (*CUP* 598).

The reference to using analogy to define the paradox appears in a note which stresses the 'essential invisibility' of God against the 'illusory analogies' of paganism (*CUP* 580). Any direct understanding of the paradox is dismissed as a *mis*understanding, which leads to the confusion of Christianity with 'something that has arisen in man's, that is humanity's, heart' and which forgets 'the qualitative difference that accentuates the absolutely different point of departure: what comes for God and what comes from man' (ibid). Any analogy which revokes the paradox of the eternal existing in time is an 'analogy of deception' which revokes itself. The only way to preserve an analogy is to respect the absolute difference of God and humanity, and to accord to God the primacy in initiating a relationship between the two – a relationship which analogy can only show to be paradoxical. Analogy does not therefore give us knowledge of God's essence, but differentiates between ourselves and God. It is a grammatical, critical tool, which guards against idolatry, and which is properly rooted in and directed towards worship.

Analogy has its place, but it is a paradoxical one. The religious writer is committed to using necessary deceptions. When Climacus is about to recount the incarnation of the god in *Fragments*, he says: 'no human situation can provide a valid analogy [Analogi], even though we will suggest one here in order to awaken the mind to an understanding of the divine' (*PF* 26). If the story is to work, then there must be something in the situation of a king loving a poor girl which awakens us to the meaning of the paradox. The deception is that such scenarios are comprehensible within the language and conventions of a given society, whereas the paradox speaks of the incarnation of that love which makes any language or convention possible at all. The linguisticality of analogy means that it must presuppose as its unintelligible origin what it seeks to make intelligible. How then can such language be used, if it is condemned to be 'invalid'? Kierkegaard's use of analogy, particularly his frequent illustration of his points by reference to human love affairs, implies that there may be a 'valid' analogy between those fundamental aspects of human experience and consciousness which resist conceptual articulation, and the qualities which faith ascribes to their unknown, self-differing source. The analogy in these cases does not grant conceptual knowledge of God, but centres on modes of relating to and communicating with others – others who themselves resist conceptual grasp. The analogy is the religious act of communication in microcosm, a sort of synechdoche within the text. It is not primarily verbal or propositional, but narrative and related to concrete acts of communication.

Moreover, whilst attempting to rule out any cognitive standpoint which could claim to understand God, Kierkegaard inverts the commonsense interpretation of metaphorical language in a way similar to Aquinas' treatment of metaphor. In 'Strengthening in the Inner Being', a discourse of 1843, he names God as Father, and adds that 'this expression is not metaphorical, imperfect, but the truest and most literal expression, because God gives not only the gifts but himself with them in a way beyond the capability of any human being' (*ED* 95). God is not 'Father' in a secondary sense, based on an extension of an earthly metaphor. Literalness is displaced, so that the word has its primary application to God. This is appropriate, because it is God's 'fatherliness' – his generative, differentiating potency and care – which is the founding possibility for earthly fatherliness:

> Therefore, even though you had the most loving father given among men, he would still be, despite all his best intentions, but a stepfather, a shadow, a reflection, a simile, an image, a dark saying about the fatherliness from which all fatherliness in heaven and on earth derives its name. (*ED* 96)

It is crucial to note that the fatherliness of God is not a static essence, but the very creative self-giving of the absolute which makes human care and nurture possible. By turning the tables on the metaphor of fatherhood, Kierkegaard can affirm the dynamic interrelation of divine and human love, whilst denying that we have any independent, self-sufficient, cognitive standpoint from which we may judge the validity of the metaphor. That validity is dependent on a divine act of communication – of giving – which makes our faltering communication possible in response. The metaphor relates to the analogy of communication, for God is known through the gift he gives. This narrative of grace resists any anthropomorphic assimilation of divine and human fatherhood, whilst pointing us to human acts of communication or giving as the effects of that divine giving. Those human acts have a significance beyond their directly perceivable content, for, in practice, they can awaken us to the possibility of the divine gift.

In the *Christian Discourses*, Kierkegaard recognizes that all our talk about God is conditioned by the finitude of our perspective:

> All our talk about God is of course human talk. However much we may strive to prevent misunderstanding by withdrawing again what we have asserted – if we would not be completely silent, we must after all employ the human measuring-rod when we as men talk about God. (*CD* 299)

But the scales of value and measurement by which we order and judge the phenomenal world cannot be straightforwardly applied to God, as if God were merely the supreme member of a continuous chain of power and wisdom:

> So then God and man resemble one another only inversely. It is not by the steps of direct resemblance – great, greater, greatest – thou dost attain the possibility of comparison, it is possible to attain it only conversely; neither is it by lifting up his head more and more that a man approaches closer and closer to God, but conversely, by throwing himself down more and more deeply in adoration. (*CD* 300)

Language 'bursts and cracks [sprænges og brister]' (ibid.) under the strain of this reversal, because it seems to be tied to the human world of relative distinctions. Language about God must preserve the paradox and difference between time and eternity, whilst returning us to the religious practice of worship.

The dialectic of difference is the dialectic of worship. As the *Postscript* states:

> Precisely because there is an absolute difference between God and man, man expresses himself most perfectly when he absolutely expresses the difference. *Worship* is the maximum for a human being's relationship to God, and thereby for his likeness to God, since the qualities are absolutely different. (*CUP* 412–13)

The believer comes to him- or herself through an act of reverent demarcation. Indeed, it is the believer who is 'the absolutely differentiating one' (*CUP* 413). There is a sense in which the difference between God and humanity has to be re-made or repeated by each individual. Worship is not the *eradication* of difference, but its *confirmation* and *repetition*. As *Sickness* states, 'God and man are two qualities separated by an infinite qualitative difference' (*SUD* 126), and 'to worship, which is the expression of faith, is to express that the infinite, chasmal, qualitative abyss between them is confirmed' (*SUD* 129). The discipline of worship preserves the believer from the presumption which leads to idolatry.

Works of Love treats the question of religious language in different terms: 'All human speech, even the divine speech of Holy Scriptures concerning the spiritual is essentially overført speech' (*WL* 199*), where 'overført' means transferred or figurative. The figure or metaphor is a term 'carried across' from its sphere of proper usage. It implies an indirectness in religious language from which Scripture itself cannot be exempt. But this also means that religious language cannot be so radically new that it has no connection with the words we use day by day:

> Yet there is something binding which they have in common – they both use the same language. One in whom the spirit is awakened does not therefore leave the visible world ... Transferred language is, then, not a brand new language; it is rather the language already at hand [det allerede givne Ord]. Just as spirit is invisible, so also is its language a secret ... The distinction is by no means directly apparent [en Paafaldenhedens Forskjel]. (*WL* 200)

How can language bind the otherness of God and the finite human world? Precisely because of what we have called the analogy of communication. Language is a given, a presupposition. Our communicative activity can awaken us to the utter givenness of our existence, and a possible relationship to the power which has established us. It is not just that language can provide this or that particular metaphor, but that the experience of language-usage can itself be the analogy for the divine language of creation and grace, though there remains between them 'en Evighedens Sprogforskjel' – 'an eternal difference of language' or 'a language difference of eternity' (*WL* 118*).

The journals echo both the difference and the closeness of divine and human language. An 1849 entry declares that 'for the proclamation of Christianity in its truth as it is in the New Testament, a divine language is required, and more than a human being is required to proclaim it' (JP 3: 3494; Pap. X(2) A 310). In a sense, Kierkegaard still hankers after a medium of communication which will fulfil his idea of authoritative speech. However, even to preserve the name of 'language' is to draw an analogy between this divine speech and the possibility of human communication. Kierkegaard wishes to preserve this speech from the egoism and abstraction which infects ordinary discourse. In a later passage he again talks of a 'divine language' and says 'Christianity uses the same words and expressions, the same language we human beings use – but it understands [by] each particular word the very opposite of what we human beings understand by it' (JP 3: 3532; Pap. XI(1) A 19). Taken strictly, this would be a nonsense. But Kierkegaard is not so much concerned with semantics as with the ethical and religious destruction of egoism and idolatry. The divine language holds out the possibility, not of a new vocabulary, but of a new 'grammar' for faith: an inversion of the rules of egotistical communication which will respect the absolute otherness of the Creator. But a language there must be, since that is the condition for any communication of trust and love.

The question of religious language cannot be a theoretical one, nor can it be segregated as a specialized discipline. The creativity of language usage, the liberating potential of communication is radically dependent on the originary communication of God. That communication can only be 'known' in faith, in the practical witnessing in life and action which Christianity demands. The way Kierkegaard treats some key religious practices and doctrines will bring out the strange inversions which this entails.

Prayer, immortality, ascension

We begin with a text from the *Eighteen Edifying Discourses*, entitled 'One Who Prays Aright Struggles In Prayer And Is Victorious – In That God Is Victorious' (1844). Here, Kierkegaard talks of one who initially seeks to gain some external advantage from his prayers. He wishes God to answer him with observable results, and therefore 'it is a matter of making oneself clear to God, of truly explaining to him what is beneficial to the one who is praying' (*ED* 388). Gradually, this importunity for the sake of external gain is transformed by the quality of the inwardness with which it is pursued. Eventually, the idea of praying *for* things is given up; the struggle becomes one of making sense of God, of demanding some clarifying word from him. The one who prays 'had given up his wish, he is reconciling himself to his pain, and yet he is a long way from *the explanation*; his struggle in prayer is for God to explain himself' (*ED* 394).

In fact, the way a person prays determines what kind of answer is received, for 'prayer is the means by which the explanation will correspond to the way he prays about it' (*ED* 397). Initially, 'the God to whom he prays is human, has the heart to feel humanly' (*ED* 387). This conception must give way to a realization that God cannot be moved, for he is unchangeable. The form of the prayer, and the form of the pray-er's inwardness change as they conform to this changed conception of God. In this way, the one who prays marks the qualitative distinction between God and himself:

> Is he not one who draws [Tegner], he who struggles in prayer with God for an explanation? Will not the explanation draw a boundary line between him and God so that face-to-face with God he begins to resemble himself? (*ED* 399)

The one who prays must become nothing 'for only then can God illuminate him so that he resembles God' (ibid.). Resemblance to God is correlated with resemblance to self, because, in being won away from the false conception that he could find happiness in a self-centred desire for external possessions and advantages, the one who prays begins to be conformed to the unchanging constancy and love of God.

Prayer does not change God, but it leads to the transformation of the one who practises it. Kierkegaard plays on the dual meaning of the Danish: 'was it not a victory that instead of receiving an explanation [Forklaring] from God he was transfigured [forklaret] in God and his transfiguration [Forklarelse] is this: to reflect the image of God' (*ED* 400). Explanation – of God or oneself – gives way to transfiguration. At the point when God's utter unlikeness to human beings becomes evident, the one who prays becomes more inward, free from the idolatry of possessions and the kind of prayer that turns God into an idol (*ED* 393). The imagery of the discourse is very passive: becoming nothing, becoming totally still, like the ocean must if the image of heaven is to sink into it (*ED* 399). But the struggle of prayer is also an active appropriation of the values of constant love. God does not intervene in the world to answer prayer. He does not change or have feelings in analogy to a human being. Indeed, it seems that the believer must leave that idea of a personal God behind, if the highest value of the religious life is to be realized. God is known negatively, in his indirect effects, effects which nevertheless transform the believer in unforeseeable ways.

God's transcendence is thus the other side of a process whereby religious meaning and value is internalized. The case of immortality is another example of this. *Christian Discourses* contains a piece called 'The Resurrection Of The Dead Is At Hand, Of The Just – And Of The Unjust', which examines the question of immortality. Kierkegaard derides the context of bourgeois cosiness within which this doctrine is usually discussed, in which proving immortality has become a game, or a matter for aesthetic judgement. The matter needs to be given 'a different turn' (*CD* 212). Kierkegaard thus proclaims that immortality is a given, which cannot be proved from finite premises. You *are* immortal, like it or not. Immortality is qualitatively different from life as we know it. It cannot be conceived as a mere continuation:

> For immortality is the judgement. Immortality is not a life infinitely prolonged, nor even a life somehow prolonged into eternity, but immortality is the eternal separation between the just and the unjust. Immortality is not a continuation which follows as a matter of course, but it is a separation which follows as a consequence of the past. (*CD* 212–13)

Like duty, immortality is not open to question, 'but the question must be whether I live as my immortality requires me to live' (*CD* 213). Kierkegaard believes that immortality has lost its power over life, because people 'have tricked it out of its authority – by wanting to *prove* it' (*CD* 213–14).

There must be no speculation about life after death. Immortality appears rather as a transcendent ethical claim upon one's life. It signifies the separation of good and evil. The doctrine functions, not as a description of the afterlife, but as an imperative, as an ideal standard of judgement upon this life.[5] It thus appears to have a practical, rather than a cognitive use. In the *Postscript*, Climacus expresses something of the same thought when he says that 'eternal happiness, as the absolute good, has the remarkable quality that *it can be defined only by the mode in which it is acquired*' (*CUP* 426–7). Precisely because it is the absolute good, it cannot be defined or described in relative terms. Its meaning emerges in the interest of the individual and in the use to which the idea is put. Earlier Climacus had stated that 'objectively the question of immortality cannot be asked, since immortality is precisely the intensification and highest development of subjectivity' (*CUP* 173). The idea of immortality raises the pitch of the individual's interest in existence, giving a kind of absolute significance to the choices we make in this life. Apart from this existential justification, immortality has none at all, for 'Immortality is the subjective individual's most passionate interest; the demonstration lies precisely in the interest' (*CUP* 174).

However, we cannot simply conclude that Kierkegaard gives an anti-realist doctrine of immortality. In the discourse we are examining, the separation between right and wrong, for which immortality seems to stand, is not something which has relative validity in this life alone:

> But the difference between right and wrong remains eternally, as does He, the Eternal, who fixed this difference *from eternity* (not like the difference

---

[5] Cf. Wittgenstein, *Culture and Value* (Oxford: Blackwell, 1980) p. 28e: 'Christianity is not a doctrine, not I mean a theory about what has happened and will happen to the human soul, but a description of something that actually takes place in human life.'

which *in the beginning* He fixed between heaven and earth), and it remains *unto eternity*, as He, the Eternal remains, he who rolls up the heavens like a garment, changes everything, but never Himself – and hence never this difference which belongs to eternity. (*CD* 215)

The difference remains 'unto eternity'. It is a presupposition of all finite life, preceding creation because it is in the nature of the Creator himself. God, though unchanging, is co-eternal with this difference. The difference is constitutive of God's righteousness and eternity:

> But the nature of righteousness possesses this perfection, that it has within itself a duplication [Fordobelse] ... Eternity, righteousness, has the distinction [Forskjellen] within itself, the distinction between right and wrong. (*CD* 215–16)

Kierkegaard is quite clear that simple eternity, like a mathematical point, is a mere abstraction. Only the eternity which has difference *within* itself can be creative.

So God is not merely an abstract ideal, but a creative power who has difference within himself. If the transcendence of God is served by resisting anthropomorphism, care must be taken not to fall into another form of idolatry – that of equating God with an eternal essence which is transparently knowable or immediately intuitable. His nature is to create, to establish difference, value and meaning. If God is the author of all communication, of all giving, then to model him on the basis of Aristotle's self-contained unmoved mover is to risk distorting his nature, to create eternity after the only image we can think of – that of static, mathematical timelessness. The difference in God is not something knowable, but the unthinkable source of his creative love. As Constantius said, without repetition, there could be no creation (*R* 133); this repetition is the condition for the creativity of our own language. Repetition is transcendence, the incomprehensible possibility of radical novelty as well as of testimony and fidelity. It opens us to the possibility of an originary, creative repetition at the heart of the divine, whose essential nature we cannot grasp because it is the rupture of all fixed essences. Such is the analogy of communication.

However, this poses a vital question: in the light of this interpretation, how can we explain Kierkegaard's repeated insistence on God's unchangeableness? In the 1855 discourse 'The Unchangeableness of God', Kierkegaard stresses this characteristic more strongly than anywhere else. He claims that:

> God is unchangeable. In His omnipotence He created this visible world and made Himself invisible. He clothed Himself in the visible world as in a garment; He changes it as one shifts a garment – Himself unchanged. (*UG* 242)

He is like a mountain before which the wanderer stops. The wanderer waits for the mountain to move, but it never will (*UG* 244). God's unchanging will is terrifying and awesome. He is 'pure clearness' (*UG* 243). To him all is 'eternally present' (*UG* 249), and as he is eternal clarity itself, 'it is not so much that He keeps a reckoning, as that He Himself is the reckoning' (*UG* 250). God does not change – the believer must change according to the eternal standard which this image of God presents.

However, in the prayer at the start of the discourse, we find that God is contrasted with the human being, who can only remain unchanged if he or she is not moved by anything. Of God Kierkegaard says 'You, however, are moved, in infinite love, by everything ... but nothing changes You, You Unchangeable One!' (SV 19: 255*). God, though unchanging, is moved by love – or rather, *as love*. So there is a kind of movement in God, by which he relates to the world creatively, unlike the self-absorbed Aristotelian unmoved mover. The movement of love implies a certain alterity, challenging the notion that God is self-contained and therefore essentially unrelated to his other. God is unchanging as a lover is constant, not in an abstract metaphysical sense – and not, therefore, in the way that an anti-realist ideal is unchanging. Kierkegaard asks that the prayer be blessed, that the one who prays it may be changed (ibid.). God's constancy in love establishes a difference between himself and creation, a difference which must be treasured, as it is the space in which human freedom and love are possible.

This interpretation is strongly supported by a remark made by Climacus in the *Postscript*. Although, as we have seen, Climacus has a residual tendency to reintroduce the systematic standpoint on the basis of God's static and eternal viewpoint on reality, his dialectic of existence and communication leads him to suggest a radical revision of this traditional notion of God:

> The existence-sphere of paganism is essentially the esthetic, and therefore it is quite in order that this is reflected in the conception of God, according to which he himself, unchanged, changes all. This is the expression for acting in the external. The religious lies in the dialectic of inward deepening, and therefore, with regard to the conception of God, this means that he himself is moved, is changed. (*CUP* 432n.)

It is precisely the static view of God which is paganism. God is changed, moved in himself, because his action – his love – is not accidental to his nature or a matter of indifference to him. God has an interest in creation, and so there is an openness in the divine life which static categories distort. Language about the unchangeableness of God has to be held together with these narratives of divine communication. The story of the incarnation focuses the unthinkable relation between the eternity of God and his communicative love. The paradox exists for the understanding; for faith, it is the way in which God's nature is narrated anew. The understanding is stuck in fixed categories. The analogy of communication sets those categories in motion again, for God can be spoken of and witnessed to in the context of the life of faith, worship and liberating communication.

A journal entry of 1846 reflects this theme. Kierkegaard claims that 'The greatest good, after all, which can be done for a being ... is to make it free. In order to do just that, omnipotence is required' (JP 2: 1251; Pap. VII(1) A 181). Only omnipotence can take itself back, withdraw its control even as it manifests its power. Between people, relationships of dependency are unavoidable to some degree:

> Only omnipotence can withdraw itself at the same time it gives itself away, and this relationship is the very independence of the receiver. God's omnipotence is therefore his goodness. For goodness is to give oneself away completely, but in such a way that by omnipotently taking oneself back one makes the recipient independent. (ibid.)

Creation thus becomes the ideal act of communication, as Kierkegaard radically re-evaluates the notion of absolute power. It is not 'power-over', the power of compulsion, but a goodness which enables the other to be free. Contrary to the popular maxim that absolute power corrupts absolutely, Christian faith claims that absolute power is absolute gift; and this can be so if absolute power flows from a source located beyond all created locations, and therefore beyond any corrupted notion of power which *we* construct. This absolute power is not available for us to comprehend or intuit in itself, but it is known by its effects – by the experience of freedom and creation as gift. The absence of God from creation is therefore the necessary correlative of his unlimited goodness. True, Kierkegaard insists that 'Omnipotence is not involved in a relation to the other' (ibid.), which seems to contradict what we have just said about the love of God. But this non-relation is in fact what makes the other's freedom possible. It is the relation of creative difference, not that of indifferent isolation. It is a kind of giving, by which the other can become 'the most delicate of all things' (ibid.), an independent creature.

According to Climacus, we recall, the highest goal for human communication is to set its recipient free. The human act indirectly reduplicates the divine creation/revelation, so that the rhetoric of Christian discipleship is inseparable from the content of Christian belief. To practise good communication is to be a co-worker in the creative work of God. This is why the self at its most creative, as an independent, language-producing conscious being, is simultaneously derivative, dependent upon an originary act of communication. In the discourse on prayer which we examined above, Kierkegaard claims that it is 'the most revolting blasphemy to say of God that he is inhuman' (*ED* 387). To deny *any* analogical link between God and humanity leaves us with nothing to say of him. To image an anthropomorphic, interventionist God, or a static, self-contained deity is to create an idol which subverts human freedom.

The way beyond this impasse is hinted at later in the discourse, when Kierkegaard again emphasizes that God is unchanging, and that 'Faith reads the understanding only as a dark saying; humanly speaking, it does not have the explanation, only in a certain deranged sense' (*ED* 395). Faith has no ultimate rational justification, because it operates via different categories. Significantly, it is a kind of *reading*, which refuses reason's claim to master the text of existence. However, this also disqualifies a non-realist 'explanation' of faith which confidently asserts that its object is of a wholly human origin. God is unchanged:

> He has not become a friend of cowardliness and softness; he has not become so debilitated over the years that he cannot distinguish between mine and thine and everything runs together before him; he is himself still the first inventor of language and the only one who holds the blessing in his hands. (*ED* 395)

To name God as 'the inventor of language' is to make a decision of faith, that through the struggle and disillusionment of prayer, God may be known as the gracious originator and communicator of creation, a creation which we encounter in human consciousness, mediated by human language. We do not come to faith through any miraculous sign, or through the discovery of additional information, but through a deeper engagement with the act of communication itself. Faith holds that God is not dispersed into the linguistic world without remainder; but only in and through that world do we participate in his creative work. This lies at the root of a remarkably positive evaluation of language which we find in the journals:

> Language is an ideality which every man has gratis. What an ideality – that God can use language to express his thoughts and thus man by means of language has fellowship with God. (JP 3: 2336; Pap. XI(2) A 147)

In and through this ideality, which is the presupposition of all thought, God's self-expression and human response can meet. Language-usage, in the context of the fellowship it makes possible and by which it is made possible, is the locus for encountering the divine.

This shows why the human act of communicating religious truth is impossible to distinguish objectively from the truth it is communicating. For us, 'mine and thine' are not so easy to distinguish, and faith does not provide us with infallible maxims to preserve us from idolatry. The truth of religion lies, not in an objective body of doctrinal information,[6] but in the praxis of

---

[6] See the *Postscript:* 'Christianity is not a doctrine, but it expresses an existence-contradiction and is an existence-communication' (379–80).

setting others free. It is inherently and actively liberating. The uncertainty, doubt and despair which are the correlatives of free existence, can become the negative basis for the self's faith that the primordial difference which produced it is not an arbitrary mechanism, but the hidden face of infinite, self-differing, communicating love. Beyond that, it cannot go. Only the 'how' of one's religious practice will demonstrate the validity of one's belief.

So Kierkegaard does not simply dispense with objective beliefs and ontology. He is making claims about the nature of God and the ultimate value of created life which do not function as subjective fictions. However, in changing the emphasis in dogmatics from a static metaphysics to communication, Kierkegaard is fundamentally challenging metaphysical realist assumptions about the role and justification of religious language. The practical emphasis of such a dogmatics makes propositional doctrinal correctness of little value, because such beliefs must serve religious practice, and not the other way round.

That this should introduce ambiguities as to the 'objective' or cognitive status of such beliefs is neither surprising nor avoidable. Consider, by way of example, the brief discussion of the Ascension in *For Self-Examination*. Towards the end of the discourse 'Christ Is The Way', Kierkegaard dismisses the attempt to counter doubt over religious truths by rational proofs of their validity. As we have already seen, he believed that this was doing no more than fighting doubt with its own weapons: 'And these reasons fostered doubt and doubt became the stronger. The demonstration of Christianity really lies in *imitation*' (*FSE* 68). Christian doctrine requires a practical justification. In following the values manifested in Christ's example, disciples can show their validity in the only way open to them. The precise doctrines they hold will depend upon the exigencies of their particular situation:

> So it is always with need in a human being; out of the eater comes something to eat; where there is need, it itself produces, as it were, that which it needs. And the imitators truly needed this Ascension in order to endure the life they were leading – and therefore it is certain. (*FSE* 69)

This sounds markedly subjectivist, until we realize that it has its context in proclaiming a gospel of infinite love in the face of persecution. It is not the case that 'anything goes', but that belief is justified in terms of its practical worth in expressing and enabling the spread of the gospel of suffering love. At the same time, there is no purely objective, purely given doctrine. The doctrine is articulated to serve that witness, and its certainty is not that of knowledge, narrowly conceived, but that of resolution and passion.

Imitation and faithful witness are the elements which resist the subjectivism of anti-realist discourse. But how does one witness to a paradox, to that which cannot be comprehended or made present? If what we have claimed about the analogy of communication is to have any validity, we must examine the issue of the incarnation more closely. For is is here that the most radical act of divine communication is attested.

The issue in fragments

The focal point of discussion in *Philosophical Fragments* is that of making the distinction between God and humanity, and thus of seeing the Christian paradox in its radicality. Early on in the work, Climacus says that 'between one human being and another μαιευσθαι is the highest; giving birth indeed belongs to the god' (*PF* 11). A human being can only assist at the birth of another into free subjectivity; the truly creative, originating power is God's alone. If for Socrates 'self-knowledge is God-knowledge' (ibid.), the Christian idea of the incarnation breaks with such an immanent religiosity. Whereas Socratic faith needs only to recollect its latent divinity, Christianity claims that the eternal no longer exists for us, and that it must be regained anew. We have lost the condition for learning the truth, and therefore time must have a decisive significance for us. If the 'moment' is to be decisive, it must be 'because the eternal, previously nonexistent, came into existence in that moment' (*PF* 13). If the learner is in untruth (i.e. in sin (*PF* 15)), the one who teaches the truth must transform him, by giving him the condition to apprehend it. This is the crux, for 'no human being is capable of doing this; if it is to take place, it must be done by the god himself' (*PF* 14–15). However, 'inasmuch as the learner exists, he is indeed created, and, accordingly, God must have given him the condition for understanding the truth' (*PF* 15), otherwise, the teacher would 'make him a human being for the first time' (ibid.). Therefore, the condition must have been lost through the learner's own fault, through a historical fall, as a result of which 'he will not be able to set himself free' (*PF* 17).

The stage is set for a hypothetical narrative of an incarnation, in which the god must take the initiative and become human in order to raise humanity up to equality with himself. However, Climacus' telling of this tale is periodically disputed by an anonymous voice within the work. The interlocutor accuses Climacus of 'plagiarism' (*PF* 35), because what purports to be a fictional hypothesis is in fact the well-known story of Christ. Climacus is accused of poetic theft, a charge which Climacus magnifies into blasphemy:

> You called my conduct the shabbiest plagiarism, because I ... robbed the deity or, so to speak, kidnapped him and, although I am only a single human being – indeed, even a shabby thief – blasphemously pretended to be the god. (*PF* 35–6)

This is the grossest impropriety: a human being tells God's story for him, takes the words out of the mouth of the Almighty. Climacus admits that no single person, nor yet humanity in general could have created this tale: 'Presumably it could occur to a human being to poetize himself in the likeness of the god or the god in the likeness of himself, but not to poetize that the god poetized himself in the likeness of a human being' (*PF* 36). In fact, the story is 'no poem at all but *the wonder*' (ibid.). The 'solemn silence' and 'awe-inspiring words' (ibid.) of the divine drown out this human wrangling about authorship.

However, charges of impropriety and forgery are not so easily dismissed. The incarnation requires the art of human narrative to make it accessible to human belief, and there seems no valid a priori reason why a human being could not have thought up the idea of incarnation itself. If, therefore, the incarnation is not to be reduced to the level of a fiction, then the believer's communication must continually mark the limits of its capability, must contain a reflection on its own boundaries. The form of *Fragments* – speculative yet fragmentary, experimental yet structured around decisive existential questions – articulates this inner tension.

This tension is brought more explicitly to the fore in the passages which describe the downfall of the understanding in its collision with its unthinkable other. Climacus signals his subversive intention by equating the understanding with an excessive passion: 'the ultimate potentiation of every passion is always to will its own downfall ... This, then is the ultimate paradox of thought: to want to discover something that thought itself cannot think' (*PF* 37). Lest the erotic connotations of this go unnoticed, Climacus goes on to say: 'It is the same with the paradox of erotic love. A person lives undisturbed in himself, and then awakens the paradox of self-love as love for another, for one missing [en Savnet]' (*PF* 38–9). Passion is constituted by a lack ('Savn'); narcissism is breached in a love for one who is absent, or who remains separate and can never be fully consumed by the lover's passion. In fact, to satisfy totally one's passion for possessing the other is simultaneously to kill the passion, by closing the gap which made it possible. This is reminiscent of Lacan's famous statement that 'man's desire is the desire of the Other',[7] in the sense that the Other represents both a relationship to *another* and a lack or breach *within* subjectivity itself. It is also a hint of the ambiguous nature of Climacus' account.

So the understanding collides with its elusive other, the other which it cannot penetrate, but which is the condition for its very existence. Climacus now makes a crucial theological step: 'let us call this unknown *the* god' (*PF* 39). The divine is present negatively. 'God' as the unknown other, comes to designate a *limit*, a *difference*, a *frontier*.[8] In other words, Climacus uses talk

---

[7] Quoted by Malcolm Bowie in *Structuralism and Since*, ed. John Sturrock (Oxford: Oxford University Press, 1979), p. 135.

[8] L. Mackey, *Kierkegaard: A Kind of Poet* (Philadelphia: University of Pennsylvania Press, 1971): 'For human reason the concept of God must ever remain a limiting concept and no more' (p. 157).

about God, not to provide us with information about a supernatural realm, but to delimit the range of self-sufficient human reason. This is the grammar of talk about God in this context. According to Mark C. Taylor, 'As the difference that "precedes" all differences, the Unknown, which is forever unknowable, is the condition of both the possibility and the impossibility of reason.'[9] God does not present himself in the world:

> What, then, is the unknown? It is the frontier that is continually arrived at, and therefore when the category of motion is replaced by the category of rest it is the different, the absolutely different. But it is the absolutely different in which there is no distinguishing mark [Kjendetegn]. (*PF* 44)

God bears no sign by which he may be differentiated as one object or person amongst others in the world. He is essentially and irreducibly other to our powers of cognition and recognition. This introduces a certain anxiety into the heart of the believer:

> But this difference cannot be grasped securely. Every time this happens, it is basically an arbitrariness, and at the bottom of devoutness there madly lurks the capricious arbitrariness that knows it itself has produced the god. If the difference cannot be grasped securely because there is no distinguishing mark, then, as with all such dialectical opposites, so it is with the difference and the likeness – they are identical. (*PF* 45)

The understanding 'confuses itself with the difference' (ibid.), in the insane presumption that it has itself produced that which it cannot think. If 'the god' merely designates the limits of the understanding, does it have any objective referent? Is this otherness no more than an effect of the believer's passion, a passion which reaches its height in this encounter with unassimilable paradox?[10] Climacus denies this, whilst maintaining, curiously, that in a sense the difference *is* produced by the individual. However, it arises from an abuse of the will, not a defect of the understanding: 'What, then is the difference? Indeed, what else but sin, since the difference, the absolute difference, must have been caused by the individual himself' (*PF* 47). *The Sickness Unto Death*, whilst asserting that man and god are 'akin [beslægtet]' in what man 'owes [skylder]' to god, goes on to add that 'Sin is the one and only predicate about a human being that in no way, either *via negationis* or *via eminentiæ*, can be stated of God' (*SUD* 122). God is the self's own ideal standard: 'Qualitatively a self is what its criterion is' (*SUD* 113–14). To exist before God is to have a more intense awareness of one's self, of its limitations and potential.

---

[9] Mark C. Taylor, *Altarity* (Chicago: University of Chicago Press, 1987), p. 343.

[10] Mackey, in *Kierkegaard*, expresses the ambiguity here well: 'Paradox is the "object" that exists only in and for the subject; it is the object absorbed in and become one with the passion of the subject' (p. 182).

'God', then, does not only signify the limitations of reason, but the failure of our wills, according to an ideal standard of perfection. Since 'God' is the limit and the standard, sin can have no meaning when applied to him. Sin is *our* difference from God. But this implies that 'God' is not simply the *cognitive* blank at the back of all our finite reasoning, but a source and standard of absolute *value*. Moreover, 'God' is not simply a static ideal, but is indirectly presented in a narrative of communication, grace and revelation. According to Climacus, faith is the 'happy passion', 'when the understanding and the paradox happily encounter each other in the moment, when the understanding steps aside and the paradox gives itself' (*PF* 59). The paradox is that the unnameable unknown, the other of reason, addresses humanity, not only through signs and discourse, but through an embodiment which reason judges to be impossible and absurd. It thus shows itself not as blank nothingness, but as creative love. The paradox *gives itself*. Recalling our earlier discussion of the love of God, Climacus writes of the gratuitous communication in which God moves himself:

> But if he moves himself, then there of course is no need that moves him, as if he himself could not endure silence but was compelled to burst into speech [udbryde i Ordet]. But if he moves himself and is not moved by need, what moves him then but love, for love does not have the satisfaction of need outside itself but within. (*PF* 24)

God does not break silence for want of an object which will reflect back his love and thus make it complete. His love is gratuitous, excessive and extravagant, and it is impossible for any brand of speculation to comprehend it or provide an overarching rational justification for it. It is the movement of God's love which determines what is and what is not to count as a 'reason' for faith.

Faith, then, makes the unprovable assertion that its own need and lack is met with the gratuitous response of God, a God who remains mysterious, and yet opens himself to the wounds of bodily and mental suffering in order to communicate the condition which will eradicate the difference of sin. Faith meets God as wholly other, and yet moved by an infinite love. It is an ambiguous passion, because it cannot know its object apart from its own projections and analogies; so it always risks creating God as an object after its own image, to satisfy finite human concerns. Ideally, 'faith is not an act of will, for it is always the case that human willing is efficacious only within the condition' (*PF* 62). God's gift is the condition for human willing to be effective. However, from our standpoint, it can be so difficult to specify the difference between faith and invention, for it does involve a creative reinterpretation of the world as the product of infinite love.

In an 'Interlude', Climacus muses on the nature of our knowledge in past events. The word he uses for 'belief' is 'Tro' – exactly that which is used for religious faith. The implied analogy between historical belief and faith is instructive. Whereas 'Immediate sensation and immediate cognition cannot deceive' (*PF* 81), 'the historical intrinsically has the *illusiveness* [Svigagtighed] of coming into existence, it cannot be sensed directly and immediately' (ibid.). The act of believing in a past event in fact reveals something of the nature of all temporal existence. Climacus has already argued that 'All coming into existence occurs in freedom, not by way of necessity' (*PF* 75). Existence is inescapably contingent and opaque to reason; the word 'Svigagtighed' has overtones of guile and fraudulence. Existence contains a 'double uncertainty': 'the nothingness of non-being and the annihilated possibility, which is also the annihilation of every other possibility. This is precisely the nature of belief' (*PF* 81). Belief, then, is an act of interpretation which reduplicates the freedom with which anything comes into existence. Thus, 'it is now readily apparent that belief is not a knowledge but an act of freedom, an expression of will ... The conclusion of belief is no conclusion [Slutning] but a resolution [Beslutning]' (*PF* 83–4).

So faith both is and is not an act of will. It must be disciplined to avoid the idolatry which capriciously manipulates religious language to its own ends; yet it must also be a free act of re-evaluating the world according to a standard to which we have no cognitive access. When one believes in a past event, one believes 'not the truth of it, for that is a matter of cognition, which involves essence and not being' (*PF* 85). It is static necessity, not the movement of existence, which 'pertains to essence' (*PF* 86). Faith does not depend upon a language which seeks correspondence with a cognitively accessible essence; on the contrary, its language must serve a practice, whereby infinite love is made compatible with sensuous incarnation, assuring us of the mysterious integrity of our divided self. Language about God has a negative role, of weaning the believer away from any identification of God with a recognizable aspect of the world. Instead, by insisting on the difference of God and the world, it relocates faith as the trust that this difference is not a void of unmeaning, but the space in which infinite love expresses its creative, liberating power – and in which it is paradoxically embodied in a single life. And Climacus insists to the last that *this* idea 'did not arise in any human heart' (*PF* 109).

The narrative of the king and the maiden which is at the heart of *Fragments* is thus self-consciously naïve. It is a fairy tale, a fiction; but as such, it witnesses to aspects of reality which conceptual discourse cannot grasp. Narrative is essential. But that narrative must be self-critical; the analogy between the divine communication and the human must respect their qualitative difference. Nevertheless, there is no doing without narrative. Climacus wants to strip the Christian gospel of its historical dress, to discuss it as a hypothetical thought-project. But even then, he must retain the narrative form which tells the story of the incarnation in however truncated a form, and which invites interpretation and imitation (*PF* 104). In this respect, the follower at second hand in later generations is no worse off than the immediate eyewitness – the paradox and the demand remain the same.

But the paradox is not merely an external miracle. It is an act of communication which takes effect in the life of the believer. In the renunciation of self-mastery, the believer is opened out to transformation into the likeness of God, into a kind of deification, for God wishes there to be equality with himself. That goal is itself paradoxical (*PF* 25). The incarnation communicates the possibility of unlimitable grace, the reconciliation of real and ideal, temporal and eternal: 'the paradox specifically unites the contradictories, is the eternalizing of the historical and the historicizing of the eternal' (*PF* 61). However, that reconciliation is not immediately visible or conceptually articulated. The paradox is only for faith (*PF* 96, 102), which is to say that only for faith is it more than a paradox or intellectual contradiction, but an act of liberating communication.[11] It is a matter for existential expression in the renunciation, suffering and witness which discipleship demands. The analogy of communication holds that the act of religious witness is indirect and fragmentary, but nevertheless faithful to the *form* of the divine witness itself. The form of our religious communication cannot be direct and easy where the divine communication was indirect and costly (see *PF* 102).

There is no sense in which the paradox may be something we create, however. The paradox of the incarnation is understood only in the light of what we have said so far about the difference which lies between God and humanity. As Climacus writes, 'the absolute paradox, precisely because it is absolute, can be related only to the absolute difference by which a human being differs from God' (*CUP* 217). Because the paradox is based upon this difference, it cannot be dismissed as a mere figure of speech:

> Does *explaining* the paradox mean to turn the expression 'paradox' into a *rhetorical* expression, into something the honorable speculative thinker says has its validity – but then in turn does not have its validity? In that case, the *summa summarum* is indeed that there is no paradox. (*CUP* 220)

The paradox is in fact the negative expression of a difference, which, because it is absolute, can have no direct presentation:

> Thus God is a supreme conception that cannot be explained by anything else but is explainable only by immersing oneself in the conception itself.

---

[11] This, I believe, is the implication of the journal passage which states that the absurd ceases to be absurd for the one who has faith (JP 1: 10; Pap. X(6) B 79). It is not that the paradox receives some conceptual resolution for faith, but that the believer learns to relate to it in ways other than the conceptual. After all, as Climacus states, 'it is and remains the paradox and does not permit attainment by speculation. That fact is only for faith' (*PF* 96).

> The highest principles for all thinking can be demonstrated only indirectly (negatively). Suppose that the paradox is the boundary for an *existing person's* relation to an eternal, essential truth – in that case the paradox will not be explainable by anything else if the explanation is supposed to be for existing persons. (ibid.)

Here, the paradox is a boundary line, which articulates human existence as a contradictory relation of time and eternity. It is a repellent anti-concept which admits no higher vantage point from which it may be explained. The paradox is the relation of time and eternity which all finite, discursive explanations must presuppose, and which they cannot transcend.

However, as we have seen, there is more to the specifically Christian idea of the paradox than this. For the Christian, 'The eternal truth has come into existence in time' (*CUP* 209). No longer is the paradox in the mere relation of time and eternity, but in the actual temporalization of eternity. The eternal becomes a temporal human being, a particular incarnation of the essential truth. Subjectivity is challenged in its self-sufficiency by a concept of faith which hinges upon its evaluation of a historical person:

> Faith's analogy to the ethical is the infinite interestedness by which the believer is absolutely different from an esthete and a thinker, but in turn is different from an ethicist by being infinitely interested in the actuality of another (for example, that the god actually has existed). (*CUP* 324)

There is an 'absolute dependence on the object of faith' (*CUP* 326). Interest no longer defines the general situation of an existing human being, but is given highly specific and, indeed, absurd form: to believe that a particular person embodies eternity.

Climacus distinguishes Christian faith ('Religiousness B') from the Socratic outlook ('Religiousness A') by developing this line of thought. Whilst the *A* position follows Socrates in equating true knowledge of self with knowledge of the divine, the *B* position rejects any such immanent way to God, which depends upon unaided human powers. It involves an irreducible alterity:

> In Religiousness *B*, the upbuilding is something outside the individual; the individual does not find the upbuilding by finding the relationship to God within himself but relates himself to something outside himself in order to find the upbuilding. (*CUP* 561)

It seems that this must decisively rule out any anti-realist interpretation of Christian language, as a passing reference to Feuerbach makes clear:

> If, however, the coming into existence of the eternal in time is supposed to be an eternal coming into existence, the Religiousness *B* is abolished, 'all theology is anthropology,' Christianity is changed from an existence-communication into an ingenious metaphysical doctrine addressed to professors. (*CUP* 579)

Interestingly, it is the anti-realist account which is condemned for its metaphysics. Christianity proclaims a transcendent and liberating breach of logic and reason, whose hegemony is only confirmed by a Feuerbachian reduction of theology into anthropology.[12] One who 'understands' the paradox:

> will confuse it with something that has arisen in man's, that is, humanity's heart, confuse it with the idea of human nature and forget the qualitative difference that accentuates the absolutely different point of departure: what comes from god and what comes from man. (*CUP* 580)

In fact, I have suggested that the paradox of the incarnation is not wholly heterogeneous to human existence, inasmuch as existence itself cannot be described without some recourse to paradoxical formulations.[13] But this does *not* eliminate the paradox; it situates it in relation to the irreducible complexity of human selfhood. The human self unites contraries in the medium of existence. Immediacy has always already been breached by the inexplicable facts of freedom and language, and human consciousness is constituted as a form of interest – a 'being-between' which admits no fixed and final formulation. Our investigation suggests that any approach to the status of religious language cannot avoid locating the problem within the horizon of the question of language as a whole. Language too expresses the contradiction of existence: as an ideality and an abstraction on the one hand, and yet as the temporal medium of communication which makes possible the freedom of the self from the immediacy of the here and now on the other. To examine the phenomenon of Christ may therefore shed light, not only on the nature of the language of paradox, but on the paradoxicality of language which is bound up with all of these questions.

The truth of Christ

Christ, we have seen, is a 'sign of contradiction' (*PC* 125), in the interpretation of which our whole self-understanding is at stake. It is in the act of faith that we draw close to the infinite love of God whilst affirming our ineradicable difference from him. Anti-Climacus affirms that only God is able to re-create us in likeness to himself:

---

[12] Kierkegaard's general attitude to Feuerbach seems to be one of admiration for an intelligent unbeliever, who shows what it is to be offended by faith (*SLW* 452; *CUP* 614); it is far from one of endorsing his conclusions. See Feuerbach's *The Essence of Christianity*, trans. Eliot (New York: Harper, 1957).

[13] 'The paradoxicalness of the incarnation thus mirrors a paradoxicalness which is generally present in human existence' (C. S.Evans, 'Is Kierkegaard an Irrationalist?', *Religious Studies* 25 (1989), p. 349).

> No teaching on earth has ever really brought God and man so close together as Christianity, nor can any do so, for only God himself can do that, and any human fabrication remains just a dream, a precarious delusion. (*SUD* 117)

Practice confirms the thought of *Fragments* that to become a Christian is 'to be transformed into likeness with God' (*PC* 63) on God's initiative. God 'wills not to be transformed into a cozy – a human god; he wills to transform human beings, and he wills it out of love' (*PC* 62). But how do we recognize God's purpose, and his incarnation in Christ? What grounds can we have for interpreting this sign in the way we do?

Christ can no more be directly recognized than can God. Indeed, the contradiction involved in his being the God-Man removes him from any possibility of being directly revealed. Simply for a human being to claim to be God is indirect communication, since there is no direct way in which to make sense of it (*PC* 134). However, this special quality of the incarnation is related to the nature of all spiritual existence:

> Spirit is the denial of direct immediacy. If Christ is the true God, then he also must be unrecognizable, attired in unrecognizability, which is the denial of all straightforwardness. Direct recognizability is specifically characteristic of the idol. (*PC* 136)

Christ cannot be manipulated by human understanding, because he disobeys its laws. But the implication is that *all* spirit participates in this mysterious, indirect presence. We have already learnt that there is no 'immediate health of the spirit' (*SUD* 25), for human consciousness is always differed in itself, always beyond mere immediacy. Now we learn that this gives us some analogy to the mystery of the incarnation, not so that we can understand it, but that we may relate it to the essentially guileful nature ('Svigagtighed', *PF* 81) of our own existence. Not only this, but spirit and sign are seen to be correlative. The transcendence of immediacy which constitutes spirit is also the definitive mark of the sign. Spirit and language imply one another, linked by the common ground of this essentially mysterious breach.

For the paradox of Christ is itself not a mere conundrum, but a *sign*, a *communication*, in which the creative, self-differing love of God is embodied:

> Reduplicated in the teacher through his existing in what he teaches, the communication is in manifold ways a self-differentiating art. And now when the teacher, who is inseparable from and more essential than the teaching, is a paradox, then all direct communication is impossible. (*PC* 123)

Incarnation is the embodied art of communication. It reveals something of the nature of all communication with signs, whilst seeking to move the recipient beyond the abstractions of theoretical discourse to a faith which repeats the movement of divine love in practice:

> The being of truth is not the direct redoubling of being in relation to thinking, which gives only thought-being ... No, the being of truth is the redoubling of truth within yourself, within me, within him, that your life, my life, his life, expresses the truth approximately in the striving for it, that your life, my life, his life, is approximately the being of the truth in the striving for it, just as the truth was in Christ a *life*, for he was the truth. (*PC* 205)

Here, a radical departure is announced. Truth as a *cognitive content* is displaced by a conception of truth as a *life*, for 'only then do I in truth know the truth, when it becomes a life in me' (*PC* 206). Existence and temporality are no longer subordinated to an eternal realm of ideas, to archetypes of which the phenomenal world is a distorted and refracted embodiment. Rather, embodiment in time is itself the condition whereby truth is created, and we are invited to create it for ourselves. 'Truth' becomes a quality of self-sacrificing love, for even in everyday communication, it is only in reciprocal trust and attentiveness that meanings can be shared and communication achieved. This is a precarious achievement, a matter in the first instance for passionate striving, not least against the wilful deceit of seduction. *Judge For Yourself!* expresses the issue clearly:

> The Savior of the world, our Lord Jesus Christ, did not come to the world in order to bring a doctrine, he did not try by way of reasons to prevail upon anyone to accept the doctrine, nor did he try to authenticate it by proofs. His teaching was really his life, his existence. (*FSE* 191)[14]

There must be an act of faith that existence can be the arena in which absolute values can be communicated and realized. Reasoning and freedom are possible only in the wake of God's communicative, creative love, of which Christ is the incarnation. Only a life, a human existence, could be, not merely the vehicle, but the embodiment of that truth, which defies theoretical or cognitive grasp, since it is a reduplication of infinite love in time. This embodiment is not direct. It is not a cancellation of freedom, but its provocation.

Such a truth requires, not admirers, but 'imitators' (*PC* 233). It must be practised since it cannot be known. Indeed, Christ himself, inasmuch as he is the God-Man, cannot be known:

> one cannot *know* anything at all about *Christ*; he is the paradox, the object of faith, exists only for faith. But all historical communication is the communication of *knowledge*; consequently one can come to know nothing about Christ from history. (*PC* 25)

---

[14] Cf. Wittgenstein, *Culture and Value*, p. 53e: 'I believe that one of the things Christianity says is that sound doctrines are all useless. That you have to change your *life*.'

But if Christ exists only for faith, what value is to be placed upon the actual historical person of Jesus? Is time and history insignificant for faith? The ideal of 'contemporaneity' suggests as much. In attempting to avoid relativizing the offence of the paradox, Anti-Climacus denies that historical proximity to Christ is of any relevance to faith. The absurdity remains the same for any would-be believer. Indeed, the relation of faith must transcend time:

> In relation to the absolute, there is only one time, the present; for the person who is not contemporary with the absolute, it does not exist at all. And since Christ is the absolute it is easy to see that in relation to him there is only one situation, the situation of contemporaneity. (*PC* 63)

Consequently, 'Christ's life upon earth, the sacred history, stands alone by itself, outside history' (*PC* 64). Climacus had already argued that nothing but the bare bones of a historical report (*PF* 104) were necessary for faith, wishing to avoid the detour through scholarship which was essentially irrelevant to the risk of faith. Now Anti-Climacus goes further in seeking to preserve the Christ event from all taint of historical relativity.

There is an undeniable tension in this. Surely, the truth which is manifest in a *life* cannot be encapsulated in a single moment of pure presence. The truth 'is' in time – not accidentally, as if it could be articulated, spoken or conceived beyond time as supernal essence – but inextricably. The truth is comprised and compromised by its temporality. There can be no 'contemporaneity' with Christ, since in its strict formulation, this would require that Christ were an atemporal ideal – and thus the polar opposite of what the paradox in fact proclaims. The 'truth' is actually an effect of a certain way of living in time, a way which Christ exemplifies for faith:

> The highest thing a man is capable of is to make an eternal truth true, being himself the proof, by a life which will also perhaps be able to convince others. Did Christ ever undertake to prove some truth or another, or to prove the truth? No, but He made the truth true, or He made it true that He is the Truth. (*CD* 104)

This passage, from the *Christian Discourses*, demonstrates the paradoxical form which must accompany writing about the paradox. How can the truth be *made true*? Was it previously untrue? Was it previously non-existent? And how can a person existing in time make an eternal truth true? These strange questions echo the most striking aspect of Kierkegaard's writing on the paradox: that even as the eternal is brought closest to time, is embodied amongst us, as one of us, so it disappears from us, becomes offensive, absurd, unrecognizable. The god is absent even as he is made most present. His presence *is* his hiddenness, the one corresponding to the other with paradoxical rigour.

The idea of contemporaneity is another ruse to wean us off the belief that greater knowledge or a more immediate acquaintance with Christ in the flesh could lessen the demands of faith. It asks us to decide for ourselves the meaning of Christ for us. The present it invokes is not the eternal present of full and self-evident meaning, but an agonized present, the moment of decision, risk and commitment. And, in a curious way, it can help preserve us from another form of idolatry – that of directly equating the words and actions of the historical Jesus with those of God. Kierkegaard was canny enough to recognize that biblical criticism was not going to deliver a recognizable divine saviour. It pursued the way of approximation, which was no basis for an eternal happiness.

The problem is this: on the one hand, Kierkegaard risks loosening Christ from any historical actuality, as a free-floating ideal of divine-human reconciliation. On the other hand, he can so insist on the historical particularity of the incarnation as to obscure its essential relationship to human selfhood – for we are each called to imitate the paradoxical embodiment of infinite love in particular form (a form which is given pattern by reference to the lowliness of Christ, a lowliness which is *both* spiritual and socio-political). And, through grace, we are each enabled to become like God, even as we preserve the absolute difference which worship expresses. This problem cannot be resolved conceptually or historico-critically, but only in the existential commitment of a witnessing faith, which must hold the particularity and universal significance of the paradox together in practice.[15]

However, witnessing does require critical vigilance if it is to avoid self-deception and idolatry. This is implied in the analogy of communication: that God's absence is the negative form of a communication which intends our liberation from idolatry and cruelty, and which makes possible a human communication which, at its best, sets the other free. Of course, this places a huge responsibility upon the shoulders of one who would write about – or witness to – religion, without the relief of recourse to cognitive evidences or sure authorities. It is a matter, not of complacently accepting a ready-made truth as a self-evident and universal, but of *making the truth true* in ethical commitment, in full awareness of the temptation to idolatry which this entails.

In Kierkegaard's texts, this means that the peripheral ambiguity and risk

---

[15] See the form of offence referred to in *Sickness*, which is said to deny Christ 'either docetically or rationalistically, so that either Christ does not become an individual human being but only appears to be, or he becomes only an individual human being' (*SUD* 131). A similar tension is evident in the *Book on Adler*. On the one hand, Kierkegaard writes that 'the paradox itself did not last throughout many years: it existed when Christ lived, and since then it has existed only whenever someone was offended and someone did in truth believe' (*OAR* 58) and, on the other hand, that 'Christianity exists before any Christian exists, it must exist in order that one may become a Christian ... it maintains its objective subsistence apart from all believers, while at the same time it is the inwardness of the believer' (*OAR* 168).

which attends all discourse, even the most banal everyday 'direct' communication, is consciously cultivated as the central motif. It may be objected that Kierkegaard declares in 1848 'The maieutic cannot be the final form, because, Christianly understood, the truth does not lie in the subject (as Socrates understood it), but in a revelation which must be proclaimed' (JP 2: 1957; Pap. IX A 221). But we must place Kierkegaard's key terms – 'truth' and 'revelation' – under interrogation. 'Truth' is known in Christianity in the form of a life, an existence, not a set of propositions. It is not a content which can be transmitted as a bit of knowledge. Moreover, this truth is paradoxical in itself – it *cannot* be communicated directly, as *Practice* makes plain. As for 'revelation', that itself is a mystery; indeed mystery is the only form under which revelation can be manifest.

This raises the question of the status of Kierkegaard's remarks in the 'Lectures on Communication', which we examined in Chapter 3. There, he distinguished religious communication from the communication of ethics by saying that the former presupposed a preliminary piece of knowledge. It seems that Kierkegaard is claiming that religion, especially in its Christian form, *does* require some objective doctrinal content, which has to be known before it can be appropriated.

However, this argument invites the same critique that we have outlined above. The *kind* of knowledge which is presupposed by religion is not the same as that of empirical science or speculative philosophy. Nor does it fit neatly into a system of credal orthodoxy, where doctrines are interpreted as descriptive propositions. To use the words of the *Edifying Discourses*, it is 'a knowledge ... that is transformed into an action the moment it is possessed' (*ED* 86). In other words, we should not introduce a false dichotomy into Kierkegaard's work, as if he were utterly 'against' knowledge in any form. In fact, he is inviting his readers to participate in a dynamic and transformed mode of 'knowing', one which is more analogous to knowledge of another person than knowledge of true propositions. In this context, the preliminary knowledge demanded by religious communication is not preliminary at all, since it can only be encountered in the movement of appropriation or offence. But it does point to the fact that, for Kierkegaard, religion and Christianity in particular, are not pure invention or self-projection. They demand subjective appropriation, but such appropriation presupposes an initial otherness. It is this otherness, this sense of gift, to which the disciple must never fail to bear witness: '*the witness itself is a gift from God*' (*ED* 98).

The nature of proclamation or witness is not that of producing objective evidences, but neither is it a matter of pure self-expression. The significance of witnessing, and the continuous indirectness of his approach can be traced throughout Kierkegaard's later works.

The poet of the paradox

Kierkegaard embarked upon a welter of self-questioning following the intense productivity of the year 1848.[16] With many works completed or in progress, he was entangled in an intricate web of reflection as to how much and in what form he should publish. The ambiguity of his position was mirrored in his deliberations over the status and justification of his peculiar brand of religious poetry. What the poet loves, the Christian calls sin, or so he wrote in the journal of that year, as he was musing on the possible creation of a series of discourses entitled 'Let not the heart in sorrow sin' (JP 6: 6277; Pap. IX A 421). He developed the thought further in another entry on the same theme: 'Ask the poet what it is that especially inspires him to songs which praise heroes and heroines – it is this very sin of the heart in sorrow' (JP 6: 6279; Pap. IX A 499). Still he believed that the religious poet was capable of doing 'the kind of writing which helps people out into the current' (JP 6: 6521; Pap. X(2) A 157). But how could this poetry make any *decisive* impression on the real world?

The Anti-Climacus figure was born out of Kierkegaard's 'reflective predicament',[17] a way of maintaining the tensions necessary for a proclamation of the Christian ideal without claiming too much for the spiritual status of the 'real' author. In the 'Editor's Preface' to *Practice*, Kierkegaard claims that, in that work, 'the requirement for being a Christian is forced up by the pseudonymous author to a supreme ideality' (*PC* 7). This formula expresses the ambiguity of the whole enterprise: there is both an affirmation of the authority of the Christian *requirement*, under which the 'editor' humbles himself, and a tacit admission that the work is a poetic venture, whose masked author seems to claim a presumptuous ability to formulate and communicate the ideal. In fact, he had already considered changing the form of *Sickness* into 'a lyrical discourse in a more rhetorical form',[18] which would reflect the nature of the writing even more explicitly. He came to the point where he was prepared to see all of his completed works published, with the proviso that 'they are kept poetic as poetic awakening' (JP 6: 6337; Pap. X(1) A 95). The decision for Christianity had to be aroused in the most decisive way that the medium of *poetry* allowed.

For Self-Examination again emphasizes Kierkegaard's self estimation: 'Instead of conceitedly making myself out to be a witness to the truth and causing others rashly to want to be the same, I am an unauthorized poet who influences by means of the ideals' (*FSE* 21). But this lays Kierkegaard open to the charge contained in *Sickness* itself: 'Christianly understood, every poet-

---

[16] See 'Historical Introduction' to *PC*, p. xi.
[17] 'Historical Introduction', *SUD* p. xvi.
[18] Ibid. p. xiv. cf. JP 5: 6136; Pap. VIII(1) A 651.

existence ... is sin, the sin of poetizing instead of being, of relating to the good and the true through the imagination instead of being that – that is, existentially striving to be that' (*SUD* 77). His escape clause is that, by putting his own name forward as the editor of the work, Kierkegaard claims that he is striving after the ideal which it presents. Whatever the facts of Kierkegaard's personal piety, however, there is something more fundamental at play here. It goes to the very heart of the question of language.

As we saw in the previous chapter, Climacus describes the apostle as one who has a direct relation with God, and the ability to use direct communication. It was argued that this was a confused notion which was undermined by Kierkegaard's own analysis of existence and communication. It seems to be linked with his desire for words to regain their 'proper' authoritative meaning. The early journal with which we began looks for powerful men to impose order and structure on a miscreant and vague language. We know that this concern stayed with Kierkegaard. In the *Postscript*, we find a lament over 'loose words' strongly reminiscent of that journal entry: 'a far greater bankruptcy is perhaps impending in the world of the mind, because the concepts are gradually being canceled and the words are coming to mean everything' (*CUP* 363). Indeed, this very inadequacy is extended as a criticism of the intrinsic incompetence of language. Words lack the ability to foster ethical seriousness. They are intrinsically 'poetic' in a pejorative sense: 'In relation to possibility, words are the highest pathos; in relation to actuality, actions are the highest pathos' (*CUP* 389–90). Words articulate a false ideality, for 'the discourse itself is always somewhat foreshortened, inasmuch as words are a more abstract medium than existing' (*CUP* 444). By means of this deceptive language, 'The poet can explain (transfigure) all existence, but he cannot explain himself' (ibid.).

As against the poet, the witness, and more especially the apostle, offer a circumvention of the otherwise inevitable detour through abstraction intrinsic to language. In *The Book on Adler*, written in 1847, Kierkegaard calls on the example of the apostle to put the immanent authority of the genius in its place. The apostle is called to witness to essential paradox, which is the 'protest against all immanence' (*OAR* 107); his authority is from another place ('andetstedsfra') (*OAR* 110). But it is an authority which can rely on no discursive proof: 'An apostle has no other proof but his own assertion, and at the most by his willingness to suffer everything for the sake of the doctrine' (*OAR* 118). However, this phrase reveals what is really at issue. For the 'doctrine' is that Christianity is *not* a doctrine, but the existential paradox of Christ. The same paradox which ruptures immanence renders any direct authority and direct communication impossible.

Even as Kierkegaard states in 1848 that the indirect form cannot be the final one, he reserves 'Unqualified indirect communication' for the God-Man (JP 2: 1958; Pap. IX A 260). By 1850, he is writing that 'Only the God-Man is in every respect indirect communication from first to last' (JP 2: 1959; Pap. X(3) A 413). But if this is the case, then all direct communication must be seen as derivative. The most decisive, essential communication is intrinsically indirect, even poetic. The direct form is only a relatively uninteresting instance of a fundamentally indirect medium. One who writes about the incarnation must be disabused of the illusion that there is a form of words, or an extra-verbal medium which will evade the detour of the sign. The tension in Kierkegaard's texts arises from his belief that 'Christianity is an *existence-communication* brought into the world by the use of *authority*' (JP 1: 187; Pap. X(2) A 119), because the two halves of this assertion are at odds with each other – unless we formulate a very different notion of authority from that which Kierkegaard seems to have in mind.

Kierkegaard is well aware that authority has no place in his own practice of religious communication. The disappearance of the author in the *Edifying Discourses* is a motif repeated throughout the authorship. It is intimately connected with the absence of authority and of a fixed, pre-ordained meaning of words. In his review of the pseudonymous literature in *Postscript*, Climacus writes 'I am only a reader' (*CUP* 252), whilst denying that an author should have any special insight into his own work, 'as if in a purely legal sense an author were the best interpreter of his own words' (ibid.). Indeed, the lack of authorial presence lends these writings a space in which ideality can be communicated, for 'The absence of an author is a means of distancing' (ibid.). Ironically, Kierkegaard repeats this theme in his own name, as he takes responsibility for the writing of the pseudonymous books in a declaration at the end of the *Postscript*:

> Thus in the pseudonymous books there is not a single word by me. I have no opinion about them except as a reader, not the remotest private relation to them, since it is impossible to have that to a doubly reflected communication. (*CUP* 626)

Kierkegaard wishes that his reader 'remembers me as irrelevant to the books' (*CUP* 629). The author is merely the occasion through whom the 'textuality' of existence is revealed. His aim is 'to read through solo, if possible in a more inward way the original text of individual human existence-relationships, the old familiar text handed down from the fathers' (*CUP* 629–30). If existence is like a text, then it cannot be understood from a vantage point outside the differentiated play of language and consciousness. Neither eternity nor authority can achieve what the speculative philosopher failed to achieve.

Even in the supposedly 'direct' accounting for the authorship found in *The Point of View for My Work as an Author*, Kierkegaard's lack of authorial control is emphasized. Here we have an author laying his soul bare, but at the beginning, Kierkegaard states that he cannot communicate his private God-relation and the explanation of authorship (*PV* 9). Even this direct accounting is made in the shadow of what remains unsaid, of what essentially cannot be said. Kierkegaard is still 'in the role of a reader' (*PV* 15) in relation to his own work. There is no claim to have understood the meaning of the authorship from the start (*PV* 72). The published summary of this book, *On My Work as an Author*, is most explicit: 'I regarded myself preferably as a *reader* of the books, not as the *author*' (*PV* 155). Kierkegaard is without authority, unable to compel people to listen to him, or even to determine what they are to make of his words.[19]

Not only does Kierkegaard erase himself from the authorship, but the pseudonymous books repeat this act in the case of their own fictional authors and characters. *Either/Or* and *Stages* provide the clearest examples of this, in the multiple layers of text, authors and editors which destabilise the idea of a coherent book from within. We are never quite sure where veracity ends and invention begins. Is 'The Seducer's Diary' the work of 'A'? Are both parts of *Either/Or* the work of one hand? Is Quidam's diary an invention of Frater Taciturnus?

'In Vino Veritas' in *Stages* gives a clear example of the way in which the text is used to call into question its own status. The narrator of this section, William Afham,[20] seems to be strangely absent from the events in which he is supposed to be a present participant. He is nowhere addressed by the other characters and makes no speech at the banquet. At the end of the section, he himself asks:

> But who, then, am I? Let no one ask about that ... I am pure being and thus almost less than nothing. I am the pure being that is everywhere present but yet not noticeable, for I am continually being annulled. (*SLW* 86)

Like the silent origin of all language, Afham is present only in his absence, in the text which results from his annulment. He steals Judge William's papers from Victor Eremita, who had himself stolen them from the Judge's house. Afham says that even the idea for the theft is not his own, for it was copied from Victor (*SLW* 86). The circulation of texts resists *all* propriety and mastery, bourgeois or ironical. No one can control the flux of meanings, for meaning is not discovered in the correspondence of word and essence, but created in the transgressive movement by which linguistic signs destroy the notion of proper essences. The originator of a text is, like Constantine, author of *Repetition*, 'a vanishing person, just like the midwife in relation to the child she has delivered' (*R* 230).

Language itself dissolves authority, and this applies as much to writing

---

[19] For a much fuller deconstruction of these texts' claim to be direct accountings for the authorship, see J. Garff, 'The Eyes of Argus', *Kierkegaardiana* 15 (1991), pp. 29–54.

[20] The very name 'Afham', meaning 'by himself', implies a kind of mysterious detachment from the events of the narrative.

about, proclaiming or witnessing to the paradox as to anything else. In fact, it applies much more so, for the paradox in its very structure, repeats in historical and particular form this inescapable duplicity of the sign, which may yet be the means for graceful communication. Kierkegaard's use of the metaphor of a text in relation to human existence relationships (*CUP* 630) suggests that sign, spirit and existence share in a common 'illusiveness' (cf. *CUP* 82), a kind of guileful evasion of rational control. Faith holds that this illusiveness, whilst it can be the opportunity for dissimulation and cruelty, is most truly manifest in the form of infinite, incarnate, suffering love. The sign is the necessary medium for articulating and realizing any ideal. Though Climacus may 'recall with some relief that Caesar had the Alexandrian library burned to the ground' (*CUP* 256), this terroristic attitude towards language is caught in its own contradictions. Language makes possible, not only abstraction and infidelity, but concrete care and sacrifice. The intrinsic impropriety of the sign is itself a sign – for faith – that God has always already committed himself to move in love towards his creatures, for God 'has only one joy: to communicate' (JP 2: 1414; Pap. X(3) A 585).

Consider Climacus' description of the religious thinker:

> One who is existing is continually in the process of becoming; the actually existing subjective thinker, thinking, continually reproduces this in his existence and invests all his thinking in becoming. This is similar to having style. Only he really has style who is never finished with something but 'stirs the waters of language' whenever he begins, so that to him the most ordinary expression comes into being with newborn originality. (*CUP* 86)

The metaphor of 'stirring the waters' derives from the gospel story of the Pool of Bethesda (John 5: 1–9), which had healing powers when its surface was disturbed. The image is suggestive of an intimacy between the thinker and the material medium of language. Religious communication proceeds from a deeper immersion in the contradictions of existence.[21] It demands a repetition, a constantly renewed commitment to the communicational world, constrained by all its material exigencies. The thinker's 'style' is not an effete veneer, but a passionate process of conversion; it is a risk-laden intervention in the relativities of human life.

The phrase 'stirring the waters' also occurs in the 'Seducer's Diary'. The seducer has seen Cordelia for the first time; weeks go by without encountering her again, and he grows impatient with fortune, demanding that it satisfies him. At the culmination of his tirade, he cries 'Let her hate me, scorn me, be indifferent to me, love someone else – I do not fear; but stir up

---

[21] Cf. 'the point is to immerse oneself, existing, in subjectivity' (*CUP* 192); 'one does not prepare oneself to become aware of Christianity by reading books or by world historical surveys, but by immersing oneself in existing' (*CUP* 560).

the water, break the silence' (*EO* 327). The Pool of Bethesda only gave healing when its waters were stirred by an angel. In a perverse way, the seducer recalls this narrative. By his invocation of chance, he seeks the opportunity for the perfect seduction, his regaining of purity. The Pool of Bethesda offers healing only for the fortunate few who can anticipate the moment to descend.

Bethesda is mentioned twice in the upbuilding discourses of 1843–4. In the first case, it is again linked with fortune, Kierkegaard arguing that faith is not like other goods, whose

> apportionment is like the water in the pool Bethesda, about which we read in Holy Scripture: Once in a while the angel descends and stirs the water, and the one who comes first – ah, yes, the one who comes first – is the fortunate one. (*ED* 11)

In the second instance, Bethesda is a positive image of the restlessness of the soul, out of which healing can come:

> Only when the water in the pool of Bethesda was stirred, only then was it healing to descend into it. This is easier to understand in the spiritual sense, because if a person's soul comes to a standstill in the monotony of self-concern and self-preoccupation, then he is bordering on soul rot unless the contemplation stirs and moves him. (*ED* 207)

The Pool encapsulates the dilemmas of religious communication. When the wind breathes on the surface of the water, when immediacy is negated, is it for the sake of arbitrary caprice, a work of chance or self-will? Or is it the breath of the life-giving Spirit of inspiration? The religious writer must risk breaking silence, to enter into the opacity of the linguistic world, where seduction and healing can wear similar masks. Language is open to different uses and abuses, and no extra-linguistic standpoint is available for us to judge between them. No chance incursion of the divine from without is adequate to religious seriousness. Paradoxically, only a disturbance *within* us awakens us from self-concern, into the concern to communicate which is at the heart of the subjective thinker's style. The way to awareness of and communication with the other is through the turmoil which rouses one's inner state from apathy to passion, and opens our monologue to be interrupted by a different language.

Kierkegaard's tendency to write of apostles and witnesses to truth as extraordinary figures masks the degree to which all believers are called to be witnesses. The restless waters of Bethesda recall the restlessness of faith which Kierkegaard refers to in *For Self-Examination*. One manifestation of that restlessness is exemplified by the witness to truth (*FSE* 19), who seeks to reform externals, whereas Kierkegaard claims only to want to encourage inward deepening in relation to Christianity. However, it became clearer and clearer to Kierkegaard that such a neat distinction could not be maintained. As *Practice* affirms, the witness to truth combines both elements in a uniquely subversive way:

> Every time a witness to the truth transforms truth into inwardness (and this is the essential activity of the witness to truth), every time a genius internalizes the true in an original way – then the established order is offended. (*PC* 87)

The witness essentially challenges the self-deification of the established order, and thus has a critical, reforming role in the public realm as well as the private one.

Indeed, this is the basis for Kierkegaard's attack on Mynster and the State Church. He derides Martensen's description of Mynster as a witness to the truth. A witness is one who suffers for the faith in opposition to the world – not a paid civic functionary: 'Christianity is heterogeneous to the world, wherefore the "witness" must always be recognizable by heterogeneity to this world, by renunciation, by suffering' (*KAUC* 11). Suffering does not result only from inner renunciation, but from bearing testimony against worldly idolatry. The witness cannot retreat into silence as Martensen is accused of doing, for that is evasion and cowardice (*KAUC* 67).

It is in this context that we can better understand Kierkegaard's misgivings about the finality of the indirect form. Consider the passage we quoted earlier, this time with a preceding sentence:

> Yet the communication of the essentially Christian must end finally in 'witnessing.' The maieutic cannot be the final form, because, Christianly understood, the truth does not lie in the subject (as Socrates understood it) but in a revelation which must be proclaimed. (JP 2: 1957; Pap. IX A 221)

The witness cannot hide behind a poetized personality, but must step forward in his or her own person, to embody the testimony to the truth which provokes rejection and suffering. The indirect method 'could be an attempt to avoid suffering for the doctrine' (JP 6: 6783; Pap. X(4) A 395) and thus Kierkegaard felt bound to claim that his Anti-Climacus works were not truly indirect, as he associated his name with them in forewords to express that he himself was striving after the ideal they presented (e.g. JP 1:679; Pap. X(2) A 624).

The nature of witnesses is well summarized by a sentence from the same journal passage in which Kierkegaard writes of the need for a detachment of religious poets to help people into the current of the ideal. Christianity, he says, 'wants to be proclaimed by *witnesses* – that is, by persons who proclaim the teaching and also existentially express it' (JP 6: 6521; Pap. X(2) A 157). But this reduplication of teaching in life is not the speciality of an elite group. *Practice* makes it clear that Christ wants imitators not admirers:

> An imitator *is* or strives *to be* what he admires, and an admirer keeps himself personally detached, consciously or unconsciously does not discover that what is admired involves a claim upon him, to be or at least to strive to be what is admired. (*PC* 241)

Christ is the prototype, and his followers' footprints must 'correspond' to his (*PC* 238).

However, we can quickly see from this that Kierkegaard has not renounced the motivation which lies behind the indirect method and which is essentially bound up with the very nature of Christian proclamation. The truth is not an intellectual content or essence, but a way to be followed, a life to be imitated. And that imitation can never be direct, for the follower will face ever new demands in new situations. Following is reduplication, a kind of artistry even though it is deadly serious. Kierkegaard wishes to guard against taking his indirect communication as a poetic fantasy, which is properly enjoyed by aesthetic or intellectual contemplation. The witness sacrifices all for the teaching. But even the witness cannot escape the risk and ambiguity which threads through the indirect work. The paradox of our embodiment of God's will in time does not become any less paradoxical; no 'authority' can cancel the need for existential resolution.

In *Practice*, Anti-Climacus affirms that 'in relation to truth there is no abridgement that leaves out the acquiring of it' and that it is 'impossible summarily to appropriate it, however wide awake one is' (*PC* 203). He goes on to make it clear that even one with the 'authority' of an apostle is still only a witness to this intrinsically indirect faith:

> Thus Christ is the truth in the sense that to *be* the truth is the only true explanation of what truth is. Therefore one can ask an apostle, one can ask a Christian, 'What is truth?' and in answer to the question the apostle and this Christian will point to Christ and say: Look at him, learn from him, he was the truth. This means that truth in the sense in which Christ is the truth is not a sum of statements, not a definition etc., but a life. (*PC* 205)

Apostle and Christian are on essentially the same level. There can be no doctrinal expert, no privileged access to the essence of God's nature. The key is performance, not knowledge.

As Derrida writes, it is of the very nature of testimony that it possesses no self-evident truth. It is not a transmission of objective knowledge, it cannot make clear and present that which is opaque and immemorial:

> For one will never reconcile the value of a testimony with that of knowledge or of certainty – it is impossible and it ought not to be done. One will never reduce the one to the other – it is impossible and it ought not to be done.[22]

---

[22] J. Derrida, *On the Name*, (Stanford, Calif.: Stanford University Press, 1995), p. 31.

In this sense, the notion of contemporaneity with Christ need not be a negation of history. Contemporaneity with Christ dislocates all our contemporaneity with ourselves, and with the established order of our day. In bearing witness to the possibility of the paradoxical transformation of humanity by grace, one is never really present to oneself. One bears witness to – a witness. Christ is the prototype, the prototype therefore of witnessing also. His witness is that through life, through abasement and suffering, one testifies to an absolute other. That testimony is poetic *and* existential, indirect and yet also an ineluctable responsibility to the Other and to the others with whom one communicates. Writing in the introduction to his translation of Levinas' *Otherwise than Being*, Adolph Lingis puts it like this: 'God is not a voice that addresses me to reveal himself and become thematizable, but enters language only in the witness I formulate, not in words that put forth my presence, but in words that expose my exposedness.'[23]

The analogy of communication thus returns us to the originary witness of God to himself – a witness which is perfected in the opacity of suffering and death. That divine act of witness, that mysterious communication/revelation awakens us to the urgency of our own singular calling, a calling to communicate with the passion which such urgency demands. The life which is gift and task indirectly corresponds to the communication of Christ, which is 'in one sense *behind* people, propelling them forward, while in another sense he *stands ahead*, beckoning' (*PC* 238). Only thus are people awakened to an absolute responsibility which cannot be exhausted by any finite end.

Summary

The question of realism and anti-realism thus looks rather different to the one we began with. Whilst we may safely reject as one-sided any crudely anti-realist or metaphysical realist reading of Kierkegaard's texts, the very fact that such readings remain possible testifies to the strange interconnection between form and content which those texts embody. The analogy of communication suggests the way in which that interconnection operates.

1. Analogy is a way of talking about God which avoids silence and certainty. It respects God's otherness whilst indirectly bearing witness to his nature. It has a critical, grammatical role in relation to religious narratives, but those narratives cannot be finally reduced to non-narrative discourse.

2. The analogy of communication bears witness to the mode of God's creation and revelation. The indirect nature of religious communication is

---

[23] E. Levinas, *Otherwise than Being*, trans. A. Lingis (Dordrecht: Kluwer, 1991), 'Translator's Introduction,' p. xxxiv.

analogous to God's indirect giving of himself, a giving which sets its recipient free. The analogy of communication has a critical function in warding off a direct relation to God which would be idolatry. However, it is itself related to narratives of divine giving and revelation. Divine communication is originary and prior to the human communication it makes possible. It is thus opaque to any rational grasp. The analogy of communication thus directs us towards existential religious practice as the primary locus for our 'knowledge' of God.

3. This is illustrated by Kierkegaard's treatment of religious practices and doctrines, and supremely by his account of the incarnation. The incarnation remains paradoxical, an intrinsically indirect communication of grace.

4. That indirect communication of grace demands an existential response of imitation and witness. When Kierkegaard says that he does not want the indirect form to be final, he means that it should not become an excuse to evade commitment; the content of faith remains indirect. It is embedded in narratives which tell of the paradoxical communication of God, which can only be 'understood' by passionate faith, by the existential response they provoke.

5. The analogy of communication protects the witness against the hubris of mistaking their communication for God's. Its critical function is thus intimately bound up with the actual practice of religious communication, a practice which should challenge authority, idolatry and the supremacy of finite ends. Kierkegaard's 'realism' is therefore inseparable from the form of his communication. It transforms the value of terms like 'reality' and 'truth' into existential ones – but all the time relating the believer to the incomprehensible gift and future of a wholly other God.

CHAPTER EIGHT

The passion of language

We have come a long way from our original question about realism and anti-realism in Kierkegaard's writings. Things no longer look so clear-cut, because both sides of that divide can lapse into undialectical crudities which Kierkegaard's texts seek to avoid. Metaphysical realism can presume to describe the essence of God, to mistake the statements of faith for propositions which directly correspond to the Divine nature. Anti-realism can betray a different form of presumption, neutralizing the otherness to which the language of faith bears witness. In both cases, there is an attempt to evade the tentativeness of faith for something more direct and controllable.

However, if we renounce all control, all authority in matters of belief, whether it be the external authority of Church and Scriptures, or the internal authority of autonomous reason, what is left? Are we surrendered into a perspectivalism which renounces any notion of a reality beyond our particular and relative perspectives, and which therefore reduces the question of truth to the undecidable one of competing rhetorics? Can faith survive in the absence of sure foundations?

These questions are especially pertinent to our study of Kierkegaard. He is important because of his renunciation of authority, his emphasis on the subjective character of faith, his exploration of the paradoxical limits of thought, and his practice of an intrinsically indirect communication. It has become possible in recent years to read Kierkegaard as a forerunner of trends in postmodern thought – and also as one who pre-empts and rejects such trends. Once again, the question of language seems to be at the heart of the problem.

A postmodern Kierkegaard?

Postmodernity is a notoriously slippery concept, varying from discipline to discipline and from context to context.[1] Whilst for some it is the logical conclusion of trends in modernity pushed to their extreme, for others it is a definitively new cultural situation – whilst for others still, it renders all such division of history into epochs unstable. Nevertheless, there are a cluster of trends and ideas which give some hint of what links these different readings

---

[1] See Hans Bertens, *The Idea of the Postmodern: A History* (London: Routledge, 1995) for a survey and references.

of postmodernity – and why Kierkegaard has appeared to some to be one of its first harbingers.

For Lyotard, postmodernity is a time of loss of faith in the grand narratives which gave some kind of unity to our sense of who we are and what the world is. Such narratives, both secular and religious, served to position us individually and collectively in a cosmic drama which gave life its direction and meaning. The realization that there is no objective way of deciding between the plurality of narratives we are invited to inhabit leads to a collapse of their intrinsic authority. Moreover, there is no rational, neutral middle ground from which competing world views might be judged. The ideal of a pure, absolute secular reason is shown up to be just another narrative. Ironically, we are most aware that narratives have lost their old objective power at a time when we have realised that we cannot escape such narratives, because there is no non-narrative site beyond them.

This is linked to an understanding of language which owes much to the work of Saussure. Saussure argued that language has no positive terms. That is, words have meaning by virtue of their relationship to and difference from other words. There is no absolute end-point to this process of definition, no anchor outside of the system of differences which constitutes language. By extension, our selfhood and our self-understandings are said to be constituted within this field of differences – in such a way as to challenge notions of a stable essence of selfhood, or a totalizing and systematic comprehension of the world. Meaning in language is always conditioned by the repetition and absence which structure the sign, as we have already seen with reference to Derrida.

Such aspects of postmodernity evoke very different readings, even among those who might accept their validity. These readings have had their impact on Kierkegaard studies in a curious way – for Kierkegaard is seen as partly legitimating the strategy of reading which is then applied to his texts. However, whilst the temptations for such a circle to become vicious are clear (our reading creates a Kierkegaard who legitimates our reading of him), it is far from obvious that such circularity can ever be totally avoided. In any case, I want to examine some recent approaches to Kierkegaard study which revolve around these questions of language, reading and narrative.

The first approach seems to turn Kierkegaard's distinctions upside down. His very attempt to secure a distinctive space for faith are read as undermining all the distinctions by which he would separate authentic language from mere chatter. The meaning of his texts becomes undecidable, even as they expose the inescapable undecidability inherent in all linguistic oppositions.

The second strand of scholarship attempts to rescue Kierkegaard from this unpromising position and to reinstate him at the centre of the Christian tradition. It does so, however, by appealing to an interpretation of Christian doctrine which links with narrative theology. If narratives go all the way down, then there is no way of justifying Christianity on any grounds outside the Christian story itself. Kierkegaard's critique of speculation anticipates this resistance to any translation of Christian categories into another conceptuality. Moreover, Kierkegaard is said to interpret Christian doctrines not as descriptive propositions, but as rules for reading and living out the Christian story, as the grammar of Christian faith.

The third approach plays on the implications of the language of absolute otherness and paradox to free Kierkegaard's texts from such a narrowly Christian understanding. Such a reading links Kierkegaard's resistance to speculation with a deep ethical impulse in his work, which resists both relativistic pessimism and Christian triumphalism. It is in this last option that we will find most promise – though not without challenging the reductionism which still haunts some of these interpretations.

Undecidability

Peter Fenves offers a reading of language and history in Kierkegaard's texts which attempts to expose the way in which Kierkegaard's language is always slipping beyond his control.[2] The distinctions Kierkegaard attempts to erect – between faith and offence, between idle chatter and authentic language use – cannot be maintained in any stable form. They break down because of the nature of language itself. Language is always haunted by the possibility of mis-communication, of idleness and meaninglessness, because it is never an immediate presentation of objects in or facts about the world. Language distances us from such immediacy from the start – so all Kierkegaard's attempts to distinguish what is fake from what is authentic are shadowed by this possibility that they are no more than a literary game, an artifice as inauthentic and speculative as the most debased chatter.

Chatter, as analysed by Kierkegaard, is idle talk. But it is not just a neatly defined and separate mode of language use. It challenges 'the very concepts of a *given* language and *already* constituted subjects'.[3] Fenves seeks to demonstrate that Kierkegaard's very denunciation of chatter relies on the fundamental characteristics of language which chatter exposes. To secure faith as a distinct category, separated from objectifying modes of knowledge which rely on evidence and probability means tearing it loose from any reference to a 'foundational discourse' which anchors it in a reality beyond language. But, as Fenves argues

> this rescue operation amounts to a total capitulation, for belief and faith are declared to have no other home than hearsay, and the sense of

---

[2] Peter Fenves, *'Chatter': Language and History in Kierkegaard* (Stanford, Calif.: Stanford University Press., 1993).

[3] Ibid., p. 2.

'presence' in the phrase 'standing in the presence of the thing itself' can only mean what is commonly called, with good reason, 'absence.' The absence of the thing about which one speaks and the absence of the speakers to themselves – their distraction, inattention, absent-mindedness – not only continue to define hearsay but come to determine the sense of any creed that removes itself from the norms of knowledge and the canonical procedures through which it is established. The fate of 'chatter' thus encircles the spread of faith.[4]

Faith can only be secured against confusion with the bankrupt concepts of speculative thought by a move which opens it up to a new confusion with the rootless and cognitively empty nature of chatter.

Similarly, Kierkegaard's appeals to silence and authenticity as remedies for chatter are shown to be self-parodies, appeals whose very enunciation breaks with the silence they recommend and thus makes them inauthentic. Fenves reads chatter as 'language no longer in the service of meaning',[5] no longer under the control of a speaking subject. Rather, chatter is 'original language' which 'outgrows its origin and corrodes the very language that is determined to bring it to a halt'.[6] Chatter is thus the system of differences which always exceeds rational grasp even as it makes what we call thinking possible by loosening us from the grip of immediacy.

As we have noted, the consequences of this reading of Kierkegaard for any settled and distinct notion of faith are devastating. In order to clear a space for faith, it must be distinguished from all modes of knowing. Faith gives access to the paradox, to that object which no merely immanent Socratic recollection or philosophical speculation could reproduce. However, even to specify this much about the object of faith is already to compromise its paradoxicality. Fenves describes how Climacus rejects the Socratic position that all difficulties are illusory because they ultimately derive from oneself. For Climacus, a real difficulty

> must come from elsewhere. And yet the attempt to locate this 'elsewhere' is as contradictory an exercise as the proposal that one pose a difficulty that no one, by definition, can pose. For to locate it is *eo ipso* to locate it within one's grasp and therefore to locate it within one's self-conception.[7]

Fenves claims that this results in a challenge to the propositional model of language and truth. Language no longer promises a correspondence between word and reality; in its irreducibly temporal form, it impels us to recognize the difference of the self to itself – for the self is always preceded and constituted by an inconceivable otherness.

---

[4] Ibid., p. 15.
[5] Ibid., p. 45.
[6] Ibid., p. 84.
[7] Ibid., p. 116.

Ultimately, faith is as paradoxical as its object, Fenves argues. If its object is the paradox, it must reject any conceptuality which would translate its object into rational terms. Faith alone gives access to the paradox, and thus faith must speak only of itself. The irony is that in so doing, faith must give up any sense of itself as a distinct and definable object: 'Faith, in speaking of itself, must be its own definitive object, but in order to be so, it must abandon itself as a determinate object.'[8] Faith itself is the paradox which refuses all comprehension.

It need hardly be said that this throws any realist reading of Kierkegaard's language about God and the paradox into crisis. Fenves draws out the implications of this in a reading of *Fear and Trembling*. In this text, he argues, we find a communication of what must remain essentially incommunicable – which is not the same as no communication at all. Rather, in its concentration on the unique singularity of the story of Abraham and Isaac, this text in fact undermines any sense of a unifying narrative structure, of a law or generality under which the case of Abraham can be subsumed. Silentio's stories of the mother weaning the child from her breast become allegories of the incomprehensibility of the story itself – allegories which suspend the opposition between the comprehensible and the incomprehensible.

Fenves thus reads Kierkegaard's texts as breached by an 'event' of pure language – chatter – in which the distinctions between comprehension and incomprehension are suspended, undecidable. His conclusion appears deeply pessimistic: 'Communication cannot escape "chatter" without itself becoming more – not qualitatively different – "chatter".'[9] The issue with which we began – that of realism versus anti-realism – becomes one more undecidable opposition. For 'With the suspension of the disjunction between subjectivity and objectivity, all other terms of opposition collapse.'[10]

There is an undoubtable element of deliberate perversity in this reading of Kierkegaard. The very category of chatter which he uses as a foil to delineate an alternative space for authentic communication is turned against him, to undermine the oppositions he seeks to erect. Such oppositions become undecidable on any grounds, and the whole field of communication becomes submerged in the swamp of chatter – which is ironically held to be 'pure' language.

The difficulty with Fenves' approach is not that he reads Kierkegaard in this way, for he is not indulging in arbitrary reflections. A summary of his book cannot do justice to the close detail with which he examines individual Kierkegaardian texts. Reading against the grain of Kierkegaard's surface meaning is only permissible when allied to this rigorous textual commentary.

The problem with Fenves' interpretation is rather that he elevates an

---

[9] Ibid., p. 233.
[10] Ibid., p. 234.

aspect of language in Kierkegaard's texts to a dominant and all-encompassing position, and, by a law of 'contamination' allows that aspect to submerge any other reading of Kierkegaard's 'theories' and usage of language. As we have seen, Kierkegaard is well aware of the paradoxes which await any attempt to theorize language. Language is the contradiction of the real and the ideal, a shattering of immediacy which makes both freedom and seduction possible. Language itself reveals its own fractures when brought into confrontation with the paradox of faith. However, Fenves seems only to read this in one direction – as a passage into a swamp of undecidable oppositions, where the self is becalmed and dissipated. For Kierkegaard, however, it presents an ethical and religious challenge which could only be answered in practical terms. His readings of the subjunctive mood, of indirect communication and witnessing bear testimony to the possibility of communication as liberation. And this communication issues not out of and into a void, but responds to the prior gift of God's communication. That gift cannot be specified on neutral theoretical grounds, but it can be encountered in the very practice of communication itself, as a possibility for creativity which no immanent, rational theory could account for.

Fenves gives only a static glimpse of the ordeal of undecidability; with the negation of all passionate distinctions, time itself is negated. To be fair, he does suggest that his reading of Kierkegaard does have some liberating potential. Kierkegaard's unwitting reduction of all language into chatter contains a prophetic promise of 'a mode of speaking in advance that does not appeal to natural or cultural regularities or even to the divine ruler of the world'.[11] Chatter sounds a note of alarm for settled notions of legality and authority. But even here, such an alarm seems strangely empty. As Fenves writes 'Everything remains in its place, yet each thing, as soon as it is spoken, is altered, struck down, shattered, "chattered".'[12] But this 'prophecy' remains an empty gesture, because all distinctions between just and unjust, real and unreal have been erased. In revealing the emptiness of all authority, chatter opens no alternative space, and indeed, it offers no threat to a capitalistic or tyrannical mode of authority which rejoices in its own emptiness, in the rhetoric of commodities or power for its own sake.

A rhetorical theology need not surrender before this implied ideology – that in the absence of all distinctions between real and unreal, only the empty rhetoric of power remains. Instead, Kierkegaard offers us an alternative 'rhetoric' which claims to repeat the creative speaking/writing of God. As such, it is not an exercise in power for its own sake. It is a work of love.

---

[11] Ibid., p. 238.
[12] Ibid., pp. 240–1.

Christian narrativism

According to Gerard Loughlin, 'all theology should presuppose what a narrative theology emphasises: the priority of the story of Jesus Christ'.[13] For Loughlin, we have to accept that we are in a postmodern situation, in which there is no independent rational viewpoint or foundation which can be the basis for deciding between different grand narratives. Theology has no foundation beyond the Christian story and the community which tells it. Allied to this is an understanding of Christian narrative as pedagogical – a training in Christian practice rather than a propositional description of a reality outside the narrative. This is not to say that narrative theology is anti-realist. Loughlin rejects Cupitt's position on the basis that it elevates a non-Christian rhetoric of the Void above the Christian story itself. Rather, narrative theologians are claiming that the criteria for reality must be determined from within the Christian narrative.

Loughlin refers to George Lindbeck as an example of orthodox Christian narrativism. Lindbeck proposes an understanding of Christian doctrine as a cultural-linguistic phenomenon, which has a grammatical role in clarifying how Christians are to read and perform their founding narrative. He distinguishes this from two alternative ways of understanding doctrine. The first, the cognitive model, asserts that 'doctrines function as informative propositions or truth claims about objective realities'.[14] The second, the experiential-expressive, 'interprets doctrines as noninformative and nondiscursive symbols of inner feelings, attitudes or existential orientations'.[15] The cognitivist model fixes doctrines as articles of knowledge divorced from their context in the Christian narrative, and makes faith into a species of knowledge. The experiential-expressivist model, on the other hand, makes faith into a vague interior reality, assertions about which become 'logically and empirically vacuous'.[16]

Lindbeck's alternative – the cultural-linguistic model – sees a religion as a total framework for understanding the world, akin to a culture or a language. It is communal, contains discursive and nondiscursive elements, and possesses doctrines which function as the logic – the grammar – in terms of which those elements can be related. Doctrines are thus deeply embedded in a concrete form of life. They are the rules for Christian practice. They do not themselves make true or false assertions, but they can shape human lives such that those lives themselves are what correspond or fail to correspond to ultimate reality.[17] Lindbeck thus wants to free doctrines from a narrow

---

[13] Gerard Loughlin, *Telling God's Story: Bible, Church and Narrative Theology* (Cambridge: Cambridge University Press, 1996), pp. xi–xii.
[14] George A. Lindbeck, *The Nature of Doctrine: Religion and Theology in a Postliberal Age* (London: SPCK, 1984), p. 16.
[15] Ibid.
[16] Ibid., p. 32.
[17] Ibid., p. 69.

cognitive model without denying the ontological reality of God as the one who is the ultimate source and goal of authentic human living.

Such an argument sheds a new light on the work of D. Z. Phillips, to whom we referred in the first chapter. Although he may not be a cognitivist, this does not make him an anti-realist in Cupitt's sense. Rather, in rejecting any non-religious cognitive foundation for religious beliefs, he is not denying that those beliefs orient us to a God who is a reality beyond the consciousness of the believer. He is questioning the whole basis for distinguishing realism from anti-realism. Belief is not a question of evidence, of entertaining an hypothesis, and it cannot be recommended or rejected on such grounds. Rather, beliefs of any kind cannot be divorced from the practices with which they are integrally bound.[18]

Several themes emerge: the priority of Christian narrative and the impossibility of an independent foundation for religious belief; an understanding of doctrines which interprets them as rules for Christian performance rather than cognitive descriptions; a rejection of crude realism without abandoning a belief that the total Christian narrative, as it is celebrated and performed, in some appropriate sense 'corresponds' to ultimate reality, to 'what God means by us'.[19]

Such positions connect with the version of ethical realism which I have attributed to Kierkegaard, and they have found resonances in some recent work on him. Steven Emmanuel appeals to Lindbeck's view of doctrine in attempting to articulate Kierkegaard's understanding of revelation. He argues that Kierkegaard rejected any dependency of faith on historical or other evidences. Faith is chosen on pragmatic grounds, based on one's infinite interest in an eternal happiness. And this pragmatic option for faith is not merely prudential – it is moulded by the choice of an ethical practice: 'the affirmation of God's existence and of one's belief in an eternal happiness is intimately linked with moral practice, or as Kierkegaard frequently expresses it, "the ethical".'[20] Such a viewpoint clearly connects with the argument of this book in seeing faith in practical and ethical terms.

Emmanuel links this with Lindbeck's interpretation of doctrines by claiming that Kierkegaard's concern for the clarification of concepts like revelation has to do with articulating their logical function in Christian belief and not reducing them to abstract speculative propositions. As Emmanuel puts it, 'Kierkegaard seems to have regarded doctrines primarily as rules for

---

[18] See D. Z. Phillips, 'On Really Believing' in J. Runzo, *Is God Real?* (Basingstoke: Macmillan, 1993), pp. 85–108: 'Theological non-realism is as empty as theological realism. Both terms are battle cries in a confused philosophical and theological debate' (p. 87).

[19] The phrase is Hugh Pyper's from 'Cities of the Dead' in George Pattison and Steven Shakespeare (eds), *Kierkegaard on Self and Society* (London: Macmillan, 1998), p. 137.

[20] Steven M. Emmanuel, *Kierkegaard and the Concept of Revelation* (Albany: State University of New York Press, 1996), p. 67.

regulating the speech and action of the religious community.'[21] Emmanuel claims that, for Kierkegaard, 'True faith is exhibited primarily in correct performance, rather than in correct belief.'[22]

Emmanuel can appeal not only to particular articulations of concepts such as authority and revelation, but also to more explicit statements in which Kierkegaard appears to distance himself from a cognitivist model of religious doctrine:

> Christianity is not a doctrine, but expresses an existence-contradiction and is an existence-communication. If Christianity were a doctrine, it would *eo ipso* not constitute an opposite of speculative thought but would be an element within it. Christianity pertains to existence, to existing, but existence and existing are the very opposite of speculation. (*CUP* 380)

Christianity makes a demand on existence, and its beliefs are not doctrines in the sense of propositions of speculative reason. Nor indeed are they expressions of interior states of mind, of innate human capacities (this was Kierkegaard's critique of Adler). Rather, they shape a distinctive way of existing, of living in time in relation to an absolute paradox which cannot be assimilated to rational categories. As we have seen, dialectics can play a regulative role, in guarding us against a false, idolatrous identification of the eternal. But dialectical thought cannot make the eternal comprehensible to the intellect. In a similar way, Christian 'doctrines' provide the rules for Christian speech and behaviour, and provide guidelines for discerning false moves in the Christian language game.

The ultimate pattern for Christian life is not a set of propositional beliefs, but the life of Jesus Christ (*FSE* 191; cf. *CD* 104). Recommending faith is not therefore a matter of accumulating evidences, but of witnessing to a way of existing in the world, shaped by the narrative of Christ's life. And that narrative, for Emmanuel, provides an all-consuming horizon of reality for the believer:

> Properly understood, the narrative of Christian revelation does not present itself as an object for historical belief; it is not intended to be understood as a falsifiable description of an historical event. Rather, it presents a radically new conceptual framework for understanding self and world.[23]

This entails a revision of the cognitivist model of truth, for 'truth is not based on the traditional picture of correspondence between mind and reality, but between self and God'.[24]

---

[21] Ibid., p. 96.
[22] Ibid., p. 97.
[23] Ibid., p. 104.
[24] Ibid., p. 105.

Such an understanding also seems to inform the work of David Gouwens. In an article entitled 'Kierkegaard's Understanding of Doctrine' he makes the point that 'It is not doctrines that refer or are true in themselves, but it is people who refer truly to God with the language of faith as shaped by the doctrines.'[25]

Gouwens develops this position in his recent book:

> Johannes Climacus insists, however, that 'Christianity is not a doctrine but an existence-communication [*Existents-Meddelse*].' Or elsewhere, 'Christianity is not a doctrine; it is an existence [*Existents*], an existing [*Existeren*].' By this he means that it is fundamentally an error to think that 'Christianity,' a phenomenon that is after all describable according to its beliefs, *is* therefore simply those beliefs. Climacus does say, it should be noted, that Christianity has beliefs. But it is precisely because those beliefs cannot be stated, analyzed, weighed, and otherwise examined in a dispassionate manner that one must say that Christianity is not simply those beliefs. By saying that Christianity is, rather, an 'existence-communication,' Climacus means that those beliefs have their home within a particular context of life, or existence, and that this context is further defined as a 'communication,' not only of beliefs, but of 'capabilities.'[26]

Gouwens associates these capabilities with the virtue-tradition of ethics. Kierkegaard is seen as inviting the reader to be trained in ethical virtues, which provide the subjective qualifications for knowing God.[27] Indeed, the ethical constitutes a 'grammar' of seeing and knowing God. For Gouwens, then, Kierkegaard steers between the twin dangers of subjectivism and objectivism in religion and ethics. The truth must be subjective – a matter of passionate response and appropriation, of upbuilding – but also a relation to what transcends the self. Religious truth requires a passionate subjectivity in order to have access to a transcendent, objectively real God.[28]

Narrative is an important category for Gouwens too. He argues that Kierkegaard gives us a narrative understanding of the self's development and that narrative provides the proper context for orienting the self to God in Christ: 'Operating here [in Kierkegaard's later writings] is a Christological pattern of thought in which the narrative of Christ, his particular life, gives the context for encountering him.'[29]

---

[25] David Gouwens, 'Kierkegaard's Understanding of Doctrine', *Modern Theology* 5 (1988–9), pp. 13–22 (quote from p.20).

[26] David Gouwens, *Kierkegaard as Religious Thinker* (Cambridge: Cambridge University Press, 1996), pp. 34–5.

[27] Ibid., pp. 104ff.

[28] This is similar to the argument of C. Stephen Evans, *Passionate Reason: Making Sense of Kierkegaard's Philosophical Fragments* (Bloomington and Indianapolis: Indiana University Press, 1992).

[29] Gouwens, *Kierkegaard as Religious Thinker*, p. 135.

Several consequences can be drawn from this broad approach as Emmanuel and Gouwens articulate it. Firstly, Christianity needs to be understood on its own terms. The Christian narrative provides a total context in which questions of truth and reality are settled. It cannot be judged by the standards of an alien conceptuality. As Gouwens states, for Kierkegaard 'Because of the breach Christ causes with the understanding, an independent or foundationalist apologetics is not possible.'[30] Secondly, the use of categories like grammar and narrative are not a departure from orthodox Christianity, much less a denial of the objective reality of God. Rather, they articulate how orthodoxy works, and how this real God is to be encountered. Gouwens puts it succinctly, when he states that 'The "how" of subjectivity does not create its own object, for faith is a *response* to that object.'[31] And Emmanuel objects to the kind of undecidability which Fenves finds in Kierkegaard's language when he claims that 'Kierkegaard's understanding of what language is and how it functions is underwritten by the assumption of God's presence; indeed, he assumes that all meaningful forms of communication presuppose real presence.'[32]

Taken together, these two emphases result in a picture of Kierkegaard as a wholly orthodox Christian, whose works simply bring to the fore the innate logic of Christian belief, and the subjective passion needed to appropriate it and live it out. Indeed, Gouwens asserts that 'Kierkegaard is best seen as a person standing at the center of the Christian tradition rather than at its fringe' and he quotes Michael Plekon in claiming that that Kierkegaard is 'a theologian in the classical, catholic, and orthodox sense'.[33] Emmanuel too is concerned to emphasize the objectivity of Christian revelation for Kierkegaard, and pits the Dane against the corruption of 'the language of orthodox Christian theology'.[34]

However, all this effort to get Kierkegaard placed at the comfortable centre of the Christian tradition smacks of special pleading. Emmanuel's appeal to 'real presence' in Kierkegaard's texts is not backed up by any extensive analysis of Kierkegaard's understanding of language. As we have seen, Kierkegaard's multi-faceted 'theorizing' and usage of language does not yield such a convenient solution. Of course, there is a powerful strand of his writing which does idealize a state in which meanings will be directly and powerfully present in words. But this strand is continually contested and undermined by the 'how' of Kierkegaard's communication. Language and the sign are bound up with themes of repetition, contradiction and absence which destabilize the classification of reality into objective and subjective aspects.

---

[30] Ibid., p. 71.
[31] Ibid., p. 126.
[32] Emmanuel, *Kierkegaard*, p. x.
[33] Gouwens, *Kierkegaard as Religious Thinker*, p. 22.
[34] Emmanuel, *Kierkegaard*, p. 127; cf. p. 117: 'The Christ-revelation is thus the starting point for a proper definition of Christian theological concepts.'

It is no real solution to this situation to raise certain motifs up from Kierkegaard's texts and give them the status of 'grammar'. The assumption is that these 'rules for reading' the Christian story have an epistemologically regulative status which grants them immunity from substantive cognitive questions. But it is disingenuous to collapse together grammar with religious doctrine in this way, because religious rules are *not* cognitively neutral in the same way as linguistic ones. Indeed, insofar as linguistic grammar affects the possible ways we experience and respond to the world, then it can hardly be said to be cognitively neutral either.

The motivation behind this is presumably to find some sure footing beyond the irony and rhetoric and indirectness which threaten to overwhelm Kierkegaard's texts. In a curious way, Gouwens is advocating a kind of foundationalism after all – a foundationalism of Christian 'grammatical' fundamentalism. The Christian story and the Christian story alone gives access to reality thanks to the validity of its doctrinal grammar. However, the instability of such an enterprise is evident from the curious twists of Gouwens's argument. Having established the priority of the Christian narrative and the impossibility of any independent apologetic, Gouwens is then faced with the problem that Kierkegaard appears to use ideas which are not strictly Christian or Biblical. Kierkegaard uses terms like 'paradox' and 'indirect communication' in a way which threatens the self-sufficiency of Christian doctrines.

Gouwens's solution to this dilemma is revealing:

> what Kierkegaard adds to those dogmatic concepts is first a set of 'metaconcepts' (the absolute paradox, the divine incognito, the impossibility of direct communication, the definition of 'faith' in contrast to knowledge) and also rhetorical strategies (like the two teachers and 'the god's poem') that 'seek to quicken awareness of the divine' by enticing, provoking, shocking.[35]

There are a number of tensions within this passage which a 'narrative' theology of Kierkegaard is unable to handle. Firstly, it opens up the prospect of an infinite regress: the Christian narrative cannot stand alone, it needs rules to guide our response to it. This is the function of credal doctrines, like the Chalcedonian definition of Christ. However, it now appears that such doctrines cannot be relied upon either. Kierkegaard needs to help them out with some metaconcepts of his own. What is to say that Kierkegaard's metaconcepts will themselves not need 'meta-metaconcepts' ('grammar'?) to put them in their proper context and so on *ad infinitum*?

The second problem is that Gouwens thinks it is possible to distinguish Kierkegaard's metaconcepts from his rhetorical strategies. But it seems clear

---

[35] Gouwens, *Kierkegaard as Religious Thinker*, p. 143.

that all the motifs he mentioned in the first category are inseparably bound up with (given their context in use by) certain rhetorical strategies. The absolute paradox is not simply stated by Kierkegaard as a regulative concept – it enters into the dialectical and narrative flow of the texts, disrupting them from within. Gouwens's distinction seems to be more about preserving the identity of Christian doctrine from relativistic rhetoric than it is about what is really going on in Kierkegaard's texts. But the service he performs is two-edged, because he makes that doctrine increasingly dependent on extra-Christian concepts, which are themselves embedded in ironically and indirectly poised rhetorical strategies.

In short, a 'pure' narrative theology is not possible, for it must always presuppose certain concepts which are elevated above the narrative – most notable the concept of 'narrative' itself. In the case of Kierkegaard, this means adopting a standpoint which tries to escape the dialectics of existence-communication, and which can therefore neatly distinguish between subjective and objective aspects of faith in such a way that the stress on the former is in no way allowed to trouble the latter. The result is a reading of Kierkegaard which, however subtle, serves merely to confirm the good consciences of the orthodox. Indeed, it is the concept of 'orthodoxy' itself which should be subjected to greatest interrogation if Kierkegaard's 'how' of communication is really taken seriously.

This is not to say that Emmanuel and Gouwens do not offer highly insightful readings of Kierkegaard which resist the one-sidedness of an approach like that of Fenves. Their work highlights the irreducibility of narrative, the regulative role of doctrines and the crucial importance of ethical practice in knowing and relating to God. These are themes which are central to my understanding of the 'analogy of communication'. However, they are also themes which call into question the whole notion of what 'orthodoxy' could mean. The paradox is mediated by narratives, but it also splinters those narratives. If doctrines do function in a regulative and grammatical way for Kierkegaard, then they must also alert us to the fact that the paradox and our paradoxical faith refuse to be 'regulated'. No context is final or definitive, not even the Christian narrative. This is not because it must bow to some pure rationality divorced from all narrative, but because its own dynamic must open us out to an otherness which it cannot contain, to a practice whose shape it cannot configure in advance – for repetition is to live forwards, not to recollect. Emmanuel and Gouwens resist Fenves and his ilk only at the price of another form of one-sidedness, affirming an untroubled orthodoxy in Kierkegaard as the only alternative to a reading of him that issues in an unbridled relativism and ironic nihilism.

Such nihilism, which is implicit in Fenves's work, *does* need to be resisted. In collapsing all the distinctions which Kierkegaard tries to articulate, it negates any sense of engagement with an otherness which cannot be captured, defined or absorbed by conceptual thought. It results in a pseudo-speculative vision in which all positions and counter-positions are absorbed a priori into its consuming 'logic'. But simply to assert Christianity against this is to fail to reckon with the ways in which that otherness, that unknown limit and difference which fissures Kierkegaard's texts, cannot be exhaustively harnessed by an orthodoxy. In ways which Kierkegaard is not fully able to control, the paradox seeks to address an other which Christian concepts do not attempt to fully represent – hence the need for metaconcepts and rhetorical strategies. What this reveals is not some higher level of successful representation, but the foundering of all attempts to represent the paradox. There is no present to re-present, there is only gift and task to be repeated.

Emmanuel argues against deconstructionist readings that Kierkegaard appeals to an 'ethics of reading'[36] which directs the reader to an undeconstructible truth. I think this is perfectly valid; my only problems with it are, firstly, that this truth cannot be equated wholly with the truth of Christianity or any other narrative and, secondly, that Emmanuel's point is one which deconstruction is fully capable of recognizing. In his later work on justice and law, Derrida has written that justice is the undeconstructible.[37] Deconstruction is solicited by an otherness which it can never master, and which obligates it from the outset to a certain ethics of reading. The issue is whether this undeconstructible truth can be identified without more ado (as Emmanuel appears to do) with notions of 'authenticity' or an 'originary text'. Such terms carry a lot of metaphysical baggage – and Emmanuel is clear that metaphysics is no substitute for ethical-religious striving.

Derrida has always claimed that simply trying to jump over metaphysics to a wholly different way of thinking just leaves you entangled in an unexamined and unacknowledged form of what you are trying to escape from. The orthodox Christian narrativism we have been concerned with seems to fall into this trap – substituting one form of speculation, one set of metaconcepts, for another. But can readers of Kierkegaard who are influenced by deconstruction do any better? Can they address the otherness which Kierkegaard's texts respond to without reducing it to an idol of our own fashioning?

Deconstruction and the other

The influence of deconstruction on interpretation of Kierkegaard's texts has been substantial. Kierkegaard's textual tactics and indirectness seem to lend themselves to a certain style of 'postmodern' reading in which authorial

---

[36] Emmanuel, *Kierkegaard*, p. 18.
[37] J. Derrida, 'Force of Law: The "Mystical Foundation of Authority"', in D. Cornell *et al.* (eds) *Deconstruction and the Possibility of Justice* (London: Routledge, 1992), pp. 14–15.

intention and authority are dethroned. Beyond this initial attraction, however, it appears that there is a considerable tension in what such readings offer in their interpretation of Kierkegaard's language about God.

Indeed, these readings seem to tread a blurred line. On the one hand, Kierkegaard's religious language may be translated without remainder into immanent terms. Language about the infinitely different God becomes language about 'difference' itself, as it structures human experience. On the other hand, such readings may resist this equation, and seek to leave open the possibility that language about God for Kierkegaard testifies to an irreducible transcendence.

We have already seen how Derrida's recent reading of *Fear and Trembling* tends to equate Kierkegaard's language about God as wholly Other into language about our responsibility to *human* others. And yet it is not clear that he is proposing a straightforward Feuerbachian reading of theology as anthropology. For he intimates that Kierkegaard is writing in a way which is troublesome not only for a supernaturalist orthodoxy, but also for a naturalistic humanism – for any discourse which claims to define and limit the answer to the question 'who is the Other?' Derrida uses the language of incarnation in a way which at once displaces the traditional Christian dogma whilst invoking a movement of grace for which humanism cannot account. And he does so in a reading of Johannes de Silentio's highly refracted text, a text which is notoriously elusive when it comes to defining its precise meaning.

The ambivalence in Derrida's approach is perhaps, then, not as crudely reductionist as we suggested earlier. But it clearly does risk a kind of reductionism evident in other writers influenced by deconstruction. Sylvia Agacinski offers a particularly clear example of the way in which such an approach can translate Kierkegaard's theological language: 'God the Father is the name for absolute excess, the name of the Other or of difference. God the Son is the name for the model sacrificial victim, the Crucified one, who, by his death, annihilates the difference Father/Son.'[38] In a sense, this is a psychologization of Kierkegaard's language, which is taken to refer to the Oedipal drama of self-development. However, in invoking 'absolute excess', Agacinski may be aware that she cannot exclude the possibility of some kind of transcendence which destabilizes any such interpretation of Kierkegaard's terms.

The problem revolves around Kierkegaard's manner of communication, which Pat Bigelow characterizes as 'to say by unsaying and unsay by saying'.[39] Such indirection makes precise conceptual definitions and demarcations tremble. Indeed, Bigelow claims that it is the very movement of language itself which leads Kierkegaard to an engagement with alterity which no conceptual system could contain:

---

[38] S. Agacinski, *Aparté: Deaths and Conceptions of Søren Kierkegaard* (Tallahassee: Florida University Press, 1988), p. 81.

[39] P. Bigelow, *Kierkegaard and the Problem of Writing* (Tallahassee: Florida University Press, 1987), p. 3.

> For Kierkegaard language is always and everywhere coming fervently, furtively, futilely up against its fugitive other, yet this other to language is always and everywhere the origin of language ... such is the nature of this thought that it can neither be said nor shown – it can only be performed. And performed by a writing concerned with such phenomena that to write about them is to be deprived of them.[40]

And this creates a problem for Kierkegaard's readers. For, despite what the narrativist authors might wish, it is far from clear that this 'performance' can be easily reconciled with orthodox Christian belief and practice.

Having said that, it is not clear just what significance we should give to Kierkegaard's Other. At times, Bigelow writes of the 'imprint' which the wholly other leaves on our experience, even though it never appears directly, and he writes in terms suggestive of a movement of grace: 'the divine is the *transcendens* pure and simple; it is never present, never immediate. Yet the divine enters into the breach – by withdrawing from it, but in such a way that by withdrawing it leaves a trace.'[41] However, it is easy to see how such language can quickly abandon any suggestion of divinity, let alone divine love. The Other becomes the founding *différance* of language, the nonoriginal origin which is beyond good and evil: 'All this goes to say that this "Unknown", exterior to everything with nothing exterior to it, signifies the origin of signification that has always already and henceforth effaced itself in lieu of signification.'[42] This tendency is repeated on a more obviously anti-realist level, as we have seen when Bigelow equates Kierkegaard's language about God with language about the future.

We have already argued that this claim represents an unwarranted overstatement by Bigelow. It only makes sense in the context of the ambiguities inherent in Bigelow's interpretation of Kierkegaard. However, it is only when he disregards his own awareness of the irreducible transcendence to which Kierkegaard witnesses that Bigelow's text can take an anti-realist turn.

Mark C. Taylor has demonstrated a similar ambiguity. In *Altarity*, it is never clear whether he wants to interpret Kierkegaard's God as just another name for an amoral *différance*, or whether he acknowledges the possibility of transcendent grace and love:

> Awareness of the wholly Other must come from elsewhere; it must be solicited by otherness itself. Kierkegaard names this soliciting Other, which calls every identity out of itself, 'God'. 'God' is an improper name for absolute exteriority that resists all interiorization and recollection ... As the difference that 'precedes' all differences, the Unknown, which is forever unknowable, is the condition of both the possibility and the impossibility of reason.[43]

---

[40] Ibid., p. 58.
[41] Ibid., p. 97; cf. p. 94.
[42] Ibid., p. 192.
[43] Mark C. Taylor, *Altarity* (Chicago: University of Chicago Press, 1987), pp. 342–3.

Is the God, the Unknown, a cipher for that which resists conceptual mastery, that structure of linguistic excess which conditions all meaning? Or is there something more? Is God the Other who solicits our selfishness and cruelty, in the sense of exposing them and making them tremble?

To apply deconstruction as a 'method' risks neutralizing its subversive dynamic. Despite the subtleties of deconstructionist readings of Kierkegaard, they can easily result in a rather static picture of Kierkegaard's texts, as no more than exemplars of an underlying structure of language. But the voice of the Other interrupts Kierkegaard's writings in ways which cannot be appropriated without a response which is at once passionate and ethical. That is not to say that we should simply swallow Chalcedonian Christian orthodoxy. But it is to acknowledge an irreducible interest at work in Kierkegaard's texts which is at once ethical and religious.

Let us consider again Derrida's reading of *Fear and Trembling*. One motivation of his text seems to be a desire to repudiate certain reductionist attacks of deconstruction – attacks which charge deconstruction with being nihilistic, relativistic and amoral. Religious language opens a way to articulate the irreducible ethical import of deconstruction. 'God' in Kierkegaard's work becomes a figure for the way in which every human other comes to us as the wholly other ('God is the name of the absolute other as other and as unique') – as demanding our duty and responsibility, and so propelling us 'into the space or risk of an absolute sacrifice'.[44]

This movement inevitably obscures the boundary between the infinite otherness of God and the infinite otherness of every human being, between religion and ethics. But it also refuses the easier options of orthodoxy's good conscience or humanism's refusal of all transcendence. If Kierkegaard's language trembles on the boundary between transcendence and immanence, then this goes a long way to accounting for all the variety of interpretations which have been placed upon his work.

We have argued that Kierkegaard's texts resist the totalizing vision implied in either anti-realism or metaphysical realism. There is no avoiding the ambiguity and indirectness of his writing, an indirectness which is polemical against systematic pretensions in thought and faith. But this way of communication is also, by analogy, a way of discipleship. It does not rest in undecidability, but calls us through it to the practice of a paradoxical faith. The analogy of communication suggests that this performance of faith is a repetition of God's enabling act of creation and communication. Faith remains a *response* to what calls it forth. This structure of response is reduplicated in ethical duty, in the risk of sacrifice, in the communication which sets the other free.

Kierkegaard offers us a notion of repetition and reduplication which is not merely the return of the same, but the enactment and embodiment of a new

---

[44] J. Derrida, *The Gift of Death* (Chicago and London: University of Chicago Press, 1995), p. 68.

possibility. Language is not a ready made collection of signs which copy the world, return us to nature or perfect our reason. Nor is it merely a structure of differences. It is a contradiction in which reflection is opened out to its other in passion and freedom. Language too is a movement of response.

The form which that response takes will depend upon the choices each person makes. But ultimately, Kierkegaard sees language as an invitation to a particular form of life: one which renounces idolatry, one which risks everything to set the other free. We do not simply act in the void, but as always already indebted to the other. And that debt is not merely an immanent transaction, a matter of relative give and take. It involves us with the Other who created us out of nothing. Language does not so much refer to God as refer us to him, the God who, as the 'inventor of language' is the one who 'holds the blessing in his hands'.

All of this implies critical questions which must still be aimed at Kierkegaard. How much does he still wish to secure a distinct 'religious' zone freed from the engagements of ethical life? How much does he want to restrict our experience of the paradoxes of thought and love to our encounter with the God-Man? Kierkegaard has to be exposed to the kind of reading Derrida proposes in order to shake some of his confidence in an unexamined orthodox christology which the nature of his texts themselves undermine. It may be that we can neither claim so much for Jesus nor deny the paradoxical structure of our *whole* experience. Kierkegaard's God-Man brings into focus a paradoxicality, a movement of grace and response, which ironically subverts his insistence on Christ alone as the absolute paradox. For one does not need to name the name of Jesus, as if salvation depended upon a hyper-Protestant conscious faith, in order to reduplicate in life that pattern of embodied love which Christ represents and solicits.[45]

Perhaps we may suggest that Kierkegaard's own rhetorical presentation of his christology works against the attempt to absolutize Christ as the suppression of all dialogue with all that is not Christ. Christ too is an indirect

---

[45] Kierkegaard would no doubt wish to resist this generalization of the significance of the God-Man as an instance of the volatilization of specifically Christian terms. See, for example, his journal entries relating to Magnus Eirikson's attempt (in striking anticipation of Derrida here) to interpret *Fear and Trembling* in a way that would be a source of edification for Jews and Muslims as well as Christians (reproduced in *CUP* II 163–5). Kierkegaard attempts to distinguish Abraham's faith by virtue of the absurd from faith *in* the absurd, that is, faith in the doctrine of the God-Man. Abraham gives us the 'formal definition of faith' (CUP II, p.164), a 'purely personal definition of existential faith' (*CUP* II 163). However, it is far from clear on Kierkegaard's *own* terms that form and content can be rigidly held apart in this way. If Abraham truly has faith, and a faith that saves, then what does faith in Christ add? At the very least, Kierkegaard's texts implicitly acknowledge a dialogue between Abrahamic faith and Christian faith, which cannot be circumvented by recourse to an arbitrary hierarchy. See also my 'Thinking About *Fire*: Derrida and Judaism', *Literature and Theology* 12, 3 (September 1998), pp. 242–55.

sign, one who issues a call, but whose own identity remains enigmatic and paradoxical. The God-Man stands as a stumbling block to any systematic presentation of faith, and thus to any objective interpretation of him. Christ too has a regulative function, one which propels us into discipleship or offence without easing our uncertainty with totalizing visions. Kierkegaard's communication about Christ is thus as paradoxical as its supposed referent. The challenge for Kierkegaard, and for those who write in his wake, is to draw out the implications of the *form* of Christian communication, and how that form impacts upon lofty claims about the exclusive truth status of its *content*. It may be that, reading Kierkegaard with a sensitivity to this question, one may find in his authorship both a sharpening of the paradoxicality and risk of Christian faith, and a spur to dialogue with what remains other than Christian. Indeed, shorn of the all-seeing speculative viewpoint, and of an authoritative grounding on scripture or magisterium, Kierkegaard's authorship invites us into an immersion into the contradictions of selfhood and communication which cannot be avoided. If Christ is the Word, that Word must be followed into the depths of the poetic. It cannot be mastered and understood from the outside.

In Kierkegaard's writing, we are confronted with a religious existential poetry, one which confounds the categories Kierkegaard himself may have wanted to fix. Though he has scathing things to say about poets, Kierkegaard retains a poetic status for himself. Moreover, he can affirm that 'God is like a poet' who 'permits everything possible to come forth', without consenting to or approving it (JP 2: 1445; Pap. XI(2) A 98). God, in other words, is hidden, because God is the creator. Only one who holds open the wound and the tear of possibility can create anything. The poet-God is the gift of himself in his own self-effacement.

The stories we tell of people and of God do not rely on factual truth for their power to change lives, awaken people to possibilities, encourage their self-activity.[46] However, there is still faith that these stories are not arbitrary constructions in the void of a meaningless universe, but that they get their sense and value because they repeat the relation that God has to creation. God is like a poet, and therefore there is no unbridgeable gulf between our storytelling, even our fiction, and the reality which it addresses and to which it responds. For Kierkegaard, Christian language is played out in the wake of the Word becoming flesh, in embodied nearness and mysterious otherness. It is that tension in the divine address itself, which validates both humility and confidence in responding to and enacting a new creation.

---

[46] As Kierkegaard recognized when discussing the stories we tell to children: JP 1: 265; Pap. II A 12. For the original suggestion that Kierkegaard's pseudonymous texts should be read as novels, see A. Henriksen, *Kierkegaards Romaner* (Copenhagen: Gyldendal, 1954). Cf. G. Pattison, 'Kierkegaard as Novelist', *Literature and Theology* 1 (1987), pp. 210–20.

Bibliography

1. Primary sources: Danish

Kierkegaard, S. (1962), *Samlede Værker*, 20 vols, 3rd edn, ed. Drachmann, Heiberg and Lange, Gyldendal, Copenhagen.
— (1909–48), *Papirer,* ed. Heiberg, Kuhr and Torsting, 20 vols, Gyldendal, Copenhagen.

2. Primary sources: English translations

Hong, H., General Editor, (1978–), *Kierkegaard's Writings*, 26 vols, Princeton University Press, Princeton, NJ.
Hong, H. and Hong, E. (eds) (1967–78), *Søren Kierkegaard's Journals and Papers*, 7 vols, Indiana University Press, Bloomington.
For translations of particular works, see Abbreviations, pp.vii–ix.

3. Secondary literature

Aarsleff, H. (1982), *From Locke to Saussure*, University of Minnesota Press, Minneapolis.
Agacinski, S. (1988), *Aparté: Deaths and Conceptions of Søren Kierkegaard*, Florida University Press, Tallahassee.
Alexander, W. (1966), *Johann Georg Hamann: Philosophy and Faith*, Martinus Nijhoff, The Hague.
Alford, S. (1984), *Irony and the Logic of the Romantic Imagination*, Lang, New York.
Andersen, P. (1963), 'Kierkegaard's Theory of Communication', *Speech Monographs* 30, pp.1–14.
Archer, Margaret *et al.* (eds) (1998), *Critical Realism. Essential Readings* Routledge, London.
Benjamin, W. (1973), *Charles Baudelaire*, NLB, London.
Bertens, Hans (1995), *The Idea of the Postmodern: A History,* Routledge, London.
Bertung, B. (1987), *Om Kierkegaard, Kvinder og Kærlighed*, Reitzel, Copenhagen.
Bhaskar, Roy (1989), *Reclaiming Reality,* Verso, London.

Bigelow, Pat (1987), *Kierkegaard and the Problem of Writing*, Florida University Press, Tallahassee.
Bowie, Andrew (1990), *Aesthetics and Subjectivity: From Kant to Nietzsche*, Manchester University Press, Manchester.
Bowie, Malcolm (1979), 'Jacques Lacan' in John Sturrock (ed.), *Structuralism and Since*, Oxford University Press, Oxford, pp. 116–53.
Braithwaite, R. B. (1955), *An Empiricist's View of the Nature of Religious Belief*, Cambridge University Press, Cambridge.
Bridges, T. (1988), 'Derrida, Kierkegaard, and the Orders of Speech', *Philosophy Today* 32, pp. 95–109.
Burrell, David (1986), *Knowing the Unknowable God*, University of Notre Dame Press, Notre Dame.
Capel, Lee (1966), 'Historical Introduction' to translation of *The Concept of Irony*, Collins, London.
Caputo, John (1980), *Radical Hermeneutics: Repetition, Deconstruction and the Hermeneutical Project*, Indiana University Press, Bloomington.
Cavell, Stanley (1969), *Must We Mean What We Say?* Cambridge University Press, Cambridge.
Clark, R. (1955), *Herder: His Life and Thought*, University of California Press, Berkeley and Los Angeles.
Cloeren, H. (1985), 'The Linguistic Turn in Kierkegaard's Attack on Hegel', *International Studies in Philosophy* 17, pp. 1–13.
Collins, J. (1983), *The Mind of Kierkegaard*, Princeton University Press, Princeton.
Condillac, E. B. de (1947), *Oeuvres Philosophiques*, ed. Le Roy, 3 vols, Presses Universitaires de France, Paris.
— (1930), *Condillac's Treatise on the Sensations*, trans. Carr, Favil, London.
— (1971), *An Essay on the Origin of Human Knowledge*, Scholars' Facsimiles and Reprints, Gainesville, Fla.
Creegan, C. (1989), *Wittgenstein and Kierkegaard*, Routledge, London and New York.
Crites, Stephen (1972), *In the Twilight of Christendom: Hegel vs. Kierkegaard on Faith and History*, AAR, Chambersburg, Pa.
Crowder, Colin (ed.) (1997), *God and Reality: Essays on Christian Non-Realism*, Mowbray, London.
Cupitt, Don (1982), *The World to Come*, SCM, London.
— (1984), *The Sea of Faith*, BBC, London.
— (1987), *The Long Legged Fly*, SCM, London.
— (1989), *Radicals and the Future of the Church*, SCM, London.
— (1990), *Creation out of Nothing*, SCM, London.
— (1991), *What is a Story?*, SCM, London.
— (1993), *The Time Being*, SCM, London.
— (1994), *After All*, SCM, London.

— (1998), *The Religion of Being*, SCM, London.
Daise, B. (1976), 'Kierkegaard and the Absoloute Paradox', *Journal of the History of Philosophy* 14 , pp. 63–8.
— (1992),'The Will to Truth in Kierkegaard's *Philosophical Fragments*', *International Journal for Philosophy of Religion* 31, pp.1–12.
Derrida, Jacques (1973), *Speech and Phenomena and other Essays on Husserl's Theory of Signs*, Northwestern University Press, Evanston, Ill.
— (1976), *Of Grammatology*, Johns Hopkins University Press, Baltimore, Md.
— (1978), *Writing and Difference*, Routledge, London.
— (1980), *The Archeology of the Frivolous*, University of Nebraska Press, Lincoln and London.
— (1981), *Dissemination*, Athlone, London.
— (1982), *Margins of Philosophy*, Harvester Wheatsheaf, New York.
— (1992),'Force of Law: The "Mystical Foundation of Authority"', in D. Cornell, M. Rosenfeld and D. G. Carlson (eds), *Deconstruction and the Possibility of Justice*, Routledge, London and New York, pp. 3–67
— (1995), *On the Name*, Stanford University Press, Stanford, Calif.
— (1995), *The Gift of Death*, University of Chicago Press, Chicago and London.
Devitt, Michael (1986), *Realism and Truth,* 2nd edn. Blackwell, Oxford.
Dooley, Mark (1998), 'Repetition and Justice: A Derridean/Kierkegaardian Reading of the Subject', in G. Pattison and S. Shakespeare (eds), *Kierkegaard on Self and Society*, Macmillan, London, pp. 139–55.
Dummett, Michael (1978), *Truth and other Enigmas*, Duckworth, London.
Dunning, S. (1984), 'Rhetoric and Reality in Kierkegaard's Postscript', *International Journal for Philosophy of Religion* 15, pp. 125–37.
— (1985), *Kierkegaard's Dialectic of Inwardness: A Structural Analysis of the Theory of Stages*, Princeton University Press, Princeton, NJ.
Dupré, L. (1963), *Kierkegaard as Theologian*, Sheed and Ward, London and New York.
Eco, Umberto (1997), *The Search for the Perfect Language*, Fontana, London.
Elrod, John (1975), *Being and Existence in Kierkegaard's Pseudonymous Works*, Princeton University Press, Princeton, NJ.
— (1981), *Kierkegaard and Christendom*, Princeton University Press, Princeton, NJ.
— (1984), 'Kierkegaard: Poet Penitent', *Kierkegaardiana* 13, pp. 84–96.
Emmanuel, Steven (1989), 'Kierkegaard on Doctrine: A Post-Modern Interpretation', *Religious Studies* 25, pp. 363–78.
— (1991), 'Kierkegaard's Pragmatist Faith', *Philosophy and Phenomenological Research* 51, pp. 279–302.
— (1991),'Kierkegaard on Knowledge and Faith', *Kierkegaardiana* 15, pp. 136–46.

— (1996), *Kierkegaard and the Concept of Revelation*, State University of New York Press, Albany.
Evans, C. S. (1976), 'Kierkegaard on Subjective Truth: Is God an Ethical Fiction?', *International Journal for Philosophy of Religion* 7, pp. 288–99.
— (1983), *Kierkegaard's 'Fragments' and 'Postscript': The Religious Philosophy of Johannes Climacus*, Humanities Press International, Atlantic Highlands, NJ.
— (1989), 'Does Kierkegaard Think Beliefs can be Directly Willed?', *International Journal for Philosophy of Religion* 26, pp. 173–84.
— (1992), *Passionate Reason: Making Sense of Kierkegaard's Philosophical Fragments*, Indiana University Press, Bloomington and Indianapolis.
Fenves, Peter (1993), *'Chatter': Language and History in Kierkegaard*, Stanford University Press, Stanford, Calif.
Ferreira, M. J. (1992), *Transforming Vision. Imagination and Will in Kierkegaardian Faith*, Oxford University Press, New York.
Feuerbach, Ludwig (1957), *The Essence of Christianity*, Harper, New York.
Fichte, J. G. (1845–6), *Johann Gottlieb Fichte's Sämmtliche Werke*, ed. I. H. Fichte, 8 vols, Berlin.
— (1956), *The Vocation of Man*, Bobbs-Merrill, Indianapolis and New York.
— (1978), *Attempt at a Critique of all Revelation*, Cambridge University Press, Cambridge.
— (1982), *Science of Knowledge with the First and Second Introductions*, Cambridge University Press, Cambridge.
Finlay, M. (1988), *The Romantic Irony of Semiotics: Friedrich Schlegel and the Crisis of Representation*, Gruyter, Berlin.
French, Peter A., Uehling, Theodore E. Jr., and Wettstein, Howard K. (eds) (1988), *Realism and Antirealism*, University of Minnesota Press, Minneapolis.
Gardiner, Patrick (1988), *Kierkegaard*, Oxford University Press, Oxford.
Garelick, H. (1964), 'The Irrationality and Supra-rationality of Kierkegaard's Paradox', *Southern Journal of Philosophy* 2, pp. 75–86.
— (1965), *The Anti-Christianity of Kierkegaard*, Martinus Nijhoff, The Hague.
Garff, Joachim (1991), 'The Eyes of Argus', *Kierkegaardiana* 15, pp. 29–54.
German, T. (1981), *Hamann on Language and Religion*, Oxford University Press, Oxford.
Goodman, Nelson (1979), *Ways of Worldmaking*, Hackett, Indianapolis, Ind.
Gouwens, David (1988), 'Kierkegaard's Understanding of Doctrine', *Modern Theology* 5 pp. 13–22.
— (1989), *Kierkegaard's Dialectic of the Imagination*, Lang, New York.
— (1996), *Kierkegaard as Religious Thinker*, Cambridge University Press, Cambridge.
Gregor Smith, R. (1960), *J. G. Hamann 1730–1788: A Study in Christian Existence with Selections from his Writings*, Collins, London.

— (1964), 'Hamann and Kierkegaard', *Kierkegaardiana* 5, pp. 52–67.
Grundtvig, N. F. S. (1941), *Værker i Udvalg*, ed. Christensen and Koch, 6 vols, Gyldendal, Copenhagen.
— (1976), *Selected Writings: N. F. S. Grundtvig*, ed. Knudsen, Fortress Press, Philadelphia.
— (1984), *A Grundtvig Anthology*, ed. Clarke, Cambridge and Centrum, Viby.
Hall, R. (1985), 'Language and Freedom: Kierkegaard's Analysis of the Demonic in "The Concept of Anxiety"', in *International Kierkegaard Commentary: The Concept of Anxiety*, ed. Perkins, Mercer University Press, Macon, Ga., pp. 153–66.
— (1993) *Word and Spirit. A Kierkegaardian Critique of the Modern Age*, Indiana University Press, Bloomington and Indianapolis.
Hamann, J. G. (1949–57), *Sämtliche Werke*, ed. Nadler, 6 vols, Herder, Vienna.
— (1955), *Briefwechsel*, ed. Ziesemer and Henkel, 7 vols, Insel-Verlag, Wiesbaden.
— (1967), *Schriften zur Sprache*, ed. Simon, Suhrkamp, Frankfurt am Main.
— (1967), *Hamann's Socratic Memorabilia: A Translation and Commentary*, Johns Hopkins University Press, Baltimore, Md.
Hannay, Alastair (1982), *Kierkegaard*, Routledge, London.
Harris, R. and Taylor, T. (1989), *Landmarks in Linguistic Thought: The Western Tradition from Socrates to Saussure*, Routledge, London and New York.
Hebblethwaite, Brian (1988), *The Ocean of Truth*, Cambridge University Press, Cambridge.
Hegel, G. W. F. (1927–30), *Sämtliche Werke, Jubiläumsausgabe*, ed. Glockner, 20 vols, Fromann, Stuttgart.
— (1971), *Philosophy of Mind*, Clarendon, Oxford.
— (1977), *Hegel's Phenomenology of Spirit*, Clarendon, Oxford.
Heiberg, J. L. (1861), *Prosaiske Skrifter*, 11 vols, Reitzels, Copenhagen.
Herder, J. G. (1969), *Herder on Social and Political Culture*, selected texts, Cambridge University Press, Cambridge.
— (1985), *Werke*, ed. Bollacher *et al.*, 10 vols, Deutscher Klassiker Verlag, Frankfurt.
Heywood Thomas, J. (1957), *Subjectivity and Paradox*, Blackwell, Oxford.
Kearney, R. (1984), 'Kierkegaard's Concept of God-Man', *Kierkegaardiana* 13, pp. 105–21.
Kellenberger, J. (1984), 'Kierkegaard, Indirect Communication, and Religious Truth', *International Journal for Philosophy of Religion* 16, pp. 153–60.
Kirrmse, Bruce (1990), *Kierkegaard in Golden Age Denmark*, Indiana University Press, Bloomington and Indianapolis.
Kripke, Saul (1980), *Naming and Necessity*, Blackwell, Oxford.

Lash, Nicholas (1986), *Theology on the Way to Emmaus*, SCM, London.
— (1988), *Easter in Ordinary*, SCM, London.
Law, David (1993), *Kierkegaard as Negative Theologian*, Clarendon, Oxford.
Lebowitz, Nancy (1985), *Kierkegaard – A Life of Allegory*, Louisiana University Press, Baton Rouge and London.
Levinas, Emmanuel (1969), *Totality and Infinity*, Duquesne University Press, Pittsburgh, Pa.
— (1987), *Collected Philosophical Papers*, Nijhoff, Dordrecht.
— (1991), *Otherwise than Being*, trans. and intro. Adolph Lingis, Kluwer, Dordrecht.
Lindbeck, George (1984), *The Nature of Doctrine: Religion and Theology in a Postliberal Age*, SPCK, London.
Locke, John (1991), *An Essay Concerning Human Understanding*, Everyman, London and Rutland.
Loughlin, Gerard (1996), *Telling God's Story: Bible, Church and Narrative Theology*, Cambridge University Press, Cambridge.
Lübcke, P. (1990), 'Kierkegaard and Indirect Communication', *History of European Ideas* 12, pp. 31–40.
McClane, E. (1977), 'Kierkegaard and Subjectivity', *International Journal for Philosophy of Religion* 8, pp. 211–32.
Mackey, Louis (1971), *Kierkegaard: A Kind of Poet*, University of Pennsylvania Press, Philadelphia.
— (1986), *Points of View: Readings of Kierkegaard*, Florida University Press, Tallahassee.
— (1989), 'Deconstructing the Self: Kierkegaard's "Sickness Unto Death"', *Anglican Theological Review* 71, pp. 153–65.
Marx, K. and Engels, F. (1984), *Marx and Engels: Basic Writings on Politics and Philosophy*, ed. Feuer, Fontana, London.
Mates, B. (1986), *The Philosophy of Leibniz: Metaphysics and Language*, Oxford University Press, Oxford and New York.
Moran, J. and Gode, A. (eds) (1966), *Rousseau-Herder: On the Origin of Language*, Frederick Unger, New York.
Neubauer, J. (1980), *Novalis*, Twayne, Boston, Mass.
Nietzsche, Friedrich (1973), *Beyond Good and Evil*, Penguin, Harmondsworth.
Norris, Christopher (1982), *Deconstruction: Theory and Practice*, Routledge, London.
— (1984),'Fictions of Authority. Narrative and Viewpoint in Kierkegaard's Writing', in *The Deconstructive Turn*, Methuen, London, pp. 85–106.
— (1989), 'The Ethics of Reading and the Limits of Irony: Kierkegaard among the Postmodernists', *Southern Humanities Review* 23, pp. 1–35.
— (1992), *Uncritical Theory: Postmodernism, Intellectuals and the Gulf War*, Lawrence and Wishart, London.

— (1997), *New Idols of the Cave: On the Limits of Anti-realism*, Manchester University Press, Manchester and New York.

Novalis (1977), *Schriften*, 3rd edn, ed. Kluckhohn and Samuel, 4 vols, Köhlhammer Stuttgart.

Owen, H. P. (1969), *The Christian Knowledge of God*, Athlone, London.

Pattison, George (1983), 'Søren Kierkegaard: A Theatre Critic of the Heiberg School', *British Journal of Aesthetics* 23, pp. 25–33.

— (1984), 'Kierkegaard and Imagination,' *Theology* 87, pp. 6–12.

— (1986), 'Friedrich Schlegel's *Lucinde*', *Scottish Journal of Theology* 38, pp. 545–64

— (1987), 'Kierkegaard as Novelist', *Journal of Literature and Theology* 1, pp. 210–20.

— (1989), 'Eternal Loneliness: Art and Religion in Kierkegaard and Zen', *Religious Studies* 25, pp. 379–92.

— (1990), 'From Kierkegaard to Cupitt: Subjectivity, the Body and Eternal Life', *The Heythrop Journal* 31, pp. 295–308.

— (1992), *Kierkegaard: The Aesthetic and the Religious*, Macmillan, London.

— (ed.) (1992), *Kierkegaard on Art and Communication*, Macmillan, London.

— (1993), '"Who" is the Discourse? A Study in Kierkegaard's Religious Literature', *Kierkegaardiana* 16, pp. 28–45.

Pattison, George and Shakespeare, Steven (eds) (1998), *Kierkegaard on Self And Society*, Macmillan, London.

Pfefferkorn, K. (1988), *Novalis. A Romantic's Theory of Language and Poetry*, Yale University Press, New Haven, Conn. and London.

Phillips, D. Z. (1970), *Faith and Philosophical Enquiry*, Routledge, London.

— (1970), *Death and Immortality*, Macmillan, London and Basingstoke.

— (1981), *The Concept of Prayer*, Blackwell, Oxford.

Pojman, L. (1977), 'Kierkegaard on Justification of Belief', *International Journal for Philosophy of Religion* 8, pp. 75–93.

— (1984), *The Logic of Subjectivity. Kierkegaard's Philosophy of Religion*, University of Alabama Press, Tuscaloosa.

— (1991), 'Kierkegaard's Epistemology', *Kierkegaardiana* 15, pp. 147–52.

Pombo, O. (1987), *Leibniz and the Problem of a Universal Language*, Nodus, Münster.

Poole, Roger (1993), *Kierkegaard: The Indirect Communication*, University of Virginia Press, Charlottesville and London.

Putnam, Hilary (1981), *Reason, Truth and History*, Cambridge University Press, Cambridge.

— (1987), *The Many Faces of Realism*, Open Court, La Salle, Ill.

— (1992), *Renewing Philosophy*, Harvard University Press, Cambridge, Mass. and London.

Rorty, Richard (1980), *Philosophy and the Mirror of Nature*, Blackwell, Oxford.
Rousseau, J. (1970), *Essai sur l'Origine des Langues*, ed. Porset, Ducros, Bordeaux.
Runzo, J. (1993), *Is God Real?*, Macmillan, Basingstoke.
de Saussure, F. (1983), *Course in General Linguistics*, Duckworth, London.
Schelling, F. W. J. (1856–61), *Sämtliche Werke*, ed. K. F. A. Schelling, 14 vols, Stuttgart and Augsburg.
— (1942) *The Ages of the World*, Columbia University Press, New York.
— (1978) *System of Transcendental Idealism (1800)*, University of Virginia Press, Charlottesville.
Schlegel, F. (1971), *Lucinde and the Fragments*, University of Minnesota Press, Minneapolis.
Shakespeare, Steven (1996), 'Stirring the Waters of Language: Kierkegaard on the Dangers of Doing Theology', *Heythrop Journal* 37, pp. 421–36.
— (1998), 'Books About Nothing: Kierkegaard's Liberating Rhetoric', in Pattison and Shakespeare (eds), *Kierkegaard on Self and Society*, Macmillan, London, pp. 97–111.
— (1998), 'Thinking About *Fire*: Derrida and Judaism', *Literature and Theology* 12, pp. 242–55
Shaw, G. (1987), *God in Our Hands*, SCM, London.
Smyth, J. V. (1985), *A Question of Eros: Irony in Sterne, Kierkegaard and Barthes*, Florida University Press, Tallahassee.
Soskice, Janet Martin (1985), *Metaphor and Religious Language*, Clarendon, Oxford.
Sturrock, J. (ed.) (1979), *Structuralism and Since: From Lévi-Strauss to Derrida*, Oxford University Press, Oxford.
Sutherland, S. (1984), *God, Jesus and Belief*, Blackwell, Oxford.
— (1984),'Søren Kierkegaard', in *Faith and Ambiguity*, SCM, London, pp. 42–75.
Taylor, Mark C. (1975), *Kierkegaard's Pseudonymous Authorship: A Study of Time and the Self*, Princeton University Press, Princeton, NJ.
— (1975), 'Language, Truth and Indirect Communication', *Tijdscrift voor Filosofie* 37, pp. 74–88.
— (1980), *Journeys to Selfhood: Hegel and Kierkegaard*, University of California Press, Berkeley and London.
— (1984), *Erring: A Postmodern A/theology*, University of Chicago Press, Chicago.
— (1984),'Self in/as Other', *Kierkegaardiana* 13, pp. 63–71.
— (1987), *Altarity*, University of Chicago Press, Chicago.
Walker, J. (1969), 'Kierkegaard's Concept of Truthfulness', *Inquiry* 12, pp. 209–24.
Walsh S. (1991), 'Kierkegaard and Postmodernism', *International Journal for Philosophy of Religion* 29, pp. 113–22.

Weston, Michael (1994), *Kierkegaard and Modern Continental Philosophy: An Introduction*, Routledge, London and New York.
Wilson, E. (1992), 'The Invisible Flâneur', *New Left Review* 191, pp. 90–110.
Wittgenstein, L. (1958), *Philosophical Investigations*, Blackwell, Oxford.
— (1980), *Culture and Value*, Blackwell, Oxford.

Index

Aarslef, H. 30n
Abelard 3
Abraham 26, 129–35, 138, 184, 225, 238n
absurd 26, 129–35, 203n, 238n
Adam 72–3, 92, 144, 160–61, 184
aesthetics 20, 24, 28, 41, 52–4, 65–70, 71, 130, 143–4, 145, 194, 204
Agacinski, S. 157n, 235
alterity *see* 'otherness'
Altizer, T. 13n
analogy 3, 27, 34, 35, 39, 51, 52, 179, 180–220, 233
Andersen, H. 136n
anti-realism 1–19, 22, 23, 24, 26, 27, 28, 54, 55, 56, 69, 74, 79, 82, 84, 85, 86109, 113, 120, 129, 137, 139–41, 158, 162, 165, 167–8, 173–4, 194, 197, 205, 219, 221–39
Antigone 107–8
anxiety 71–2, 106, 126, 128
Aquinas 180–85, 187
Aristotle 31, 33, 71, 182, 193
Augustine 3, 4
author 20–21, 27, 76, 107, 156, 170, 179, 183–5, 213–14
authority 64, 76–7, 175, 185, 211–20, 221, 226, 239
Ayer, A. 5, 11n

Bacon, F. 30
Bataille, G. 132, 136
Benjamin, W. 86n
Berkeley, G. 3, 4
Bertens, H. 221n
Bhaskar, R. 7–8, 11–12
Bigelow, P. 112n, 133, 173–4, 295–6
body 25, 38–9, 50–52, 92, 95, 100, 108, 149
Boethius 3
Böhme, J. 42
Bowie, A. 41n, 69
Bowie, M. 199n

Braithwaite, R. 11n
Brown, C. 10n
Burrell, D. 180–2

Capel, L. 127n
Carnap, R. 5
Cavell, S. 64
Christ *see* Jesus
Clarke, R. 35n
Cloeren, H. 57n
communication 18–20, 22, 25–7, 38, 40–43, 47, 50, 54, 56–7, 70, 74, 75–8, 79–85, 92, 105, 107–8, 112, 121, 125, 128, 134–8, 156, 171, 174–5, 180–220, 221, 225–6, 229–30, 235, 237, 239
Condillac, Abbé de 32, 36
consciousness 4, 22, 24–5, 28, 36, 45, 47, 51, 53, 56–62, 65, 71–2, 75, 83, 128, 154, 158, 160, 162, 172, 205
Copenhagen 48, 86
Corsair 21
Crites, S. 164n
Cupitt, D. 13–15, 17, 167n, 173n, 227, 228

demonic 26, 67, 73, 128–9, 130, 131, 157
Derrida, J. 10, 18, 29, 33–4, 35n, 43n, 61–2, 67, 131–3, 136n, 139, 156n, 158n, 177, 218, 222, 234–5, 237, 238n
Descartes, R. 29, 58, 84
despair 64, 73107n, 145, 172, 197
Devitt, M. 5, 6
Don Giovanni 65–6
Dooley, M. 131n
doubt 29, 58, 59–63, 84, 160–61, 197
Dummett, M. 5, 6
Dupré, L. 164n

Eco, U. 28n
Edwards, R. 175n

Index

Elrod, S. 48n
Emmanuel, S. 228–9, 231–4
empiricism 3, 4, 11, 25, 29–35
Erikson, M. 238n
eros 21, 25, 40, 43, 52, 69, 89, 92, 96, 107, 199
eternity, eternal life 16, 19, 20, 46, 49, 118–19, 124, 152–6, 158, 165, 170, 174–6, 191–2, 193, 203–4
ethical realism 27, 139–79, 228
ethics 12, 20, 23–4, 25–6, 28, 38, 43, 54, 56, 67, 70, 75–8, 79, 81, 85, 105–7, 129–35, 145–50, 183, 204, 228, 230, 234, 239 *see also* 'ethical realism'
Evans, C.S. 14n, 164, 205n, 230n
Eve 92
existence 23, 25–7, 33, 38, 47, 49, 52, 58, 62–3, 74, 119, 158–62, 163, 166, 171, 174–5, 178, 202, 204–5, 207, 212–13, 215, 229–30

faith 1, 14n, 15–16, 23–4, 26–7, 40–41, 49, 54, 58, 61, 64–5, 79, 81–2, 84, 118, 124–5, 150–58, 160–61, 164–5, 169, 175, 185, 194, 196, 201–4, 207–9, 221, 223–9, 237–9
Faust 65, 67
Fenves, P. 223–6
Feuerbach, L. 173n, 205, 235
Fichte, J. 3, 25, 44, 141–3, 159
Finlay, M. 101n
flâneur 86–7
freedom 27, 33, 35–6, 42, 46, 52–3, 57, 60, 72, 84, 128, 143, 147, 150, 158, 167–8, 171, 177, 183, 194–5, 202, 205, 207, 226, 237
Frege, G. 4

Gardiner, P. 14n, 164n
Garff, J. 214n
God-Man *see* Jesus
Goodman, N. 10
Gouwens, D. 230–34
Gregor-Smith, R. 29n
Grundtvig, N.F.S. 21, 48–51
Gyllembourg, Mme 110

Hamann, J. 25, 29, 35, 38–40, 41, 42, 54, 57, 83

Hannay, A. 112n
Harris, R 33
Hart, D. 13n
Hebblethwaite, B. 13–14
Hegel, G. 3, 25, 45–8, 52, 57, 59, 65, 127, 132, 141, 143, 160n
Heiberg, J. 25, 48, 50–52, 65
Henriksen, A. 21, 239n
Herder, J. 35–8
Heywood-Thomas, J. 167n
Homer 66

idealism 3–4, 6, 10, 24–5, 43–8, 50, 58, 70, 81, 141–3, 158–9, 185
idolatry 15, 27, 137, 139, 165, 174, 183, 185, 186–7, 189–90, 202, 206, 209, 220, 237
imagination 34, 46, 89, 172–3
immediacy 25–6, 28, 33, 36, 41, 45, 47, 53, 56, 58–60, 64, 65–70, 71, 78–80, 83, 90–95, 96–7, 100, 107–9, 113, 120–25, 130, 138, 148, 160, 205–6, 224, 228
immortality *see* eternal life
incarnation 1, 13, 27, 39, 50, 53, 54, 67, 79–82, 100, 108, 139, 187, 194, 198–210, 235, 239
indicative 74, 88
individual 14, 24, 45, 111, 130, 147
interest 61–2, 71, 162, 165–6, 168, 175–6, 192, 204–5
irony 25–6, 38, 41–3, 54, 67, 69, 73, 75–7, 78, 104, 126–9, 141–6, 178

Jesus/Christ/God-man 20, 26, 27, 39, 50, 79–82, 84, 107, 115, 118, 142, 167, 184, 198–210, 229–31, 238–9
Job 126

Kant, I. 3, 29, 41n, 52, 53, 56, 57, 63
Kierkegaard, M. 21
Kirmmse, B. 48
knowledge 4–5, 7–8, 15, 22, 26, 29, 31, 33, 58, 60, 76–9, 82, 110, 137–8, 152–3, 161, 174, 180, 197, 202, 207, 210, 220, 223–4, 227
Koch, H. 48n
Kripke, S. 7

Lacan, J. 199
language games 10, 17

Lash, N. 180–83
Law, D. 13, n, 21
leap 71–2, 73, 84, 161
Leibniz, G. 30–1, 33, 54
Levinas, E. 43n, 140, 167n, 219
Lindbeck, G. 18n, 227
Lingis, A. 219
Locke, J. 30–32, 34, 54, 159
Loughlin, G. 18n, 227
Lyotard, J. 222

Mackey, L. 19, 61n, 164n, 199n, 200n
maieutic 76, 170, 198, 210, 217
Malantschuk, G. 164n
Martensen, H. 48n, 125–6, 217
Marx, K. 104–5
memory 47, 49
metaphor 17, 34–5, 44, 100, 187–90
Møller, P. 104
Mozart, W. 65
music 56, 65–70, 83, 96, 99
Mynster, J. 217
myth 37, 49, 52, 53, 92, 93, 96, 98–100

narrative 16, 18–19, 27, 44, 54, 96, 100, 125, 129, 133, 138, 185–6, 194, 202–3, 219, 222, 227–34
nation 37, 49, 53
nature 31–9, 41–3, 51–2, 56–7, 90–93, 99, 107–8, 120–25, 169
Neubauer, J. 43
Newmark, K. 75
Nietzsche, F. 29, 86
nihilism 18, 38, 40, 43, 60, 67, 78, 81, 85–6, 88, 103–4, 106–7, 109, 137, 160, 233
nominalism 2–3, 4, 6, 30, 31
Norris, C. 6n, 10n, 12n
Novalis 41–3, 66

O'Flaherty, W. 38
objectivity 1–5, 8, 11–15, 17, 22–4, 26, 29–30, 42–7, 51, 59, 62, 76, 82, 142, 162, 163–9, 192, 200, 225, 230–31
Ockham, W. 2
Olsen, R. 21, 133–4
organism 51–3, 59, 90
otherness 23–4, 27, 47, 54, 57, 58, 61, 73, 84, 106, 115, 31, 134, 137–41, 158–9, 161–2, 164, 171, 173, 178, 181, 190, 194, 199–200, 204, 210, 219, 224, 233–7
Owen, H. 181

parabasis 74–5, 78
paradox 13n, 19–20, 22, 24–7, 54, 56, 58, 63, 79, 81–2, 108, 129–35, 166–7, 175, 186–8, 194, 197–220, 224–6, 229, 233–4, 238–9
passion 22–4, 26, 36–7, 84, 110, 134, 165–6, 168, 184, 199, 200, 237
Pattison, G. 14n, 65n, 70n, 104n, 143n
Pfefferkorn, K. 95n
Phillips, D.Z. 15–17, 228
pietism 48
Plato 84
Plekon, M. 231
poetry 27, 37, 42, 65, 88–9, 92, 95n, 95–7, 99–100, 103, 135–7, 144, 174, 199, 211–20, 239
Pojman, L. 166n
Pombo, O. 30
Poole, R. 65n
postmodernism 18, 27, 75, 221–3
press 21
public 21, 86–9, 110–11
Putnam, H. 8–12, 14–15, 23, 81n, 141
Pyper, H. 228n

Quine, W. 9

rationalism 29–35, 38
reader 76, 80
realism 1–19, 22–4, 26–7, 54, 56–7, 65, 69, 71–3, 81n, 82, 84–6, 109, 115, 120, 129, 137, 158, 219, 221–39
recollection 34, 46, 58, 63, 88–90, 176, 224
reductionism 5, 8–9, 11–12, 21, 24–6
reference 4, 6–10, 42–3, 72, 75, 230
reflection 22, 25, 28, 33, 50, 60, 68, 70, 80, 89, 96, 98, 123, 142, 158, 160–61, 172
relativism 7–9, 11–12, 23, 40, 233
repetition 34, 39, 61n, 62–3, 65–8, 71, 83, 108, 155–6, 173, 176–7, 193, 233, 237
representation 2, 18–19, 25–6, 28, 31–2, 43, 45–6, 54–5, 57, 63, 68–9, 73, 84–5, 89, 92, 99, 107, 137–8, 174

revelation 37–8, 40, 42, 50, 64, 73, 77, 79, 140, 170, 184, 185, 210, 217, 219–20, 228–9
rhetoric 18, 22, 24–6, 75, 79, 127, 164, 203, 211, 226, 232–3
romanticism 24–6, 38, 41–3, 70, 84, 143–4, 185
Rorty, R. 10, 14
Rousseau, J. 35–6
Russell, B. 4

Saussure, F. 222
Schelling, F. 3, 25, 41, 44, 52–4, 90, 159
Schlegel, F. 41, 43, 70, 75, 98n, 99n, 101n, 143
scripture 39, 185, 209, 221
seduction 25–6, 39, 70, 76, 86–109, 110, 113, 132, 134, 215–16, 276
selfhood 24–7, 44, 52, 55–6, 60–61, 65, 115, 124, 145–50, 154–6, 179–3, 200, 205, 209, 222, 224
sensuality 46, 52–3, 64–70, 83, 92, 95–6, 99
sexuality 37
sign 3, 9, 16, 28, 30–33, 36, 38–40, 44, 46–7, 50, 61n, 62, 215, 222
sign of contradiction 26, 79–82, 84, 205–6
silence 26, 64, 83, 95–7, 99, 107–8, 110–38, 201, 216, 224
sin 56, 64, 71–3, 106, 118, 198, 200, 211–12
Socrátes 127, 198, 204, 217
Soskice, J.M. 80n
speculation 14, 17, 23, 44, 50, 57–8, 64, 71, 73–4, 84, 133, 203n, 234
speech 36–8, 42, 45, 47, 50, 102, 157
spirit 37, 39, 42, 45–7, 49–51, 56, 60, 67–8, 71–3, 83–4, 90, 92, 96, 99–100, 108, 109, 146–7, 151, 169, 171, 189, 206, 215
Sponheim, S. 118n

structuralism 14, 18–19
subjectivity 1–2, 8, 11–13, 15, 19, 22–4, 26, 42–7, 76, 82, 106, 142, 162–9, 192, 199–200, 204, 225, 230–31
subjunctive 74, 88, 144, 226
Sutherland, S. 14
symbol 46
system 22, 40, 44, 47, 52, 58, 107, 158–61, 168, 171, 174–8

Taylor, M.C. 13n, 20–21, 63n, 112n, 132, 133n, 164n, 200, 236
Taylor, T. 33
temporality 38–9, 47, 49, 57, 63, 66, 68, 83–4, 96, 118, 124, 131, 152–6, 158, 170, 202–4, 207–8
Tieck, L. 143
transcendence 13–14, 16–17, 58–9, 61, 71, 73, 108, 156, 172, 176, 180–81, 186, 193, 235–7
transparency 28, 30, 52–3, 63–5, 69, 83, 101, 117–18, 160, 171
Trendelenburg, F. 160n
truth 1–19, 22–7, 30, 43–4, 46, 53–4, 56–61, 70, 74, 82–4, 99, 109, 129, 136, 162, 163–5, 167, 175, 196, 198, 207, 210, 218, 230

verification 5–6, 8, 11, 19, 164

Walker, J. 167n
Weston, M. 141
Wilson, E. 86–7
witness 25, 27, 82, 84, 152, 184, 190, 197, 210, 216–20, 226
Wittgenstein, L. 9–11, 15–17, 192, 207n
woman 25–6, 41–3, 90–97, 100, 106, 113–15, 119–20, 134, 137–8, 149
worship 42–3, 96, 122, 186–9, 209
writing 36, 47, 50, 76, 87–8, 101–2, 157

For Product Safety Concerns and Information please contact our EU
representative GPSR@taylorandfrancis.com
Taylor & Francis Verlag GmbH, Kaufingerstraße 24, 80331 München, Germany

www.ingramcontent.com/pod-product-compliance
Lightning Source LLC
Chambersburg PA
CBHW071820300426
44116CB00009B/1380